AF215330

Hallstätter See (p68), Austria

Charles Bridge (p93), Prague

CENTRAL EUROPE
THE JOURNEY BEGINS HERE

My first job as a journalist after graduating university in the 1980s took me to Vienna, and that's where my love affair with this part of Europe began. This was before 1989, when the countries in this guide were divided by barbed wire. The fall of communism across the former Eastern Bloc brought the countries of Central Europe back together. Ever since, it's been fascinating to watch how the various countries and cultures have rediscovered aspects of their common Central European identity, while at the same time retaining the qualities that make each of them distinct. Not that long ago, those former political divisions would have made it impossible to publish a coherent guidebook to this region. These days – precisely because of how those divisions have melted away – Central Europe has emerged as the most exciting region on the continent.

Mark Baker

@markbakerprague

Mark writes about travel and culture and is the author of Čas proměn *(Time of Changes), a personal account of the 1989 anti-communist revolutions and what came after. He's a passionate blogger about all things Central European. Mark curated the Czechia and Slovenia chapters.*

My favourite experience is crossing the **Charles Bridge** (p93) in Prague. I love to wander the Old Town's closed-in, cobblestone streets and then emerge back out onto the open bridge – hopefully on a sunny day.

4

ALEXANTON/SHUTTERSTOCK

lonely 🌐 planet

Central Europe

Poland
p209

Germany
p113

Czechia
p84

Slovakia
p238

Austria
p53

Hungary
p182

Switzerland
p276

Slovenia
p259

**Mark Baker, Marc Di Duca, Kata Fári, Kerry Walker,
Luke Waterson, Nicola Williams, Barbara Woolsey**

CONTENTS

**Matterhorn (p291),
Switzerland**

**Wawel Royal Castle
(p221), Poland**

WHO GOES WHERE

Our writers and experts choose the places which, for them, define Central Europe.

JERZY/SHUTTERSTOCK

The distinctive blend of 20th-century history, compelling museums, windswept beaches and filling Baltic food make **Gdańsk** (pictured; p229) my favourite place in Poland. It's a city I never grow tired of returning to.

Marc Di Duca

@marcdiduca

Marc has written travel guides for over two decades, covering destinations from Siberia to the Caribbean. He curated the Poland chapter.

ZGPHOTOGRAPHY/SHUTTERSTOCK

My favourite experience in Hungary is pausing halfway across the sage-green **Liberty Bridge** (pictured; p191) to marvel at Budapest's incredible beauty. It gives you a perfect view of the winding Danube, Gellért Hill and Hungary's Statue of Liberty, Castle Hill and the iconic Royal Palace, plus the stunning riverside Parliament.

Kata Fári

@kata.fari

Kata is a Budapest-based writer who sings the praises of the world's best places online and in print. She curated the Hungary chapter.

There are higher mountains in Austria, but few are more upliftingly beautiful than the **Tennengebirge** (pictured; p67) – ragged spires of limestone that fling up above the village of Werfen and Eisriesenwelt, the world's largest accessible ice caves. Walking high on this karst plateau, you are often alone with your thoughts, footsteps and the occasional screech of a golden eagle wheeling overhead.

Kerry Walker

@kerryawalker

Kerry is a lifelong fan of the Austrian Alps, an avid hiker and the author of multiple Lonely Planet guidebooks. She curated the Austria chapter.

My favourite experience is crunching over the crevasses, roped to a guide, on the mammoth **Aletsch Glacier** (pictured; p292), which will be gone by 2100. The rumbling of water flowing deep beneath your feet is an emotive song to the glacier's immensity and fragility. Should you trip and fall, razor-sharp ice crystals can shred the skin of your hands like glass. Yet, on this monumental sea of ice on a hot day in July, 80 cu metres of ice melt every second.

Nicola Williams

@tripalong

Nicola lives on Lake Geneva. She is a travel writer and editor, specialising in France, Italy and Switzerland for Lonely Planet, the Telegraph *and other publications. She curated the Switzerland chapter.*

MARTINA STRIHOVA/SHUTTERSTOCK

Slovakia is filled with marvels but it's the **Malé Karpaty** (Small Carpathians; pictured; p246) in particular that hold me in thrall. Dense, untrammelled forest means you can traipse across Western Slovakia and scarcely cross a road.

Luke Waterson

lukeandhiswords.com

Luke is an adventure writer specialising in Slovakia, Scandinavia, the UK and Latin America. He wrote the Slovakia chapter.

NOPPASIN WONGCHUM/SHUTTERSTOCK

My favourite experience was – to my astonishment – waking up at 6am on a Sunday to visit the famous **Fischmarkt** (pictured; p141) in Hamburg. Strolling the 300-year-old harbour market was well worth sacrificing sleep for, along with rousing live music in the Fish Auction Hall and starting the day with a fish sandwich (surprisingly, the perfect breakfast).

Barbara Woolsey

@xo.babxi

Based in Germany for over a decade, Barbara has authored over 30 Lonely Planet guidebooks. When not researching, she's DJing in Berlin's renowned nightclubs. She curated the Germany chapter.

Salzburg, Austria
Mozart, Maria and a resplendent baroque Altstadt (p63)

Český Krumlov, Czechia
Jewel box of a town in Bohemia (p100)

Cologne, Germany
Energetic yet ancient Roman city (p131)

Munich, Germany
World-class beer and museums (p145)

Geneva, Switzerland
Lakeside living and belle époque romance (p280)

Lake Bled, Slovenia
Mountain peaks, perfect lakes and blue-green rivers (p268)

Postojna Cave, Slovenia
One of Europe's longest cave systems (p270)

Prague, Czechia
Czechia's breathtaking capital (p88)

Gdańsk, Poland
Northern capital with a fascinating past (p229)

BALTIC SEA

LITHUANIA

Pomeranian Bay

Gulf of Gdańsk

Kaliningrad

RUSSIA

Gdańsk

Great Masurian Lakes

Koszalin

Olsztyn

Białystok

BELARUS

Nemunas

Toruń

Białowieża National Park

Poznań

POLAND

Warsaw

Zielona Góra

Łódź

Lublin

Wrocław

Odra

Vistula

Kraków, Poland
Poland's best-preserved city (p218)

Sudeten Mountains

Elbe

Prague

UKRAINE

Kutná Hora

Oświęcim

Kraków

Przemyśl

Ostrava

CZECHIA

Ołomouc

Zakopane

Bardejov

High Tatras, Slovakia
Mesmeric mountains and medieval townscapes (p251)

Malá Fatra National Park

Tatra Mountains

Poprad

Levoča

Telč

Brno

Trenčín

Slovenský Raj National Park

Košice

Tisa

České Budějovice

Banská Štiavnica

SLOVAKIA

Melk

Vienna

Bratislava

Eger

Tokaj

Sopron

Esztergom

Vác

Debrecen

AUSTRIA

Győr

Visegrád

Lake Tisza

Budapest

ROMANIA

Graz

HUNGARY

Kecskemét

Budapest, Hungary
Scenic beauty, high culture, hot nightlife (p186)

Maribor

Tihany

Siófok

Keszthely

Lake Balaton

Kiskunsági Nemzeti Park

SLOVENIA

Szeged

Zagreb

Pécs

SERBIA

CROATIA

Vienna, Austria
Palaces, coffeehouses and galleries galore (p56)

Lake Balaton, Hungary
Warm days at Central Europe's largest lake (p201)

9

OUTDOOR ADVENTURES

Central Europe is made for outdoor adventure. The region is bursting with natural features that invite exploration in every season. The Alps and Tatras have endless hiking, skiing and climbing possibilities, while Slovenia's Soča River promises heart-quickening canyoning and whitewater rafting. In Austria and Switzerland, cable cars sail above glaciers and meadows burst with wildflowers. Lakes like Hungary's Balaton and Slovenia's Bohinj are pure summertime fun.

Epic Hikes

The region's mountain ranges and rugged peaks are laced with well-marked trails, leading to amazing flora, fauna and views.

Go Spelunking

Subterranean karst landscapes, dripstone formations and unique underground rivers and lakes – particularly in Slovenia – can be seen on stunning caving excursions.

Water Sports

Wherever you go, you'll find plenty of ways to keep cool, from stand-up paddleboarding to canyoning.

BEST OUTDOOR EXPERIENCES

Admire the **❶ Postojna Cave** (pictured left; p270) system in Slovenia; tour the caverns while riding an underground mini-train.

Explore Switzerland's **❷ Jungfrau Region** (pictured far left; p291), with its mountain peaks, glaciers, lakes and gorges. The area features some of the country's most spectacular scenery.

Ride the funicular from the medieval Altstadt in **❸ Innsbruck** (p74) up to the 2334m Hafelekar. Walking trails head off in all directions, including the ridge-top 'Goethe Trail', a 10km, five-hour out-and-back.

Ski or snowboard in Germany's **❹ Garmisch-Partenkirchen** (p152) or simply enjoy the view. To reach the summit, hop the cogwheel train 'Zugspitzbahn'.

Go whitewater rafting along Slovenia's heavenly **❺ Soča River** (p269) and ponder the origins of the water's wonderful green-blue colour.

MAGICAL OLD TOWNS

Central Europe's bounty of old towns grew wealthy in the Middle Ages when they were stopovers along major trade routes. Merchants in Prague, Kraków and Salzburg built grand markets and churches in the architectural styles of the day: Gothic, Renaissance and baroque. Some town centres survived the ravages of war; others were painstakingly rebuilt to the last brick.

BEST OLD TOWN EXPERIENCES

Stroll the backstreets and main market square of the historic heart of **❶ Kraków** (p224), which thankfully escaped the ravages of WWII.

Swoon at the resplendent baroque Old Town (Altstadt) of **❷ Salzburg** (p63), where every corner feels steeped in Mozart's music and imperial majesty.

Admire Dresden's painstakingly reconstructed Old Town. Nothing symbolises its astounding rebirth more than the solemn **❸ Frauenkirche** (p164).

Gawk at the perfectly preserved ramparts and half-timbered houses of **❹ Rothenburg ob der Tauber** (pictured above left; p153), along Germany's 'Romantic Road'.

Step back into the 14th century in **❺ Prague** (p88) while crossing statue-lined Charles Bridge or standing on the sprawling Old Town Square (pictured above right; p94).

Alleyways & Cobblestones

A big part of the fun of exploring old towns is to trace old alleyways that were laid out in the Middle Ages.

Medieval Rivalries

The rising merchant class saw themselves as rivals to the aristocracy and built soaring churches and town halls to demonstrate their growing wealth.

Rebuilt & Restored

Many of Central Europe's most beautiful old towns – Gdańsk, Warsaw, Nuremberg and Dresden – were faithfully rebuilt after WWII.

Auschwitz-Birkenau (p223), Poland

BEST MODERN HISTORY EXPERIENCES

Reflect at Berlin's **❶ Holocaust Memorial** (p120) and pass through Checkpoint Charlie.

Pay your respects at **❷ Auschwitz-Birkenau** (p223), a symbol of humanity's darkest chapter.

Visit Gdańsk's uplifting **❸ European Solidarity Centre** (p232), which celebrates the 1980s labour movement that led to the fall of communism.

Gawk at Budapest's **❹ Memento Park** (p192) and its kitsch-filled collection of Soviet-inspired statues.

Tour the **❺ Warsaw Rising Museum** (p216) and the POLIN Museum, which bear witness to a one-time war-ravaged city.

20TH-CENTURY HISTORY

Central Europe served as the main staging ground for two of the 20th century's biggest tragedies: the horrors of WWII and the separation of Europe into a communist East and democratic West. Memories linger long in this part of the world, and amateur historians will find much to learn in these epic events.

World War II Battleground

WWII started with Germany's attack on Poland and much of the war was fought in Central Europe. The region is dotted with battlefields and memorials.

Behind the Iron Curtain

From 1949 to 1989, the Iron Curtain ran straight down the middle of Central Europe, separating Austria, Switzerland and much of Germany from Czechoslovakia, Poland and Hungary.

BREATHTAKING NATURE

With the Alps stretching across four Central European countries – Switzerland, Austria, Germany and Slovenia – it's no surprise that nature is a strong drawcard here. The Carpathians, meanwhile, form an equally impressive arc across Slovakia and parts of southern Poland. Add to that the age-old forests, high-altitude glaciers, scenic valleys, frothy rivers, pristine lakes, limestone caves and fascinating rock formations, and you have a natural paradise.

Mountain Majesty

From the jagged High Tatras (pictured) of Slovakia to the snow-covered Alps, Central European peaks offer boundless vistas and pure, high-altitude air.

Limpid Lakes

Slovenia's turquoise Lake Bled (pictured) is a real-life postcard. Hungary's Lake Balaton and Switzerland's urban lakes invite sailing, swimming and serenity.

Caverns & Springs

Slovenia's Škocjan and Postojna cave complexes and Hungary's vast thermal springs are examples of how nature's artistry runs deep.

BEST NATURE EXPERIENCES

Gaze at the ❶ **High Tatras** (p251), Slovakia's natural jewel. Admire the range's jagged granite peaks, mirror-like lakes and deep forests.

Drive Austria's ❷ **Grossglockner Road** (p69) while manoeuvring around the country's highest peak: the 3798m Grossglockner.

Feel the power of Germany's highest cascade, the ❸ **Triberger Wasserfälle** (p158), a major highlight of the Black Forest.

Take in the sweep of the Danube River in the ❹ **Wachau Valley** (p61), where castle ruins stand watch over terraced vineyards. It's the most picturesque section of Central Europe's central river.

Let Slovenia's iconic ❺ **Lake Bled** (p268) mesmerise you: the glacial lake is crowned by a fairytale island church and medieval cliffside castle.

CANDASTOCK/SHUTTERSTOCK

Schloss Neuschwanstein (p152), Germany

STATELY CASTLES

Many of Central Europe's magnificent castles began life as fortified bastions to safeguard the land holdings of the local noble family – in some cases, this meant the king and queen themselves. Over the centuries, these castles and palaces evolved into luxurious residences, showing off the family's wealth and taste.

A Pile on Every Hilltop

From robust fortresses and crumbling piles of bricks to grandiose Renaissance residences, some regions have a castle on nearly every hilltop.

Elegant Royal Residences

Less visually arresting than multi-turreted castles, town palaces – such as the Hofburg in Vienna – are every bit as luxurious and impressive.

BEST CASTLE EXPERIENCES

Soak up the magic of ❶ **Schloss Neuschwanstein** (p152), cradled by Alpine foothills and the inspiration for the Disney castle.

Ride the funicular to tour ❷ **Ljubljana Castle** (p262), which has towered over the Slovenian capital for hundreds of years.

Take in the castle of ❸ **Český Krumlov** (p100), which testifies to the wealth of southern Bohemian nobility.

Admire the scope of Slovakia's ❹ **Spiš Castle** (p253), a vast medieval ruin with spectacular views.

Vienna's town palaces, such as the ❺ **Hofburg** (p58), symbolise the power of the ruling Habsburgs.

CITY LIGHTS

Central Europe is home to some of the continent's most exciting cities. Vienna, Berlin, Zürich and Geneva have fabulous museums and cultural institutions, and are also home to trendsetting clubs and bars. Former communist capitals like Prague, Warsaw and Budapest, while no slouch in the culture department, remain fascinating test cases of cities still in transition.

Captivating Capitals

Formerly forgotten, Eastern Bloc capitals like Prague, Bratislava, Budapest and Warsaw (pictured) have now emerged as some of Central Europe's most energetic and attractive cities.

Most Livable

Cities like Vienna, Zürich (pictured), Geneva and Munich have recently found themselves atop lists of the world's most-livable cities for their excellent cultural institutions, transport and healthcare.

Second Cities

Don't pass up Central Europe's second-tier cities – those that are neither a country's capital nor its biggest city – like Hamburg, Cologne, Graz and Brno.

BEST URBAN EXPERIENCES

Walk through the leafy centre of ❶ **Ljubljana** (p262) and along its pretty riverside, enlivened by Jože Plečnik's dazzling bridges.

Gather in Munich's ❷ **Englischer Garten** (p149) for the beloved ritual of music, conversation, and beer.

Enjoy the waterfront of ❸ **Zürich** (p287), where locals swim, sail and sunbathe along the Zürichsee by day, then fill the bars by night.

Visit Vienna's ❹ **Belvedere** (p59) to see Gustav Klimt's most famous work, *Der Kuss* (The Kiss).

Attend a music festival in ❺ **Poznań**, Poland's cultural dynamo. (p227)

HEARTY CUISINE

Central Europe encompasses a variety of culinary traditions, but one similarity is that meals tend to be filling, flavourful and meaty. Expect hearty soups, big plates of pork, beef or chicken, and signature sides that can include oversized bread dumplings, grains like barley, and creative potato casseroles and salads. Vienna's influence is felt in the ubiquity of dishes like *Tafelspitz* (slow-cooked beef) and schnitzels: breaded and fried pieces of veal, pork or chicken.

Back to the Roots

Central European cooking features simple ingredients – root vegetables, potatoes and fruits – that traditionally have been grown locally.

Ornate Coffee Houses

Vienna's grand coffee houses elevate java to high art. Find similarly elaborate cafes in former Austro-Hungarian Empire cities like Budapest, Bratislava and Prague.

Alpine Feasts

Swiss cuisine stands out for its fondue, raclette and *rösti* (grated, fried potatoes), ideally served in a mountain chalet.

BEST CULINARY EXPERIENCES

Fill up with goulash and a shot of *pálinka* (fruit brandy) at one of the many excellent restaurants in ❶ **Budapest** (p186).

Lose count of how many pierogi you eat as you sample these meat- and cheese-stuffed dumplings at a Polish milk bar *(bar mleczny)* in ❷ **Kraków** (p218).

Sip the 'new' wine (this year's harvest), while noshing on delicious cold cuts and cheese, in one of the many *Heurigen* (wine taverns) around ❸ **Vienna** (p61) .

Chug down some original Pilsner-Urquell beer at the ❹ **brewery** (p99) in Plzeň (Pilsen), where modern-style lager was invented in the 19th century.

Enjoy some hearty Bavarian food in a ❺ **Munich** beer hall (p147) while seated on benches packed with locals, everyone holding steins of golden *Helles*.

COUNTRIES

Find the places that tick all your boxes.

Germany
p113

Germany

**TRANQUIL LANDSCAPES AND
FESTIVE TRADITIONS**

This is a country that's serious about
simple pleasures. The German take on
fun and adventure is just like its beer:
an age-old recipe that never wavers
from tradition and values good taste.
Germany offers a breath of fresh air in
forests, beer gardens and laid-back
cities.

Czechia

**BREATHTAKING CASTLES AND
EVEN BETTER BEER**

Prague is arguably Europe's prettiest
capital as well as an exciting urban
centre, with excellent museums,
lovely parks and cutting-edge clubs
and restaurants. Outside the capital,
the country is filled with beauty.
And wherever you go, you'll likely be
mug-in-hand. No one does beer like
the Czechs.

Poland
p209

Czechia
p84

Slovakia
p238

Slovakia

MAJESTIC MOUNTAINS, CASTLES AND MEDIEVAL MARVELS

Epic hikes in the High Tatras, caving in the Slovak karst and cycling through primeval beech forests are all good reasons for travellers to add Slovakia to their bucket list. While Slovakia appeals most to lovers of the outdoors, don't sleep on Bratislava: its old town is filled with gems.

Poland

A WARM, WELCOMING AND RESILIENT NATION

The home of Chopin has a turbulent history marked by both triumph and tragedy. Warsaw was painstakingly and miraculously rebuilt after WWII, while colourful Kraków is known for its medieval old town, cultural riches and modern nightlife. Elsewhere, woods, rivers, mountains and lakes offer loads of fresh-air fun.

Switzerland

ALPINE TRADITION, OUTDOOR ACTION AND URBAN FUN

No other place inspires exploration like Switzerland – a country that gave the world melt-in-the-mouth chocolate, cyberspace and an overdose of God-like landscapes. Where else can you follow flower trails around glittering lakes, cross crevasse-riddled glaciers and corkscrew up vertiginous alpine passes like James Bond – all in a weekend?

Slovenia

RELAXING TOWNS AND PRISTINE NATURE

Tucked between the Alps and the Adriatic, Slovenia has everything under the sun when it comes to the great outdoors. Hiking, swimming, cycling, skiing, horse riding, rafting, ballooning, caving and canyoning are all possible. Lake Bled looks like something out of a fairy tale, but don't skip the lively capital, Ljubljana.

Switzerland
p276

Austria

WHERE CULTURE HITS THE HEIGHTS

No country waltzes so effortlessly between urban and outdoors. One day you're cresting alpine summits, the next you're swanning around imperial Vienna. For such a tiny country, Austria is big on inspiration. This is the land where Mozart was born and the Habsburgs ruled over their sprawling 600-year empire.

Hungary

STUNNING ARCHITECTURE AND THERMAL SPAS

A landlocked country with an undying love for water, Hungary is home to healing thermal spas, the world's largest swimmable thermal lake and Central Europe's largest lake. Budapest, standing astride the Danube, is a stunning capital, with astonishing architecture, exciting nightlife and excellent restaurants.

Austria
p53

Hungary
p182

Slovenia
p259

ZGPHOTOGRAPHY/SHUTTERSTOCK

Budapest (p186)

ITINERARIES

The Essential East

Allow: 14 days   **Distance:** 2000km

From the regal streets of Kraków to majestic Prague Castle, and the thermal baths of Budapest to the urban flourishes of Ljubljana, this journey offers a whirlwind adventure through six cities that not so long ago found themselves on the other side of the Iron Curtain. Consider an overnight train for some of the legs.

① WARSAW ⏱ 2 DAYS

Start off in the **Polish capital** (p212). Ease into your introduction to Central Europe's formerly communist countries by exploring the city's beautifully restored Old Town (pictured). Take pictures at the Royal Castle, gawk at the Palace of Culture & Science or visit the POLIN Museum of the History of Polish Jews. Eat pierogi (dumplings) to your heart's content before taking a train to Kraków.

② KRAKÓW ⏱ 3 DAYS

Stay two nights to fully absorb the regal atmosphere of the Polish kingdom's former capital and one of the country's most **beautiful cities** (p218). Explore the Old Town and Wawel Castle (pictured), then wander around Kraków's famed Jewish quarter, Kazimierz.

🚂 **Detour:** Plan a day trip to harrowing **Auschwitz-Birkenau Memorial & Museum** (p223) or the spectacular **Wieliczka Salt Mine** (p223).

③ PRAGUE ⏱ 2 DAYS

Spend the next two days admiring the cache of medieval buildings in **Prague** (p88). Cross Charles Bridge and admire Prague Castle rising high above the Vltava River. Prague's Old Town Square (pictured) and Astronomical Clock are pure theatre, while cafes and pubs buzz with energy. Don't forget to imbibe some tantalising Czech beer. Re-board the train for Bratislava.

FROM LEFT: SOURLAND STUDIOS/LONELY PLANET, SANGA PARK/SHUTTERSTOCK, SERGII FIGURNYI/SHUTTERSTOCK

Warsaw

START

POLAND

Berlin
Potsdam
Poznań
Zielona Góra
Łódź
Lublin
Leipzig
Wrocław
2h 45min
Vistula
Dresden
Litoměřice
Sudeten Mountains
Elbe
Auschwitz-Birkenau
Memorial & Museum
Kraków
Przemyśl
Terezín
Prague 3
6h 30min
Ostrava
Wieliczka Salt Mine
Loket
Karlovy Vary
Plzeň
Kutná Hora
Olomouc
Oświęcim
Zakopane
CZECHIA
Telč
Brno
4h
Trenčín
Tatra Mountains
Levoča
Košice
Český Krumlov
České Budějovice
SLOVAKIA
Banská Štiavnica
Slovenský Raj National Park
Linz
Melk
Vienna
Bratislava 4
2h 30min
Vác
Eger
Tokaj
Salzburg
Bad Ischl
Sopron
Győr
Visegrád
Budapest 5
Debrecen
AUSTRIA
Grossglockner (3798m)
Graz
Tihany
Keszthely
Siófok
6h
Lake Balaton
Danube
Kiskunsági Nemzeti Park
Kecskemét
HUNGARY
ROMANIA
Werfen
Lienz
Klagenfurt
Maribor
Pécs
Szeged
SERBIA
Bled
END
Ljubljana 6
Zagreb
SLOVENIA
CROATIA
Lake Tisza
Tisa
200 km
100 miles
N 0

4 BRATISLAVA ⏱ 2 DAYS

After Prague, the cobbled Old Town in **Bratislava** (p242) will feel much, much smaller, but also less touristy. The main squares are framed by baroque palaces and Gothic towers and have a quirky cafe culture. Climb to Bratislava Castle (pictured) for sweeping views, visit St Martin's Cathedral, then cross the river to modern galleries like the Danubiana Meulensteen Art Museum.

5 BUDAPEST ⏱ 3 DAYS

Brace yourself for beauty and get your camera ready. The architecture in **Budapest** (p186) is astonishing. Spend your time wandering the historic Castle District, soak your muscles at the splendid Széchenyi Baths, take a sightseeing cruise on the Danube River (pictured) and enjoy Budapest's buzzing nightlife in District VII. Long-haul buses are better than trains for the tour's last leg.

6 LJUBLJANA ⏱ 2 DAYS

End your journey in **Ljubljana** (p262), a national capital that looks and feels much more like a provincial river town. Stroll and sip coffee along the banks of the Ljubljanica River (pictured), cross Jože Plečnik's famed Triple Bridge, and ride the funicular (or walk up) to Ljubljana Castle. Toast the end of your trip with Slovenian specialties at the Michelin Bib Gourmand restaurant **Gostilna Na Gradu** (p264).

A Germany Sampler

PLAN YOUR TRIP

ITINERARIES

Allow: 12 days   **Distance:** 1400km

This itinerary is all about exploring the best of Germany and highlights the blend of tradition and innovation that make the country so fascinating. Thanks to Germany's excellent transport infrastructure, the tour is easy to follow by train or bus.

Frauenkirche (p164), Dresden

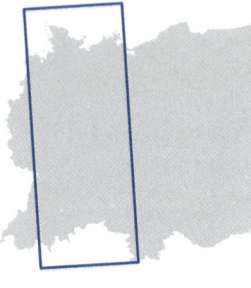

❶ HAMBURG ⏱ 2 DAYS

Start in **Hamburg** (p139), Germany's largest port and a vibrant, forward-looking city. Wander the Speicherstadt, the world's largest warehouse complex, and see the striking Elbphilharmonie, a modern concert house that rises over the Elbe River. Follow the trail of the Beatles, who once performed here. Dine on north German specialties at restaurants like **Laufauf** (p141).

❷ BERLIN ⏱ 3 DAYS

There's plenty to see in **Berlin** (p118). First-timers should start off in the Historic Mitte and trace the past through evocative landmarks, like the Holocaust Memorial and Checkpoint Charlie (pictured), while celebrating today's reunified republic at the Reichstag and Brandenburger Tor (Brandenburg Gate). Next up: head south to the former seat of Saxon royals.

❸ DRESDEN ⏱ 1 DAY

In **Dresden** (p164), begin by marvelling at the reconstructed Frauenkirche, a magnificent cathedral resurrected from WWII rubble. Take in the Residenzschloss, a Renaissance palace that was once home to Saxony's rulers for 400 years, then pop over to the Albertinum, a former arsenal and now home to the Galerie Neue Meister, filled with masterpieces.

④ NUREMBERG ⏱ 2 DAYS

Nuremberg (p155) is a historic city that was painstakingly rebuilt following WWII. The city played a key role in Adolf Hitler's rise, and at the Memorium Nuremberg Trials, you can see the famous courtroom in which the Allies tried high-ranking Nazis after the war. Stroll the Old Town and indulge in Nuremberg's distinct version of bratwurst.

⑤ MUNICH ⏱ 2 DAYS

Bavaria's cosmopolitan **capital** (p145) has a well-earned reputation as a city of art and beer. Explore the museums of the Kunstareal and relax in the English Garden. Wander from the famous piazza Marienplatz to the Viktualienmarkt farmers' market.

➳ **Detour:** Take the train south to **Garmisch-Partenkirchen**, home to Germany's tallest mountain, the **Zugspitze** (p152).

⑥ STUTTGART ⏱ 2 DAYS

Finish the trip in the southwestern city of **Stuttgart** (p156), another fascinating urban juxtaposition of old and new. Car fans will certainly want to visit the Mercedes-Benz Museum (pictured) and Porsche Museum.

➳ **Detour:** Stuttgart makes a decent base for the **Nationalpark Schwarzwald** (Black Forest National Park; p158). Stay the night at a secret nature camp only accessible on foot.

27

ITINERARIES

Alpine Majesty

Allow: 12 days   **Distance:** 800km

This Alpine route connects the most scenic regions of Austria and Switzerland while passing over spectacular mountain ranges. The stops mix high-altitude towns, lakeside villages and fabulous resorts. It's easiest by car, though if you're travelling in winter (November–March) some roads and passes may be closed due to inclement weather.

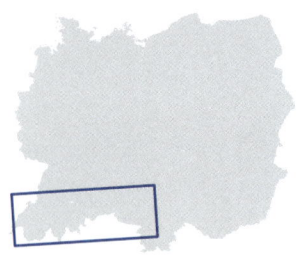

① SALZBURG, AUSTRIA
⏱ 2 DAYS

Baroque **Salzburg** (p63) charms with fortress views, rococo palaces and music that fills the tiny lanes. Walk to the Benedictine abbey Stift Nonnberg, then continue the short but scenic walk to Festung Hohensalzburg (pictured). Enjoy some Mozart magic or follow the Sound of Music trail.

🔶 _Detour:_ Take a day trip to **Werfen** (p67) and the world's largest ice caves.

② KITZBÜHEL, AUSTRIA
⏱ 2 DAYS

The fabled ski resort at **Kitzbühel** (pictured; p76) is scenic year-round, but the place really sparkles in winter. If there's snow on the ground, slalom down Hahnenkamm and Kitzbüheler Horn. In autumn, cows parade home crowned with flowers for the Almabtrieb festivities. The Alpine huts, folk music and crisp mountain air combine with snow and schnapps to create indelible memories.

③ INNSBRUCK, AUSTRIA
⏱ 2 DAYS

Continue on to **Innsbruck** (p73), Tyrol's provincial capital. It's an impressive mix of imperial grandeur and alpine adventure. Stroll the alleys of the Altstadt, then soar by funicular (pictured) to the surrounding summits for sweeping views and hair-raising pistes. Visit Empress Maria Theresia's baroque Hofburg and Emperor Maximilian's ornate Hofkirche. Splurge on farm-fresh, foraged goodness at **Die Wildern** (p74).

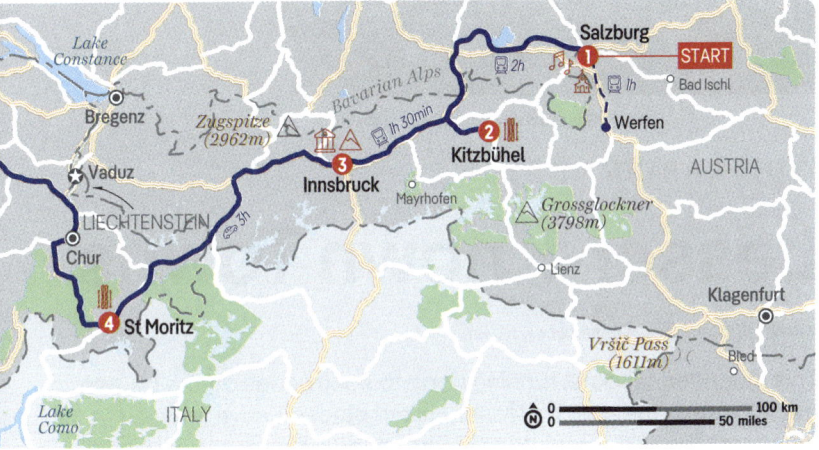

4 ST MORITZ, SWITZERLAND
⏱ 2 DAYS

Carry on to **St Moritz** (pictured; p293), arguably Switzerland's best-known alpine resort, drawing the rich and famous for more than 150 years. The town is framed by aquamarine lakes and pine forests, and manages to balance the glamour with high-altitude solitude. Follow lonely passes that corkscrew high into the mountains or brave the Olympic Bob Run.

5 INTERLAKEN, SWITZERLAND ⏱ 2 DAYS

Victorian glamour meets big mountains in snug Interlaken, surrounded by the pearly white peaks of Eiger, Mönch and Jungfrau. The town thrills with every heart-pumping alpine sport you care to name. First port of call is **Outdoor Interlaken** (p291), a well-equipped adventure shop that can set you up for paragliding (pictured), skydiving, bungee jumping, rafting and canyoning.

6 ZERMATT, SWITZERLAND
⏱ 2 DAYS

Park your car in the village of Täsch and board the shuttle train up to **Zermatt** (pictured; p290). Here, all eyes are on the Matterhorn. Ride the vintage Gornergratbahn to 3089m for panoramic glaciers and peaks, or cross into Italy via the Matterhorn Alpine Crossing cable car. Toast the view with cheese fondue on the terrace of the Kulmhotel Gornergrat.

Banská Štiavnica (p249), Slovakia

ITINERARIES

Lesser-Known Towns

Allow: 10 days   **Distance:** 1250 km

This meandering route, running north to south, goes off the beaten track to reach the region's lesser-visited places. Leave yourself plenty of time to appreciate the ever-changing landscapes, from the mountains and mining valleys of Polish Silesia and Slovakia through Moravia and on to the wine-growing regions of Hungary.

❶ WROCŁAW, POLAND ⏱2 DAYS

Start in **Wrocław** (pictured; p225), the largest city on this tour. Explore the Rynek, one of Europe's most beautiful squares, and visit the Old Town Hall. Climb the tower steps of the 14th-century Church of St Elizabeth. Wander over to Cathedral Island (Ostrów Tumski), where in 1000 CE Wrocław's first church was built.

❷ OLOMOUC, CZECHIA ⏱2 DAYS

Venture south over the Czech border to the atmospheric college town of **Olomouc** (p106). Stroll the elegant squares and wonder at the UNESCO-listed Holy Trinity Column (pictured). See the unusual Astronomical Clock on the Town Hall and visit baroque churches. Stop for a hearty meal and beer at a traditional pub like **Hanácká hospoda** (p106).

❸ BRNO, CZECHIA ⏱2 DAYS

Continue on to **Brno** (p103), Moravia's capital city, home to thousands of students. Explore the underground Labyrinth under the Vegetable Market and visit the spooky Ossuary at the Church of St James (pictured). Climb up to Špilberk Castle or tour the Villa Tugendhat, a masterpiece of modernist architecture. Take a break at one of Brno's trendy coffee bars.

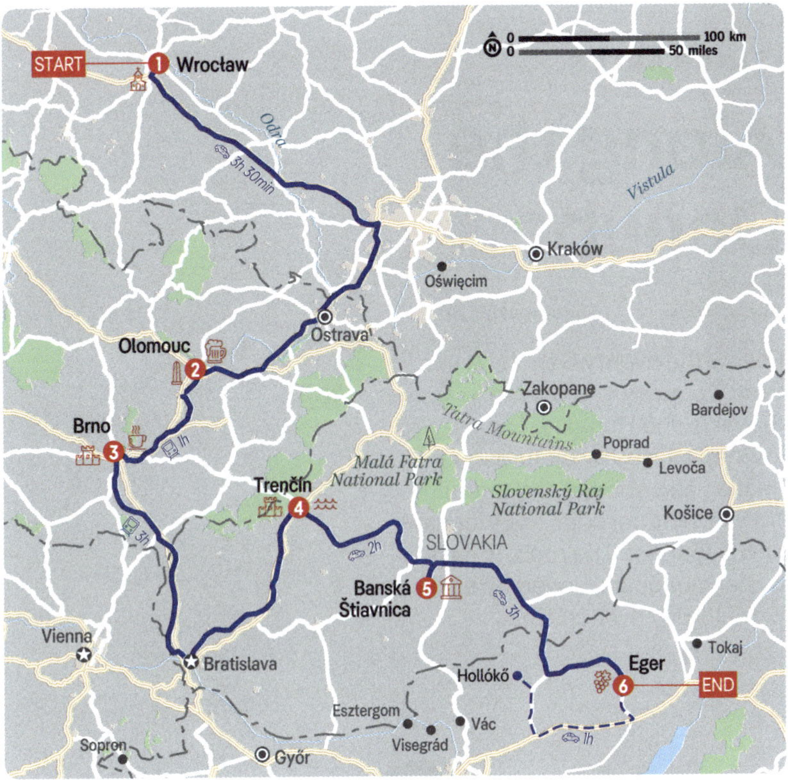

START ❶ Wrocław

3h 30min

Odra

Vistula

Kraków

Oświęcim

Olomouc ❷

Ostrava

Brno ❸

1h

Zakopane

Bardejov

Tatra Mountains

Poprad

Levoča

Malá Fatra National Park

Trenčín ❹

2h

Slovenský Raj National Park

Košice

SLOVAKIA

Banská Štiavnica ❺

3h

3h

Vienna

Bratislava

Eger ❻ END

Tokaj

Hollókő

Esztergom

Vác

1h

Sopron

Győr

Visegrád

100 km
50 miles

❹
TRENČÍN, SLOVAKIA
⏱ 2 DAYS

Next up is the graceful river town of **Trenčín** (p259). The crag-top Trenčín Castle (pictured) affords views across the Váh River valley, while the town's main square, brimming with Renaissance façades, arcades and fountains, earned the town the European Capital of Culture designation in 2026. Walk the riverfront or linger in shaded cafes to soak up the vibe.

❺
BANSKÁ ŠTIAVNICA, SLOVAKIA ⏱ 1 DAY

Press on to the 13th-century mining settlement of **Banská Štiavnica** (p249). Sparkling like the silver once found in its hills, this town is a trove of burghers' houses from the 16th to 18th centuries. Visit the hillside chapel complex Kalvaria (pictured) and the dignified Old Castle. Delve into mining heritage at the Open-Air Mining Museum, 2km west of town.

❻
EGER, HUNGARY ⏱ 1 DAY

Finish the tour in hilly northern Hungary, home to world-famous vineyards. The town of **Eger** (p202) is a wine-lover's fantasy come true. About 2km southeast is the Valley of the Beautiful Women, with dozens of wine cellars (pictured).

🚗 *Detour: About an hour west is* **Hollókő** *(p203) known for the whitewashed folk architecture of its Old Village (Ófalu).*

ITINERARIES

Along the Danube

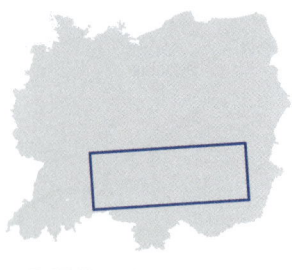

Allow: 8 days   **Distance:** 850km

Follow the mighty Danube River from Germany into Austria, Slovakia and Hungary. The journey passes by picturesque castles and abbeys and through historic cultural hubs like Vienna and Budapest. The route is easy by car, but best enjoyed on a bike or multi-day river cruise.

1 REGENSBURG, GERMANY
⏱1 DAY

Start in **Regensburg** (p155), which has two millennia of architectural heritage. Roman walls and Gothic spires meet the quickening flow of the Danube near the start of its long journey to the Black Sea. Explore the Dom St Peter (pictured) and stroll across the 12th-century Stone Bridge. Linger over beer and sausages along the river.

2 MELK, AUSTRIA ⏱1 DAY

Head southeast for a long drive to the riverside town of **Melk** (p61), one of Europe's finest ensembles of baroque architecture. Perched high above the Danube, Stift Melk (pictured) dazzles with golden stucco, frescoes and terraces opening to vineyard views. Wander the abbey, then descend to the water to watch boats glide through the heart of the Wachau Valley.

3 DÜRNSTEIN, AUSTRIA
⏱1 DAY

Hike or bike along the river to nearby **Dürnstein** (p62), an impossibly photogenic town atop a bend of the Danube. It's famous for its Kuenringerburg (pictured), the ruins where Richard I of England – yes, the Lionheart – was once imprisoned. Climb the trail to the castle for sweeping valley views or sample apricot liqueur and crisp white wine in the village.

4
VIENNA, AUSTRIA
⏱ **2 DAYS**

Follow the river's flow to
Austria's grand capital,
Vienna (p56), which blends
imperial elegance with big-city
rhythms. Seek out the Gothic
masterpiece Stephansdom
and admire its patterned roof
and panoramic tower, stroll
the Ringstrasse and linger
in one of the many coffee
houses (pictured), where faded
Habsburg grandeur meets
modern-day creative energy.

5
BRATISLAVA, SLOVAKIA
⏱ **1 DAY**

Slovakia's **capital** (p242) is the
ideal mid-sized city, big enough
for a swag bag of significant
sights yet small enough for
a relaxing stroll. Explore the
Old Town's cobbled lanes and
pastel façades, then climb up to
Bratislava Castle (pictured) for
sweeping river vistas. Modern
galleries and bridges add a
touch of contemporary flair.

6
BUDAPEST, HUNGARY
⏱ **2 DAYS**

Budapest (p186) is an
architectural treasure trove with
a fin-de-siècle feel. Cross the
Chain Bridge between Buda and
Pest, bathe in the Széchenyi
Baths and watch lights shimmer
along the Danube. Enjoy the
panorama from Castle Hill or
the Ferris Wheel (pictured) of
Budapest – the ride is most
impressive at night.

WHEN TO GO

Central Europe entices year-round; summer is the high season.

Central Europe enjoys a continental climate, with four distinct seasons. Winters are cold, grey and occasionally harsh. Snow blankets the streets and rooftops, and temperatures can dip to –10°C. Yet in many ways, it's a magical time, particularly around Christmas, when the region turns into a winter wonderland with fairy lights, crackling fireplaces and the scent of mulled wine filling the air. Skiers carve tracks at world-class resorts in Switzerland and Austria, and even Slovenia, Slovakia, Czechia and Poland have decent slopes. When winter's final breath fades, the region revives in spring (March to May). Flowers bloom and temperatures hover from 10°C to 20°C. Summer is in full swing from June to August. The days are long and temperatures can climb to 35°C. Autumn (September to November) turns the landscape into a riot of red, orange and yellow, while daytime temperatures dip to a comfortable 10°C to 18°C, perfect for outdoor activities.

⊛ I LIVE HERE

THE HIGH TATRAS

Agnieszka Guspiel is a linguistics teacher at Kraków's Jagiellonian University.

I've always loved hiking in Gorce National Park, with its views of the Tatra Mountains. It's just a short drive from Kraków – close enough to reach between exams but far enough to get away from it all. Hike through meadows of crocuses in May, stuff yourself with wild blueberries in August or try ski touring in winter. Turbacz is the highest peak (1310m) and beautiful on crisp autumn days.

CHRISTMAS MARKETS

No one celebrates Christmas quite like the countries of Central Europe. Festive, open-air markets spring up in nearly every town and city. Some of the best are in Vienna, Salzburg (Austria), Prague, Nuremberg (Germany), Dresden (Germany) and Budapest.

FROM LEFT: SCSTOCK/GETTY IMAGES, PYTY/SHUTTERSTOCK

Christmas market, Salzburg (p63)

Weather through the Year (Prague)

JANUARY	FEBRUARY	MARCH	APRIL	MAY	JUNE
Avg. daytime max: **2°C**	Avg. daytime max: **4°C**	Avg. daytime max: **9°C**	Avg. daytime max: **14°C**	Avg. daytime max: **19°C**	Avg. daytime max: **22°C**
Days of snow/ rainfall: **6**	Days of snow/ rainfall: **5**	Days of snow/ rainfall: **6**	Days of snow/ rainfall: **6**	Days of rainfall: **9**	Days of rainfall: **10**

EMBRACE THE SHOULDER SEASONS

The shoulder seasons – March to May and September to October – are the best times to travel in Central Europe. The weather is pleasant, while crowds and prices drop off. If you're on a shoestring, lodging is cheapest in winter.

The Big Festivals

Carnival is big across the whole of Central Europe, but one of the craziest celebrations is the pre-Lenten **Kurentovanje** (*kurentovanje.net*) in Ptuj, Slovenia. ❄ **February**

Symphony orchestras and chamber music ensembles around the world perform at the **Prague Spring International Music Festival** (*festival.cz*). ☁ **May**

With a multicultural lineup and diverse events, the **Pohoda Festival** (*pohodafestival.sk*) is Slovakia's biggest music gathering. ☁ **July**

World-class opera, classical music and drama take the stage in Salzburg at the unmissable **Salzburger Festspiele** (*salzburgerfestspiele.at*). Book months ahead. ☁ **July/August**

Hungary's biggest festival is the **Sziget Music Festival** (*szigetfestival.com*), the country's Glastonbury, held in Budapest. ☁ **August**

Accept no substitutes. Munich's **Oktoberfest** (*oktoberfest.de/en*) is still the ultimate beer-swilling, stein-swinging party. ☀ **September/October**

Lesser-Known Celebrations

Experience baroque brilliance at Germany's **Thüringer Bachwochen** (*thueringer-bachwochen.de*). ☁ **April/May**

Kraków's **Jewish Culture Festival** (*jewishfestival.pl*) hosts some 200 events. ☁ **June/July**

The **Ljubljana Festival** (*ljubljanafestival.si*) is tops on the Slovenian social calendar, bringing music, theatre and dance to the city. ☁ **June to September**

Pool parties, jam sessions, dance classes: anything flies at Switzerland's **Montreux Jazz Festival** (*montreuxjazzfestival.com*). ☁ **July**

In Austria, the **Bregenzer Festspiele** (*bregenzerfestspiele.com*) brings choreographed opera to an open-air stage on Lake Constance. ☁ **July/August**

The 11-day **Locarno Film Festival** (*locarnofestival.ch*) in Switzerland screens movies on the main square. ☁ **August**

Prague (p88)

FÖHN WIND

Originating in the Alps, the *Föhn* is a warm, dry down-slope wind in Austria and Germany that sparks quick temperature swings. While it provides relief from cold weather, it can also cause headaches and discomfort for those sensitive to pressure shifts.

JULY	AUGUST	SEPTEMBER	OCTOBER	NOVEMBER	DECEMBER
Avg. daytime max: **24°C**	Avg. daytime max: **24°C**	Avg. daytime max: **19°C**	Avg. daytime max: **13°C**	Avg. daytime max: **7°C**	Avg. daytime max: **3°C**
Days of rainfall: **10**	Days of rainfall: **9**	Days of rainfall: **7**	Days of rainfall: **6**	Days of snow/rainfall: **6**	Days of snow/rainfall: **6**

LEFT: GILITUKHA/GETTY IMAGES; RIGHT: BFA/NETFLIX

Hiking, High Tatras (p251), Slovakia

GET PREPARED FOR CENTRAL EUROPE

Useful things to load in your bag, your ears and your brain.

Clothes

Layers Winter can be cold and the ground icy, so several layers of warm clothing and flat shoes (for slippery cobbles) are essential, along with a scarf, gloves and hat. In summer, wear layers you can peel off.

Waterproofs Be prepared for rainfall year-round.

Dressy clothes Central Europeans tend to dress up in the evenings for concerts and high-end restaurants, but jeans are fine for upmarket clubs and restaurants – so long as you pair them with a nice shirt or blouse and a blazer or summer jacket.

Hiking gear Pack sturdy boots, trekking poles, sunscreen and a wide-brimmed hat, thermal layers, a waterproof outer shell

Manners

Clinking glasses During a toast, especially when lifting a glass of beer or spirits, always maintain eye contact.

Bon appétit! When dining with others, it's polite to say *bon appétit* (*Guten appetit* in German-speaking countries) before digging in.

Tap water (*Leitungswasser* in German-speaking countries) is still relatively uncommon, especially in upmarket places. Order mineral water (still or sparkling) instead.

and a daypack. In winter, you'll need ski gear and snow boots.

READ

Fatelessness (Imre Kertész; 1975) Harrowing tale of the Holocaust by Nobel Prize–winning author from Hungary.

The Joke (Milan Kundera; 1967) Kundera's debut follows the repercussions of a joke in Soviet-occupied Czechoslovakia.

The Glass Room (Simon Mawer; 2009) Entertaining look at Czechoslovak life in the interwar years of the 20th century.

The Radetzky March (Joseph Roth; 1932) Chronicles the decline of the Austro-Hungarian Empire.

Words

Czech/Slovak
Hello. Ahoj. *uh-hoy*
Thank you. Děkuji. *dye-ku-yi* (Czech); Ďakujem. *dyuh-ku-yem* (Slovak)
Yes. Ano. a*h-no*
No. Ne. *ne* (Czech); Nie. *ni-ye* (Slovak)
Goodbye. Na shledanou. *nah-sklu-dah-noh* (Czech); Dovidenia. *doh-vee-deh-nyah* (Slovak)
Beer. Pivo. *pee-voh*

German
Hello (standard German). Hallo. *hah-loh*
Hello (Austria). Servus. *sehr-voos*
Hello (Austria and southern Germany). Grüß Gott. *gruess-got*
Hello (Switzerland). Grüezi. *grue-tsi*
Thank you. Danke. *dahn-keh*
Yes. Ja. *yah*
No. Nein. *nine*
Goodbye. Auf wiedersehen. *auf-vee-der-zayn*
Beer. Bier. *beer*

Hungarian
Hello. Jó napot. *yoh nah-pot*
Thank you. Köszönöm. *kew-sew-newm*
Yes. Igen. *ighen*
No. Nem. *nehm*
Goodbye (informal). Szia. *see-yah*
Beer. Sör. *shur*

Polish
Hello. Cześć. *cheshch*
Thank you. Dziękuję. *jyen-koo-ye*
Yes. Tak. *tak*
No. Nie. *nye*
Goodbye. Do widzenia. *doh-veed-zeh-nyah*
Beer. Piwo. *pee-voh*

Slovenian
Hello. Zdravo. *zdrah-vo*
Thank you. Hvala. *hvah-la*
Yes. Da. *da*
No. Ne. *ne*
Goodbye. Nasvidenje. *nahs-vee-deh-nyeh*
Beer. Pivo. *pee-voh*

WATCH

All Quiet on the Western Front (Edward Berger; 2022; pictured) Powerful portrayal of the experiences of German soldiers during WWI.

The Informant (HBO; 2022) The story of university students in communist Hungary, one of whom is an informant.

The Third Man (Carol Reed; 1949) Classic film noir set in shadowy postwar Vienna.

Schindler's List (Steven Spielberg; 1993) Oscar winner set in WWII Kraków.

Closely Watched Trains (Jiří Menzel; 1966) Brilliant adaptation of a WWII classic that put Czech New Wave on the map.

LISTEN

Papp László Aréna Live (Azahriah; 2023) Live album from Hungary's hottest singer-songwriter, currently a Gen Z icon.

Fantaisie-Impromptu (Chopin; 1834) Poland's greatest composer and virtuoso pianist at his best.

O Brother, Shut the Door (Karel Kryl; 1969) Echoes the hopelessness that many Czechoslovaks felt after the 1968 Warsaw Pact invasion.

Eine kleine Nacht Musik, K 525, (Wolfgang Amadeus Mozart; 1787) The most uplifting and recognisable composition for a chamber ensemble.

HINTERHAUS PRODUCTIONS/GETTY IMAGES

Berlin (p118)

Greet People in Central Europe

Central Europeans are friendly, warm and more than happy to show off their country. That said, interactions between people in these parts are governed by unspoken, formal niceties that you might not be familiar with. Here are some pointers for getting to know the locals.

Use Titles and Formal Address

An instinctive formality is deeply woven into the social fabric. Introductions invariably begin with a firm handshake, unwavering eye contact and the judicious use of titles and surnames. When meeting new people, respect and use titles such as 'Doctor' or 'Professor'. Don't jump to first names until invited to do so. All languages employ two forms for addressing people: formal ('Sie' in German, usually 'Vy' in Slavic languages) for strangers and informal ('du' in German, and 'ty' in Slavic languages) for addressing family, friends and children.

First Encounters

Be on time. If running late, give advance notice. Focus small talk on innocuous interests like travel, sports and food. It's always best, particularly in today's polarised times, to avoid politics or religion. Any display of interest in the local culture is likely to be appreciated. Generally speaking, allow time for personal relationships to develop. Friendships in this part of the world tend to grow slowly, but they gradually give way to genuine feelings of warmth and affection.

Overtourism

Parts of Central Europe have become popular destinations – maybe too popular. In summer, Vienna, Prague, Kraków, Budapest and other cities heave with visitors. Smaller destinations, like Slovenia's Lake Bled, Austria's Hallstatt and Český Krumlov in Czechia, become nearly unrecognisable. Generally, Central Europeans will go out of their way to help visitors. Bear in mind, though, that locals can get chippy when overwhelmed by the sheer number of outsiders. If you find yourself on the wrong end of a stressed-out server or shopkeeper, try to show empathy for the situation. Reacting in an angry or demanding tone won't get you far.

THEATRICALITY

Day-to-day interactions between strangers in Central Europe can sometimes reflect levels of politeness and theatricality that border on the absurd. The dialogue between a butcher and a customer in Vienna, for example, might begin like this:

Butcher: And what would the gracious lady like today?

Customer: If it's permitted, I'd like 20 decagrams of your excellent ham, please.

It's understandable, however, when you consider the role that large multi-ethnic empires played in the development of social mores. These societies prized hierarchy and relied on courtesy to navigate the complex layers of class and authority.

FOTOKON/SHUTTERSTOCK

Foamy pilsner, Plzeň (Pilsen; p98), Czechia

HOW TO...
Drink Beer in Central Europe

Central Europe is home to some of the world's best beer – and most enthusiastic beer drinkers. Czechia leads the world in annual per capita beer consumption at around 130 litres per person, with Austria, Germany, Poland and Slovenia not far behind. Beer here comes with its own regional rituals. Below is a short primer.

Respect the Pour

Experienced bartenders will be well-schooled in how best to pour their local brew. Depending on the type, the beer may be served very cold or closer to room temperature, with relatively little froth or with a big head of creamy foam (such as with a pilsner in pubs in Czechia and Germany). It's bad form to question the pour or ask for the beer to be served differently.

Toasting

Before drinking, raise your glass, offer a hearty 'Cheers!' and clink glasses. If you're drinking from a mug or pint, clink from the side or rim. For taller, narrower glasses, clink from the bottom. Once you've clinked, take an immediate sip before putting your glass down as toasting without sipping is considered rude. During the toast, maintain direct eye contact with each person in turn (the mythical consequences for not doing this are severe). Never cross arms across the table while toasting – another transgression that's sure to bring bad luck.

Ordering Another Round

Once you've started drinking, finish the beer to the last sip to show appreciation. Leaving a half-finished beer at the table is not done. Never pour the contents of a half-drunk beer into another glass to top it up. There's probably no faster way to get deported. Likewise, it's bad form to water down or mix a traditional beer with anything else. The exception is a *Radler*, a mix of pale lager and a lemon-line soft drink. In a good pub, there's usually no need to wave down the server to ask for another round. He or she will ask at the appropriate moment if you'd like another. It's common practice to buy a round for friends, with each person in turn taking the next round. When settling up, servers normally expect a tip of around 10%.

REGIONAL STYLES

Central European brewers have dozens of different styles, each featuring a different colour, body, taste and finish. Some of our faves:

Pils (Pilsner) Bottom-fermented, with a crisp, hoppy bite and creamy crown. Beloved in Czechia and throughout Central Europe.

Light Pale lager. Depending on the brewer, the taste leans more or less bitter. The standard order *(Helles)* in much of Germany and Austria.

Dark Roasted malts give these beers a darker colour and sweeter taste.

Wheat Top-fermented, with fruity, spicy notes, reminiscent of bananas or cloves.

Craft Hop-forward, high-alcohol IPAs and pale ales.

39

SAHARA FROST/SHUTTERSTOCK

Döner Kebab

THE FOOD SCENE

Central Europe welcomes travellers with flavourful, hearty food and knock-out (sometimes literally) wine, beer and spirits.

While each country in Central Europe has its own unique cuisine, dishes across the region share many aspects. Cooks everywhere tend to emphasise comfort and simplicity over sophistication, with a strong reliance on local agriculture and livestock. Recipes also reflect the region's geography, characterised by long winters and fertile fields. The long dominance of Austria's Habsburg Empire is also evident on menus everywhere. That said, each country brings its own identity to the mix. In Germany and Czechia, hearty dishes like roast pork with bread dumplings and sauerkraut or beef goulash often define the midday meal. Poland adds its own take on dumplings (pierogi), usually stuffed with curd cheese or cabbage. Hungarian cooks add a dash of paprika to their national dish, goulash. In Austria, find beautifully turned out schnitzels (breaded and fried veal or pork cutlets) and potato salad. Slovakia adds a rustic touch. The local specialty is potato dumplings with a tart sheep's cheese *(bryndzové halušky)*. Switzerland's potato and cheese dishes also reflect this comfort-first philosophy.

Hungarian Cuisine: The Regional Standout

While each of the national cuisines of Central Europe feature exceptional dishes, the region's underrated culinary star might well be Hungary. Traditional Hungarian fare is rich, hearty and scrump-

Best Central European Dishes	EISBEIN/ SCHWEINSHAXE, AUSTRIA & GERMANY	VEPŘO-KNEDLO-ZELO, CZECHIA	SPARGEL, GERMANY	GOULASH, HUNGARY
	Broiled or grilled pork hock.	Roast pork with bread dumplings and sauerkraut.	Steamed white asparagus, drizzled with brown butter.	Rich soup of beef cubes, vegetables and paprika.

tious – and also *spicy*. Hot peppers and paprika play starring roles here, while only serving as bit players in the other countries. Paprika features heavily in Hungary's two best-known dishes, goulash and chicken paprikash – a chicken stew that also tosses in plenty of sour cream for good measure. And while Hungary may be landlocked, look out for its signature fish soup *(halászlé)*. Hungarian cooking draws plenty of inspiration from its former invaders, like Austria and Turkey, as well as minority communities like its Jewish population.

In Poland: Know Your Kiełbasa

Sausage plays a big role in every country in Central Europe, but Poland's vast range of *kiełbasa* (sausages) stands out. Usually made from pork, they are often eaten as a snack or part of a light lunch or dinner, and served with a side of brown bread and mustard. It's helpful to know some of the local favourites. *Wiejska kiełbasa* are the most popular. These are thick cylinders of pork, spiced with garlic and marjoram. *Kiełbasa myśliwska* (hunters' sausage) are smoked and air-cured and flavoured with juniper. Also air-cured are *kabanosy*, thin

sausages seasoned with caraway. *Krakowska*, a speciality of Kraków but found across Poland, are thick and seasoned with pepper and garlic. *Biała* are thin and white. These are traditionally sold uncooked and then boiled in soups like the barley broth *żurek staropolski*. Whatever you pick, you can't lose.

Oktoberfest

FESTIVALS TO FEAST AT

Aufsteirern Festival *(p71; September)* The biggest Styrian celebration of food, wine, crafts and costume, filling Graz's Old Town.

Oktoberfest (p149; September/October) The world's largest beer festival, where six million people down steins of Märzen beer in Munich's Theresienwiese.

Budapest Wine Festival (p187; September) One of Budapest's most atmospheric events, held in the courtyards of Buda Castle.

Tihany Lavender Festival (p201; June/July) A harvest celebration, featuring handmade goods, lavender-infused foods and family picnics.

Pezinok Wine Festival (p244; September) Western Slovakia's biggest wine event. Vineyards are open for tastings and the streets fill with parades and folk music.

Prekmurska gibanica

LEFT: YESPHOTOGRAPHERS/SHUTTERSTOCK, RIGHT: KATJEN/SHUTTERSTOCK ©

PIEROGI, POLAND	BRYNDZOVÉ HALUŠKY, SLOVAKIA	PREKMURSKA GIBANICA, SLOVENIA	CHEESE FONDUE, SWITZERLAND
Crescent-shaped dumplings with a variety of fillings.	Dumplings with sheep's cheese and smoked bacon.	Layered pastry, today a national treasure.	Melted Alpine comfort shared with bread.

Currywurst

Germany's Culinary Landscape

Germany's culinary heritage reads like a flavour map of its regional and cultural mix. Bavarian cuisine is catnip for carnivores, with everything from crispy roast pork to sausages galore. The Black Forest is your ticket to *Maultaschen*, a Teutonic twist on ravioli, and the irresistible Black Forest gateau. Coastal regions sing the praises of fresh and smoked fish. In the Rhineland, *Sauerbraten*, a tangy pot roast, is a cherished dish, while Thuringia serves up bratwurst perfection. Berlin spices things up with its cult-fave currywurst. In Saxony, the buttery Dresdner Stollen cake reigns supreme.

The Importance of Seasonal Foods

Locals take genuine pride in homegrown produce. On weekend mornings across the region, locals comb the stalls of their closest farmers' market to find whatever's in season. In spring, they might be eyeing the asparagus, wild garlic or fresh herbs. Later in summer, cherries, strawberries, peaches and plums make an appearance – often destined for dumplings or strudels. Towards the end of the growing season, shoppers turn their attention to mushrooms, squash and root vegetables used to season soups and roasts.

Schnapps & Spirits

On most days, wine and beer are the most common drinks in Central Europe. It won't be long, though, before you're offered a glass of the region's famous brandy or schnapps. According to specious medical 'research', such fiery spirits are a cure-all for whatever ails you, and locals are generous in doling them out.

Most brandies are distilled from fruit, and each country has its own preference. In Czechia and Slovakia, look for *slivovica* ('slivo') from plums. Hungarians and Austrians often go for the slightly sweeter but still potent apricot schnapps. In Germany, sample brandies made from cherries (*Kirschwasser*) and pears (*Williamsbirne*). In Poland, vodka reigns supreme. It's enjoyed ice cold and neat – prepare for some serious side-eye if you add orange juice.

HOLIDAY MEALS

The important Christmas and Easter holidays come with their own deep-rooted culinary traditions. At Christmas, family tables are topped with traditional symbolic dishes. In Czechia, homemakers spend days and weeks baking special cookies. Christmas Eve dinner invariably involves fried carp and potato salad.

In Poland, the Christmas Eve feast, dubbed the *wigilia*, typically also features carp, but here with pierogi and clear beet soup. Austrian and German homes fill with the aromas of fruit cake (*stollen*), sweet cakes (*lebkuchen*) and roast goose. In Hungary, poppy-seed rolls (*bejgli*) are a Christmas obsession. Swiss families gather over fondue or raclette, sharing cheese, bread and good cheer.

Equally important, Easter traditions typically revolve around special braided breads. Family meals feature baked ham or, in some areas, lamb. Painted eggs are cherished everywhere. In Slovenia, homemakers bake *potica*, a beloved walnut roll.

Specialities

Street Food

Bratwurst or Currywurst (Germany & Austria) Flavoured sausages and a classic late-night German nosh.

Burek (Slovenia) Flaky pastry with cheese or meat, found at bakery counters and late-night stands.

Döner Kebab (Germany & Austria) Turkish import of pita kebab stuffed with cabbage and lamb mince. For added spice, order it 'mit scharf'.

Kranjska Klobasa (Slovenia) Slovenian sausage, culturally protected within the EU.

Lángos (Hungary & Slovakia) Deep-fried disc-shaped dough with various toppings – usually sour cream and cheese.

Leberkäse (Germany) A kind of Bavarian meatloaf sliced thick into a crusty roll.

Obwarzanki (Poland) Bagel-like bread rings, sold from street carts.

Zapiekanka (Poland) A long baguette topped with mushrooms, cheese and ketchup and a staple of Kraków nightlife.

Sweet Treats

Koláč (Czechia) Sweet pastry filled with fruit or poppy seeds.

Zapiekanka

Krapfen (Germany & Austria) Deep-fried doughnuts, filled with jam or cream. Especially popular around Carnival season.

Kürtőskalács (Hungary) Called chimney cake in English, this cylindrical dough is baked over an open fire and rolled in cinnamon, vanilla sugar or sweet toppings. Also common in Prague (known in Czech as *trdelník*).

Ovocné knedlíky (Czechia) Sweet dumplings, stuffed with berries, plums or apricots, and drizzled with butter and sugar.

Pączki (Poland) Doughnuts, often filled with custard.

Sacher Torte (Austria) The ultimate chocolate cake – rich, iced and with a layer of tangy apricot jam.

MEALS OF A LIFETIME

Modrá Hviezda (p245) On the up way to Bratislava Castle, features high-end takes on traditional Slovak food.

420 Restaurant (p94) Directly across from Prague's Astronomical Clock, but it feels like a find.

Stand25 (p192) Freestyle Hungarian cuisine, overseen by Bocuse d'Or–winning chef Tamás Széll.

JAZ by Ana Roš (p264) Michelin-starred chef Ana Roš brings her inventive dishes to Ljubljana at affordable prices.

Restauracja Lwia Brama (p226) Modern Polish fare in an inviting medieval cellar on Wrocław's Cathedral Island.

Gasthaus zur Oper (p58) This contemporary venue serves perfectly prepared house recipe *Wiener Schnitzel*.

THE YEAR IN FOOD

SPRING

Upon awakening from winter, food becomes lighter, brighter and greener. Colourful vegetables, soft fruit and fresh herbs abound; Central Europe takes its Easter feasts seriously.

SUMMER

Meals become social gatherings and spill onto balconies, porches and picnic blankets. People start preserving by pickling, drying, fermenting and jarring everything that grows.

AUTUMN

Misty autumn days dish up a feast of mushrooms and game. Fizzy young wine is served in Austria *(sturm)* and Czechia *(burčák)*. Goose lands on tables for St Martin's Day (11 November).

WINTER

Slow-cooked, hearty dishes take centre stage. Meals are made to fill and nourish. Hot, spiced wine *(glühwein)* makes its appearance at Christmas markets and special breads and cookies warm kitchens.

Kitzbühel (p76), Austria

TRIP PLANNER

SKIING IN CENTRAL EUROPE

No matter whether you're a slalom expert, a freerider or a beginner, there's a slope for you. Austria and Switzerland have world-class facilities, but skiing is also popular in Czechia, Poland, Slovakia and Slovenia – often with the added benefit of cheaper lift passes and accommodation.

Lift Passes

Lift passes everywhere will take a big chunk out of your budget. Count on paying anywhere from €50 to €75 for a one-day pass, with reductions for longer-term passes. Prices vary; passes for less-known places may be as little as half of what's charged in the big-name resorts. The passes often give access to one or more ski areas and nearly always include shuttles. Kids usually pay half-price, while those under five or six ski for free (bring a passport as proof of age). At many resorts, lift passes are hands-free, with a built-in chip that barriers detect.

Properly insured?

Before you hurtle down that black run, make sure you're insured and read the small print: mountain-rescue costs, medical treatment and repatriation can quickly add up.

Equipment Hire & Ski School

Skis, boots, poles and helmets – resorts often rent everything you might need. Expect to pay from €30/165 per day/week for skis, with additional charges for top-of-the-range gear and boot hire. Many resorts also have one or more ski schools, and often offer instruction in English. In Austria, group lessons for both adults and children start from €120 per day (two hours in the morning, two hours in the afternoon). Costs may be lower in other places. Usually, the more lessons you take, the cheaper the rate per day.

CZECHIA

Czechia may not be the first place you think of when looking for a winter-sports destination, but this largely mountainous country offers lots of winter fun, especially if you are into less-obvious activities such as

Plan your ski trip to Central Europe using these handy websites.

Bergfex (bergfex.com) A great website with piste maps, snow forecasts and details of ski resorts in Austria, Switzerland, Germany and Slovenia.

If You Ski (ifyouski.com) Resort guides, ski deals and information on ski hire and schools. Best for Austria and Switzerland.

On the Snow (onthesnow. co.uk) Reviews of Central European ski resorts, plus snow reports, webcams and lift-pass details.

Sno (sno.co.uk) A handy Top 10 resort guide ranked according to theme and level, plus deals on holidays and hotels.

---

cross-country skiing and hiking. For downhill skiing, the resorts of northern Bohemia, near the Polish border, are the best, with the full range of hire centres, après-ski options and luxury accommodation available. Notable resorts include **Harrachov** (skiareal.com), **Pec pod Sněžkou** (skiresort.cz) and **Špindlerův Mlýn** (skiareal.cz).

GERMANY

Skiing is popular in southern Germany. Both downhill and cross-country skiing are possible at Feldberg, site of the Black Forest's highest peak at 1493m. It's family-friendly and offers ski hire. Afterwards, hit the après-ski bars in small resort towns such as Todtnau and Feldberg. Also check out the ski resorts of Garmisch-Partenkirchen in Bavaria if you're keen on more winter adventures.

POLAND

The mountain ranges of southern Poland are the places to ski, though you can go cross-country skiing in other locations as well, especially around the Masurian Lakes. The Tatras have the most resorts, and the country's winter sports capital of Zakopane is the most popular. Here, several ski areas (pkl.pl) range from flat tracks for cross-country skiers to alpine slopes that are suitable for everyone from newbies to shredders. Mt Kasprowy Wierch (1987m) has the most challenging slopes in this region, and the skiing season sometimes extends into early May.

SLOVAKIA

Don't sleep on Slovakia. The High Tatras resorts – Tatranská Lomnica on the eastern side, the Smokovec resorts in the middle and Štrbské Pleso to the west –all come alive in winter. From Tatranská Lomnica, Slovakia's most hair-raising cable car ascends to Lomnický štít, the nation's second-highest summit at 2634m. Take a six-seat chairlift to Štart, then the gondola to Skalnaté pleso. **Ski Resort Tatranská Lomnica** (vt.sk) has dramatic pistes: the black run from Lomnické sedlo is Slovakia's steepest.

SLOVENIA

Skiing rivals hiking as the most popular recreational pursuit in Slovenia. Most of Slovenia's ski areas are small and relatively unchallenging, but they do have the attraction of lower prices. Recommended ski areas include **Kranjska Gora** (kranjska-gora.si), with some 20km of pistes. **Vogel** (vogel.si/en/winter) sits above shimmering Lake Bohinj, with dazzling views of Mt Triglav and reliable snow cover. **Krvavec** (rtc-krvavec.si/skiing) is located in the hills northeast of the city of Kranj. As it's only an hour's drive from Ljubljana, it's best avoided at the weekends.

TOP SKI RESORTS IN AUSTRIA

Ski Amadé
In Salzburgerland, Austria's biggest ski area covers a whopping 760km of pistes. Its 25 resorts are divided into five snow-sure regions, with every sort of terrain, from gentle cruising on tree-lined runs to off-piste touring.

Ski Arlberg
Tyrol's famous ski area has 300km of signposted pistes. The star is St Anton am Arlberg, beloved by expert skiers and boarders.

Kitzbühel
The legendary Hahnenkamm mountain, 233km of groomed slopes and upbeat nightlife make Kitzbühel as popular as ever.

Zillertal 3000
Mayrhofen is the showpiece of Zillertal 3000, which has 202km of slopes. Besides being an intermediate paradise, Mayrhofen has Austria's steepest black run.

FROM LEFT: BRUNOCOELHO/SHUTTERSTOCK, JAN VON NEBENAN/SHUTTERSTOCK

Lake Bled (p268), Slovenia

THE OUTDOORS

Central Europe is an adventure waiting to happen – if you're after an outdoor experience that feels authentic, raw and undiscovered, that is.

With mountains covering so much of Central Europe, it's no wonder the outdoors holds such an attraction here. The Alps are at their highest in Switzerland, with jagged, Toblerone-like peaks such as the Matterhorn, and they continue their march through southern Germany, across Austria and into Slovenia. Hike, bike, ski or simply ride the gondolas and funiculars to enjoy the Alpine views. Other mountains, like Slovakia's High Tatras, promise just as much adventure. In mid-summer, lakes and rivers lure bathers and boaters.

Walking, Hiking & Cycling

It's safe to say that walking and hiking are Central Europe's most popular active pur-

suits. Across the region, networks of clearly signposted paths link valleys, lakes and peaks, making hiking suitable for everyone from casual walkers to seasoned trekkers. Many trails are colour-coded to let hikers gauge the level of difficulty. Pick up detailed maps at tourist offices or bookstores.

Trails in the mountains of Austria, Switzerland, Slovenia and Slovakia are the most challenging and rewarding, but beautiful, serene trails cut through landscapes of all types. Some of the regional highlights include Slovakia's Slovenský Raj National Park, where ladders and chain-assists line the trails of the waterfall-filled park. In Slovenia's Julian Alps, near the Italian border, paths lace the high-altitude region, centered

---

Underground Adventures

POSTOJNA CAVE, SLOVENIA
Explore this 24km-long **cave system** (p270), a series of two-million-year-old caverns, halls and passages.

HOSPITAL IN THE ROCK, HUNGARY
Walk around the maze of wards in this underground **hospital** (p190) turned nuclear bunker in Budapest.

BRNO'S UNDER-GROUND, CZECHIA
Find your way through the **Labyrinth under the Vegetable Market** (p104), 8m beneath cabbage vendors.

on iconic Mt Triglav. In Switzerland's Jungfrau Region, the many routes pass through a spectacular playground of peaks and valleys. In Germany's Black Forest, meanwhile, timeworn paths lead from bucolic villages to misty peaks. And in Kitzbühel in Austria, peak-to-peak hiking is served by cable cars.

Many trails are also suited for mountain biking. In summer, ski resorts turn into downhill terrain parks, offering plenty of banked turns, jumps and on-site rentals. And urban cycling across cities in Germany and Austria is a way of life. Cyclists often outnumber pedestrians in cities like Berlin, Vienna and even Ljubljana.

Feldberg (p159), Germany

Skiing & Snow Sports

Skiing is one pursuit where Central Europe is truly world class. Resorts here range from the world-famous to smaller family-friendly affairs. The best facilities are in Austria and Switzerland, where state-of-the-art resorts combine reliable snow, modern lifts and festive après-ski traditions. In Switzerland, car-free Zermatt, beneath the Matterhorn, has year-round skiing on a glacier, plus a charming village atmosphere. Slovakia's High Tatras have well-equipped resorts near Štrbské Pleso and Tatranská Lomnica. In Germany's Black Forest, Feldberg features gentler runs that are ideal for beginners.

On the Water

Central Europe has an impressive range of water-based activities, from lakes and rivers to spas. For the best of the latter, hit one of Budapest's famed historic bathhouses. Natural lakes like Austria's Wörthersee or Slovenia's Lake Bohinj lure open-water swimmers, kayakers and stand-up paddle-boarders each summer. Enormous Lake Balaton in Hungary might well be the best of all. Switzerland's Lake Geneva and Zürich's lake and riverside lidos attract swimmers from May to September. For those seeking more adventure, the Julian Alps in Slovenia feature heart-stopping white-water rafting and canyoning opportunities in serene mountain settings.

WIELICZKA SALT MINE, POLAND	**HALLSTATT SALT MINE, AUSTRIA**	**EISRIESENWELT ICE CAVES, AUSTRIA**	**SLOVENSKÝ RAJ, SLOVAKIA**
Marvel at the beauty of the huge underground **salt mine** (p223) in Kraków, where even the chandeliers are salt.	A fascinating experience in the world's oldest **salt mine** (p68), complete with miner slides and tunnels.	Poke around these **caves** (p67) and discover a wonderworld of frozen chambers and sculptures.	Cave and hike through **Slovenský Raj National Park** (p253) to find gorges, ladders, and limestone passages.

National Parks

1. Bavarian Forest National Park, Germany (p155)
2. Black Forest National Park, Germany (p158)
3. Malá Fatra National Park, Slovakia (p250)
4. Slovenský Raj National Park, Slovakia (p253)
5. Strunjan Landscape Park, Slovenia (p271)

Swimming

1. Bains des Pâquis, Switzerland (p282)
2. Lake Balaton, Hungary (p201)
3. Lake Bohinj, Slovenia (p269)
4. Titisee, Germany (p159)
5. Wörthersee, Austria (p72)
6. Zürich, Switzerland (p287)

ACTION AREAS

Where to find Central Europe's best outdoor activities.

BALTIC SEA

LITHUANIA

RUSSIA

Gulf of
Gdańsk

Kaliningrad

Pomeranian
Bay

Gdańsk

Great
Masurian
Lakes

Koszalin

Olsztyn

Białystok

BELARUS

Toruń

Białowieża
National Park

Poznań

Warsaw

POLAND

Zielona
Góra

Łódź

Lublin

Wrocław

Odra

Sudeten Mountains

Vistula

Elbe

Prague

Kraków

Przemyśl

Kutná Hora

Ostrava

Oświęcim

UKRAINE

Olomouc

Zakopane

CZECHIA

Brno

Malá Fatra
National Park

Bardejov

Telč

Poprad

České
Budějovice

Slovenský Raj
National Park

Levoča

Trenčín

Košice

Banská
Štiavnica

SLOVAKIA

Tisza

Vienna

Bratislava

Eger

Tokaj

Melk

Esztergom

Vác

Debrecen

Sopron

Visegrád

Lake
Tisza

AUSTRIA

Győr

Budapest

ROMANIA

Graz

HUNGARY

Kecskemét

Maribor

Tihany

Keszthely

Siófok

Kiskunsági
Nemzeti Park

SLOVENIA

Lake
Balaton

Szeged

Zagreb

Pécs

SERBIA

CROATIA

Skiing/Snowboarding

1. Garmisch-Partenkirchen, Germany (p152)
2. High Tatras, Slovakia (p252)
3. Grindelwald, Switzerland (p292)
4. Kitzbühel, Austria (p76)
5. Zermatt, Switzerland (p290)
6. Zillertal, Austria (p76)

Vineyards/Wineries

1. Deutsche Weinstrasse (p175)
2. Eger, Hungary (p202)
3. Pezinok, Slovakia (p244)
4. Tokaj, Hungary (p203)
5. Wachau Valley, Austria (p62)

Walking/Hiking

1. Aletsch Glacier, Switzerland (p292)
2. Feldberg, Germany (p159)
3. Goethe Trail, Austria (p75)
4. High Tatras, Slovakia (p251)
5. Zillertal, Austria (p76)
6. Savica Waterfall, Slovenia (p269)
7. Vrátna Valley, Slovakia (p249)

0 — 200 km
0 — 100 miles

49

CENTRAL EUROPE

THE GUIDE

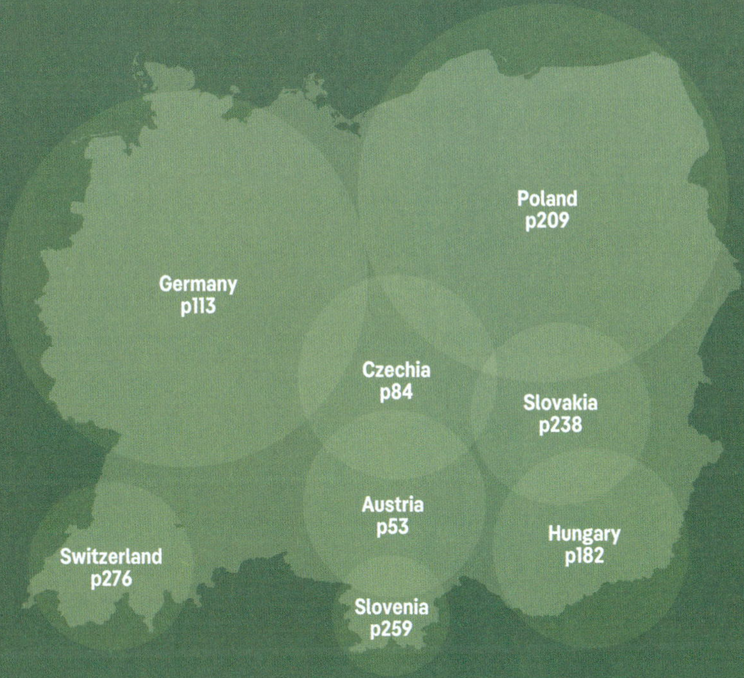
Poland
p209
Germany
p113
Czechia
p84
Slovakia
p238
Austria
p53
Hungary
p182
Switzerland
p276
Slovenia
p259

Chapters in this section are organised by countries, with each country split into hubs and their surrounding areas. Each hub includes unique experiences, local insights, insider tips and expert recommendations. It's also your gateway to the surrounding area, where you'll see what and how much you can do from there.

Grossglockner Road (p69), Austria

PYTY/SHUTTERSTOCK

For places to stay
in Austria, see
p79

LUDMILA KIERKMEER/SHUTTERSTOCK

Above: Stift Melk (p61), Melk; Right: Skiing, Kitzbühel (p76)

Curated by
Kerry Walker

Austria

WHERE CULTURE HITS THE HEIGHTS

No country waltzes so effortlessly between urban and outdoors as Austria. One day you're cresting alpine summits, the next you're swanning around imperial Vienna.

For such a tiny country, Austria is ridiculously big on inspiration. This is the land where Mozart was born, Strauss taught the world to waltz and Julie Andrews grabbed the spotlight with her twirling entrance in *The Sound of Music*. It's where the Habsburgs ruled over their spectacular, sprawling 600-year empire.

These past glories still shine in the resplendent baroque palaces and chandelier-lit coffee houses of Vienna, Innsbruck and Salzburg. Over centuries, the Habsburgs channelled immense wealth into the fine arts and music, collecting palaces the way others do stamps. You'll feel their cultural reverberations today – be it hearing the work of classical masters echo at lavishly gilded concert halls, eyeballing avant-garde art in born-again baroque riding stables, or catching a summer music festival against an uplifting lakeside or mountain backdrop.

Beyond its storybook cities, Austria's trump card is its astonishing natural beauty, which waltzes joyously from the romance of the vine-strewn Wachau to the crystal-clear lakes of Carinthia. Whether you're schussing down the legendary slopes of Kitzbühel, spotting an ibex in the fiery light of sunset as you crest a mountain ridge in Hohe Tauern National Park, or freewheeling along the banks of the mighty Danube, you'll find the kind of landscapes to which no well-orchestrated symphony or singing nun could ever quite do justice.

GEVISION/SHUTTERSTOCK

THE MAIN AREAS

Find Your Way

Austria's public transport network is a dream, with swift, inexpensive trains linking towns and cities, and buses filling the gaps. Car hire gives you greater freedom to explore the country's remotest corners.

CAR

Autobahn (motorways) are well maintained. You can only drive on them with a *Vignette* (motorway tax), available from border crossings and petrol stations. Be prepared for exposed, sharply twisting roads in the Alps.

TRAIN

Austria's rail network is fast, efficient, inexpensive and wide-reaching. Österreiche Bundesbahn (ÖBB; *Austrian Federal Railway; oebb.at*) is the main operator. The best deals are *Sparschiene*, heavily discounted tickets sold up to six months ahead.

Vienna, p56

Baroque streetscapes and imperial palaces set the stage for Vienna's artistic and musical masterpieces alongside its coffee-house culture and vibrant epicurean and design scenes.

Graz & the South, p70

Castle-topped Graz beguiles with medieval looks and edgy art, while beyond rolling hills, vines, orchards and pristine mountain lakes entice.

Salzburg, p63

Legends have been made and born on these grand baroque streets, where you can explore Mozart's 'hood, climb to a medieval castle and catch one of Europe's greatest summer festivals.

Innsbruck & Tyrol, p73

Cultured Innsbruck is the springboard for mountains that make you want to yodel out loud, from summer's patchwork pastures to Christmas-card scenes in winter.

GERMANY

CZECHIA

SLOVAKIA

HUNGARY

SLOVENIA

ITALY

SWITZERLAND

LIECHTENSTEIN

Munich

VIENNA · Bratislava
Eisenstadt
Neusiedler See
Neusiedl am See
Szombathely

Laa an der Thaya
Mistelbach
Retz
Hollabrunn
Horn
Gmünd
Zwettl
Krems an der Donau
St Pölten
Tulln
Danube (Donau)
Amstetten
Baden bei Wien
Wiener Neustadt
Neunkirchen
Oberpullendorf
Oberwart
Feldbach

Freistadt
Linz
Enns
Steyr
Mürzzuschlag
Kapfenberg
Hartberg

České Budějovice

Passau
Landshut
Braunau am Inn
Ried
Mattighofen
Wels
Lambach
Gmunden
Ebensee
Bad Ischl
Liezen
Nationalpark Kalkalpen
Theben
Judenburg
Knittelfeld
Leoben
Graz
Wolfsberg
Leibnitz
Radkersberg
Maribor

Rosenheim
Kufstein
Wörgl
Kitzbühel
Zell am See
Saalfelden
Mittersill
Jenbach
Zell am Ziller
Hoher Dauchstein
Radstadt
Bad Gastein
Tamsweg
Murau
St Veit an der Glan
Feldkirchen
Völkermarkt
Klagenfurt

Bischofshofen
Bad Hofgastein
Salzburg
Hohe Tauern National Park
Grossglockner
Spittal an der Drau
Lienz
Drava
Villach

Sonthofen
Immenstadt
Memmingen
Bregenz
Dornbirn
Feldkirch
Bludenz
Arlberg
St Anton am Arlberg
Landeck
Imst
Innsbruck
Wildspitze
Ötztaler
Zugspitze

Konstanz
St Gallen
Chur
Vaduz
Schesaplana
Piz Buin

Merano
Bressanone
Bolzano

A1 A2 A3 A4 A5 A8 A9 A10 A12 A13 A14

50 miles

100 km

N

ROBERT NIEDRING/GETTY IMAGES

Cycling in the Zillertal (p76)

Plan Your Time

Austria looks deceptively small on a map, but as most of it is vertical there's always a mountain pass, alpine view or hidden hamlet to discover. Avoid peak season for better deals.

Vienna to Salzburg

● Begin with palaces, parks, galleries and world-class concert halls in **Vienna** (p56). An hour west is **Wachau** (p61) on the River Danube, home to twin-spired baroque abbey **Stift Melk** (p61). Next stop is UNESCO-stamped **Hallstatt** (p68). Continue west to **Werfen** (p67) and the **Eisriesenwelt** (p67) ice caves, before rounding out with fortress-topped **Salzburg** (p63).

Into the Tyrolean Alps

● Admire soaring peaks in **Innsbruck** (p73). Roam the Altstadt's medieval lanes, before breezing up to 2334m **Hafelekarspitze** (p75). Skip east to **Swarovski Crystal Worlds** (p75) in Wattens. Detour south to the **Zillertal** (p76) for mountain biking, hiking, whitewater rafting and skiing. From here, head east to **Kitzbühel** (p76) for more action on Olympic slopes.

SEASONAL HIGHLIGHTS

SPRING

Meadows and parks bloom. Snow polishes the highest Alps, but there's cycling and hiking in valleys. Easter markets dazzle.

SUMMER

Light, warm days entice hikers. Cities host open-air festivals, including Vienna's **Donauinselfest** (p59).

AUTUMN

New wine in *Heurigen* (taverns) and highs like **Steirischer Herbst festival** (p71). Cows descend from pastures at the **Almabtrieb** (p78).

WINTER

Alpine slopes buzz, Christmas markets sparkle and Vienna waltzes into ball season. Salzburg gets orchestral at **Mozartwoche** (p65).

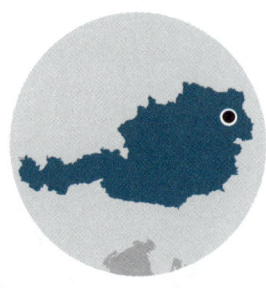

Vienna

REGAL HISTORY | HIGH CULTURE | CUTTING-EDGE ARTS

GETTING AROUND

Vienna's historic centre and inner districts are easy to explore on foot, including the Hofburg, museum complexes, modern neighbourhoods with landmarks and low-key nightlife. Schloss Schönbrunn can be easily reached by bus, tram and metro from the centre. Get information at *wienerlinien.at*.

☑ TOP TIP

There's an easy way to know when you've left the circular centre. The grandiose architectural loop of the Ringstrasse surrounding the Innere Stadt, completed on one side of the Danube Canal, is a great orientation point. Beyond this boulevard border, you enter the fringes of the inner districts.

Few cities in the world waltz so effortlessly between past and present, urban and outdoors like Vienna, a capital that has clocked up Mercer's 'most liveable city in the world' for many consecutive years. Its splendid historical face is easily recognised: grand imperial palaces and bombastic baroque interiors, revered opera houses, magnificent squares and art-vault museums curated over the 600-year reign of the Habsburgs.

But Austria's capital isn't bound by its vintage time bubble. Dig deeper, and you'll see a multifaceted Vienna on a spectrum from grandeur to gritty that bridges the classical and the contemporary. You'll need to cover some ground, though – which is easy to do via Vienna's excellent and cheap public transport system.

A stone's throw from Hofburg (the Imperial Palace), the MuseumsQuartier houses provocative and high-profile contemporary art behind a striking basalt facade. In the Innere Stadt (Inner City), up-to-the-minute design stores sidle up to old-world confectioners, and Austro-Asian fusion restaurants stand alongside traditional *Beisln* (small taverns).

Seeking Out Stephansdom

Vienna's symbolic landmark cathedral

Vienna's Gothic masterpiece **Stephansdom** *(stephanskirche. at)* soars above. A mosaic of 230,000 glazed roof tiles crests in between, stamped with the imperial double-headed eagle. It's free to venture into the vaulted, prismatic glass site. You have to pay to enter the central **nave** *(adult/child €7/3, cash only)* for a closer look at the 16th-century sandstone masterwork on the **Pilgramkanzel** (Pilgrim pulpit) and the commanding baroque black marble **High Altar** consecrating the holy space some 100 years later.

Austria's largest bell, the 21-tonne *Pummerin*, is accessible via an elevator journey to the **North Tower** *(adult/child €7/3)*

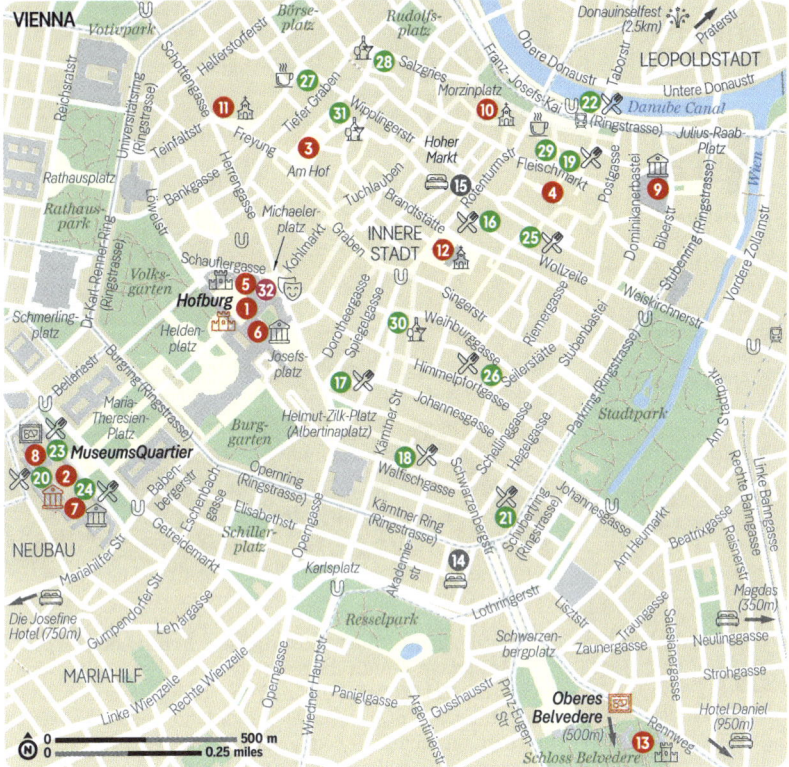

★ HIGHLIGHTS
1 Hofburg
2 MuseumsQuartier

● SIGHTS
3 Am Hof
4 Heiligenkreuzerhof
5 Kaiserappartements
6 Kaiserliche
   Schatzkammer
7 Leopold Museum
8 mumok

9 Österreichische
   Postsparkasse
10 Ruprechtskirche
11 Schottenkirche
see 5 Sisi Museum
12 Stephansdom
13 Unteres Belvedere

● SLEEPING
14 Hotel Imperial
15 Hotel Lamée

● EATING
16 Figlmüller
17 Gasthaus Reinthaler
18 Gasthaus zur Oper
19 Griechenbeisl
20 Halle
21 Meissl & Schadn
22 Motto am Fluss
23 MQ Kantine
24 MQDaily
25 Parémi
26 Tian

**● DRINKING
& NIGHTLIFE**
see 7 Café Leopold
27 Die Cafetière
28 Dino's Apothecary Bar
29 Fenster Café
see 15 Lamée Rooftop Bar
30 Loos American Bar
31 Needle Vinyl Bar

● ENTERTAINMENT
32 Spanische
   Hofreitschule

platform overlooking Stephansplatz. Sweeping city views from the **South Tower** *(adult/child €6.50/2.50)* require enough stamina to climb 343 precarious, winding steps to access the peering **Türmerstube** (tower room).

Step into the Middle Ages

Medieval squares and backstreets

Narrow trader alleys, age-old market squares and hidden courtyards – pockets of the Innere Stadt are a window into

COFFEE IN THE 1ST DISTRICT

Michael Prem, owner of sustainable coffee roastery Prem Frischkaffee *(frischkaffee.at),* shares his favourite coffee spots.

Café Exchange: A special place in Österreichische Postsparkasse, where you can breathe in the atmosphere of Otto Wagner while enjoying a daily lunch menu, homemade cakes and coffee brews crafted by award-winning baristas.

Parémi: French bakery combining impeccable coffee with Vienna's best croissant.

Fenster Café: Unique hole-in-the-wall cafe near Schwedenplatz serves its own roast. This is not a space you can enter, but it is the place to get a speciality brew when passing by.

MYROSLAVA BOZHKO/SHUTTERSTOCK

Am Hof

medieval Vienna. Start in **Blutgasse**, **Franziskanerplatz** and **Ballgasse**, beautiful streets hidden behind Stephansdom.

Palatial **Am Hof** stands upon the grand designs of 1154, when the Duke of Bavaria, Heinrich II, retreated to Vienna and built the palatinate compound. He commissioned Vienna's oldest monastery church, **Schottenkirche**, on neighbouring Freyung in 1170.

The courtyard curiosity of **Heiligenkreuzerhof** has its foundations in the 1135-founded Heiligenkreuz Abbey. A time-warp passage between Schönlaterngasse and Grashofgasse, today's courtyard was added in 1771. Neighbouring **Ruprechtskirche**, from 1200, is the oldest in Vienna, overlooking Schwedenplatz and perched on an elevated weave of cobbled alleys that chart the prettiest route down to the Danube Canal.

Habsburg Grandeur at the Hofburg

A palace to out-pomp them all

Nothing epitomises the Habsburgs' extravagant reign more than the humongous 240,000-sq-metre **Hofburg**. Home to

 EATING IN INNERE STADT: WIENER SCHNITZEL

Figlmüller: Proclaimed inventors, where the original *Wiener Schnitzel* (breadcrumbed veal cutlet) has been served since 1905. *11am-10.30pm* €€

Meissl & Schadn: Before feasting, watch the schnitzel beaten and baked through the open salon kitchen in front of the restaurant. *11.30am-11pm* €€€

Gasthaus Reinthaler: It's like time stopped still in this 1977 *Beisl,* one of the historic district's last remaining authentic taverns. *11am-11pm Mon-Fri* €€

Gasthaus zur Oper: Contemporary venue of classic culinary institution Plachutta serves perfectly prepared house recipe *Wiener Schnitzel. 11.30am-midnight* €€

the imperial family for 700 years until 1918, the palace is a tapestry of heritage across its 18 wings and 19 courtyards, showcasing a staggering collection of cultural artefacts and art masterpieces.

Roll back the times in the **Alte Burg** (Old Castle). Enter the **Sisi Museum** and **Kaiserappartements** *(Imperial Apartments; sisimuseum-hofburg.at; adult/child €20/12)* via the marbled Emperor's Staircase – as visitors seeking an audience with Emperor Franz Joseph I once did – and meander through resplendent rooms of court life accompanied by a 75-minute audio guide. Move to the bedazzling belt of living spaces, including bedrooms and bathrooms, studies and saloons, preserved with their chandeliered ceilings, decked walls, regal red silk upholstery and royal gold embellishments.

Burrowed within the wings of the **Schweizerhof** (Swiss Courtyard) are the coveted crown jewels of Austria. The **Kaiserliche Schatzkammer** *(Imperial Treasury; kaiserliche-schatzkammer.at; adult/child €18/free)*. Make a beeline to the bejewelled Crown and Holy Lance of Emperor Rudolf II (Room 2), and the distinguished insignia of the Order of the Golden Fleece (Room 15).

The Hofburg residents today are world-famous white Lipizzaner stallions. Classical skills of horse-riding art and equestrianism have been practised at the UNESCO-listed **Spanische Hofreitschule** *(Spanish Riding School; srs.at; adult/child from €26/reduced)* since 1565. Horses dance gracefully in musical performances in the baroque **Winter Riding School** arena.

Baroque at the Belvedere

Find the world's most famous kiss

Prince Eugene of Savoy's 1723 baroque palace is a masterpiece; the art connoisseur filled it with his collections, which Empress Maria Theresia turned into the Imperial Picture Gallery in 1777, opening Vienna's first public museum. The dual complex is a trove of Austrian art from the Middle Ages to the present day and displays the world's largest collection of Klimt works.

Begin at the **Oberes Belvedere** *(adult/child €21/free; 9am-7pm)*. Top billing goes to Gustav Klimt's most famous work, *Der Kuss* (The Kiss), which, of his 22 paintings here, never leaves the gallery. Stroll the terraced, fountain-splashed, sculpture-strewn gardens down to the **Unteres Belvedere** *(adult/child €18/free, Combi ticket adult/child from €31.50/free; 10am-6pm)* to explore Prince Eugene's illustrious world. He commissioned

BEST FREE MUSIC FESTIVALS

The city of music has events throughout the year, though summer to autumn is when festivities abound.

Film Festival Rathausplatz: Open-air music films from concert and stage greats, plus pop-up eats at the City Hall square. *Jul-Sep*

Kultursommer Wien: Music, theatre and dance performances are staged at parks, squares and gardens across the city. *Jun-Aug*

Gürtel Night Walk: Up-and-coming artists and local bands perform outside the Gürtel (belt) road of bars. *last weekend in August*

Donauinselfest: Europe's biggest free open-air music festival brings the party to the Donauinsel (Danube Island). *last weekend in June*

 EATING IN THE HISTORIC CENTRE: OUR PICKS

Motto am Fluss: Canal-anchored boat with cafe and restaurant serving contemporary Austrian cuisine. *6-11pm Mon-Sat, to 10.30pm Sun, bar to midnight* €€

Griechenbeisl: Feast on *Wiener Schnitzel* and *Kaiserschmarrn* (sweet pancake) in the city's oldest *Beisl. noon-11pm* €€

Tian: This Michelin-star gourmet vegetarian restaurant is rooted in rare ingredients and experimental cooking. Book well ahead. *6am-11pm Tue-Sat* €€€

Die Cafetière: Revived mid-century modern cafe and purveyors of the tastiest Viennese cheese-and-ham toastie. *7.20am-6pm Mon-Fri, 9am-4pm Sat* €€

mumok

TOP TIPS FOR VISITING MQ

You'll need half a day for just one main museum. Bear in mind that mumok and Kunsthalle Wien are closed on Monday; Leopold Museum on Tuesday. Kunsthalle Wien has free entry 5pm to 9pm Thursday.

Should you wish to dig deeper into the world's largest cultural district, hook onto the one-hour **Secret MQ tour** *(mqw.at/programm/secret-mq-tour-1-1; English tours 3pm Sat).* Rest and refuel with organic plates at **MQ Kantine**, takeaway bites and beverages from **MQDaily**, Italian cuisine at **Halle** and Southeast Asian fare at **Café Leopold**.

baroque starchitect Johann Lucas von Hildebrandt to design the opulent summer residence.

A Cultural Dive into the MuseumsQuartier

Tune into Vienna's on-the-pulse arts scene

The former baroque imperial stables have been reborn as **MuseumsQuartier** *(MQ; mqw.at; courtyard open 24/7, museum entry times vary),* one of the world's largest cultural districts with its arsenal of 11 exhibition spaces.

For modernist art in a brightly lit marble interior, hit the **Leopold Museum** *(leopoldmuseum.org),* where star exhibits include the world's most comprehensive Egon Schiele collection and Gustav Klimt's *Death and Life* masterwork. Across the way, **mumok** *(mumok.at)* presents a galaxy of contemporary art: from expressionism to the experimental pop of the 1960s and 1970s, and the taboo and tragic in 20th-century Viennese actionism.

Save on individual entry with the MQ Fab 5 ticket *(€39);* discounted or free entry for children across all museums.

 DRINKING IN THE HISTORIC CENTRE: BARS

Dino's Apothecary Bar: Dark wood-panelled, low-light, classic cocktail bar. Extensive experimental menu. *5pm-2am Tue-Thu, to 3am Fri & Sat*

Loos American Bar: Celeb magnet and cult-status bar designed by Viennese modernism architect Adolf Loos. *noon-4am*

Lamée Rooftop Bar: The chic and colourful rooftop bar of Hotel Topazz Lamee, with one of the best views of Stephansdom. *11am-1am Sun-Thu, to 2am Fri & Sat*

Needle Vinyl Bar: A trendy, retro-styled, record-spinning bar lounge, mixing music and signature cocktails. *5pm-2am*

Beyond Vienna

Waltz beyond the Austrian capital to find some of the country's greatest treasures – from grand abbeys to romantic castle ruins.

Providing popular day-trip material from Vienna, Lower Austria possesses the country's most vibrant cultural landscape: a combination of vineyards and art, monasteries and low wooded hills. Through this enchanting scene flows the mighty Danube, which forms the famous Wachau – one of Europe's most fascinating valleys, watched over by castles and medieval villages.

The stretch of Danube between Krems and Melk is arguably the loveliest along the entire length of this long, long river. Both banks are dotted with ruined castles and medieval towns, and lined with terraced vineyards. You can also indulge in some of Austria's best wines, and local and seasonal dishes at low-key but enormously welcoming *Heurigen* (wine taverns).

Melk

TIME FROM VIENNA: **45MIN**

Benedictine abbey: the Wachau's baroque masterpiece

Perched on a granite outcrop overlooking the Danube, **Stift Melk** *(stiftmelk.at; adult/child €16/8)* is one of Europe's finest ensembles of baroque architecture. Built on the site of a castle, which Leopold II of Babenberg gave to Benedictine monks from Lambach in Upper Austria, it's a huge and imposing place.

The abbey church shines with frescos by baroque master Johann Michael Rottmayr, and Paul Troger, a highly influential painter who ditched the characteristic dark palette of baroque painting in favour of lighter, more vibrant colours. His huge, illusionistic ceiling painting is in the abbey's **Marble Hall**. Around two dozen monks reside in the abbey and surrounding parishes. English-language guided tours of the abbey take place two or three times a day and last around 50 minutes.

The Wachau by boat

Taking a cruise along the Danube is almost part and parcel of spending time in the **Wachau Valley**. It's a nice, lazy way to spend half a day, and the views from the upper deck, enhanced and unobstructed, are very enjoyable – so order yourself a cool spritzer from the onboard bar, sit back and watch the world go by. Tables on the upper deck tend to fill up fast. You can easily combine a boat cruise with a return journey by train or bicycle; don't forget to reserve a place for your bike

GETTING AROUND

Lower Austria is the largest of the country's nine states; however, given Vienna's proximity, transport links are frequent and efficient. There are good rail connections between Vienna and Krems via St Pölten. Along with the famous **Danube Cycle Path**, many areas of Lower Austria are fantastic for cycling, and bikes can easily be rented locally. Bring walking boots, too, as trails above the river lace hills and vines.

ON YOUR BIKE

The **Danube Cycle Path** is one of Europe's greatest long-distance cycle routes – and one of its most beautiful sections is between Krems and Melk, through the UNESCO-listed Wachau Valley. The path follows both banks of the Danube, so you can cycle along one bank and return along the other. Even better, you can take your bike on a boat from Krems to Melk, visiting Dürnstein and Spitz – or on a train from Krems to Emmersdorf (the town opposite Melk), stopping at Dürnstein, Spitz and other places. This makes it nice and easy to combine a river cruise or train ride through the area's legendary vineyards, stopping to soak up some of the Wachau's celebrated cultural sites while sampling its excellent wines.

TRABANTOS/SHUTTERSTOCK

Kuenringerburg castle, Dürnstein

when you book). **DDSG Blue Danube** (*ddsg-blue-danube.at*) offers cruises on the river between Krems and Melk, calling at Dürnstein and Spitz.

Dürnstein

TIME FROM VIENNA: 1HR 10MIN

Romantic castle ruins

The pretty little town of Dürnstein stands on an impossibly photogenic curve in the Danube, backed by low hills. Rising high above the town, **Kuenringerburg** is the castle where Richard I of England – yes, the Lionheart – was once imprisoned. He ended up here due to a dispute with Leopold V, Duke of Austria, during the Third Crusade. Leopold had Richard incarcerated on his way back from the Holy Land. Leopold was excommunicated for imprisoning a fellow Crusader, and was obliged to have Richard released (following the payment of a sizeable ransom – 35 tonnes of silver).

Only ruins of the castle remain, but they can still be visited, and the view is lovely. It takes 20 minutes to walk up from town following a clearly marked trail.

EATING & DRINKING IN THE WACHAU: OUR PICKS

Gasthof Prankl: Deservedly popular, with delicious food and local wines, in a 500-year-old former ship-owner's house in Spitz. *8am-10pm Fri-Tue* €€

Landgasthaus Essl: Refined dining on Danube's right bank between Spitz and Dürnstein. *11.30am-2.30pm & 6-11pm Wed-Fri, 11.30am-3.30pm & 6-11pm Sat, 11.30am-4pm Sun* €€€

Gasthof Goldenes Schiff: Family-run traditional restaurant and guesthouse, right in the centre of town, with a nice big terrace. *11.30am-8pm Thu-Tue* €€

Klosterhof Spitz: Set in a vineyard on the east side of Spitz, with tables in an atmospheric brick-vaulted interior. *11.30am-7pm Wed-Sun* €€

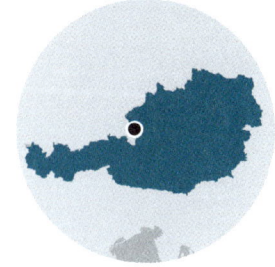

Salzburg

BAROQUE BRILLIANCE | MOZART'S BIRTHPLACE | ALPINE BACKDROP

The joke 'If it's baroque, don't fix it' could be a perfect maxim for Salzburg: the storybook Altstadt burrowed below steep hills looks much as it did when Mozart lived here 250 years ago. Beside the fast-flowing Salzach River, which divides the city in two, your lifted gaze is raised bit by bit to graceful domes and spires, the formidable clifftop fortress and the mountains beyond. It's a backdrop that did the lordly prince-archbishops and Maria proud.

Beyond Salzburg's two biggest money-spinners – Mozart and *The Sound of Music* – hides a city with a burgeoning arts scene, wonderful food, manicured parks, quiet side streets where classical music wafts from open windows, and concert halls that uphold musical tradition 365 days a year. Everywhere you go, the scenery, the skyline, the music and the history send your spirits soaring higher than Julie Andrews' octave-leaping vocals.

> ☑ **TOP TIP**
>
> During the summer holidays (July and August), Salzburg gets swamped. In December, when the city brims with Christmas markets and festival sparkle, it can get busy and expensive, too. Come in spring or autumn for cheaper flights, lower room rates and fewer crowds.

Salzburg on High

Get a ringside city view

Salzburg is at its most entrancing from above, with domes, spires and rooftops spreading out before you and the turquoise Salzach River unfurling into the mountains. One of the most memorable ways to see the city away from the masses is to get out and stride. Puff up the Nonnbergstiege to Benedictine abbey

 GETTING AROUND

Walking is the only way to get a true feel for Salzburg's pedestrianised backstreets. This is one of Austria's most cycle-friendly cities, with a superb network of bike paths along the river, making the transition from city to mountains seamless. Rent touring and e-bikes at **aVelo** at Staatsbrücke.

Getting around by public transport *(salzburg-verkehr.at)* is quick, easy and inexpensive. If you're planning on zipping about town, a *Tageskarte* day pass is better value than single tickets.

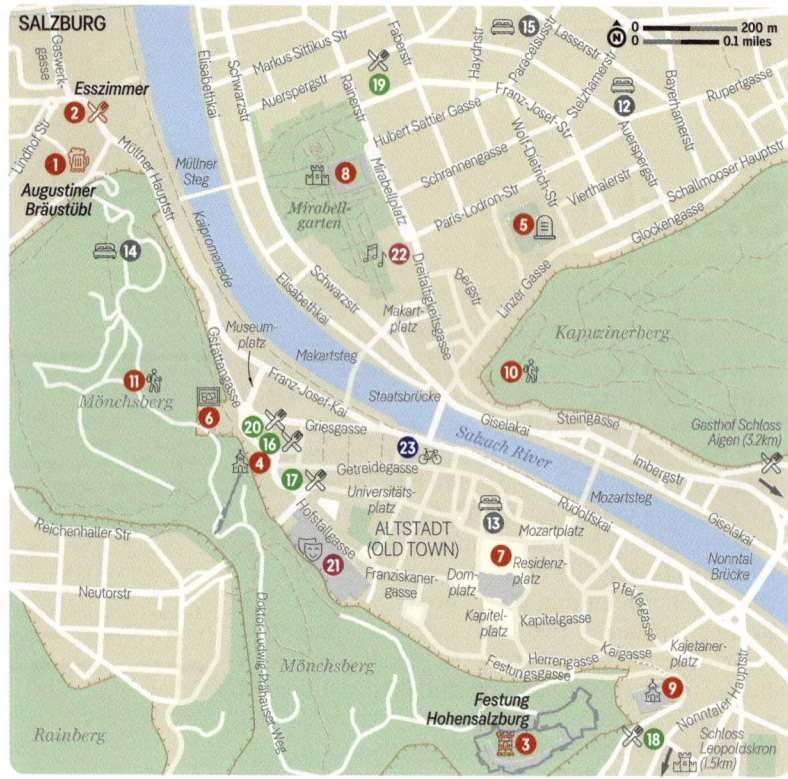

HIGHLIGHTS
1 Augustiner Bräustübl
2 Esszimmer
3 Festung Hohensalzburg

SIGHTS
4 Bürgerspitalkirche St Blasius
5 Friedhof St Sebastian
6 Museum der Moderne

7 Residenzplatz
8 Schloss Mirabell
9 Stift Nonnberg

ACTIVITIES
10 Kapuzinerberg
11 Mönchsberg

SLEEPING
12 Hotel & Villa Auersperg
13 Hotel am Dom

14 Schloss Mönchstein
15 YoHo

EATING
16 Afro Café
17 Blaue Gans Restaurant
see 14 Glass Garden
18 Green Garden
19 Heart of Joy
20 Humboldt

ENTERTAINMENT
21 Felsenreitschule
22 Mozarteum
see 8 Schlosskonzerte

TRANSPORT
23 aVelo

Stift Nonnberg (p66), then continue your short but scenic walk along Hoher Weg and Festungsgasse to **Festung Hohensalzburg** (*festung-hohensalzburg.at; adult/child €13.60/5.20*). The city's crowning-glory fortress has dress-circle views of the baroque Altstadt. Time your walk for midday to hear bells ring out across the city.

You can easily devote an afternoon to wandering the 540m peak of **Mönchsberg**, the cliffs that give Salzburg its dramatic edge. Its sheer, wooded heights are crisscrossed by walking trails. A highly scenic hike leads 3km on from Festung Hohensalzburg, past the **Museum der Moderne** (*museumder moderne.at; adult/child €14/free*) and through woods of beech,

Capuchin abbey

MOZART MAGIC

Mozart's symphonies, sonatas and concertos live on in Salzburg.

Mozarteum: Opened in 1880 and revered for its supreme acoustics, the Mozarteum highlights the life and works of Mozart through chamber music (October to June), concerts and opera. *mozarteum.at*

Mozart Week: In late January, when much-lauded orchestras, conductors and soloists celebrate Mozart's birthday with an 11-day music feast.

Schlosskonzerte: A fantasy of coloured marble, stucco and frescos, the baroque Marmorsaal (Marble Hall) at Schloss Mirabell is the exquisite setting for chamber-music concerts *(adult/child from €42/28)* where internationally renowned soloists and ensembles perform works by Mozart and other well-known composers such as Haydn and Chopin. *schlosskonzerte-salzburg.at*

sycamore, linden and oak, to the jovial monastery-founded brewery **Augustiner Bräustübl** *(augustinerbier.at)*. Here you can rest up with a cold foamy one under the chestnut trees in the beer garden.

A leap over the river to the Right Bank brings you to the forested, 640m-high hump of **Kapuzinerberg**, which frames the Altstadt like a postcard. Paths twist past Way of the Cross chapels to the Capuchin abbey at the top. Despite the glorious views, it's rarely busy – hence the reason it is still home to a colony of nimble-footed chamois, which you might spot if you're lucky (and quiet).

The Hills Are Alive

The Sound of Music trail

Ever since Hollywood box-office smash *The Sound of Music* hit big screens in 1965, Salzburg has been inseparable from the world's most famous singing nun. Channel your inner Julie Andrews by devising your own self-guided tour of the movie locations. Start at the very beginning with a cable-car ride to the summit of **Untersberg** *(untersbergbahn.at; return cable car adult/child €34/17)*, where Maria makes her twirling entrance through blooming alpine pastures and the Trapp family flee from the Nazis at the end.

 EATING IN SALZBURG: BEST ROMANTIC RESTAURANTS

Gasthof Schloss Aigen: This 15th-century country manor does Austrian home cooking with panache. *5.30-10pm Thu, 11.30am-10pm Fri-Sun* €€	**Blaue Gans Restaurant:** In 650-year-old vaults, this restaurant riffs on regional cuisine in season-spun dishes. *noon-midnight Mon-Sat* €€	**Glass Garden:** Ingredient-driven sensations at Hotel Schloss Mönchstein's glass-domed, Michelin-starred restaurant. *noon-10pm Thu-Mon* €€€	**Esszimmer:** Andreas Kaiblinger puts an innovative spin on market-driven French cuisine at this art-slung, Michelin-starred stunner. *noon-10pm Tue-Sat* €€€

ESCAPE THE CROWDS

Hildegard Strohmeyer, an official Salzburg city and hiking guide *(hildastroh. com)*, divulges some peaceful spots.

Friedhof St Sebastian: Mozart's father, Leopold, and wife, Constanze, are buried in this cemetery, established in 1600 as an Italian 'campo santo'. Its centrepiece is the mausoleum of Prince-Archbishop Wolf-Dietrich of Raitenau.

Bürgerspitalskirche St Blasius: The civic hospital church near Getreidegasse has an inner courtyard with Renaissance arcades. A Gothic church with 12th-century roots, it impresses with its vault, stained-glass windows and mystical interior.

Waldbad Anif: Rent a bike to pedal south along the Salzach River to this emerald-green lake, perfect in summer.

Schloss Mirabell gardens and Festung Hohensalzburg (p64)

At the foot of Mönchsberg's cliffs, the **Felsenreitschule** is the dramatic backdrop for the **Salzburger Festspiele** (Salzburg Festival) in the movie, where the Trapp Family Singers win the audience over with 'Edelweiss' and give the Nazis the slip with 'So Long, Farewell'. Close by is **Residenzplatz**, where Maria belts out 'I Have Confidence' and playfully splashes the spouting horses of the Residenzbrunnen fountain. Hoof it uphill from here to Benedictine **Stift Nonnberg** *(nonnberg.at; free)*, where the nuns waltzed on their way to mass, including the ever-problematic Maria. To see the abbey at its most atmospheric, arrive for the 6.45am Gregorian chant.

Palaces, you say? Romantically rococo **Schloss Leopoldskron** *(schloss-leopoldskron.com)*, a 15-minute stroll south of the centre, is where the lake scene was filmed. Its Venetian Room was the blueprint for the Trapps' opulent ballroom, where the von Trapp kids bid their heart-melting farewells. Now you can stay the night in its elegant hotel.

Back in town, the Pegasus fountain, gnomes and steps with fortress views in the **Schloss Mirabell** *(salzburg.info; free)* gardens might inspire a rendition of 'Do-Re-Mi' – especially if there's a drop of golden sun.

⊘ EATING IN SALZBURG: TOP LUNCH SPOTS

Afro Café: Go for fair-trade coffees, lavish brunches and creative day specials at this Afro-chic cafe. *9am-8pm Mon-Sat €*

Green Garden: Tapping into plant power, this vegan cafe rustles up tasty Buddha bowls, brunches and superfood salads. *1-9pm Wed-Fri, 10am-9pm Sat & Sun €*

Heart of Joy: Ayurveda-inspired cafe: all-vegetarian, part-vegan, mostly organic menu of bagels, salads, homemade cakes, juices, daily specials. *8am-7pm €*

Humboldt: Like a blast of nouveau alpine chic, the vibe is cool yet cosy. A good buzz and all-organic, season-driven menu. *10.30am-11pm €€*

Beyond
Salzburg

Salzburg is the curtain-raiser to Alps that will make your heart soar and cinematic backdrops that will prompt you to yodel out loud.

You don't need to venture far from Salzburg for high alpine drama. For a memorable day trip, take the quick train ride to Werfen, which thrills with a showstopping medieval castle and the world's biggest ice caves, Eisriesenwelt. Here cliff-skimming trails thread through the rugged peaks of the limestone Tennengebirge, where eagles wheel, winds blow and silence reigns.

Further east, the Salzkammergut wows with alpine and subalpine lakes, deeply carved valleys, high hills and rugged, steep mountains rising to almost 3000m. Rugged paths wind to mountain-top restaurants, caves and salt mines, where the region's 'white gold' once filled the coffers of Habsburg rulers. Swinging south, the unmissable road trip is the Grossglockner Road, helter-skeltering below the country's highest peak, 3798m Grossglockner.

Places
Werfen p67
Hallstatt p68

Werfen
TIME FROM SALZBURG: **40MIN** 🚗 OR **1HR** 🚆

Cue the world's biggest ice caves
High above Werfen, the pointed peaks of the Tennengebirge rise like a theatre curtain of solid limestone over the river-woven Salzach Valley. Take the cable car, then hoof it up the steep, scree-strewn trail to **Eisriesenwelt** *(eisriesenwelt.at; adult/child €42/21)*, open from May to October. Stepping through the huge 20m-wide gash in the rock, feeling the frosty blast of 0°C air and seeing the ice twinkle is like pushing through the wardrobe into Narnia.

An old-fashioned carbide lamp illuminates your passage through this pitch-black, glittering underworld of frozen tunnels and passageways, where you will be blown away by the scale and beauty of the ice. But most impressive of all is the echoing, cathedral-like **Eispalast** (Ice Palace), with icicles as big as organ pipes and ice-veined walls.

Big views and birds of prey at Burg Hohenwerfen
Slung high on a wooded clifftop and cowering below the gnarly peaks of the Tennengebirge, **Burg Hohenwerfen** *(burg-hohen-werfen.at; adult/child incl lift €17.90/6.10, with guided tour €20.90/7.60)* is visible from afar. For 900 years this turreted beauty of a castle has guarded the Salzach Valley. You'll be mostly captivated by the mountain views from the 16th-century belfry,

GETTING AROUND

Much of the region beyond Salzburg is accessible by public transport (bus and train), removing the need to hire a car unless you crave the independence. There are regional and S-Bahn trains from Salzburg running frequently to Hallein (15 minutes) and Werfen (40 minutes). The two-hour journey to Obertraun often involves a bus-train combo via Bad Ischl.

WATER & WHEELS ON HALLSTÄTTER SEE

Swimming:
Hallstätter See reaches about 24°C from June to August. Obertraun and Untersee (near Steeg) have free public beaches with facilities.

Cycling & kayaking:
Hire touring bikes, mountain bikes and e-bikes at Dormio Resort Obertraun. For standard city/e-bikes per hour, expect to pay €20/30. There's a charging station at the cable car valley station. Kayak hire for the first hour is €10, and €5 after that.

Lake Connections:
Hallstättersee Schifffahrt (*hallstattschifffahrt. at*) connects the train station on the eastern shore with the town of Hallstatt year-round, timed to trains. From May to September it does southern-end lake circuits and boat rental.

GOXCENTUNG/SHUTTERSTOCK

Saltzwelten Funicular, Hallstatt

but the dingy dungeons (displaying the usual nasties, such as the iron maiden and thumbscrew) are equally worth a look.

Time your visit to catch the stunning **falconry show** *(11.15am & 3.15pm daily)* in the grounds, where falconers in medieval costume release eagles, owls, falcons and vultures to wheel in front of the ramparts. The brisk walk up from Werfen takes 20 minutes, or you can cheat by catching the lift.

Hallstatt
TIME FROM SALZBURG: **1HR 30MIN**

Descending into the salt mine

On the western shore of its exquisitely pretty lake, Hallstatt is famous for its salt mine, where mining began over 7000 years ago. Today miners still dig white gold out of the earth. After a short ferry ride across the lake from the train station, you reach a jetty that is a 15-minute walk from the **Saltzwelten Funicular** *(salzwelten.at; adult/child €24/12)*. It's a dramatic ascent into a strange alpine valley with mirrors reflecting the green landscape, a **Skywalk** with stupendous views, and an Iron Age burial ground.

From the top station, it is another 15-minute walk to the mine. After donning protective clothing, you begin the bilingual 90-minute mine tour in **Salzwelten** *(salzwelten.at/en/ hallstatt; funicular & tour adult/child €43/21)*, taking you around 2km through shafts, down miners' slides, and to an illuminated underground lake. Along the way you learn all about the formation of salt, salt mining, and conditions of the miners.

 EATING IN WERFEN: OUR PICKS

Pizzeria im Markt: Pizzas fly out of the oven perfectly thin and crisp at this cosy pick in Werfen's heart. *10am-10pm* €

Oedlhaus: At Eisriesenwelt, this 1574m woodsy hut fortifies walkers with grub like *Gröstl* (pan-fried potatoes, pork and onions) and mountain views. *8am-4pm* €€

Stiege No 1: Venison, asparagus, wild garlic – the menu sings of the seasons. In summer, sit in the lantern-lit garden. *11am-10pm Wed-Sun* €€

Obauer: Two Michelin-starred restaurant, with alpine, homegrown and locally foraged ingredients. *6-9pm Wed, noon-9pm Thu-Sun* €€€

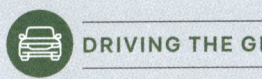 **DRIVING THE GROSSGLOCKNER ROAD**

Get up close and personal with the Austrian Alps on this sky-high road trip.

START	END	LENGTH
Bruck	Heiligenblut	48km; 5–6hr

Leaving **1 Bruck**, enter the mountainous Fuschertal, passing Fusch and **2 Wildpark Ferleiten**. Once through the tollgate, the road climbs steeply to **3 Hochmais** (1850m), where glaciated peaks like Grosses Wiesbachhorn (3564m) crowd the horizon. The road zigzags up to **4 Haus Alpine Naturschau** (2260m), which spotlights local flora and fauna. Further on, a 2km side road spirals up to **5 Edelweiss Spitze** (2571m), the road's highest viewpoint. Get your camera handy for **6 Fuscher Törl** (2428m), with smashing views, and gemstone-coloured lake **7 Fuscher Lacke** (2262m) nearby. Here is a small exhibition on the road's construction, built by 3000 men during the Great Depression (1930–35). The road wriggles on through high meadows to **8 Hochtor** (2504m), the top of the pass. Next there's a steady descent to **9 Schöneck**. Branch off west onto the 9km Gletscherstrasse, passing waterfalls and Achtung Murmeltiere (Beware of Marmots) signs – you may spot one of the burrowing rodents. The Grossglockner massif slides into view on the approach to flag-dotted **10 Kaiser-Franz-Josefs-Höhe** (2369m), with memorable views of bell-shaped Grossglockner (3798m) and the rapidly retreating Pasterze Glacier. Allow time for the glacier-themed exhibition at the visitor centre and the Wilhelm-Swarovski observatory. Round out your road trip in **11 Heiligenblut**, where a 15th-century pilgrimage church lifts gazes to Grossglockner.

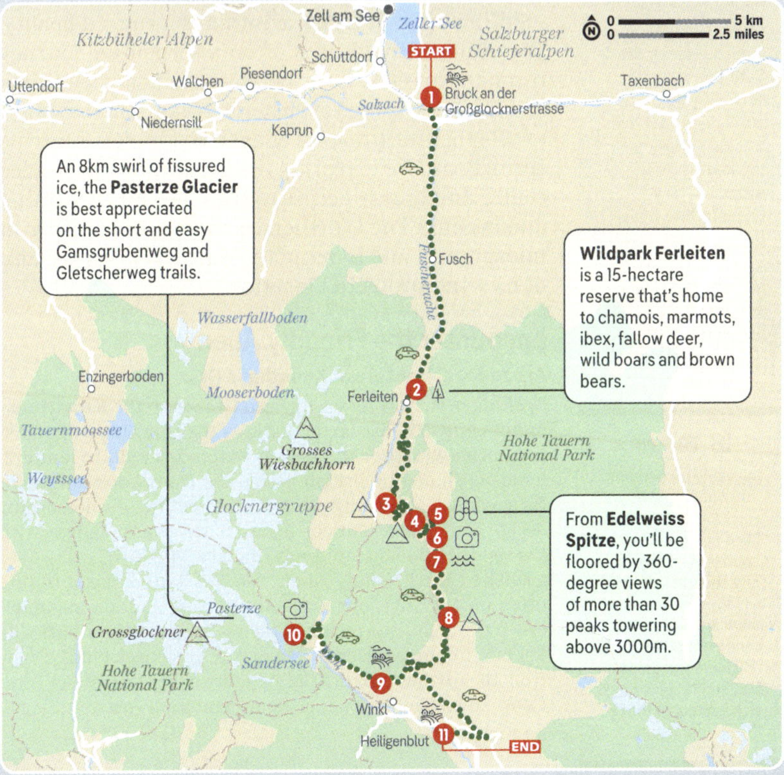

An 8km swirl of fissured ice, the **Pasterze Glacier** is best appreciated on the short and easy Gamsgrubenweg and Gletscherweg trails.

Wildpark Ferleiten is a 15-hectare reserve that's home to chamois, marmots, ibex, fallow deer, wild boars and brown bears.

From **Edelweiss Spitze**, you'll be floored by 360-degree views of more than 30 peaks towering above 3000m.

Graz & the South

LAKES | MOUNTAINS | CULTURAL COOL

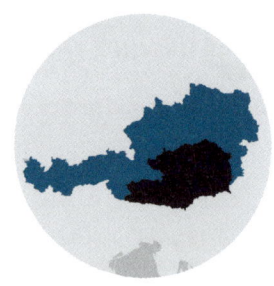

Though Austria's south receives just a trickle of visitors compared to other regions, if you make it this far you'll be richly rewarded. Styria wings you from rolling vineyards, pumpkin fields, wildlife-rich national parks and snow-streaked limestone peaks to the beautiful sweep of the River Mur. UNESCO-listed Graz, Austria's second city, is one of its most vibrant, fizzing with avant-garde arts and a food scene buoyed by abundant farmers markets and local produce.

Sidling up to Styria, Carinthia is a rugged beauty. Travelling through it is often a serpentine journey through carved valleys, between soaring mountains and along the shores of glistening lakes. On the shores of Wörthersee, graceful Klagenfurt makes a terrific springboard for exploring, with a grand Renaissance centre and breezy access to the lakes for swimming and cycling. The Wörthersee reaches about 25°C in midsummer, and is one of the warmest lakes because of its wind-protected location.

Encounter the Friendly Alien

Art and architecture at Kunsthaus Graz

Nothing better expresses modern Graz than the **Kunsthaus** (*adult/child €12/free*) on the banks of the Mur. Opened in 2003 to coincide with the city's stint as European Capital of Culture, it was designed by British architects Peter Cook and Colin Fournier. It's a dazzling piece of architecture, its biomorphic design and intense blue colouring contrasting strikingly with the red-tiled gabled buildings that surround it.

Dubbed the Friendly Alien, the *Kunsthaus* has a rolling program of exhibitions focusing on contemporary and modern art, which have included the work of such luminaries as Sol LeWitt and Ai Weiwei. Make sure you check out the view from the furthest nozzle (the 'naughty nozzle', architect Peter Cook called it) in the upper-floor exhibition space.

GRAZ

⭐ **HIGHLIGHTS**
1 Dom
2 Kunsthaus Graz
3 Schlossberg

⚫ **SLEEPING**
4 Das Weitzer
5 KAI 36
6 Schlossberg Hotel

🟢 **EATING**
7 Altsteirische Schmankerlstube
8 Geniesserei am Markt
9 Mohrenwirt
10 Scheucher

To the Top of the Schlossberg

Graz' unassailable fortified hill

Schlossberg (*graztourismus.at*), the city's green hill, stands at 473m high above the left bank of the Mur. The old medieval castle underwent a makeover in the mid-16th century courtesy of Italian architect Domenico dell'Allio, who turned it into an impregnable Renaissance fortress. The best way to approach Schlossberg is by skipping up the zigzagging steps from Schlossbergplatz, where it towers above you. Or take the **Schlossbergbahn** (*adult/child €3.20/1.60*) funicular, which was built in 1894 and has a gradient of 61%.

At the top, you'll find the **Bell Tower**, with its 5-tonne bell known as Liesl, the restored casemates and the Schlossberg

---

BEST FESTIVALS IN GRAZ

This university town has a flurry of festivals, from the International Storytelling Festival (May) to Assembly, the city's Festival of Fashion (September) and Klangnacht, a mesmerising light and sound festival (October).

Elevate: Bills itself as a festival of 'music, arts and political discourse'. *Mar*

Design Month: All of Graz' creative energy condensed into a one-month festival. *May*

Springfestival: Live electronic music and art installations. *Late May/early June*

Aufsteirern: (*aufsteirern.at*) Traditional festival with music, dance, handicrafts and good food. *Sep*

Steirischer Herbst: Edgy, contemporary performing-arts festival, which has been running for over half a century. *Sep/Oct*

EATING IN GRAZ: OUR PICKS

Mohrenwirt: Traditional dishes with a contemporary twist: organic, seasonal local produce. Michelin Bib Gourmand. *11.30am-11pm Wed-Sat* €€

Geniesserei am Markt: Beside the Kaiser-Josef-Platz farmers market. Lunch or the 6pm 10-course surprise menu (book ahead). *9am-10pm Tue-Sat* €€€

Altsteirische Schmankerlstube: Seasonal Styrian and classic Austrian in a homely setting. Vaulted ceiling and wood panelling. *10am-11pm* €€

Scheucher: Michelin-listed restaurant famed for its dry-aged steaks. *11am-2.30pm & 6am-10pm Mon-Fri, 6am-10pm Sat* €€€

branch of the Graz Museum. But the main thing to do up here is enjoy the view over the rooftops of Graz in the beautiful garden on the **Bürgerbastei** – a restored bastion below the clock tower.

Historic Highs in Klagenfurt
Evocative architecture and altar painting

Renaissance romance lives on in Klagenfurt's historic centre. On **Neuer Platz** square is the 16th-century **Dragon Fountain**. This blank-eyed, wriggling statue is modelled on the lindwurm (dragon) of legend, said to have resided in a swamp here long ago, devouring cattle and virgins.

Nearby is the Renaissance **Landhaus** (state parliament), where the highlight is the **Grosser Wappensaal** (Heraldic Hall; landesmuseum.ktn.gv.at; adult/child €7/free), with its magnificent trompe l'oeil gallery painted by Carinthian artist Josef Ferdinand Fromiller (1693–1760). Steps from here, on Pfarrplatz, is the **Stadthauptpfarrkirche St Egid** (kath -kirche-kaernten.at/pfarren/pfarre/C3080; free), where a climb to the 90m-high tower affords a bird's-eye view of town and the surrounding mountains.

Backtracking brings you to the **Dom** (cathedral; kath-kirche -kaernten.at/pfarren/pfarre/C3074; free), with its ornate marble pulpit, sugary pink-and-white stucco and standout altar painting in the chapel by Paul Troger dedicated to St Ignatius.

Swimming & Cycling Wörthersee
Make a splash in Carinthia's biggest lake

Framed by wooded hills and shimmering turquoise-blue, Wörthersee is an instant heart-stealer. In summer all the action is on the lake – open-water swimmers, canoeists, kayakers and stand-up paddleboarders love its placid, tepid waters.

If you prefer to pedal rather than paddle, the 40km **R4 bike route** wraps around the entire shoreline. It's an easy, well-marked ride ticking off swimming spots, beaches and viewpoints. You can hire road and e-bikes at stations in the region, including at the Klagenfurt **tourist office** on Neuer Platz. Boats departing for destinations around the Wörthersee leave from a quay just north of **Strandbad Klagenfurt** (Klagenfurt Bathing Beach). Check times at woertherseeschifffahrt.at.

PLAYING YOUR GUEST CARDS RIGHT

Play your guest cards right and you won't need to pay for travelling by regional train around Carinthia. As well as offering various discounts, the free **Wörthersee Plus Card** (woerthersee. com/card; year-round) entitles overnight visitors to free train travel throughout Carinthia, including the S1, connecting Friesach in the north with Lienz (in Tyrol, west of Carinthia). It is valid both days of a one-night stay in a participating hotel.

The **Erlebnis Card** (visitvillach.at/de/ erlebnis-card.html), Villach's free card, also includes regional travel anywhere in Carinthia and on a few special bus services for the duration of your stay.

The **Kärnten Card** (kaerntencard.at; adult €60-89, child €31-46) provides discounts or free admission but not free transport; available in one-, two- and five-week timeframes.

EATING IN KLAGENFURT: OUR PICKS

Princs: Lively kitchen serves pizzas, plates of pasta and 'street food'. Kitchen closes at 9pm. Also with a popular bar. *10am-midnight Mon-Thu, to 2am Fri & Sat* €€

Dolce Vita: Local flagship restaurant-*bistretto* with northern Italian cuisine and a local seasonal menu. *11.30am-3pm & 6.30-10pm Mon-Fri* €€

Ricardo: Portuguese, tapas, vegetarian (and vegan) dishes, and steaks in a relaxed setting, with outdoor seating. *11.30am-2pm & 6-11.30pm Tue-Sat, 6-11.30pm Mon* €€

Gasthaus im Landhaushof: Classic Austrian cuisine, with outdoor seating in the yard and a kitchen open all day. *11am-9pm Mon-Sat, to 3pm Sun* €€

Innsbruck & Tyrol

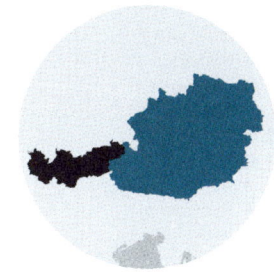

LIVING HISTORY | HABSBURG CULTURE | HIGH ALPS

Tyrol's capital is a sight to behold. Rising like a theatre curtain above the city, the rock spires of the Nordkette range are so breathtakingly close that when you fly here, it feels as though you're going to smash right into them. It isn't just an illusion: within minutes you can whizz from the late-medieval Altstadt, presided over by a Habsburg palace, to 2000m above sea level and be up among crags where alpine choughs glide and cowbells tinkle.

Beyond Innsbruck, it's all about the outdoors, whether you're pelting down an Olympic bob run, schussing down the legendary slopes of Kitzbühel, cycling the Zillertal or hiking in the Alps with a flawlessly blue sky overhead. Welcome to a place where snowboarders brag under the low beams of a medieval tavern about awesome descents; where *Dirndls* and *Lederhosen* have street cred; and where *Volksmusik* (folk music) features on club playlists.

Palace of Dreams

MAP p74

Discover imperial Innsbruck

Grabbing attention with its pearl-white facade and cupolas, the **Hofburg** *(burghauptmannschaft.at; adult/child €9.50/ free)* imperial palace was built for Archduke Sigmund the Rich in the 15th century, expanded by Emperor Maximilian I in the 16th century and given a baroque makeover by Empress Maria Theresia in the 18th century.

Take a romp around the lavish rococo state apartments and you'll be astounded by the 31m-long **Riesensaal** (Giant's Hall), a feast of frescos, weighty chandeliers and Habsburg portraits. Right opposite is the **Hofkirche** *(tiroler-landesmu seen.at; adult/child €14/free)*, one of Europe's finest royal court churches. Top billing goes to the crazily ornate black-marble tomb of Emperor Maximilian I (1459–1519), a masterpiece of German Renaissance sculpture. The twin rows of 28 giant bronze figures guarding the sarcophagus include Dürer's legendary King Arthur. Touching the statues is now forbidden,

GETTING AROUND

Innsbruck's compact, pedestrianised, alley-woven Altstadt is a pleasure to explore on foot. Most sights are here, and ultramodern funiculars race you up into the mountains. For outlying sights, such as Bergisel and Schloss Ambras, hop on one of the **IVB** *(ivb. at)* buses; for multiple journeys, invest in a 24-hour ticket. Public transport is free with summer's Welcome Card, the guest card you receive with stays of more than two nights.

☑ **TOP TIP**

Tourist information centres on Burggraben, at the Stadtturm and the Hauptbahnhof are handy first ports of call for maps, tickets, ski passes and information.

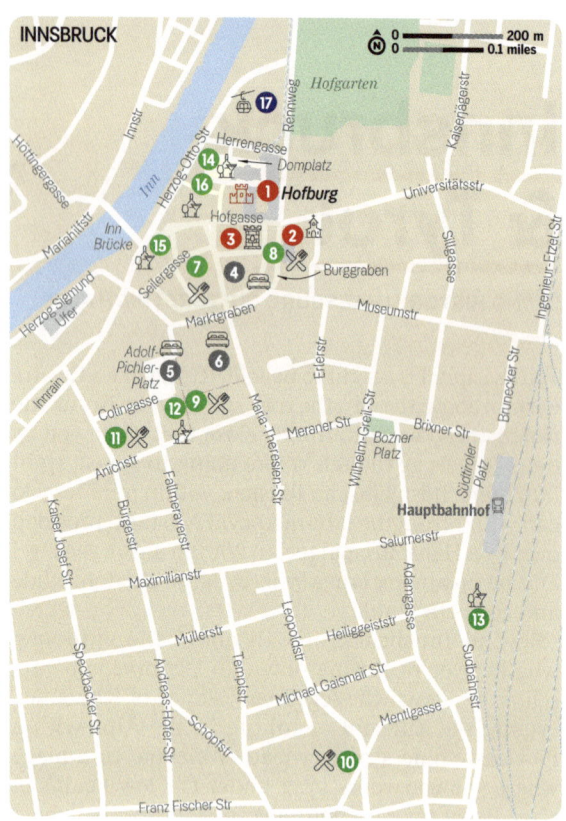

HIGHLIGHTS
1 Hofburg

SIGHTS
2 Hofkirche
3 Stadtturm

SLEEPING
4 Hotel Weisses Kreuz
5 Penz Hotel
6 Stage 12

EATING
7 Die Wilderin
8 Il Convento
9 Lichtblick
10 Olive
11 Oniriq

DRINKING & NIGHTLIFE
12 360°
13 Cloud One
14 Fuchs & Hase
15 In Vinum
16 Moustache
see 6 Stage 12

TRANSPORT
17 Nordkettenbahnen

but numerous inquisitive hands have already polished parts of the dull bronze, including Kaiser Rudolf's codpiece!

Innsbruck on High

MAP p74

From city to slopes

You'll be itching to head into the mountains on Innsbruck's doorstep. Zaha Hadid's space-age funicular **Nordketten-bahnen** *(nordkette.com; top of Innsbruck return ticket adult/child €52/31.20)* floats to the slopes in no time, stopping at Hungerburg, where you switch to a cable car to Seegrube and,

 EATING IN INNSBRUCK: OUR PICKS

MAP p74

Olive: Vegetarians and vegans are in their element at this cute bistro with vintage furniture. Book – it gets busy. *5-11pm Mon-Sat* **€**

Die Wilderin: A modern hunter-gatherer restaurant, where season-spun menus play up farm-fresh and foraged ingredients. *5pm-midnight Tue-Sun* **€€**

Il Convento: Tucked into the old city walls, this Italian job has dishes like clam linguine and braised veal, and a well-stocked cellar. *11.30am-midnight Mon-Sat* **€€**

Oniriq: Explosive Austrian flavours are given a foraged twist in ingredient-led tasting menus at this stylishly monochrome pick. *6-11pm Wed-Sat* **€€€**

finally, 2256m Hafelekar. A 15-minute uphill trudge brings you to 2334m **Hafelekarspitze**, where alpine choughs ride the breeze and gnarly limestone mountains rise in great waves. The views are riveting, reaching all the way to 3798m Grossglockner when it's clear.

Walking trails head off in all directions, including the ridge-top **Goethe Trail**, a 10km, five-hour, out-and-back stomp over meadow and mountain to the **Pfeishütte**. The steep, technically demanding **Nordkette Single Trail** draws hardcore downhill mountain bikers. In winter, the most central place to pound powder is the **Nordpark**. Fearless skiers ride the **Hafelekar Run**, one of Europe's steepest runs, with a 70% gradient.

Life in the Fast Lane

MAP p77

Pick up speed, Olympian-style

For a minute in the life of an Olympic bobsleigh racer, ride the **Olympia Bob** (*knauseder-event.at; bobsleigh ride summer/winter €55/120, skeleton €65*) at the foot of Patscherkofel mountain in **Igls**.

Zipping around 14 curves and picking up speeds of up to 120km/h, the 1.3km bob run, built for the 1976 Winter Olympics, is a single minute of pure hair-raising action. From December to March, you can either join a four-person bobsleigh or throw yourself headfirst down the run on a skeleton. Otherwise, join a pro-bobsled driver from April to October for the summer version. See the website for dates, times and bookings. To reach the bob run, take Bus J from Innsbruck Landesmuseum to Igls Olympiaexpress.

Swarovski Sparkle

MAP p77

Enter a crystal world

The dinky village of **Wattens**, a 30-minute bus ride east of Innsbruck, is the glittering heart of the Swarovski crystal empire. **Swarovski Kristallwelten** (*kristallwelten.swarovski.com; adult/child €26/8*) shines as one of Austria's most-visited attractions.

Against the backdrop of the Alps, the fantasy world begins outdoors with an ivy-swathed giant's head spouting water, a dazzling crystal cloud, bejewelled with 800,000 crystals, floating above a mirrorlike pool, and a stunning modernist, black-and-white carousel glimmering with 15 million crystals by Spanish designer Jaime Hayon. Inside, the Chambers of Wonder zoom in on Alexander McQueen's wintry *Silent Light,*

SKY-HIGH VIEWS

Stadtturm: Onion-domed medieval tower in the heart of the Altstadt. Puff up 133 steps for 360-degree views over Innsbruck's rooftops to the surrounding mountains.

360°: Knockout view of the skyline from the balcony skirting this spherical bar. Nicely chilled spot for a coffee/sundowner.

Lichtblick: Dinner at this slickly minimalist, backlit, glass-walled restaurant takes in the entire sweep of the city and its mountain backdrop.

Buzihütte: This woodsy alpine hut has a peak-gazing terrace for digging into traditional faves like *Käsespätzle* (cheese noodles).

Cloud One: On the 13th floor of Motel One, this glass-fronted bar has tremendous views. Shake your own cocktail or go for a signature pomegranate margarita.

 DRINKING IN INNSBRUCK: OUR PICKS ──────── MAP p74

Fuchs & Hase: This vaulted bar is a mellow pick for an expertly mixed cocktail, proper coffee or glass of natural wine. *5pm-1am Tue & Wed, 3pm-1am Fri & Sat*	**Stage 12:** Backlit, gold-kissed bar with a terrace for summer imbibing, a vintage popcorn machine and talented mixologists. *noon-midnight Sun-Thu, to 1am Fri & Sat*	**Moustache:** Retro bolthole, with a terrace overlooking Domplatz. Go for cocktails, craft beers and finger food. *10am-2am Tue-Sun, 4pm-2am Mon*	**In Vinum:** Snug Altstadt wine bar: relaxed choice to sample Austria's finest wines; see website for details of the regular tastings. *11am-midnight Mon-Sat, 4-10pm Sun*

CITY TO SLOPES

The money-saving **Innsbruck Card** *(24/48/72hr €69/79/89, child half price)* gets you one visit to Innsbruck's main sights and attractions, a return cable car or funicular journey, a guided city walk and unlimited use of public transport, including the Sightseer and Kristallwelten shuttle bus.

Heading to the slopes? The surrounding region is brilliantly connected by public transport. Distances are generally short and fares inexpensive. Many connections are covered by free guest cards you receive locally, so check this before shelling out on tickets. In winter, Innsbruck's money-saving **Ski Plus City Pass** wraps up 346km of pistes in 12 ski areas around Innsbruck and the glacier-capped Stubaital, and opens the doors at 22 sights and attractions.

BIKEMP/SHUTTERSTOCK

Hikers, Kreuzjoch

South Korean artist Lee Bul's perspective-bending *Into Lattice Sun* and Mexican-Canadian artist Rafael Lozano-Hemmer's *Pulse Voronoi,* a light fantastic walk through 7000 shards of crystal inspired by a Big Bang–style blast.

Outdoor Action in the Zillertal   MAP p77

Hit the slopes

In a stupendously wild pocket of Tyrol, an hour's train ride from Innsbruck, the Zillertal is ripe for outdoor adventure. In summer, hiking trails vein the landscape. Memorable rambles in Zell am See include the 8km round hike to **Zellberg** via the wispy Talbach falls, and the tougher 14km, five-hour stomp up to the 2558m-high, cross-topped summit of **Kreuzjoch**, the highest peak in the Kitzbühel Alps. Mountain bikers are in their element on the 30km **Zillertal Radweg**. For bigger thrills, the **Aktivzentrum** *(aktivzentrum-zillertal.at)* is a one-stop shop for pulse-quickening sports, from paragliding to whitewater rafting and river bugging in raging waters.

When the snow falls, **Mayrhofen**, at the head of the valley, has the downhill edge, with 204km of well-groomed slopes, terrific off-piste and the **PenkenPark** for boarders. One ticket covers the lot: the **Zillertal Superskipass** *(zillertal.at; adult/child €79/35.50).*

Snow Legends in Kitzbühel   MAP p77

World Cup winter wonderland

Winter sparkles brightly in Kitzbühel, right up there among the world's best ski resorts. When flakes blanket the mountains,

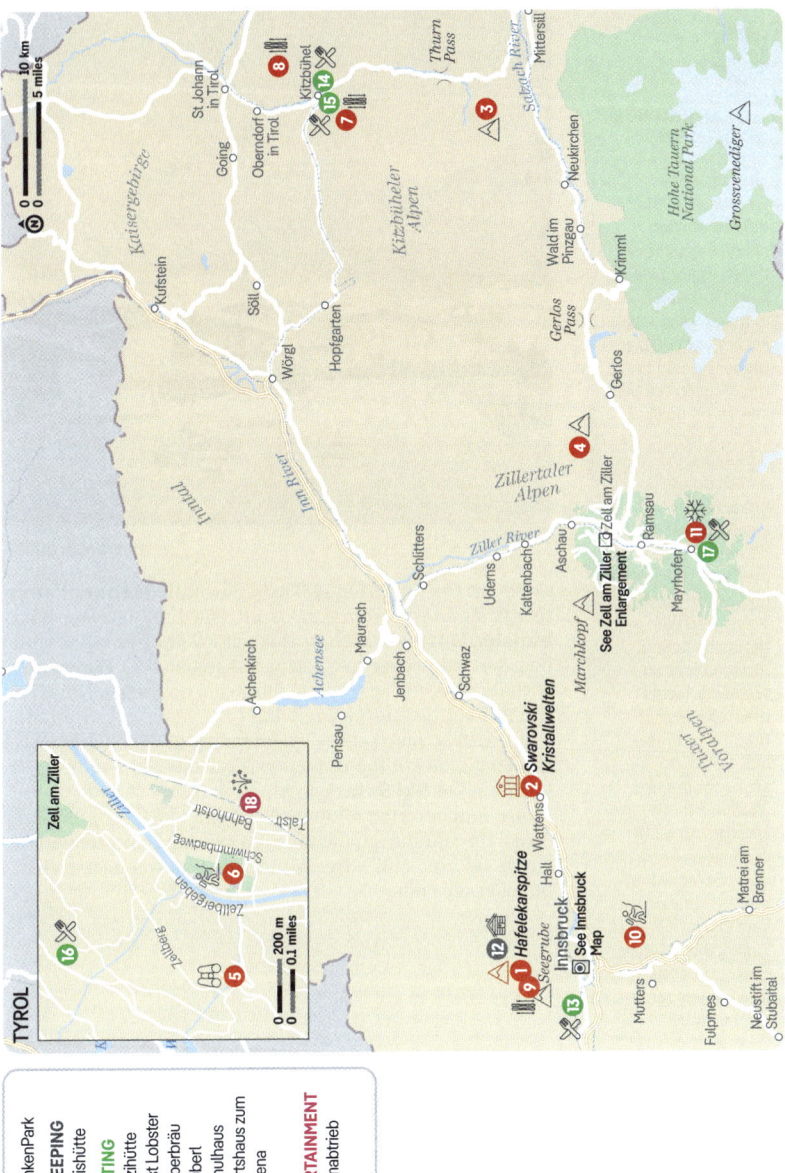

TYROL

HIGHLIGHTS
★ Hafelekarspitze
1 Swarovski
2 Kristallwelten

SIGHTS
3 Hanglalm
4 Kreuzjoch
5 Zellberg

ACTIVITIES
6 Aktivzentrum
7 Hahnenkamm
8 Kitzbüheler
Horn
9 Nordpark
10 Olympia Bob

11 PenkenPark

SLEEPING
12 Pfeishütte

EATING
13 Buzihütte
14 First Lobster
15 Huberbräu
Stüberl
16 Schulhaus
17 Wirtshaus zum
Griena

ENTERTAINMENT
18 Almabtrieb

THE COMING HOME OF THE COWS

In autumn, the Zillertaler celebrate the **Almabtrieb**, or coming home of the cows from their summer pastures to their winter digs in cosy barns. It's a proper taste of the rural Alps to see the cows strut down from the mountains adorned with heavy and elaborate floral headdresses and jangling giant bells.

The centuries-old event is a valley-wide party with feasting, *Volksmusik* with the jaunty melody of accordions and yodelling, locals dressed in *Tracht* (traditional dress), and plenty of schnapps before another harsh, long, snowbound winter of shovelling cow dung. Some of the best celebrations are held in the villages of Fügen, Gattererberg, Hart and Gerlos from mid-September to early October.

Mayrhofen (p76)

skiers hit the slopes for 233km of downhill. **Hahnenkamm** *(bergwelt-hahnenkamm.at)* is intermediate heaven, **Kitzbüheler Horn** *(kitzski.at)* is much loved by novices, while boarders slide over to Snowpark Kitzbühel at **Hanglalm**, with its rails, kickers, boxes, tubes and obstacles. The **Kitz-Ski Pass** *(2-day pass adult/child €125.50/63)* covers all lifts.

But with so much snow, where to begin? If you're up for a challenge, tackle the tremendously scenic, hut-to-hut, lift-to-lift, 35km **Ski Safari**, linking the Hahnenkamm to Pass Thurn and covering 6000m of vertical. Marked by elephant signs, the full-day alpine tour is a cracking overview to the entire ski area and a free ski bus schleps you back to Kitzbühel at the end.

EATING IN THE ZILLERTAL & KITZBÜHEL: OUR PICKS

Wirtshaus Zum Griena: *Schlutzkrapfen* (cheese-filled pasta) and *Speckknödel* (bacon dumplings) at 400-year-old chalet in Mayrhofen.
3-11pm Mon & Thu-Sun €€

Schulhaus: Panoramically perched above Zell am Ziller, this old schoolhouse has sublime views and a Tyrolean seasonal menu.
6-11pm Fri €€

Huberbräu Stüberl: Old-world Kitzbühel haunt with vaults and pine benches, delivering Austrian classics like schnitzel, goulash and dumplings.
9am-11pm €€

First Lobster: Oyster shells mounted on brick walls are a nod to the terrific fish and seafood on the menu at this slick, bistro-style restaurant.
4-11pm Mon-Sat €€

Places We Love to Stay

€ Budget €€ Midrange €€€ Top End

Vienna
MAP p57

Hotel Lamée €€ Glamorous art deco–styled hotel near Stephansplatz, with a city-view rooftop bar.

Die Josefine Hotel €€ Boutique 49-room hotel with *Great Gatsby* vibes; home of stylish Barfly's speakeasy.

Hotel Daniel €€ Smart-luxury, minimalist-style hotel next to Belvedere, with one of the best brunches in town. Vespas and bikes for hire.

Magdas €€ Social business hotel integrating refugees. The sustainable, upcycled design supports NGOs and local artists.

Hotel Imperial €€€ Palatial hotel brimming with decadent features, from the royal staircase to rooms.

Melk & Dürnstein

Hotel Schloss Dürnstein €€€ Opulent rooms in a 17th-century castle – the height of luxury in the Wachau.

Hotel Richard Löwenherz €€€ Beautifully converted from a former medieval convent in Dürnstein, complete with serene monastery garden.

Salzburg
MAP p64

YoHo € Backpacker dream: comfy bunks, cheap beer and *The Sound of Music* screened daily.

Hotel & Villa Auersperg €€ Fuses late-19th-century flair with contemporary. Relax in the vine-swaddled garden or rooftop spa with Kapuzinerberg views.

Hotel am Dom €€ Antique meets boutique at an Altstadt hotel in an 800-year-old building.

Schloss Mönchstein €€€ On a fairytale perch atop Mönchsberg and set in hectares of wooded grounds, this 16th-century castle is honeymoon material.

Werfen

Weisses Rössl € Good-value *Pension* (B&B) has great views of the fortress and the Tennengebirge from its rooftop terrace.

Landgasthof Reitsamerhof €€ Rousing views of the Tennengebirge peaks at a sunny yellow, geranium-bedecked chalet just south of Werfen.

Hallstatt

Camping am See € Camping, glamping and upmarket wagons in Obertraun; lake location with beach and sauna-on-wheels.

Hallstatt Hideaway €€€ Modern, beautifully textured suites just back from the lake in Hallstatt. Sauna and private garden on the lake itself.

Graz
MAP p71

Das Weitzer €€ Excellent hotel beside the River Mur and near the Kunsthaus, with a cafe, rooftop sauna and flower-filled lobby.

Schlossberg Hotel €€ Swish art hotel in the former late-16th-century royal carpentry workshops, with an impressive art collection.

Klagenfurt & Wörthersee

Sandwirth €€ Contemporary, comfortable and central, these parquet-floored rooms and apartments are ideal for families.

Seehotel Porcia €€€ In Pörtschach, right on the Wörthersee, with a private beach and elegantly decorated rooms in antique style, some with lake views.

Innsbruck
MAP p74

Hotel Weisses Kreuz €€ This 500-year-old hotel oozes history, with creaking beams, wood-panelled parlours and a twisting staircase.

Stage 12 €€ Design-driven pick lodged in a 16th-century townhouse, with mountain-view rooms, a 6th-floor spa and an upbeat cocktail bar.

Penz Hotel €€€ Behind a sheer wall of glass, this contemporary design hotel has minimalist-chic rooms and a rooftop bar for sunset cocktails.

Zillertal

Schulhaus €€ Charismatic schoolhouse panoramically perched above Zell am Ziller. Rustic rooms, mountain views and a slow-food menu.

Alpenhotel Kramerwirt €€ Big on alpine flair, this rambling 500-year-old chalet in Mayrhofen has warm-hued rooms and a rooftop spa.

Kitzbühel

Snowbunny's Hostel € This friendly, laid-back hostel is a bunny-hop from the slopes.

Villa Licht €€ Pretty gardens, spruce modern apartments with pine trappings, balconies with mountain views – this charming Tyrolean chalet has the lot.

Practicalities

HEALTH

The World Health Organization (WHO) recommends all travellers should be covered for diphtheria, tetanus, measles, mumps, rubella, polio and hepatitis B. A UK Global Health Insurance Card (GHIC) or European Health Insurance Card (EHIC) from your healthcare provider covers most emergency medical care in Austria. This is no substitute for good insurance.

ANDRZEJ ROSTEK/SHUTTERSTOCK

LGBTIQ+ TRAVELLERS

Progressive and diverse, Vienna is home to the country's biggest gay community. Positive change is afoot elsewhere, too, though there is still some discrimination, especially in staunchly conservative, Catholic pockets of the country.

VISAS

Austria is part of the Schengen Agreement. Citizens of the EU, Eastern Europe, Israel, USA, Canada, Central and South America, Japan, Korea, Malaysia, Singapore, Australia and New Zealand don't need visas for stays of up to three months.

ACCESSIBLE TRAVEL

Austria scores highly with accessible travel, but a trip still requires careful planning. Ramps into buildings are common but not universal; most U-Bahn stations have wheelchair lifts, but on buses and trams you'll often be negotiating gaps and steps.

MOUNTAIN SAFETY

Every year people die from landslides and avalanches in the Alps. Always check weather conditions before heading out; consider hiring a guide when skiing off-piste. For challenging hikes, ensure you have the proper equipment and fitness. Inform someone at your accommodation where you're going and when you intend to return.

OPENING HOURS

Opening hours vary through the year and can differ between cities and small villages.
Banks 9am–3pm Monday to Friday
Cafes 8am–11pm
Post offices 8am–noon and 2–6pm Monday to Friday
Pubs & bars 5.30pm–midnight
Restaurants 11am–2.30pm & 6–11pm
Shops 9am–6.30pm Monday to Friday, to 5pm Saturday
Supermarkets 8am–8pm Monday to Friday, to 5pm Saturday

PUBLIC HOLIDAYS

New Year's Day 1 January
Epiphany 6 January
Easter Monday March/April
Labour Day 1 May
Whit Monday 6th Monday after Easter
Ascension Day 6th Thursday after Easter
Corpus Christi 2nd Thursday after Whitsunday
Assumption 15 August
National Day 26 October
All Saints' Day 1 November
Immaculate Conception 8 December
Christmas Day 25 December
St Stephen's Day 26 December

Language

The national language of Austria is German. Let's get to grips with the basics here.

Basics

Hello. Servus. *ser*-vus
Hello. Grüss Gott. grewss-got
Good morning. Moagn. *mwah*-gen
Goodbye. Auf Wiedersehen. owf *vee*-der-zay-en
Bye. Tschüss./ Tschau. chüs/chow
Yes. Ja. yah
No. Nein. nain
Please. Bitte. *bi*-te
Thank you. Danke. *dang*-ke
Excuse me. Entschuldigung. ent-*shul*-di-gung
Sorry. Entschuldigung. ent-*shul*-di-gung
What's your name?
Wie ist Ihr Name? (pol) *vee* ist eer *nah*-me
Wie heißt du? (inf) vee haist doo
My name is ...
Mein Name ist ... (pol) main *nah*-me ist ...
Ich heiße ... (inf) ikh *hai*-se ...
Do you speak English?
Sprechen Sie Englisch? (pol) *shpre*-khen zee *eng*-lish
Sprichst du Englisch? (inf) shprikhst doo *eng*-lish
I don't understand. Ich verstehe nicht. ikh fer-*shtay*-e nikht

Directions

Where's (the station)?
Wo ist (der Bahnhof). vor ist (der *bahn*-hawf)
What's the address?
Wie ist die Adresse? vee ist dee a-*dre*-se
Could you please write it down?
Könnten Sie das bitte aufschreiben? *kern*-ten zee das *bi*-te owf-*shrai*-ben

Can you show me (on the map)?
Können Sie es mir (auf der Karte) zeige *ker*-nen zee es meer (owf dair *kar*-te) *tsai*-gen

Signs

Ausgang Exit
Eingang Entrance
Damen Women
Herren Men
Heiß Hot
Kalt Cold
Offen Open
Geschlossen Closed
Kein Zutritt No Entry
Rauchen Verboten No Smoking
Verboten Prohibited

Time

What time is it? Wie spät ist es? vee shpayt ist es
It's (10) o'clock. Es ist (zehn) Uhr. es ist (tsayn) oor
morning Morgen *mor*-gen
afternoon Nachmittag *nahkh*-mi-tahk
evening Abend *ah*-bent
yesterday gestern *ges*-tern
today heute *hoy*-te
tomorrow morgen *mor*-gen

Emergencies

Help! Hilfe! *hil*-fe
Go away! Gehen Sie weg! *gay*-en zee vek
I'm ill. Ich bin krank. ikh bin krangk
Call the police! Rufen Sie die Polizei! *roo*-fen zee dee po-li-*tsai*
Call a doctor! Rufen Sie einen Arzt! *roo*-fen zee *ai*-nen artst

NUMBERS
1
eins *ains*
2
zwei *tsvai*
3
drei *drai*
4
vier *feer*
5
fünf *fünf*
6
sechs *zeks*
7
sieben *zee·ben*
8
acht *akht*
9
neun *noyn*
10
zehn *tsayn*

NATALI GLADO/SHUTTERSTOCK

Arriving

Vienna is the main transport hub for Austria, operating services worldwide. The airport is 19km southwest of the city centre. Most low-cost and European carriers operate from Terminal 1, while Terminal 3 is for long-haul flights. Salzburg, Innsbruck and Graz have small, minimal-fuss airports, operating flights to numerous destinations across Europe.

By Rail
Bordering eight countries, Austria's super-central location makes international rail travel a breeze. Vienna is an hour from Bratislava, Innsbruck is 3½ hours from Verona, Linz is four hours from Prague. You get the idea – Europe really is your oyster here.

By Car
There are numerous entry points from Germany, the Czechia, Slovakia, Hungary, Slovenia, Italy and Switzerland. Border crossing points are open 24 hours. Austria is compact – driving from Bregenz in the west to Vienna in the east takes just six hours (traffic permitting).

MONEY

Currency: Euro (€)

CREDIT CARDS

Visa and Mastercard (EuroCard) are more widely accepted than Amex and Diners Club. Upmarket shops, hotels and restaurants will accept cards. Credit cards allow you to get cash advances at ATMs and over-the-counter at most banks. Train tickets can be bought by credit card in main stations.

TAXES & REFUNDS

Mehrwertsteuer (VAT) in Austria is typically 20%. Look for the 'Global Refund Tax Free Shopping' sticker to reclaim about 13% on single purchases over €75 (by non-EU citizens/residents); see *globalrefund.com*. Refund desks are at major department stores, as well as Vienna and Salzburg airports.

TIPPING

Bars About 5% at the bar and 10% at a table.

Hotels One or two euros per suitcase for porters and valet parking in top-end hotels.

Restaurants About 10% (unless service is abominable).

Taxis About 10%.

Getting Around

Austria's public transport network is a dream, with swift, inexpensive trains linking towns and cities, and buses filling the gaps. Car hire gives you greater freedom to explore the country's remotest corners.

Train
Austria's rail system is excellent and inexpensive with a discount card. Österreiche Bundesbahn *(ÖBB; Austrian Federal Railway; oebb.at)* is the main operator. The best deals are *Sparschiene,* heavily discounted tickets sold online up to six months ahead.

JULIA MOUNTAIN PHOTO/SHUTTERSTOCK

Car
You'll find all the major car-hire companies at airports, including Sixt, Hertz and Enterprise. The minimum age for hiring small cars is 19. A valid licence is necessary. Autobahn (motorways) are well maintained. You can only drive on them with a *Vignette* (motorway tax), available from border crossings and petrol stations.

Mountain Railways
When trains stop in the Alps, the only way is up on a *Seilbahn* (funicular) or *Bergbahn* (cable car). Costs quickly mount, meaning it's often cheaper to buy a weekly pass (a ski pass in winter) or use a discount card. Some guest cards get you a free ride.

DRIVING ESSENTIALS

Drive on the right.

Bus
Rail routes are often complemented by Postbus *(postbus.at)* services, useful in inaccessible mountainous regions. Buses are fairly reliable, and usually depart from train stations. Aim for weekday travel; services are reduced or nonexistent on weekends.

Bike
Thousands of kilometres of well-signposted bike routes shadow rivers and lakeshores and twist up the Alps. Bike/e-bike rental is ubiquitous and many ÖBB stations rent wheels. Most regional trains transport bikes in the baggage car (you'll need a bicycle ticket). On long-distance trains, reserve online/ use the ÖBB app.

Winter tyres are obligatory November to mid-April.

Speed limit is 50km/h: built-up areas, 100 km/h: open roads and 130 km/h: motorways.

Curated by
Mark Baker

Czechia

BREATHTAKING CASTLES AND EVEN BETTER BEER

Find dramatic historical architecture, charming towns,
quirky sights and a vibrant, youthful culture.

Since the fall of communism in 1989 and the opening up of Central and Eastern Europe, Prague has evolved into one of Europe's most popular travel destinations. And for very good reason. Czechia's capital city offers an intact medieval core that transports you back – especially when strolling the hidden streets of the Old Town – some 600 years. The 14th-century Charles Bridge, linking two historic neighbourhoods across a slow-moving river – with Prague Castle pitched dramatically in the backdrop – is one of the continent's most beautiful sights. But Prague is not just about history. It's a vital urban centre with a rich array of cultural offerings, including fantastic museums, concert halls, restaurants and clubs.

Outside the capital, in the provinces of Bohemia and Moravia, castles and palaces abound – including the audacious hilltop chateau at Český Krumlov – which illuminate the stories of powerful dynasties whose influence was felt throughout Europe. Bohemia was famous in the 19th century for its regal spas, and Karlovy Vary still shows off this old-school splendour. Beer afficionados will make a beeline for Plzeň (Pilsen), where modern-day lager was first invented. Moravia lies a bit further off the beaten path. The provincial capital of Brno abounds in student-fiilled bars and cafes and ghoulish underground sights. The city of Olomouc has much of the architectural beauty of Prague, with just a fraction of the crowds.

FOTOKON/SHUTTERSTOCK

THE MAIN AREAS

PRAGUE	**BOHEMIA**	**MORAVIA**
Czechia's breathtaking and energetic capital. **p88**	Castles, historic spa resorts, beers and bones. **p97**	Underground adventure and baroque beauty. **p103**

For places to stay in Czechia, see p108

Above: Charles Bridge (p93), Prague; Left: Beer, Plzeň (p98)

Find Your Way

A sampling of the best of Czechia. We've picked out some of the must-see sights in Prague, plus highlights for excursions further afield into the provinces of Bohemia and Moravia.

Moravia, p103

Experience Czechia without the tourists, including visiting a vibrant provincial capital and an underappreciated baroque beauty.

Prague, p88

Immerse yourself in centuries-old historic architecture, followed up with a pint at a pub or a classical concert.

Bohemia, p97

Discover castle-topped hills and charming historic towns, and then treat yourself to possibly the world's best beer tour.

TRAINS & BUSES

You won't need a car to get around. The extensive train and bus network can take you to all the places covered here. We've noted where either the train or bus might be faster or cheaper.

CAR

Don't use your own vehicle to get around Prague. The city's metro and trams are much more practical. Outside the capital, a car gives you flexibility to explore the country at your own pace.

GERMANY

POLAND

SLOVAKIA

AUSTRIA

Dresden
Chemnitz
Děčín
Ústí nad Labem
Most
Chomutov
Louny
Žatec
Kladno
Karlovy Vary
Mariánské Lázně
Plzeň (Pilsen)
Beroun
Domažlice
Klatovy
Příbram
Písek
České Budějovice
Český Krumlov
Český Krumlov State Castle
Šumava National Park
Třeboň
Jindřichův Hradec
Tábor
Benešov
Mladá Boleslav
Kutná Hora
Sedlec Ossuary
Havlíčkův Brod
Jihlava
Třebíč
Pelhřimov
Chrudim
Hradec Králové
Ústí nad Orlicí
Litomyšl
Svitavy
Šumperk
Olomouc
Přerov
Kroměříž
Blansko
Brno
Labyrinth under the Vegetable Market
Villa Tugendhat
Nový Jičín
Opava
Ostrava
Frýdek-Místek
Rožnov pod Radhoštěm

PRAGUE
Prague Castle
Old Town Square

Bohemian Switzerland National Park

BOHEMIA

MORAVIA

Elbe
Labe River
Vltava River
Morava River
Odra

Munich

Katowice

N

0   100 km
0   50 miles

BORIS STROUJKO/SHUTTERSTOCK

Prague (p88)

Plan Your Time

Three days is sufficient for Prague, and you can then pick and choose what you'd like to see in Bohemia or Moravia. With a car you can cover the highlights in a week.

Three Days in Prague

● Experience the exciting combination of a glorious past and energetic present in Prague. Take in the grandeur of **Prague Castle** (p89), cross **Charles Bridge** (p93) and wander Prague's Old Town. Take in the spectacle of **Old Town Square** (p94) and the **Astronomical Clock** (p94) and then explore the **Prague Jewish Museum** (p94). Spend a third day on the train going to see spectacular **Karlštejn Castle** (p96).

A Week in Czechia

● Begin in **Prague** (p88) before heading west for the spa scene at **Karlovy Vary** (p97). Balance the virtue and vice ledger with a few brews in **Plzeň** (p98), before heading south to **Český Krumlov** (p100). Take in the 'Bone Church' in **Kutná Hora** (p101) and then head east to enjoy the underground sights of **Brno** (p103). From Moravia's largest city, it's just a skip to stately **Olomouc** (p106).

SEASONAL HIGHLIGHTS

SPRING
Trees and flowers start budding in April and the country comes alive after the long winter. May and June days are often warm and sunny.

SUMMER
Hot, sunny days are perfect for escaping the city. That said, it's high season. Thousands of visitors stream through Prague daily.

AUTUMN
September and October tend to be quieter but still offer reliably good weather. Locals decamp to the forests to pick mushrooms.

WINTER
The Christmas and New Year's holidays enliven the long, cold winter. Hotel rates drop, but some attractions, including gardens, close.

Prague

RIVETING HISTORY | STIRRING VIEWS | REGAL ARCHITECTURE

☑ **TOP TIP**

Prague can get very crowded, particularly in midsummer and over major holidays. To avoid disappointment, book things like meals at popular restaurants as well as theatre and concert tickets as far in advance as possible.

The ups and downs of centuries past, of empires, wars, plagues and prosperity, are etched into Prague's soul like the lines carved onto the facades of its Gothic towers and Renaissance palaces. Some 35 years ago, Prague re-emerged on the European stage after languishing for years under communism, and the world was agog. Those years trapped behind the Iron Curtain left the city looking neglected and rundown, but it was obvious Prague's rich history and intrinsic beauty – the hypnotic, visual tension between Charles Bridge and Prague Castle – had survived intact.

Indeed, that's the real pleasure of a trip to Prague now that the scaffolding is down and the appeal is obvious to everyone: to take in the beauty as you wander slowly from Prague Castle down through the historic Malá Strana quarter, across Charles Bridge, over the Vltava River and into the arms of the Old Town.

Prague Castle & Hradčany

The hilltop neighbourhood of Hradčany, home to Prague Castle, retains a whiff of exclusivity centuries after the emperors and kings who once lived here have gone. The main attractions include the Prague Castle complex and stately St Vitus Cathedral, which stands within the castle walls. Strahov Monastery has been here since at least 1140; the

 GETTING AROUND

Prague has an excellent public transport system of metros, trams, buses and night trams, but when it comes to moving around the relatively compact historic neighbourhoods of Staré Město (Old Town), Malá Strana and Prague Castle, it's more convenient – and more scenic – to travel by foot. Use the metro to cover longer distances or to convenient stations located near Staré Město, Malá Strana and central Wenceslas Square. Use the tram for shorter stretches. Tram 22 runs to near Prague Castle and can spare you the climb up to the castle district.

Old Royal Palace

monks' adjoining library is one of the most beautiful in Europe. Scattered among the incredible palaces are pubs, restaurants and breathtaking views out over Malá Strana and the Old Town.

Take in sprawling Prague Castle

Looming high above the Vltava River, **Prague Castle** *(hrad.cz; tours from adult/child 300/200Kč),* with its serried ranks of spires and palaces, dominates the city. Within its walls lies a fascinating collection of historic buildings, museums and galleries, home to some of Czechia's greatest artistic and cultural treasures. The grounds of the castle complex are free to enter, though to see the interiors (including adjoining St Vitus Cathedral) requires a combined admission ticket. Buy tickets online at **Ticketportal** *(ticketportal.cz)* or at the **castle information centre**.

The high point for most visitors is the **Old Royal Palace**, situated in the castle's third courtyard. This is one of the oldest surviving parts of the castle, dating from 1135. Don't miss the **Vladislav Hall** (Vladislavský sál), which is famous for its beautiful, late-Gothic vaulted ceiling. Beyond the Old Royal Palace, the **Basilica of St George** is Czechia's best-preserved Romanesque basilica. You can also stroll **Golden Lane**, where writer Franz Kafka stayed at No 22 (from 1916 to 1917).

EARLY STORY OF HRADČANY

Hradčany got its first royal residents in the 9th century. A ducal palace was built here to accommodate the early ruling Přemyslid dynasty. The 12th century saw significant expansion. A grander ducal palace was completed. In 1140, the Premonstratensian Monastery was founded in Strahov. In the 14th century, Emperor Charles IV rebuilt the castle to more properly represent Prague's status as seat of the Holy Roman Empire. He also embarked on construction of St Vitus Cathedral.

In 1541, a tragic fire engulfed the district and damaged many buildings, including the castle and cathedral. Yet the fire created large, empty lots that eventually gave way to today's mega-palaces, including the **Schwarzenberg Palace** and the **Archbishop's Palace**.

EATING & DRINKING NEAR PRAGUE CASTLE: OUR PICKS

Klášterní Pivovar Strahov: Convivial pub near Strahov Monastery serves its own St Norbert beers – and very good Czech food. *10am-10pm* €€

Vinobona Wine & Bistro: Tiny, romantic spot; perfect for breakfast/ lunch. Dress smartly for pricier dinner tasting menu. *9am-3pm, 6-10pm Thu-Mon* €€€

Kuchyň: Book well in advance to secure one of the popular terrace tables. Excellent Czech standards. *11.30am-11pm* €€

Lobkowicz Palace Café: The best pit stop for drinks and light meals within the Prague Castle complex. Superb views from the back balcony. *10am-6pm* €€

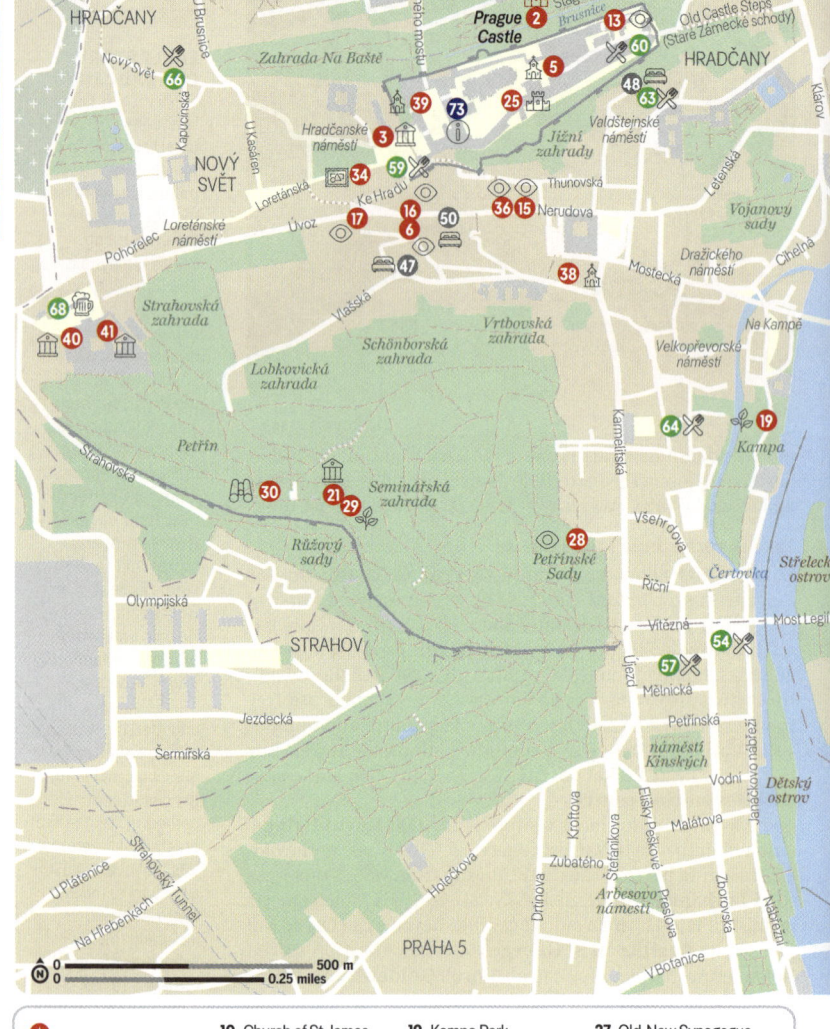

⭐ HIGHLIGHTS

1 Old Town Square
2 Prague Castle

🔴 SIGHTS

3 Archbishop's Palace
4 Astronomical Clock
5 Basilica of St George
6 Bretfeld Palace
7 Ceremonial Hall
8 Charles Bridge
9 Church of Our Lady Before Týn
10 Church of St James
11 Church of St Nicholas
12 Estates Theatre
13 Golden Lane
14 House at the Stone Bell
15 House at the Three Fiddles
16 House of the Golden Horseshoe
17 House of the Two Suns
see 1 Jan Hus Statue
18 K (David Černý Sculpture)
19 Kampa Park
see 7 Klaus Synagogue
see 69 Kůň (David Černý Sculpture)
20 Maisel Synagogue
see 1 Marian Column
21 Mirror Maze
22 Municipal House
23 National Museum
24 National Museum Annex
see 7 Old Jewish Cemetery
25 Old Royal Palace
26 Old Town Hall
27 Old-New Synagogue
28 Petřín Funicular Railway
29 Petřín Hill
30 Petřín Lookout Tower
31 Pinkas Synagogue
32 Prague Jewish Museum
33 Rudolfinum
34 Schwarzenberg Palace
35 Spanish Synagogue
36 St John of Nepomuk House
37 St John of Nepomuk Statue

38 St Nicholas Church
39 St Vitus Cathedral
40 Strahov Library
41 Strahov Monastery
42 Velvet Revolution
   Memorial
43 Wenceslas Statue

● SLEEPING
44 Ahoy! Hostel
45 Design Hotel Josef
46 Dominican
47 Dům U Velké Boty
48 Golden Well Hotel

49 Icon Hotel
50 Little Quarter Hostel
51 Mosaic House
52 Sophie's Hostel

● EATING
53 420 Restaurant
54 Café Savoy
55 Čestr
56 Garden's
57 Ichnusa Botega Bistro
58 Kantýna
59 Kuchyň

60 Lobkowicz Palace Café
61 Mincovna
62 Naše Maso
63 Terasa U Zlaté Studně
64 U Modré Kachničky
65 V Kolkovně
66 Vinobona Wine & Bistro

● DRINKING
& NIGHTLIFE
67 Duplex
68 Klášterní Pivovar
   Strahov

● ENTERTAINMENT
see 33 Dvořák Hall
69 Lucerna Music Bar
70 National Theatre
71 Prague State Opera
72 Reduta Jazz Club
see 22 Smetana Hall

● INFORMATION
73 Castle Information
   Centre

● TRANSPORT
74 Praha Hlavní Nádraží

BEST VENUES FOR CLASSICAL MUSIC

Rudolfinum: Gorgeous neo-Renaissance building with **Dvořák Hall**, home of the Czech Philharmonic Orchestra. The season runs September–June. *(rudolfinum.cz; standing tickets from 200Kč)*

Smetana Hall: Centrepiece stage of the Municipal House and home of the Prague Symphony Orchestra. *(fok.cz; tickets from 400Kč)*

Church of St James: Features a splendid pipe organ. Pop in on Sunday mornings at 10am for a free organ recital. *(praha.minorite.cz; free)*

Church of St Nicholas: Chamber concerts here are visually splendid (though acoustically average). *(svmikulas.cz; tickets from 300Kč)*

Estates Theatre: Branch of the National Theatre hosting occasional baroque music concerts. *(narodni-divadlo.cz; tickets from 400Kč)*

St Vitus Cathedral

Admire towering St Vitus Cathedral

Built over almost 600 years, **St Vitus Cathedral** *(katedrala svatehovita.cz)* is one of Central Europe's most richly endowed cathedrals. It is pivotal to the country's cultural life, housing treasures that range from the tombs of St Wenceslas and Charles IV to the baroque silver tomb of St John of Nepomuk and the ornate Chapel of St Wenceslas. Step inside to see the massive nave flooded with colour from stained-glass windows created by eminent Czech artists of the early 20th century – note the one by Alfons Mucha in the third chapel on the northern side. The high points include the **tomb of St Vitus** and spectacular silver **tomb of St John of Nepomuk**. The **Wallenstein Chapel** contains the graves of cathedral architects Matthias of Arras and Peter Parler. The most beautiful of the side chapels is the **Chapel of St Wenceslas**. Its walls are adorned with gilded panels containing polished slabs of semiprecious stones.

The world's prettiest library?

Tucked away in a quiet corner of Hradčany, the **Strahov Monastery** *(strahovskyklaster.cz; library tours adult/child 150/80Kč)* has stood here since 1140, when it was founded by Duke Vladislav II. The biggest attraction is the magnificent **library**. Guided tours allow you to peer into the two baroque halls. The stunning interior of the two-storey 'Philosophy Hall' features floor-to-ceiling walnut shelving. The older 'Theology Hall' is even more breathtaking.

Malá Strana (Lesser Town)

Visitors are often surprised to discover that Malá Strana (Lesser Town) is in some ways more beautiful than Staré Město (Old Town). In the 17th and 18th centuries, noble families built their sumptuous palaces and plotted out spacious gardens here. The neighbourhood is home to many top sights, including the impressive baroque of St Nicholass Church and the elegant Wallenstein Garden. The best way to explore is to amble along the cobblestoned backstreets, or through **Kampa Park** along the river, and admire the handsome buildings and tiny squares.

Walk across Charles Bridge

Who knew a bridge could ever be this beautiful or that mounting 30 baroque statues along its edges might elevate a handsome Gothic structure into a public work of art? **Charles Bridge** *(Karlův most, free)* is a world-class attraction. The bridge began life in 1357 when Emperor Charles IV commissioned Peter Parler (architect of St Vitus Cathedral) to replace an older, 12th-century bridge that had been washed away by floods. The new bridge was completed in 1390. The statues came three centuries later, when the bridge's first monument, the Crucifix near the eastern end, was mounted in 1657. The most famous figure is the monument to **St John of Nepomuk**. Tradition says if you rub the bronze plaque, you'll one day return to Prague.

Take in grand St Nicholas Church

Praguers generally have a love-hate affair with baroque architecture. Everyone, though, loves **St Nicholas Church** *(Kostel svatého Mikuláše; stnicholas.cz; adult/child 140/80Kč)*; its big green dome can be seen from just about anywhere in the centre. The building was begun by famed baroque architect Christoph Dientzenhofer; his son Kilian continued the work and Anselmo Lurago finished the job in 1755. Mozart himself tickled the ivories on the 2500-pipe organ in 1787. Take the stairs up to the gallery to see Karel Škréta's emotive, 17th-century *Passion Cycle* paintings. On the ceiling, Johann Kracker's 1770 *Apotheosis of St Nicholas* is Europe's largest fresco.

Climb Petřín Hill

This 318m-high **Petřín** is one of Prague's largest green spaces. It's great for quiet, tree-shaded walks and fine views over the 'city of a hundred spires'. Climb up or take the **Petřín Funicular** to find the views and a handful of kid-friendly attractions. The **Petřín Lookout Tower** *(adult/child 220/150Kč)*, a 60m-high Eiffel Tower lookalike (though smaller at a ratio of 1:5), offers dramatic vistas. Just near the lookout tower is a **Mirror Maze** *(adult/child 120/80Kč)*. Younger children will get a kick out of the distorting funhouse mirrors and labyrinth.

Staré Město (Old Town)

Staré Město, Prague's Old Town, has been the city's beating heart for more than 1000 years. The grand buildings, churches and squares, the Old Town Hall and Astronomical Clock

HOUSE SIGNS OF NERUDOVA

Steep Nerudova street leads from Malá Strana to Prague Castle. It has a long, rich history – much of it written on the playful symbols that adorn the fronts of the houses. The **House at the Three Fiddles** (Nerudova 12) once belonged, fittingly, to a family of violinmakers. **St John of Nepomuk House** (No 18) is adorned with an image of the patron saint himself. **Bretfeld Palace** (No 33) was a social hot spot, entertaining the likes of Mozart and Casanova. The **House of the Golden Horseshoe** (No 34) is named after St Wenceslas' horse, allegedly shod with gold. Czech writer and journalist Jan Neruda, after whom the street is named, lived at the **House of the Two Suns** (No 47) from 1845 to 1857.

EATING IN MALÁ STRANA: OUR PICKS

U Modré Kachničky: This feels like an old-fashioned hunting lodge, with quiet, candlelit nooks. The traditional roast duck is very good. *noon-11pm* €€€

Terasa U Zlaté Studně: Perched atop a Renaissance mansion close to the castle, the 'Golden Well' has truly fine dining. *noon-4pm & 6-11pm* €€€

Ichnusa Botega Bistro: Superb Italian food and wines ferried to Prague directly from the owner's homeland of Sardinia. *11am-10pm* €€

Café Savoy: Elegant Viennese-style coffeehouse, with terrific Czech specialties and homemade desserts. *8am-10pm Mon-Fri, from 9am Sat & Sun* €€

IN THE FOOTSTEPS OF KINGS

The **Royal Way** (Královská cesta) was the former processional route followed by the Bohemian kings on their way to St Vitus Cathedral for coronation. The first king to ride the route was the Habsburg ruler Albert II, in 1438; the last was Emperor Ferdinand I of Austria, in 1836.

The coronation route ran right through the heart of Staré Město. It began at the Powder Gate. From here, the route followed Celetná to Old Town Square and the adjacent Little Square (Malé náměsti). From the squares, the route traced Karlova street to Charles Bridge and then across to Malá Strana. On the Malá Strana side, the coronation route proceeded along Mostecká street to Malostranské náměstí (Lesser Town Square) before climbing up Nerudova to Prague Castle.

stand as testimony to the growing wealth and influence over the centuries of Prague's merchants and artisans. This splendour came to rival that of the kings and noble families on the other side of the river. The best way to take in Staré Město's sights is to wander at will. The street plan appears to have little logic at all; perfect for getting lost in.

Explore Old Town Square

One of Europe's most beautiful and busiest urban spaces, **Old Town Square** has been Prague's principal public square since the 10th century and was its main marketplace until the beginning of the 20th century.

The most important building, the **Old Town Hall** (*staromestskaradnicepraha.cz; tower adult/child 300/200Kč*), was founded in 1338 to serve as Staré Město's independent seat of government. These days it no longer has a formal governing function. The main admission ticket includes entry to the tower, which affords dramatic views of the square below. The Town Hall's best-known attraction is the **Astronomical Clock** *(free)* on its south-facing exterior. On the hour, from 9am to 9pm, spectators are treated to a 45-second mechanised marionette display straight out of the Middle Ages.

Beyond the Old Town Hall, the most dramatic structure on the square is the twin-spired **Church of Our Lady Before Týn**, across the way, which stands incongruously behind a row of baroque facades. The 14th-century **House at the Stone Bell** is considered the square's oldest building. Find another important church, the baroque **Church of St Nicholas**, wedged into the northwestern corner.

Two pieces of statuary in the middle of the square are integral to this public space. Praguers love the dramatic art nouveau depiction of Czech religious reformer **Jan Hus** by Ladislav Šaloun. The newer **Marian Column** was only installed in 2020, and it's fair to say locals haven't quite warmed up to it yet.

Tour Prague's Jewish Museum

The **Prague Jewish Museum** (*jewishmuseum.cz; from adult/child 600/400Kč*) isn't simply one museum but a grouping of historic synagogues and an ancient burial ground. The holdings constitute possibly the world's biggest collection of sacred Jewish artefacts, many rescued from synagogues destroyed by Nazi Germany during WWII. The crumbling **Old Jewish Cemetery** is a must. The weatherworn headstones mark just a fraction of the thousands buried here. Other important sites include the **Old-New Synagogue**,

EATING IN STARÉ MĚSTO: OUR PICKS

420 Restaurant: Opulent dining room with baroque statues. Traditional Czech dishes given fusion upgrade. Book ahead. 11.30am–10.30pm €€€

Mincovna: Best of an average bunch of restaurants on Old Town Square. Decent pork knee, schnitzels and duck. 11.30am–11pm €€

Naše Maso: Tiny butcher with stand-up tables at the forefront of Prague's rush to embrace the foodie philosophy of locally sourced meat. 11am–10pm €€

V Kolkovně: Operated by Pilsner Urquell Brewery. Stylish, modern take on traditional Prague pub; fancy-ish versions of classic Czech dishes. 11am–midnight €€

Old Town Square

Pinkas Synagogue, **Maisel Synagogue**, **Spanish Synagogue**, **Klaus Synagogue** and **Ceremonial Hall**. One basic admission ticket allows entry to all of the main monuments, including the Old-New Synagogue. Buy tickets via the museum website or at the Museum Reservation Centre (Maiselova 15).

Admire art nouveau elegance

The **Municipal House** (*obecnidum.cz; guided tours adult/ child 320/270Kč*) is Prague's most exuberantly art nouveau building. The building, constructed between 1906 and 1912, was a lavish joint effort by around 30 leading Czech artists, including Alfons Mucha. Every detail of its design and decoration was carefully considered. Guided tours in English can be booked via the website or at the venue box office. The tour's highlight is the octagonal Lord Mayor's Hall, the windows of which overlook the main entrance.

Nové Město (New Town)

The busy streets of Prague's main commercial area are where Prague starts to feel like a real city (and less like a living museum). Nové Město translates as 'New Town', but there's little 'new' about it. It was laid out by Emperor Charles IV in the mid-14th century to alleviate overcrowding in Staré Město. Nové Město is home to the city's most important public gathering

EPIC HISTORY OF WENCESLAS SQUARE

Wenceslas Square has witnessed a great deal of Czech history. In 1848, during the revolutionary anti-Habsburg upheavals of that year, a giant mass was held here. In 1918, at the end of WWI, thousands gathered to celebrate the creation of the newly independent Czechoslovakia from the ruins of the old Austro-Hungarian Empire.

For many Czechs (and Slovaks), Wenceslas Square will forever be linked to the 1989 Velvet Revolution. Not far from the square, on Národní street, find a **memorial** to the spot where demonstrators and riot police first clashed on 17 November. In the days afterwards, angry citizens gathered on the square night after night to protest and cheer on the efforts of dissident leader Václav Havel.

 EATING IN NOVÉ MĚSTO: OUR PICKS

Kantýna: Choose your own piece of meat at the counter for the chefs to prepare, and enjoy it in an opulent former bank building. *11.30am-11pm* €€	**Čestr:** Splurge-worthy steakhouse behind the 'New Building' of the National Museum. Pair a meal with a trip to the museum or State Opera. *noon-11pm* €€€	**Garden's:** A passage opposite the entrance to the Lucerna Palace leads to a secret garden. Book ahead. *11am-10pm Mon-Sat, to 8pm Sun* €€	**Hostinec na Výtoni:** Duck is a beloved staple of Czech cuisine and at this picturesque inn by the river they do it better than anyone else in town. *11.30am-11pm* €€

area, Wenceslas Square, as well as many excellent museums, restaurants, hotels and concert venues. Many of the great moments of Czech history took place here.

Tour the National Museum

Nové Město's most important building looms high above Wenceslas Square. The neo-Renaissance bulk of the **National Museum** *(nm.cz; adult/child 300/200Kč),* designed in the 1880s as an architectural symbol of the Czech National Revival, highlights not only the history of the Czech lands from the 8th to 20th centuries, but presents thorough exhibitions on natural history, the 'miracles of evolution' and much more. The holdings are divided into two buildings. In addition to the main historical building, the **annex** is home to two more attractions: the interactive Children's Museum and the Museum of the 20th Century, narrating last century's gripping events.

See Kafka's head on a swivel

Nové Město is home to two of Czech artist David Černý's *(davidcerny.cz)* most-popular installations. Don't leave Prague without checking out **K**, a giant rotating bust of Franz Kafka. The bust gives a mesmerising show, as Kafka's face rhythmically dissolves and re-emerges.

The Lucerna Palace shopping arcade holds Černý's oddest installation: **Kůň** (Horse). A giant dead horse – with St Wenceslas sitting astride – hangs from the marbled atrium. It's a wryly amusing counterpart to the more imposing equestrian statue of the Bohemian patron **St Wenceslas** on Wenceslas Square.

Outside of Prague   TIME FROM PRAGUE: **45MIN**

Tour majestic Karlštejn Castle

Once you've had your fill of Prague, one fun, easy day trip is to catch the train out to Karlštejn, 35km southwest of the capital, to see magnificent **Karlštejn Castle** *(hrad-karlstejn.cz; basic tour adult/child from 300/240Kč).* This glorious pile was conceived by Emperor Charles IV in the 14th century and wouldn't look at all out of place on Disney World's Main Street. After seeing the interior, stroll through the charming town that surrounds the structure.

Two main guided tours of the castle are available, but most visitors opt for the shorter, hourlong 'basic' tour. This option provides a good introduction. You'll get glimpses into the Knight's Hall – still daubed with the coats of arms and names of the knight-vassals – as well as views of Emperor Charles IV's bedchamber, the Audience Hall and the Jewel House.

Bohemia

HISTORIC SPA | BREATHTAKING ARCHITECTURE | BIRTHPLACE OF BEER

Czechia's western province of Bohemia, with its forests and rolling hills, surrounds Prague on all sides. The region is peppered with unique sights and UNESCO World Heritage listings. To the west, the lustrous spa region – centred on Karlovy Vary – attracted the rich and famous from all around Europe in the 19th and early 20th centuries and still has the impressive architecture to match. To the south, the medieval resplendence of Český Krumlov and its glorious Renaissance castle rival Prague in terms of wow factor. Just south of Prague, the sweet aroma of hops drifts in the air in the city of Plzeň (Pilsen), where lager was invented in the 19th century and brewing traditions are still based on Bohemia's crystal-clear water and award-winning Saaz hops. Other highlights in this incredibly varied wedge of Central Europe include the magnificent former silver-mining town of Kutná Hora. People come here not just to tour the old mines but to visit the shocking, must-be-seen-to-be-believed 'Bone Church'.

Places
Karlovy Vary p97
Plzeň (Pilsen) p98
Český Krumlov p100
Kutná Hora p101

☑ TOP TIP

If you've only got time for one destination in Bohemia, make it Český Krumlov, one of Europe's prettiest small towns. Plan to stay overnight, as the three-hour travel time from Prague each way can be too long for a comfortable day trip.

Karlovy Vary

TIME FROM PRAGUE: 1½HR 🚆

Karlovy Vary, or simply 'Vary' to Czechs, perhaps more than any other town in Central Europe best captures the lost glamour and elegance of 19th-century spa culture. The

---

GETTING AROUND

Bohemia is well covered by buses and trains, though if you don't have your own wheels, the destinations listed here are probably best approached as a return trip from Prague. Whether the train or bus is best depends on the destination. For Karlovy Vary and Český

Krumlov, opt for the bus, while Plzeň and Kutná Hora both lie an easy train journey away. For drivers, roads are good but get crowded on weekends. The D5 motorway whisks you from Prague to Plzeň in under an hour.

SOUVENIRS FROM KARLOVY VARY

Becherovka: This strong-tasting herbal liquor, made to a secret recipe, is available at every bar and grocery store.

Moser Glass: Visit the **Moser Glasswork Shop** at the Grandhotel Pupp for an eternal reminder of your trip.

Spa cups: Among the most popular Bohemian souvenirs are these curiously shaped sipping cups, available from spa kiosks.

Porcelain: Head to **Porcelain Pokorný** *(nábřeží J Palacha 924/6)* for a wide choice of locally produced wares.

Spa wafers: Typical Czech-spa tooth-rotters available at stalls in the spa zone.

Petrified roses: Roses left in the spring water accumulate mineral residue, essentially turning to stone; buy one from kiosks in the Vřídelní Colonnade.

promenades, colonnades and grand neoclassical buildings dazzle the eye. In the resort's heyday, royals like Russia's Peter the Great and members of the Habsburg monarchy hobnobbed here with the greatest thinkers, writers and composers of their time. These days, visitors come to admire the architecture and stroll the impressive colonnades, sipping on the health-restoring sulphurous waters from spouted ceramic drinking cups.

Stroll the colonnades

The best way to experience Karlovy Vary is to get out walking and see the magnificent colonnades up close. Start your stroll at the northern end of the spa area, whose entry is marked by the landmark communist-era **Hotel Thermal** (1976), built in the modern 'brutalist' style.

Inside, you'll find **Saunia** *(saunia.cz)*, with access to the hotel's famous rooftop pool and views across the town. Walk south into the spa zone to find the cast-iron **Park Colonnade**. Then continue for 300m along the Teplá River to the biggest and most impressive colonnade, the neo-Renaissance **Mill Colonnade**, with five different springs.

Keep walking along Lázeňská street to the impressive **Market Colonnade**; one of its two springs, the pramen Karla IV (Charles IV Spring), is the spa's oldest. The street Stará Louka continues south for more splendour. At the end of the stroll stands the magnificent **Grandhotel Pupp**, the resort's choicest hotel.

Hit Vary's high points

For the best high-level views of pretty Karlovy Vary, make your way up to the **Diana lookout tower**, reached by **funicular railway** from behind the Grandhotel Pupp. The tower is free to climb and affords memorable views across the spa and the surrounding forested hills. There's a restaurant and cafe here and other attractions, including a worthwhile **Butterfly House** *(papilonia.cz)*.

Plzeň (Pilsen)

TIME FROM PRAGUE: 1HR

Bohemia's second-biggest city of Plzeň (Pilsen) is a grainy, industrial place with a couple of stellar attractions that make it worth the trip from Prague. Beer drinkers will head straight for the Pilsner Urquell Brewery and Brewery Museum to pay homage to the place where modern lager was first produced (and still made to the original recipe). Parents with kids in

EATING IN KARLOVY VARY: BEST FOR A SPECIAL MEAL

La Hospoda: Upscale take on a traditional Czech pub, serving staples as well delicacies like baked goose and roast boar. *11am-10pm* €€

Ukrajina: Serves the huge, local Ukrainian refugee community, offering filling fare from their war-torn home country. *11am-10pm* €€

Tusculum: The best lunch or dinner option in town, Tusculum features organic, locally sourced ingredients. Lots of vegetarian options. *noon-10pm* €€

Embassy Restaurant: The restaurant of the Embassy Hotel plates up top-notch Czech standards for Munich prices. *noon-10pm* €€€

Pilsner Urquell Brewery

tow may bypass the brewery in favour of Techmania, a giant, hands-on science museum and arguably the best children's attraction in the country.

Learn how lager is made

The number one reason people come to Plzeň is to visit the famous **Pilsner Urquell Brewery** *(prazdroj.cz; entry 380Kč)*, where Pilsner lager was first cooked up in 1842. Arguably Czechia's best known and most copied beer, it was 'invented' when a Bavarian brewer named Groll, whose task it was to upgrade the slurry the locals were forced to drink, came up with a new way of brewing. The drink – pils lager – quickly spread to Prague's pubs and the world beyond. Entry to the brewery is by guided tour. Highlights include the old cellars (dress warmly) and a glass of unpasteurised nectar (tasting far better than the Urquell you get in pubs). Get beer merch at the brewery shop.

Across the Radbuza River, close to the town's big main square, is the **Brewery Museum** *(prazdrojvisit.cz; entry 150Kč)*, which offers an insight into how beer was made (and drunk) in the days before Pilsner Urquell. Highlights include a mock-up of a 19th-century pub, a huge, wooden beer tankard from Siberia and a collection of beer mats.

THANKS, AMERICA!

At the end of WWII, the area around Plzeň was liberated from Nazi Germany by the US army (not the Soviet Red army), and the people here have never forgotten. Throughout the communist era this was a problematic event – the communists even went so far as to claim Soviet troops in US uniforms freed Plzeň.

After the Velvet Revolution it became possible to talk more openly about how WWII ended in this part of Europe. Plzeň goes further than that, organising its May **Slavnosti Svobody** (Liberation Festival) with a dwindling number of US soldiers who were here in '45 as guests of honour. The 'General Patton' and 'Díky, Ameriko!' ('Thanks America!') monuments are permanent reminders of the US Army's greatest moment in Bohemia.

 EATING IN PLZEŇ: OUR PICKS

Lokál pod Divadlem: The Plzeň branch of a popular pub-restaurant serving Czech standards and good beer. *11am-11.30pm* €

Na Spilce: The pub-restaurant at the Urquell Brewery is a great place to end the day in Plzeň. *11am-10pm* €€

U Salzmannů: Plzeň's oldest tavern, with a proud tradition of serving well-chilled Urquell and belly-filling Bohemian cuisine. *11am-11pm* €€

Šenk na Parkánu: At the Brewery Museum, the beer at this typically Czech pub-restaurant is tops, but so is the traditional food. *11am-late* €€

EGON SCHIELE IN ČESKÝ KRUMLOV

Art fans may be interested in knowing the celebrated Austrian expressionist painter Egon Schiele (1890–1918) loved Český Krumlov and had a deep connection to the town through his mother, Marie Soukupová, who was born here. Schiele himself lived in Krumlov in 1911, spending most of his time painting his *Dead Towns* pictures, a far cry from the explicit nudes for which he is famous. However, things did not go well when he returned to those naked female forms. He raised the ire of the townsfolk by hiring underage girls as nude models and was eventually chased out of town.

Get 'technical'

The interactive **Techmania Science Centre** (*techmania.cz; adult/child/family 280/280/1040Kč*) is one of the best ways to entertain kids that Czechia has to offer. If you arrive in the morning, you can almost guarantee you'll be dragging your reluctant-to-leave offspring out of the door at closing time eight hours later.

It's based in a huge, former heavy-engineering workshop, and kids are free to roam all day, trying out myriad experiments as they go. Sit back and relax as your little ones mess about with magnets, splash around in the water world, become TV news presenters in front of a green screen, see if they can out-run a cheetah and build towers out of thousands of wooden blocks. There are also excellent science demonstrations, a 3D planetarium and full-sized historic trains manufactured at the Škoda engineering works.

Český Krumlov

TIME FROM PRAGUE: **3HR**

Wrapped around a tight bend in the Vltava River, deep in Bohemia's south, the must-see town of Český Krumlov is a gem in every sense of the word. It's a Prague in miniature – a UNESCO World Heritage Site, with a huge castle complex, an old town, Renaissance and baroque architecture and hordes of tourists milling through the streets – but all on a smaller scale. You can walk from one end of town to the other in 20 minutes.

Lose yourself among cobbled lanes

The best way to see the town is simply to wander the Inner Town. Pass through the narrow streets packed with tiny shops and cafes to reach **Svornosti Square**, a small, painfully pretty piazza where there's always something going on – this is the focus of the Five-Petalled Rose Celebrations and the venue for the town's Christmas market. The town hall rests on six Gothic arches on the square's northeast flank, one of them providing shelter for the tourist office. There are also a few hotels and restaurants occupying prime spots. Radiating out from Svornosti are cobbled lanes, alleyways and streets that are sheer joy to explore.

Explore Krumlov's XL castle

Wherever you wander, you can't miss Český Krumlov's dramatic **Renaissance castle** (*zamek-ceskykrumlov.cz; tours adult/child from 300/90Kč*), which stands atop a promontory high above town. The castle began life in the 13th century and acquired its present appearance in the 16th to 18th centuries under the

 EATING IN ČESKÝ KRUMLOV: OUR PICKS

Krumlovský Mlýn: This huge, heavy-beamed tavern right on the tourist trail serves Bohemian staples and has seating next to the Vltava. *11am-10pm* €€

Krčma v Šatlavské: Slightly upmarket medieval cellar with a meat-heavy menu. Reservations essential. *11am-midnight* €€

U Dwau Maryí: Old Bohemian recipes washed down with mead and ale at this tavern where time has stood still. *11am-10pm* €€

Cikánská Jizba: Raucous, tightly-packed pub-restaurant that's been around forever. Nightly gypsy music. *5pm-midnight Mon-Sat* €€

Český Krumlov

stewardship of the noble Rožmberk and Schwarzenberg families. The interiors are accessible by guided tour only, though you can stroll the grounds unsupervised. Note there are over 360 rooms in the castle, though the tours examine only a small fraction.

Three tour routes are available: Tour 1, the standard tour, takes in the opulent Renaissance and baroque interiors; Tour 2 visits the Schwarzenberg portrait galleries and their 19th-century apartments. Tour 3 explores the chateau's nearly perfectly preserved baroque theatre.

Even if you don't take the tour, part of the fun here is getting lost in the passages, arcading and gangways on the south side, which lead to the **Cloak Bridge** – an amazing Renaissance structure rising incredibly high above the gorge.

Kutná Hora

TIME FROM PRAGUE: 1HR

Enriched by silver ore, the medieval city of Kutná Hora became the seat of Wenceslas II's royal mint in 1308 and once rivalled Prague in importance. By the 16th century, the mines began to run dry, and the town's demise was hastened by the Thirty Years' War. Kutná Hora became a UNESCO World Heritage Site in 1996, luring visitors with a smorgasbord of historic sights. One of those sights is the Sedlec Ossuary, aka the 'Bone Church', a chapel decorated with thousands of stacked human bones.

FIVE-PETALLED ROSE CELEBRATIONS

Bohemia's biggest medieval bash is the **Five-Petalled Rose Celebrations** (slavnostipetilister-uze.cz), a three-day Renaissance party that takes place each June. The entire historical centre is roped off (you need a ticket to get in even if you are just sightseeing) and countless events take place in every street, park and courtyard.

The biggest day is the Saturday, which sees a huge procession featuring many a silly costume somehow squeeze its way through the crooked medieval streets. In the evening, the focus is on Svornosti Square, where there are sword fights, puppeteers, medieval music and tons of food and drink. In other places there are demonstrations of horsemanship, archery, folk music, street theatre and more food.

EATING IN KUTNÁ HORA: OUR PICKS

Restaurace V Ruthardce: Old Bohemian tavern with heavy Czech favourites and views of the St Barbara Cathedral. *11am-11pm* €€

Dačický: An old Bohemian, wood-panelled beerhall with lager and dumplings galore. *11am-8pm* €€

U Šneka Pohodáře: Enjoy a pizza and a Bernard beer at the 'Easy-going Snail'. *11am-10pm* €

Kavárna na Kozím plácku: Cute cafe with big timber beams and mismatched 1950s furniture. *9am-7pm* €

FIVE CENTURIES IN THE MAKING

It took over 500 years to complete Kutná Hora's Cathedral of St Barbara. Construction began in 1380 under Jan Parléř, son of Petr Parléř, Charles IV's favoured architect.

The Hussite Wars soon intervened and work was interrupted, but between 1489 until his death in 1506 another star architect Matěj Rejsek (of Prague's Prašná brána fame) added the cathedral's impressive vaulting, and another architectural superstar Benedikt Ried (of Old Royal Palace at Prague Castle fame) finished off the naves after that. But when the silver ran out, construction work was abandoned completely in 1558, and for three centuries nothing much happened. It was only in the late 19th century that the cathedral was completed in neo-Gothic style.

MIKHAIL MARKOVSKIY/SHUTTERSTOCK

Sedlec Ossuary

Gasp at a ghoulish spectacle

When the Schwarzenberg royal family purchased the Sedlec Monastery (about 2.5km northeast of the town centre) in 1870 they allowed local woodcarver František Rint to get creative with the bones in the crypt (the remains of an estimated 40,000 people), resulting in the spooky **Sedlec Ossuary** *(Kostnice; sedlec.info; adult/child 220/150Kč),* a remarkable 'bone church'. The skeletons found their way into the church when the surrounding cemetery was reduced in size. The human remains here are mostly plague victims and those who perished in the Hussite Wars of the 15th century. Garlands of skulls and femurs are strung from the vaulted ceiling, while in the centre dangles a vast chandelier containing one of each bone in the human body.

Tour the old silver mines

Originally part of the town's fortifications, the Hrádek (Little Castle) was rebuilt in the 15th century as the residence of Jan Smíšek, administrator of the royal mines, who grew rich from silver mined illegally under the building. It now houses the **Czech Silver Museum** *(cms-kh.cz; adult/concession 90/60Kč).* There are two guided tours; the second includes a visit down an ancient silver mine.

Gaze up at the miners' cathedral

Kutná Hora's greatest monument is the Gothic **Cathedral of St Barbara** *(chramsvatebarbory.cz).* It rivals Prague's St Vitus in size and magnificence, its soaring nave culminating in elegant, six-petalled ribbed vaulting, and the ambulatory chapels preserve original 15th-century frescoes, some of them showing miners at work. Take a walk around the outside of the church; the terrace at the eastern end enjoys the finest view in town.

Moravia

URBAN FUN | BEAUTIFUL BAROQUE | SPOOKY UNDERGROUND

Venture into Czechia's easternmost province, Moravia, for a rurally resplendent flip on its western counterpart, Bohemia. Here, instead of industry as in the west of the country, tradition and folklore take centre stage. A dedication to vineyards and wine surpasses breweries, and big-hitter sites fill tiny towns, chronicling the former dynasties of medieval Moravia to the Habsburg Empire.

At Moravia's core is its provincial capital of Brno. The province's gateway and trendsetting student city carves a somewhat rebellious, artistic path in creating a new identity above ground, while showing off its historic cache beneath. Come here to experience the pleasures of urban Czechia – with its sights, restaurants and bars – but without the crowds of Prague.

Olomouc, to the northeast, was Moravia's first capital and a former Habsburg stronghold. This relatively sleepy city conceals its baroque beauty in a bubble – the prettiest city in the region is surprisingly overlooked. This is the place for peaceful walks through resplendent public squares while surrounded by grand churches and statues. An active student scene keeps the bar and cafe scene fresh.

Brno

TIME FROM PRAGUE: 2HR 🚆

Prague may garner more attention, but Brno isn't trying to compete. Sure, the city isn't as pretty as Prague, but it feels somehow more authentic. Brno's vibrancy comes from its university students and start-ups that fill the city with youthful energy and creative enterprise. While Brno boasts a grand town hall and hilltop castle, many of the biggest attractions lie below ground, where history is burrowed in medieval labyrinths and subterranean cellars and crypts. Architecture buffs won't want to miss touring the early-20th-century functionalist icon, the Villa Tugendhat.

Places

Brno p103
Olomouc p106

GETTING AROUND

Both Brno and Olomouc are easily reachable by train or bus from Prague. Brno is accessible by bus or train from Vienna, Budapest and Bratislava. Long-distance and international bus companies like Flix and RegioJet use a small bus station opposite the Grandhotel Brno in the centre of the city. By car, Czechia's main D1 motorway links Prague with both Brno and Olomouc, though parking is limited. Within Moravia, fast trains run between Brno and Olomouc.

☑ TOP TIP

Guided tours of Brno's UNESCO-listed **Villa Tugendhat** (p104) are very popular and often oversubscribed. Buy tickets in advance of travelling.

MORE ON MENDEL

It's fascinating to think that the foundations of modern genetics were laid not in a high-tech lab but on a simple lawn. Between 1856 and 1863, Gregor Mendel cross-bred pea plants in a monastery garden, studying how combinations and traits like colour and size were inherited. Being a humble monk with a green-thumbed hobby, his work was largely overlooked by the scientific community at the time.

It wasn't until the mid-20th century when genetics was studied in the context of DNA and chromosomes that Mendel's pioneering research gained the recognition it deserved. His initial observations revealed the patterns of generational inheritance and predictable ratios – discoveries now known as 'Mendel's Laws'.

Poke around Brno's underground

The fun of a visit to Brno is the chance to explore the many underground passages etched into the earth here over the centuries. Make your way first to the central **Vegetable Market** (Zelný trh), a fixture since the 13th century. Just next to the market find the entrance to a kilometre-long maze of chambers and passageways in a multilevel den from the Middle Ages. Tour the cellars of old city merchants and alchemists on a one-hour walk through the **Labyrinth under the Vegetable Market** (podzemibrno.cz; adult/child 180/90Kč). The nearby **Ossuary at the Church of St James** (podzemibrno.cz; adult/child 160/80Kč) is a more sombre walk through history: find a floor-to-ceiling, bone-stacked burial shaft of some 50,000 people who perished in the Thirty Years' War of the 17th century and the plagues. For something even more ghoulish, the **Capuchin Crypt** (hrobka.kapucini.cz; adult/child 120/70Kč), below the Church of the Discovery of the Holy Cross on Capuchin Square, holds a truly macabre encounter. For over 100 years, until 1784, the Friars of the Christian Capuchin Order were given a simple – respectful – burial here as mummified remains.

Climb up for Old Town vistas

Brno's medieval **Old Town Hall** (Stará radnice) features a 13th-century vaulted treasury and 16th-century judicial-themed, fresco-daubed hall, but be sure to climb the 173 wooden stairs through the clocktower centriole to the 63m-high panoramic **Renaissance pavilion** (gotobrno.cz; adult/child 90/50Kč), and take in the city spires and pastel veneers.

Wander the halls of spooky Špilberk Castle

The mid-13th-century fortification of **Špilberk Castle** (spilberk.cz; adult/child 160/95Kč) turned 18th-century notorious Habsburg lockup is today a museum complex. Top exhibitions include the **Prison of Nations** with dungeon and torture exhibits; the eight-part, artefact-packed **Brno on Špilberk** timeline from medieval stronghold to the Capital of Moravia; and a preserved 18th-century **Baroque Pharmacy** set-up. Other rooms are chock-full of artworks from Austrian Moravia to the modern day.

Tour the UNESCO-listed Villa Tugendhat

Brno was no exception to the 1920s interwar boom in modern architecture, with **Villa Tugendhat** being its greatest example of functionalist architecture. This simple, purist-style living

EATING IN BRNO: OUR PICKS

Bucheck: Teeming food truck tucked off the side of the Vegetable Market (Zelný trh) serving banging pulled-pork burgers. 11.30am until sold out Tue-Sun €

Lokál U Caipla: Traditional Czech eats from goulash soup to grilled meats served with a perfectly poured beer. 11am-midnight Mon-Thu, to 1am Fri & Sat, to 1pm Sun €€

Eggo Truck Brno: Punk rock tunes with your mimosa or coffee-fuelled breakfast or brunch at this uber-cool bistro. 9am-1pm Mon, 8am-2pm Tue-Sat, 9am-1pm Sun €

Cà Phê Cô: Of all the Vietnamese restaurants in Brno, this trendy joint has the tastiest street-food style pho, rolls, rice and banh mi. 11am-10pm €€

Venus of Dolní Věstonice

space, designed by German-born architect Ludwig Mies van der Rohe, was completed in 1930 for the Jewish industrialist family of Greta and Fritz Tugendhat, though they had to flee eight years later. Entry is by a 60- or 90-minute **guided tour** *(tugendhat.eu; adult/child 400/250Kč),* ideally booked at least a month in advance. However, free garden access is without reservation, linking to the art nouveau **Villa Löw-Beer** that belonged to Greta's parents.

Admire the world's oldest ceramic figurine

The **Moravian Museum** *(mzm.cz; adult/child 170/110Kč)* has a repository of six million natural history, archaeology and ethnography artefacts housed in the reconstructed 1616 Diet-richstein Palace. Collections span the Palaeolithic era to the Middle Ages, and despite the lack of English text, come here for the museum's prized exhibit: the 30,000-year-old **Venus of Dolní Věstonice** – considered to be oldest ceramic figu-rine in the world, found during an excavation in the South Moravian village in 1925.

Discover the origins of genetic science

In the mid-19th century, Augustinian monk Gregor Mendel began experimenting with pea plant breeding in a monas-tic garden in a suburb of Brno; humble observations that

BRNO'S BEST COFFEE

Adam Neubauer, three-time Barista of the Year from Brno's top coffee shop, MONOGRAM Espresso Bar, shares his favourite spots. *monogramespresso-bar.cz*

Take 5 If you want to feel like a local, head to this place in the eastern Židenice neighbourhood. There's great coffee, excellent pastries, and friendly owners behind the bar. **Kafe Fridrich** Head north of the centre to this cosy cafe. They serve tasty coffee and incredible vegan sweet treats – the banana bread is possibly the best in the city. **Typika** Brno's recently opened hangout has a coffee garden in the courtyard of the Moravian Gallery. Spacious and comfortable; you might end up staying a few hours. **Kimono** This small and hip espresso bar has a stylish wood-panelled interior and serves top brew classics and speciality coffees.

DRINKING IN BRNO: OUR PICKS

Super Panda Circus: Find the door behind the circus curtain, ring the buzzer and indulge in this unique, hidden cocktail world. *7pm-2am Mon & Tue, 6pm-2am Wed-Sat*

Bar, Který Neexistuje: The 'bar that doesn't exist' is the city's trendy-decked cocktail bar behemoth. *5pm-2am Sun-Tue, to 2.30am Wed & Thu, to 3.30am Fri & Sat*

4pokoje: This neon-lit, exposed-brick hipster hangout turns buzzing early-hours bar after its daytime bistro persona. *5pm-1am Mon & Tue, to 3am Wed, to 4am Thu-Sat*

Schrott: Brewery and bar with courtyard garden in an old industrial building with unique upcycled scrap decor. *3pm-1am Mon-Sat, 3pm-midnight Sun*

WHY I LOVE OLOMOUC

Becki Enright, Lonely Planet writer

There's Prague's showy magnificence and Brno's alternativeness, but what is it about Olomouc that makes it unmatched by any other Czech city? Its cobblestone core is a cultural evolution – you can walk through the riverside gardens below the old walls, have coffee in an old Jesuit commune, step inside baroque, Renaissance and art nouveau houses, dine in part of the old fortress and admire modern murals. I love Olomouc because it has nothing to prove; it's grand without being flashy. Like its Holy Trinity Column construction, the city's admiration comes from its own people; for us visitors, its modesty is its majesty.

Hercules' Fountain, Olomouc

unknowingly founded genetic science. Only after his death was Mendel revered as the 'Father of Genetics' for his discovery. The **Mendel Museum** *(mendelmuseum.muni.cz; adult/child 130/100Kč),* an institution of the Masaryk University, is in the precinct of the abbey where Mendel lived and details his life's work and the story of his revolutionary findings through audiovisual exhibits and personal objects.

Olomouc

TIME FROM BRNO: 1HR

Somehow, Olomouc has evaded discovery; Czechia's prettiest city outside Prague flies entirely under the radar. Once the seat of the Czech monarchy and Moravia's first capital before it moved to Brno, the town is plump with grandeur. Its well-preserved urban core is a municipal conservation area, protecting its main squares ringed with baroque buildings, fountains and the centrepiece UNESCO World Heritage monument the Holy Trinity Column. Olomouc was a barricaded city and Habsburg military centre until the end of the 19th century, and is now fringed by remnants of the medieval and crown fortresses.

Admire squares, fountains & UNESCO monuments

The star of Olomouc's main **Upper Square** (Horní náměstí) is the 32m-high **Holy Trinity Column** (Sloup Nejsvětější Trojice), an 18th-century devotional masterpiece carved by

EATING & DRINKING IN OLOMOUC: OUR PICKS

Hanácká hospoda: Modern-twist beer hall in an old Renaissance palace, with contemporary-traditional Czech classics and share platters. *hours vary* €€

Long Story Short: From fortress bastion and military bakery to contemporary cuisine eatery, with small bites, grill plates and veggie dishes. *8am-10pm Mon-Sun* €€

Konvikt Bistro & Bar: Trendy hangout in a former 17th-century Jesuit house with ecclesiastical trims. Come here for the veggie-laden lunch menu. *8.30am-10pm Mon-Fri* €

Café na cucky: Have breakfast and brunch in this arty lounge cafe that's also a gallery and theatre space. *1-9pm Mon, 8am-9pm Tue-Sat, 9am-7pm Sun* €

local artists with depictions of 18 saints, 12 light bearers, 12 apostles, and the Assumption of Mary and the Holy Trinity. It took 37 years to build. The largest and tallest baroque sculpture in Europe, it was inscribed on the UNESCO World Heritage list in 2000.

The Gothic-towered, 15th-century **Town Hall** (Radnice) is known for its **Astronomical Clock,** renovated in the 1950s communist era in the style of socialist realism. The mosaic is topped by the folk tradition *Ride of the Kings* and worker murals at its base. Its moving procession of proletariat workers can be seen at noon. South of the action, **Lower Square** (Dolní náměstí) is an alfresco square of cafes punctuated with the 1715 Marian Plague Column.

Around these landmarks are six mythological baroque fountains built between 1683 and 1735. On Upper Square: the **Hercules' Fountain** (Herkulova kašna) and **Caesar's Fountain** (Caesarova kašna), and **Mercury's Fountain** (Merkurova kašna) north of it. On Lower Square: **Neptune's Fountain** (Neptunova kašna) and **Jupiter's Fountain** (Jupiterova kašna). The Rome-inspired **Tritons' Fountain** (Kašna Tritonů) is on the road to the cathedral.

Visit palaces, cathedrals & churches

The city's origins trace back to **Ostrava Castle** on **Wenceslas Square** (Václavské náměstí). Little remains of the medieval site where the Přemyslid dynasty ended with the assassination of King Wenceslas III in 1306. Some ruins are visible in the **Archdiocesan Museum**, packing 1000 years of Olomouc Archdiocese culture into art collections and the Romanesque **Bishop's Palace** *(muo.cz; adult/child from 250/150Kč).*

The bastion is the 100m-high **St Wenceslas Cathedral** *(Katedrála sv Václava; katedralaolomouc.cz),* a 12th-century Romanesque basilica rebuilt in Gothic style, with a crypt entombing Olomouc bishops. The adjacent **Archbishop's Palace** *(arcibiskupskypalac.cz; tours 180/120Kč)* has been the headquarters for Olomouc archbishops since 1685 and was where Franz Joseph I was declared Emperor of Austria in 1848.

The Olomouc Archdiocese's significance is reflected in its mass of Roman Catholic churches. The 15th-century Gothic **St Maurice** (Chrám sv Mořice) houses Central Europe's largest organ with 10,000 booming pipes. The tri-domed 17th-century **Church of St Michael** (Kostel sv Michala) glimmers with neo-baroque interiors, while the 18th-century **Church of the Virgin Mary of the Snow** (Kostel Panny Marie Sněžné) pops with colourful stucco. The tiny **Chapel of St Jan Sarkander** (Kaple sv Jana Sarkandra) was built in 1909 upon the prison site where priest John Sarkander was tortured to death in 1620 for refusing to divulge confessions. His canonisation as Moravia's patron saint occurred in 1995 in Olomouc with Pope John Paul II.

OLOMOUC'S PRESTIGIOUS PUNGENT CHEESE

Love it or hate it, you haven't been to Olomouc until you've tasted its culinary speciality. *Olomoucké tvarůžky* is a distinctive Czech delicacy, a matured cheese with a pungent aroma and piquant flavour. This tiny yellow dairy disk is a Haná region tradition dating back to the 15th century; it is considered Czechia's oldest cheese and an integral part of Moravian heritage. You'll find it on menus around the city, served fresh, fried, spread and garnished. The cheese is so important that it is celebrated annually at the Olomouc Cheese Festival in April: a mix of folk pageantry, chef presentations and musical revelry, with cheese and its best accompaniment, beer.

Places We Love to Stay

€ Budget €€ Midrange €€€ Top End

Prague
MAP p90

Malá Strana (Lesser Town)

Little Quarter Hostel €
Gleamingly clean and perched halfway between Charles Bridge and Prague Castle. Book early.

Dům U Velké Boty €€ The quaint 'House at the Big Boot' is set on a quiet square, five minutes' walk from the castle and Charles Bridge.

Golden Well Hotel €€€ A secluded, elegant Renaissance house that is a popular choice for honeymooners in Prague.

Staré Město (Old Town)

Ahoy! Hostel € A pleasant, welcoming and peaceful hostel (definitely not for the pub-crawl crowd).

Design Hotel Josef €€ The work of London-based Czech architect Eva Jiřičná; the minimalist theme is evident in the stark white lobby with glass staircase.

Dominican €€€ Housed in the former monastery of St Giles, this luxury hotel is bursting with character and is full of delightful period details.

Nové Město (New Town)

Sophie's Hostel € Chic step up from a typical hostel; contemporary style, with oak-veneer floors and stark, minimalist decor. Book way in advance.

Icon Hotel €€ Pretty much everything in this gorgeous

boutique hotel on a hidden street behind Wenceslas Square has a designer stamp on it.

Mosaic House €€ Modern, clean and eye-catching, fully in keeping with the hotel's 1930s functionalist design ethos.

Bohemia

Karlovy Vary

Villa Basileia €€ Long-established guesthouse by the Teplá River, with very cosy rooms and a restaurant within walking distance of the city's sights.

Hotel Romance Puškin €€ Superb spa-area location, with very comfortable rooms and a cooked breakfast.

Pension Villa Rosa €€ Perched high above the river, the family-run Villa Rosa combines traditionally furnished rooms with a spectacular location.

Plzeň (Pilsen)

Hotel Astory € The most convenient hotel for the main train station and the Prazdroj Brewery, with clean and well-kept 21st-century rooms.

Hotel Rango €€ Plzeň's most character-packed boutique hotel, with sumptuous rooms, a great restaurant and a convenient location.

Český Krumlov

Hotel Myší Díra €€ This hotel has a superb location overlooking the river, and bright, spacious rooms with

lots of blonde wood and quirky handmade furniture.

Hotel Konvice €€ An attractive, old-fashioned hotel with romantic rooms and period furnishings. Many rooms have impressive old wood-beamed ceilings.

Moravia

Brno

10-Z Bunker € An extraordinary stay in a former nuclear fallout shelter, foregoing comforts for a more authentic experience, even if just for one night.

Hotel Avion €€ Reconstructed functionalist-style hotel designed by Czech architect Bohuslav Fuchs. A National Cultural Monument with colour block rooms and a design museum.

Barceló Brno Palace €€€ Prestigious heritage building from the 1850s turned luxury hotel with 199 rooms, a courtyard lobby bar and fine-dining restaurant.

Olomouc

Miss Sophie's Olomouc €€ Restored 14th-century listed monument building with eight boutique-antique rooms. The in-house cafe serves a local coffee roast and homemade food.

Long Story Short €€ Sophisticated hostel with dorms and private rooms. The on-site cafe, bistro and bakery nods to the site's former use as a military bakery.

Practicalities

LGBTIQ+ Travellers
Czechs are generally tolerant of same-sex couples. Prague is the most open-minded city; the industrial areas of north Bohemia and north Moravia have the most conservative views. Rarely will openly gay couples experience any kind of negative reaction. Same-sex registered partnerships have been possible since 2006.

Health
Tap water is safe to drink and there are no serious threats to health. Watch for ticks, though, when hiking or camping in forests and grasslands. Ticks can carry two serious diseases: tick-borne encephalitis and Lyme disease. Use repellents, cover exposed legs and periodically check your skin for bites.

Insurance
Insurance is not compulsory to travel to Czechia but it's good to have. Consider a policy that covers flight cancellation and medical care. Alternatively, or additionally, EU travellers can apply for the European Health Insurance Card (EHIC) that covers emergency medical treatment free of charge.

Public Toilets
Public toilets are more plentiful in Prague than elsewhere in the country. Nearly all Prague metro stations have a public toilet. Most public toilets charge either 10Kč or 20Kč. Have small change ready.

EGOTRIPONE/SHUTTERSTOCK

Charles Bridge (p93), Prague

Opening Hours
Banks 8am–5pm Monday to Friday
Bars noon–2am
Clubs 11pm–4am Thursday to Saturday
Restaurants 11am–10pm
Supermarkets 7am–10pm
Shops 9am–5pm Monday to Friday, 9am–1pm Saturday

Accessible Travel
Authorities have made steady progress in making Czechia accessible to all, though challenges remain. Prague's airport is mainly barrier-free and has 20 contact points from which passengers with disabilities can call for assistance. As for getting around Prague, many (but not all) metro stations have lifts. Choose accommodation carefully, as only the most modern hotels have fully accessible facilities.

Public Holidays
New Year's Day 1 January
Easter Monday March/April
Labour Day 1 May
Liberation Day 8 May
Sts Cyril & Methodius Day 5 July
Jan Hus Day 6 July
Czech Statehood Day 28 September
Republic Day 28 October
Struggle for Freedom & Democracy Day 17 November
Christmas Eve/Day 24/25 December
St Stephen's Day 26 December

Language

An accent mark over a vowel in written Czech indicates it's pronounced as a long sound. Note that air is pronounced as in 'hair', aw as in 'law', oh as the 'o' in 'note', ow as in 'how', uh as the 'a' in 'ago', kh as the 'ch' in the Scottish loch, and zh as the 's' in 'pleasure'. Also, r is rolled in Czech and the apostrophe (') indicates a slight y sound.

Basics

Hello. Ahoj. *uh·hoy*
Goodbye. Na shledanou. *nuh·skhle·duh·noh*
Excuse me. Promiňte. *pro·min'·te*
Sorry. Promiňte. *pro·min'·te*
Please. Prosím. *pro·seem*
Thank you. Děkuji. *dye·ku·yi*
Yes. Ano. *uh·no*
No. Ne. *ne*
What's your name? Jak se jmenujete *yuhk se yme·nu·ye·te*
My name is … Jmenuji se … *yme·nu·yi se …*
Do you speak English? Mluvíte anglicky? *mlu·vee·te uhn·glits·ki*
I don't understand. Nerozumím. *ne·ro·zu·meem*

Transport

bus	autobus	*ow·to·bus*
plane	letadlo	*le·tuhd·lo*
train	vlak	*vluhk*

One … ticket jízdenku … *yeez·den·ku*
to (Telč), do (Telče), *do (tel·che)*
please. prosim. *pro·seem*
one-way. jedno-směrnou. *yed·no·smyer·noh*
return. zpátečni. *zpa·tech·nyee*

Emergencies

Help! Pomoc! *po·mots*
Go away! Běžte pryč! *byezh·te prich*
Call the doctor/police! Zavolejte lékaře/policii! *zuh·vo·ley·te lair·kuh·rzhe/po·li·tsi·yi*
I'm lost. Zabloudil. *zuh·bloh·dyil*
I'm ill. Jsem nemocný. *ysem ne·mots·nee*
Where are the toilets? Kde jsou toalety? *gde ysoh to·uh·le·ti*

Eating & Drinking

What would you recommend? Co byste doporučil/doporučila? (m/f) *tso bis·te do·po·ru·chil/do·po·ru·chi·luh*
Do you have vegetarian food? Máte vegetariánskájídla? *ma·te ve·ge·tuh·ri·ans·ka yeed·luh*
I'd like the bill/menu, please. Chtěl/Chtěla bych účet/jídelníček prosím. (m/f) *khtyel/khtye·luh bikh oo·chet/yee·del·nyee·chek … pro·seem*
I'll have … Dám si … *dam si …*
Cheers! Na zdraví! *nuh zdruh·vee*

Shopping & Services

I'm looking for … Hledám … *hle·dam …*
How much is it? Kolik to stojí? *ko·lik to sto·yee*
That's too expensive. To je moc drahé. *to ye mots druh·hair*
bank. banka. *buhn·kuh*
post office. pošta. *posh·tuh*
tourist office. turistická informační kancelář. *tu·ris·tits·ka in·for·muhch·nyee kuhn·tse·larzh*

NUMBERS

1
jedan *ye·dan*

2
dva *dva*

3
tři *trzhi*

4
čtyři *chti·rzhi*

5
pět *pyet*

6
šest *shest*

7
sedam *se·dam*

8
osm *o·sm*

9
devět *de·vyet*

10
deset *de·set*

Tram, Prague (p88)

Arriving & Getting Around

Václav Havel Airport Prague is the main air gateway. From the airport, taxis and public transport quickly bring you to the centre. Prague's main train and bus stations are connected to major European cities and the gateways for onward travel within Czechia.

Public Transport in Prague
The public transport network of metros, trams and buses is comprehensive and relatively cheap. Buy tickets at ticketing machines in metro stations or on tram cars, and validate tickets in special yellow stamping machines.

Prague Ticket Costs
Tickets for Prague's buses, trams, metro and trolleybuses are timed with 30-minute (30Kč) and 90-minute (40Kč) validity. One-day (120Kč) and three-day (330Kč) passes are also available and can make for good value.

Driving Essentials
Hire cars at Prague airport or points around the country, and drive on the right. The speed limit is 50km/h in urban areas, 90km/h on secondary roads and 130km/h on motorways. The blood alcohol limit is 0g/L.

Long-Haul Train & Bus Travel
Train and bus routes cover the entire country and are practical for moving around. Trains are best for covering large distances, such as from Prague to Brno or Olomouc. Buses are more practical for shorter distances and select routes, as from Prague to Karlovy Vary or Český Krumlov. Most trains depart from **Praha Hlavní Nádraží** (main station). Most buses use Prague's **Florenc Bus Station**.

MONEY
Currency: Czech crown (Koruna česká; Kč)

CHANGING MONEY
Avoid private exchange booths at Prague airport or around heavily touristed areas, as these places invariably charge high commissions. Instead, withdraw cash from bank ATMs using your own debit or credit card. Czech ATMs require a four-digit PIN.

CARD PAYMENTS
Paying with credit or debit cards is common around the country and often preferable to cash. The only exceptions might be smaller shops in outlying areas. Ticket machines at Prague metro stations and on trams also allow for card payments.

TIPPING
Tipping is not widespread in Czechia but very much appreciated in restaurants and cafes. Tip 10% to reward good service or round up to the nearest 10Kč or 100Kč increment (depending on the amount).

For places to stay in Germany, see p176

CANADASTOCK/SHUTTERSTOCK

Brandenburger Tor (p118), Berlin

Curated by
Barbara Woolsey

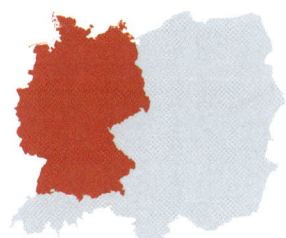

Germany

TRANQUIL LANDSCAPES AND FESTIVE TRADITIONS

Travel in Germany is just like its culture: direct and efficient. In a world of options, Germany is serious about the joy of simple pleasures.

Germany's take on fun and adventure is just like how it brews its beer: an age-old recipe that never wavers from tradition and values good taste. If you're on a roller-coaster, multicountry Eurotrip, what Germany offers is a breath of fresh air (literally) in forests, beer gardens and laid-back cities where parks and nature are a must.

Getting from A to B is efficient on the autobahn, the world's fourth-longest highway system, and a train network where high-speed and wide-spanning regional services tick like clockwork. There's something undeniably artistic in the way scenery unfolds here; the corrugated, dune-fringed coasts of the north; the moody forests, romantic river valleys and vast vineyards of the centre; and the off-the-charts splendour of the Alps, carved into rugged glory by glaciers and the elements. All of these are integral parts of a magical natural matrix that's bound to give your legs a good workout.

Experiencing Germany is all about your belly, too. Local food is so much more than sausages and pretzels. Beyond the clichés awaits a cornucopia of seasonal palate-teasers and ingredients varying greatly from region to region. Dishes are a formidable means of consuming Germany's culture and history, and understanding its regional differences. In many ways, the country is akin to its hodgepodge dinner staples like *Eintopf* (one-pot stew) and *Auflauf* (casserole) – a vibrant mix of flavours and influences offering new surprises in every bite.

THE MAIN AREAS

BERLIN
Germany's nonconformist capital. **p118**

POTSDAM
Palaces and gardens galore. **p130**

COLOGNE
Energetic yet ancient Roman city. **p131**

DÜSSELDORF
Germany's fashion capital. **p136**

HAMBURG
Northern charms – medieval and maritime. **p139**

LÜBECK
Sweets and picture-book streets. **144**

MUNICH
World-class beer and museums. **p145**

BAVARIA
Modern fairytale landscapes. **p150**

STUTTGART & THE BLACK FOREST
Fast cars and enchanting greenery. **p156**

BREMEN & LOWER SAXONY
Dramatic scenery and architecture. **p160**

DRESDEN & LEIPZIG
Historical elegance, countercultural stride. **p164**

CENTRAL GERMANY
Intellect and innovation on the heartland. **p167**

FRANKFURT AM MAIN
Manhattan vibes on the Maine. **p169**

113

Find Your Way

Wherever you go in Germany's north, water is a loyal travel buddy. Hop on a car or train for a couple of hours, and landscapes shift from wild nature to quaint countryside and lively small-city life.

Berlin, p118

Berlin's alternative spirit, eclectic food scene, layered history and anything-goes nightlife enthral. Cavernous museums and industrial nightclubs outnumber rainy days.

Hamburg, p139

Germany's largest port boasts cosmopolitan vibes and urban dwellers with cash to spend. Urban renewal, counterculture and a vibrant nightlife create excitement.

CAR

Useful for travelling at your own pace or visiting nature-heavy regions and national parks where public transport is meagre. Frequent rest stops make for comfortable journeys – and the experience of blasting down speed-limit-free autobahn.

TRAIN

An extensive network of long-distance and regional trains have frequent departures. The national operator Deutsche Bahn has a monopoly on tracks and can be fairly expensive; private operators offer some deals. Carriage chaos ensues on weekends and public holidays.

AIR

Only useful for longer distances, such as Hamburg to Munich or Berlin to Munich. It's sometimes cheaper than trains but not necessarily faster when you factor in check-in, security and getting into the city centre; trains drop you right into the downtown action.

Central Germany, p167

Germany's heartland of nature and history. Ancient beech forests, rococo castles atop vine-clad hills, historic redoubts of German culture and lively university towns all await.

Bavaria, p150

Traditional Germany bottled into one region. Intoxicating landscapes – rolling vineyards, storybook forests and alpine peaks – spiked with castles, palaces and breweries along the way.

Munich, p145

Its reputation as the 'City of Art and Beer' is well earned. Attack the art quarter's museums and galleries; drink up beer-garden vibes and brewhouse traditions.

Stuttgart & the Black Forest, p156

Exciting thrills from fast Swabian cars to the outdoor action of Black Forest firs. Hike, swim and ski, then sink into healing thermal waters.

Cologne, p131

Feel your spirits soar in the cathedral's luminous beauty, then come back to earth with a Kölsch beer, fantastic shopping and museums.

Frankfurt am Main, p169

Europe's de facto financial hub offers fine dining and art museums against an iconic skyline; further out, regional discoveries span mystical villages, castles and forests.

100 km
50 miles

115

Plan Your Time

Seeing Germany's different landscapes makes for a special journey. Beyond capitals like Berlin and Munich, countryside and small-city life are worth exploring – especially where scenic rivers run through.

MAJONIT/SHUTTERSTOCK

Kölner Dom (p131), Cologne

Weekend in the Capital

● A few days in **Berlin** (p118) is all it takes for key cultural highlights and a high-level perspective on German history. In Historic Mitte, trace the past against evocative landmarks: sobering WWII commemoration at the **Holocaust Memorial** (p120), Cold War divide at **Checkpoint Charlie** (p120), and finally, celebrating today's reunified Republic of Germany at the **Reichstag** (p120) and **Brandenburger Tor** (p118).

● On the UNESCO-listed **Museumsinsel** (p123), former Prussian palaces are prime for discovering ancient Egyptian history as well as globetrotting ethnology and Asian art at the **Neues Museum** (p123) and **Humboldt Forum** (p124) respectively. On an easy day trip to Potsdam, **Sanssouci Palace** (p130) and **sumptuous gardens** (p130) drive home Prussian glory days.

SEASONAL HIGHLIGHTS

Germany embraces all seasons, with events spread across the year. Weather and even public holidays range wildly across states.

MARCH
Longer-lingering daylight puts a spring in even the most gruff Germans' steps. Fresh **herring** hits coastal menus, and dishes prepared with **Bärlauch** (wild garlic) are all the rage.

APRIL
The Easter Bunny? Pfff. Germany's springtime mascot is the village Asparagus Queen, ushering in the nation's favourite cream-coloured crop. From markets to menus, **white asparagus** is everywhere.

MAY
Surprisingly warm and sunny, May is perfect for clinking in **beer gardens**. It's also packed with public holidays; trains and highways become awfully busy.

A Week's Southerly Quest

● Exploring southern Germany is an odyssey meandering high and low. Over two weeks, make your first impression in **Munich** (p145), Bavaria's cosmopolitan capital, visiting world-class museums of **Kunstareal** (p148) and tipping beer in **Englischer Garten** (p149). Wander from the famous piazza, **Marienplatz** (p145), to the truly urban **Viktualienmarkt** (p147) farmers market.

● Next, chase the superlative and fantastical within the Bavarian Alps: Germany's highest point, the **Zugspitze** (p152), and the Disney-inspiring **Schloss Neuschwanstein** (p152). Along the southern border, continue following fairy tales into the **Black Forest** (p158) and along the **Romantic Road** (p154). Backtrack to **Stuttgart** (p156) to discover further German legends – the **Porsche** (p156) and **Mercedes-Benz** (p157) museums.

A Few Days in the East

● Challenge historical assumptions about eastern Germany, chasing cultural highlights that reveal royal elegance and artsy modern gumption. Spin through **Berlin** (p118), Germany's wild-child capital with its eclectic neighbourhoods, iconic nightlife and GDR history. Hop over to **Dresden** (p164), exploring its baroque elegance and treasure troves of art.

● From there, it's just a zip over to **Leipzig** (p166), dubbed the City of Heroes for its role in razing the Berlin Wall. Immerse yourself in a cultural heritage to a soundtrack by Bach, Mendelssohn and Wagner, as well as today's modern rhythms of industrial nightlife and contemporary art. Some say 'Hypezig' is the better Berlin; go ahead and judge for yourself.

JUNE
it's **festival season** and there's fresh, local produce in supermarkets. Life moves fully outdoors upon summer solstice's blessed 9.30pm sundown.

JULY
School's out, and peak season begins. Pre-book accommodation – mountain or coast. Dip into lakes, rivers and Baltic or North Sea waters.

SEPTEMBER
It's sunny, but not hot. Summer is over but **wine** and autumn festivals (also, **Oktoberfest**) ease the season out. Changing leaves excite.

DECEMBER
Cold, sun-deprived days are brightened by **Advent** festivities, **Christmas markets** and twinkle-light canopies across streets, beer halls and restaurants.

Berlin

WORLD-FAMOUS MUSEUMS | MONUMENTAL HISTORY | GASTRONOMY

☑ TOP TIPS

Today, the site of the **Führerbunker** lies beneath an unremarkable car park, revealing its grim history only by a modest information panel. A diagram outlines the vast bunker network alongside construction data and the site's post-WWII fate. The Soviets blew up the interior in 1947, sealing off one of the darkest chapters of the 20th century.

Berlin is a city built on sand, water and the refusal to sit still. From its orderly Prussian foundations to its roaring industrial boom, through wartime destruction, Cold War division and the euphoric tearing down of the Wall, it's reinvented itself more times than most capitals can fathom. Former French culture minister Jack Lang said it well when he quipped that Paris will always be Paris, but Berlin will never be Berlin. True, although that's the city's magic. It's always becoming.

What keeps Berlin magnetic is sheer variety. Swoon over Nefertiti on Museum Island in the morning, raise your pinkie at afternoon tea at posh Hotel Adlon and sip natural wine in a trendy bar by evening. Street art decorates Berlin's facades like a second skin; weekend flea markets are a citywide ritual. Even club culture still exudes global pull, from marathon Berghain techno sessions to summer raves and sex-positive parties.

Historic Mitte

MAP p119

Symbol of division and unity

Brandenburger Tor (Brandenburg Gate) is Berlin's most famous – and most photographed – landmark. Trapped right behind the Berlin Wall during the Cold War, it symbolised division for decades before becoming an emblem of German reunification when the hated barrier fell in 1989. Today, it's a photogenic backdrop for New Year's Eve parties, concerts, festivals and mega-events, including FIFA World Cup finals.

⊙ GETTING AROUND

Berlin is a sprawling city, but key areas are compact. Most blockbuster sights are found between Alexanderplatz and Zoo Station. Walking around Berlin's *Kieze* (neighbourhoods) is a joy, but to travel between them you'll need the excellent public transport – or a bicycle. Bike lanes, rental stations and app-based bike- and e-scooter-sharing services abound. Bicycles may be taken aboard specially marked U-Bahn, S-Bahn and tram carriages but require a separate *Fahrradkarte* (bike ticket).

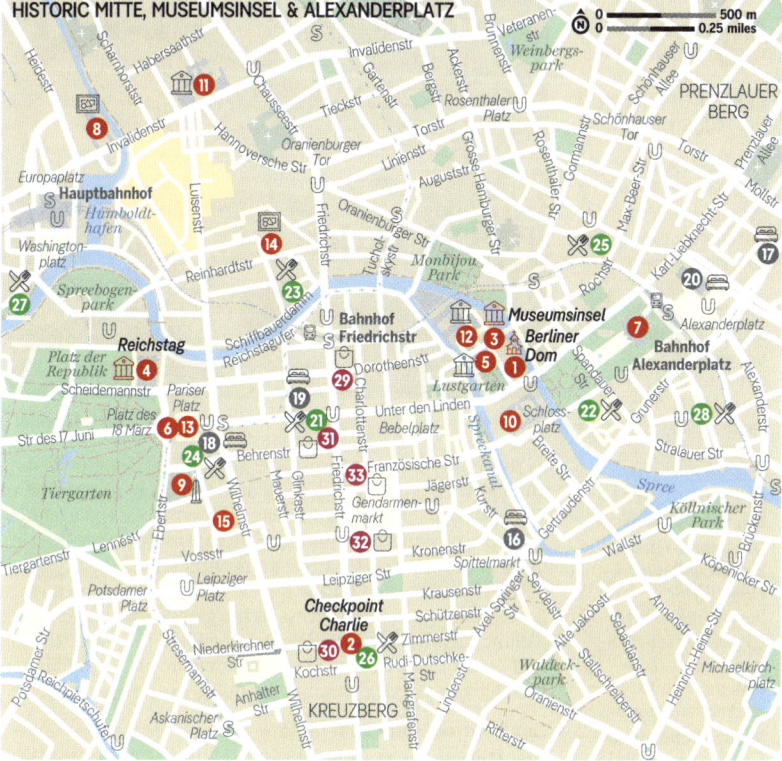

HISTORIC MITTE, MUSEUMSINSEL & ALEXANDERPLATZ

Crowned by the Quadriga (Johann Gottfried Schadow's sculpture of the Roman goddess of victory), the Brandenburg Gate looks over **Pariser Platz**, which was completely flattened in WWII. Look around now: the US, French and British embassies and the venerable **Hotel Adlon** once again frame the square.

Beacon of German democracy

It's been burned, bombed, rebuilt, buttressed by the Berlin Wall, wrapped in fabric and finally reimagined by Norman Foster

BEST SHOPPING IN HISTORIC MITTE

Frau Tonis Parfum:
This made-in-Berlin perfume boutique offers scent tests to help you choose a matching fragrance plus bespoke blends.

Ritter Sport Bunte Schokowelt:
Colourful flagship store with classic, limited-edition, vegan, organic and personalised chocolate bars, and a bean-to-bar exhibit.

Dussmann – Das Kulturkaufhaus:
Eldorado for bookworms, with a huge music selection, free concerts and high-profile book readings and signings.

Rausch Schokoladenhaus: Emporium of truffles and pralines with replicas of Berlin landmarks and a cafe with a view of Gendarmenmarkt.

KPM Berlin: Store and outlet for handmade porcelain from the royal KPM manufactory, established by Frederick the Great in 1763.

Holocaust Memorial

as the modern seat of Germany's parliament, the Bundestag. Topped with a glistening glass dome, the iconic **Reichstag** *(bundestag.de; free)* now stands as the symbolic and architectural heart of the surrounding Federal Government District, built in the 1990s after German reunification.

Reserve a time slot online for the lift to the rooftop terrace for fabulous views and access to the glass dome. Resembling a giant glass beehive, the glistening cupola is open at the top and bottom, and hovers directly above the plenary chamber, serving as a visual metaphor for political transparency.

Confronting Holocaust history

The **Holocaust Memorial** *(stiftung-denkmal.de; free)* was dedicated in 2005 to commemorate the six million Jewish victims of the Holocaust. Designed by New York architect Peter Eisenman, the football-field-size area is filled with 2711 concrete stelae, rising in sombre silence from undulating ground and inviting quiet reflection on loss, absence and memory.

You're free to access this massive concrete maze at any point and make your individual journey through it. Lose yourself in the narrow passageways and connect with its metaphorical sense of disorientation, claustrophobia and oppression. Remember that this is a space for respectful reflection.

Alfa, Bravo...Checkpoint Charlie

Checkpoint Charlie was the principal Cold War–era border crossing for foreigners and diplomats between the American

 EATING IN HISTORIC MITTE: OUR PICKS MAP p119

India Club: Curries are culinary poetry at this elegant North Indian outpost led by top toque Manish Bahukhandi. *5-11.30pm Wed-Mon €€€*

Crackers: Cosmopolitan gastro-cathedral where the lofty ceiling matches the dishes made with sustainably sourced provisions. *6pm-1am €€€*

Ganymed Brasserie: Paris meets Berlin at this charming and historic all-day riverside spot for French classics and seafood. *9am-midnight €€€*

Zollpackhof: Hearty German fare and Bavarian beer in a riverside beer garden or historic dining room with a crackling fireplace. *noon-11pm €€*

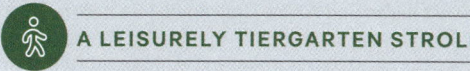

A LEISURELY TIERGARTEN STROLL

Clear your head with a spin around Tiergarten, one of the world's largest inner-city park.

START	END	LENGTH
Potsdamer Platz	Tiergarten S-Bahn station	6km; 2hr

From **1** **Potsdamer Platz**, make your way to **2** **Luiseninsel**, an enchanting enclosed garden adorned with statues and flowerbeds. Follow the waterway west to **3** **Rousseau-Insel**, a teensy island and memorial to 18th-century French philosopher Jean-Jacques Rousseau.

Continue to the **4** **Siegessäule** (Victory Column) to climb up to the skirt hems of its gilded Victoria statue for fabulous city views. Following Spreeweg north takes you past snowy-white **5** **Schloss Bellevue**, a palace originally built for Frederick the Great's brother and now the residence of the German president.

Meander along the Spree River, then check out the latest art exhibit at the **6** **Akademie der Künste**.

Walk south through the park to reach the Neuer See, a romantic lake fronted by the charming **7** **Café am Neuen See** restaurant and beer garden.

Stroll north on Tiergartenufer along the Landwehrkanal until you reach Schleuseninsel to strike see the wacky **8** **Rosa Röhre**, a massive piglet-pink pipe snaking around a university research facility painted cornflower-blue.

Then arrive at the magnificent **9** **Charlotten-burger Tor**, a counterpart to the Brandenburg Gate. If you're hungry, drop by **10** **Capt'n Schillow**, a quirky fish-focused restaurant boat moored below the gate. Otherwise follow Strasse des 17 Juni east to wrap up your tour at **11** **Tiergarten S-Bahn station**.

On Sundays you can browse **Berliner Trödelmarkt**, Berlin's oldest flea market, which sets up along Strasse des 17 Juni.

The **Hansaviertel quarter** is a showcase of modernist 1950s buildings designed by Gropius, Niemeyer and other big mid-century architects.

A **memorial** below Lichtenstein Bridge marks where the body of revolutionary Rosa Luxemburg was thrown into the Landwehr Canal after her 1919 murder.

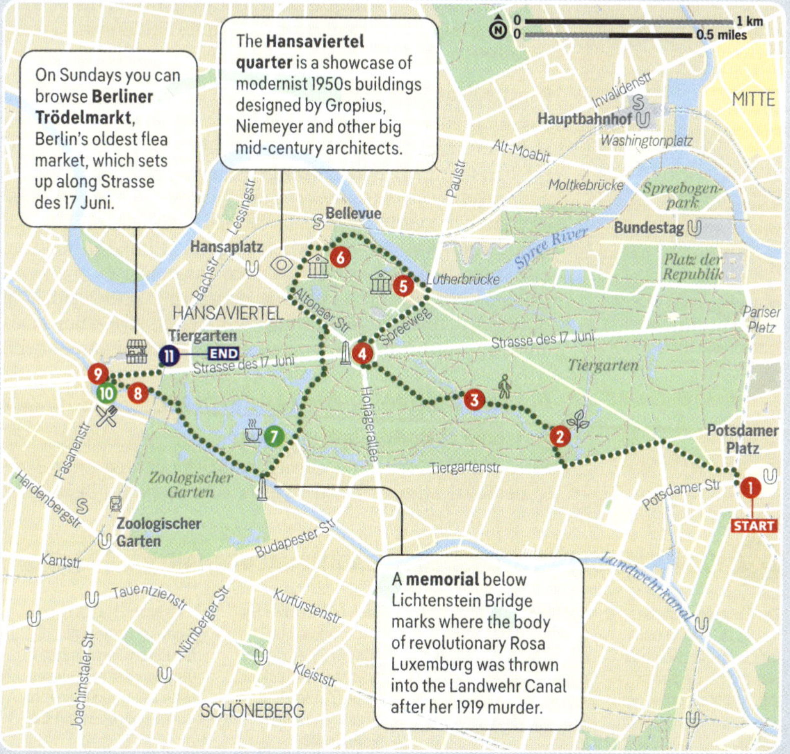

sector in West Berlin and Soviet-controlled East Berlin. It got the name 'Charlie' because it was the third Allied checkpoint to open – hence the third letter in the NATO phonetic alphabet.

These days, the recreated checkpoint, complete with young men in uniform posing for tips, may scream 'tourist trap', but there are a few genuinely worthwhile exhibits that help you connect with this historic site.

For a crash course in Cold War milestones, check out the photos and documents of the free outdoor **Checkpoint Gallery**. Stories of daring escapes across the Wall are at the heart of the **Mauermuseum** (*mauermuseum.de; adult/child €18.50/12.50*).

Edgy art in a Nazi bunker

Pick up on the vibes of war, vegetables and whips still clinging to the labyrinthine warren now housing the **Sammlung Boros** (*Boros Collection; sammlung-boros.de; adult/student €18/10*), one of Berlin's most exciting private art spaces. A fresh exhibition rolls out every four years. Tours (also in English) run for 90 minutes and tend to sell out fast, so book early.

All aboard the art train

Housed in a grand old train station, **Hamburger Bahnhof – Nationalgalerie der Gegenwart** (*hamburgerbahnhof.de; adult/child €16/free*) is one of Germany's top spots for contemporary art. Its collection spans the full arc of post-1960s art movements – conceptual art, pop art, minimalism, Arte Povera, Fluxus – particularly from the US and Europe. It's an engaging mix of the iconic and the unexpected.

Pantheon of natural wonders

Fossils and minerals don't quicken your pulse? Well, how about Oskar, the world's tallest mounted dino and star of the **Museum für Naturkunde** (*Museum of Natural History; museumfuernaturkunde.berlin; adult/child/under 6yr €11/5/free*). Towering 13m high, the long-limbed brachiosaurus welcomes you along with an entire squad of Jurassic buddies, all 150-million-year-old expats from Tanzania.

Beyond the dino drama, you can take a cosmic journey from the Big Bang to today, discover a huge wet collection and bug models so magnified you'll never look at house flies the same again.

Museumsinsel & Alexanderplatz

MAP p119

An island of world-class museums

Flirt with an Egyptian queen, count the carved figures on a medieval altar or be mesmerised by Monet's landscapes.

MEDIEVAL REBOOT

The area west and south of the TV Tower was once the bustling heart of medieval Berlin. Back in the 13th century, traders set up shop along the Spree, giving rise to the twin towns of Berlin and Cölln. Many of the old buildings and crooked lanes survived until WWII, but in the aftermath, East German city planners bulldozed most of what remained, sparing only a few token landmarks like the Marienkirche that now stands forlorn in a sea of open space. Ironically, just a few years later, in honour of Berlin's 750th anniversary in 1987, the same government decided to rebuild the city's medieval cradle. And so, the twee **Nikolaiviertel** was born, a patchwork of relocated historic buildings and prefab replicas dressed in medieval drag.

 EATING AROUND MUSEUMSINSEL: TRADITIONAL GERMAN MAP p119

Zur Letzten Instanz: Rustic 1621 lair famous for Berlin classics, now elevated by regional ingredients. *noon-3pm Tue-Sat, 5.30-11pm Mon-Sat* €€

Sphere: Berlin–Brandenburg cuisine (schnitzel, *soljanka*, veal dumplings) from star chef Tim Raue in the TV Tower. *9am-11pm* €€€

Fischer & Lustig: Fish-centric home cooking like crisp pike-perch amid understated nautical decor or in the beer garden. *11.30am-midnight* €€

Lebensmittel in Mitte: Load up on hearty southern German fare in this woodsy restaurant with a deli you'll want to raid. *noon-midnight* €€

SEANPAVONEPHOTO/GETTY IMAGES

Fernsehturm (p124)

Welcome to **Museumsinsel** *(Museum Island; smb.museum; day pass adult/child €24/free)*. Berlin's renowned repository of 6000 years of art, artefacts and sculpture from Europe and beyond is spread across five grand buildings.

The grand neoclassical **Old Museum** holds historical antiquities and the **New Museum** has a show-stopping Egyptian collection. The Greek-temple-style **Old National Gallery** is a tribute to 19th-century European art while the palatial **Bode-Museum** brings together several period-spanning collections under one grand roof. Note that the **Pergamonmuseum**, Museum Island's crown jewel, will remain closed for renovation until at least 2027.

Iconic Egyptian collection

For over 60 years, the **Neues Museum** *(New Museum; smb. museum; day pass adult/child €24/free)* sat in ruins. But today it's one of the city's most celebrated attractions and a standout on Museumsinsel.

With her elegant neck and eternal good looks, Egyptian queen Nefertiti is definitely the head-turner of the **Egyptian Museum and Papyrus Collection**. Berlin's world-renowned Egyptian collection shares a roof with the **Museum of Pre- and Early History**, a rather clunky name for a trove of fascinating finds from the Stone Age to the Middle Ages.

The entire museum building was a wartime ruin resurrected by David Chipperfield, who ingeniously incorporated salvaged remnants.

Pantheon-inspired antiquities

The Neues Museum shares top billing on Museumsinsel with the **Altes Museum** *(Old Museum; smb.museum; day pass adult/child €24/free)*. The first museum to open on Museumsinsel

---

DOWN INTO THE UNDERBELLY

Berliner Unterwelten *(berliner-unterwelten. de; adult/child from €17/13)*, a nonprofit committed to preserving the city's hidden depths, is your gateway to exploring Berlin's mysterious underbelly on a guided tour. The most popular is 'Dark Worlds', a 90-minute descent into a civilian air-raid shelter beneath Gesundbrunnen U-Bahn station. Inside, you'll pick your way through claustrophobic rooms, narrow corridors and heavy steel doors, and past haunting wartime relics like hospital beds, gas masks and guns. The guides bring alive the chilling reality of ordinary Berliners cooped up here, crammed and scared, as the bombs rained down on the city. The minimum age is seven; children under 14 must be accompanied by an adult. Tickets are only available online.

BERLIN'S BEST FLEA MARKETS

Our picks beyond the Mauerpark (all are held on Sunday).

Trödelmarkt Arkonaplatz, Mitte: Ride the retro frenzy with upmarket furniture, accessories, clothing, vinyl and books at this weekly market.

Flohmarkt Boxhagener Platz: Fun finds and bargains abound at this year-round Friedrichshain charmer.

Nowkoelln Flowmarkt, Neukölln: Canal-side hipster market with handmade treasures and impromptu concerts every other Sunday from April to December.

NK Kranoldplatz Flohmarkt, Neukölln: Idyllic vintage, art and bric-a-brac market held every other Sunday from mid-March to mid-November.

Flohmarkt am Rathaus Schöneberg: Hunt for deals and collectables next to where JFK gave his *'Ich bin ein Berliner'* speech.

in 1830, its Pantheon-inspired rotunda is the centrepiece. The ground level is home to sculptures, vases, tomb reliefs and jewellery that delve into Greek mythology, daily life in cities and the royal courts, and the importance of theatre. Two sculptures are standouts: the *Praying Boy* behind the rotunda and the *Berlin Goddess* off to the right. Upstairs, the busts of Caesar and Cleopatra are especially striking.

Atop Germany's tallest structure

No matter where you are in Berlin, chances are you'll spot the **Fernsehturm** *(tv-turm.de; adult/child from €29.50/19.50)*. The TV Tower – Germany's tallest structure – is as iconic to the city as the Eiffel Tower is to Paris. It has stretched its slim frame to a dizzying 368m (including the antenna) since its 1969 debut.

Up top, pinpoint city landmarks from the glass-fronted **observation deck** at 203m, complete with a bar and a slow spin (twice an hour). The TV Tower's newest attraction is the rotating restaurant **Sphere** (p122); it's now helmed by Tim Raue, whose two-starred eponymous restaurant, **Restaurant Tim Raue** *(tim-raue.com)*, has long made foodies swoon.

Explore Berlin's royal cathedral

Spirituality meets spectacle at the **Berliner Dom** *(berliner dom.de; adult/student €10/7.50)*, which pulls quadruple duty as church, museum, concert hall and royal crypt. Inside, the former royal court church is gilt to the hilt, featuring an altar of marble and onyx, a 7269-pipe Sauer organ and lavish chapels, including one housing the sculpted sarcophagi of Friedrich I and Sophie Charlotte. For more dead royals, albeit in less extravagant coffins, head down to the crypt. There's an optional leg workout: a 270-step climb to the dome for glorious 360-degree views.

Berlin's newest cultural hub

After 20 years of debate, planning, construction and delays, Berlin's newest culture hub finally fully opened in 2022. Housed in a replica of the baroque Prussian city palace, the **Humboldt Forum** *(humboldtforum.org; prices vary, many exhibits free)* was named after Enlightenment-era brothers Wilhelm and Alexander von Humboldt. At its heart lie the dazzling collections of the **Ethnologisches Museum** and the **Museum für Asiatische Kunst** – your ticket to tapping into centuries of culture and creativity from across Africa, Asia, the Americas and Australia. It's open Wednesday to Monday.

Prenzlauer Berg

MAP p125

From death strip to urban living room

No other park in Berlin has pulled quite as radical a transformation as the **Mauerpark** *(mauerpark.info)*. Once part of the Berlin Wall death strip, it now pulses with a free-spirited vibe, especially on Sundays during the outdoor season. That's when thousands of locals, expats, tourists and bleary-eyed clubbers flood in to forage for treasure at the **Flohmarkt**

GESUNDBRUNNEN

Volkspark
Humboldthain

SIGHTS
1 Gedenkstätte Berliner Mauer
2 Mauerpark

ACTIVITIES
3 Berliner Unterwelten

SLEEPING
4 Myer's Hotel Berlin
5 Soho House Berlin

DRINKING & NIGHTLIFE
6 August Fengler
7 Bryk Bar
8 Pluto

9 Prater

ENTERTAINMENT
10 Bearpit Karaoke

SHOPPING
11 Flohmarkt im Mauerpark
12 Trödelmarkt Arkonaplatz

im Mauerpark, snack at street-food stalls, chill in the beer gardens or stake out **Bearpit Karaoke** in the amphitheatre

Legend of a divided city

Though dismantled over 30 years ago, the Berlin Wall continues to capture our collective imagination. You'll find answers to just about any Wall-related question at the **Gedenkstätte Berliner Mauer** *(Berlin Wall Memorial; stiftung-berliner-mauer.de; free)*. Along with the superb 1.4km-long outdoor exhibition, visit the **Documentation Centre**'s exhibition – called '1961/1989. The Berlin Wall' – for a concise, engaging history (it's closed on Mondays).

BUDGET-FRIENDLY SIGHTSEEING

One of Berlin's best bargains is a DIY city tour aboard buses 100, 200 and 300, whose routes pass by many of the capital's greatest hits, all for the price of a standard public transport ticket (tariff AB). You have two hours to ride, hop off or switch lines. Better yet, get the 24-hour ticket to explore without the rush.

Bus 100 travels between Berlin-Zoo station and Alexanderplatz, and provides glimpses of landmarks such as the Gedächtniskirche, the Siegessäule, the Reichstag and the Brandenburg Gate.

Bus 200 also links Berlin-Zoo station and Alexanderplatz through a more southerly route via Potsdamer Platz.

Bus 300 connects the Philharmonie and U-Bahn/S-Bahn station Warschauer Strasse via Alexanderplatz and the East Side Gallery.

 DRINKING IN PRENZLAUER BERG: OUR PICKS ──────── MAP p125

Prater: Berlin's oldest beer garden (1837) offers custom pilsner and snacks; also has a woodsy beer hall with a full menu. *noon-11.30pm*

Bryk Bar: Sophisticated neighbourly cocktail lab, with classic and next-gen drinks, some starring the house-made Bryk gin. *7pm-1am Tue-Sat*

Pluto: Unpretentious wine bar with burgundy walls, serving biodynamic European wines and seasonal small plates. *5pm-late Thu-Mon*

August Fengler: The flirty party vibe, wallet-friendly prices and mix of locals and visitors make this 1936-born spot a Berlin classic. *6pm-4am*

GERMANY BERLIN

BEST MURALS IN KREUZBERG

Astronaut/ Kosmonaut Mural: Victor Ash's monumental stencil-style piece was inspired by the US–Soviet space race.

Pink Man Mural: A lone terrified figure crouches on the finger of Blu's scary creature built from writhing pink bodies.

Rounded Heads Mural: Berlin artist Nomad's faceless figure hugs a hooded character in his signature pictogram style, inspired by punk and hip-hop culture.

Yellow Man Mural: Brazilian twins Os Gemeos painted a yellow-skinned, gender-neutral figure in eccentric attire, blending folklore with social messaging.

Nature Morte: Belgian artist ROA's depiction of animal carcasses reflects on the life-and-death cycle of native species within the urban environment.

Charlottenburg & Western Berlin

MAP p127

Pandas, pythons and piranhas

Zoo Berlin (*zoo-berlin.de; adult/child €25/12.50*), established in 1844, holds the triple crown as Germany's oldest, most species-rich and most visited animal park. Its biggest heart-throbs are panda twins Meng Hao and Meng Tian, born here in 2024, and their parents, on loan from China. To catch the antics of bears, gorillas, hippos, sea lions and other zoo inhabitants, plan your visit around feeding times, posted on-site and online. Special mention goes to the zoo's architecture, in particular the ornate **Elephant Gate** on Budapester Strasse.

Where history and commerce collide

In the 1950s and '60s, as Berlin rebuilt itself, Breitscheidplatz became a hub of modern urban life in the western half of the divided city. Its main landmark is the **Kaiser-Wilhelm-Gedächtniskirche** (*gedaechtniskirche-berlin.de; free*), once a majestic neo-Romanesque church that was crushed by WWII bombs. The ruined west tower has been preserved as an antiwar memorial, with photographs and artefacts in the **Gedenkhalle** (Hall of Remembrance) showcasing the church's former grandeur.

Outside, look down at the golden crack in the steps north of the church: the **Mahnmal am Breitscheidplatz** is a simple, striking memorial to the victims of the 2016 terror attack here.

From Hitler to Hertha BSC

Berlin's monumental **Olympiastadion** (*olympiastadion.berlin; adult/student/under 14yr €11/8/6, tours €17-25*), built by the Nazis for the 1936 Olympic Games, is one of the city's few surviving Third Reich architectural relics. Revamped for the 2006 FIFA World Cup, the coliseum-like venue is now a state-of-the-art space for concerts, sports and major events. It's also the home turf of Berlin soccer team, Hertha BSC.

On non-event days (check the website first), explore the stadium with an optional multimedia guide (*€4*). To see the locker rooms and stadium roof, join a guided tour (some are offered in English).

In the footsteps of Prussian royalty

Schloss Charlottenburg (*spsg.de; day pass to all open buildings adult/student/under 7yr €19/14/free*) is an exquisite palace ensemble and the best place in Berlin to soak up the grandeur of the Hohenzollern clan, who ruled Brandenburg and later Prussia from 1415 to 1918. A visit is especially pleasant in summertime when you can fold a picnic in the palace park into a day of peeking at art, treasures and period rooms. It's closed on Mondays.

DRINKING IN CHARLOTTENBURG: CLASSIC PUBS

MAP p127

Zwiebelfisch: Cosy pub popular with artsy barflies, exemplifying Charlottenburg at its boho best since the 1960s. *noon-2am*

Schleusenkrug: Next to a canal lock, Schleusenkrug has a charming 1950s interior but truly rocks the beer-garden season. *11am-10pm*

Diener Tattersall: Signed stills of celeb patrons decorate this artist pub founded by a heavyweight boxer. *6pm-2am Mon-Sat*

Dicke Wirtin: Stuffed with knick-knacks, this long-standing pub doles out homemade schnapps and hearty local fare. *11am-midnight Wed-Mon*

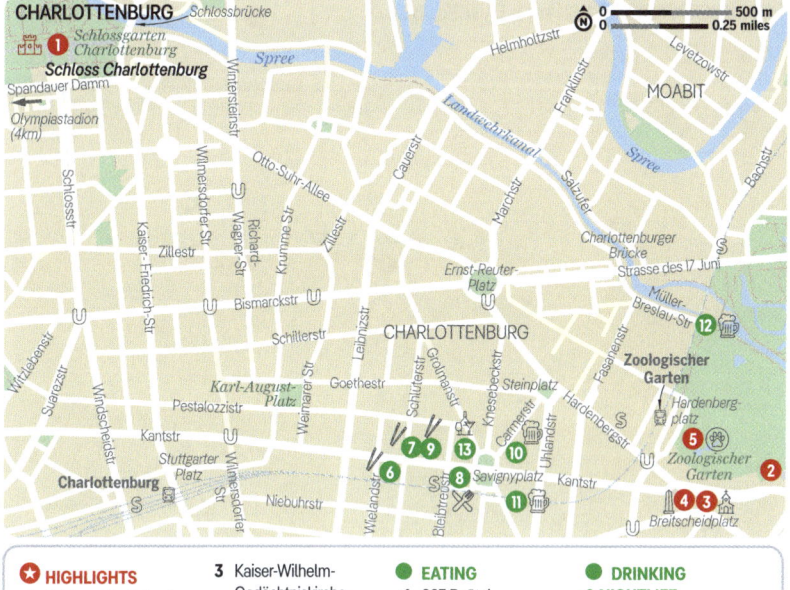

HIGHLIGHTS
1 Schloss Charlottenburg

SIGHTS
2 Elephant Gate – Zoo Berlin Entrance

3 Kaiser-Wilhelm-Gedächtniskirche
4 Mahnmal am Breitscheidplatz
5 Zoo Berlin

EATING
6 893 Ryōtei
7 Good Friends
8 Lo Fūfu
9 Madame Ngo

DRINKING & NIGHTLIFE
10 Dicke Wirtin
11 Diener Tattersall
12 Schleusenkrug
13 Zwiebelfisch

Kreuzberg

MAP p128

Beacon of enlightenment

The **Jüdisches Museum** (*jmberlin.de; free),* Europe's largest Jewish museum, is an eye-opening destination for anyone curious about Jewish history and culture, regardless of background or belief. The building alone is a showstopper: the zigzagging, zinc-clad masterpiece by American-Polish architect Daniel Libeskind stands as a powerful metaphor for the fractured yet enduring journey of the Jewish people in Germany over the past 1700 years.

Street-food pioneers

Berlin has embraced the global street-food frenzy with the fervour of a newfound convert. It all started back in 2013 with

EATING ON KANTSTRASSE (CHINATOWN): OUR PICKS

MAP p127

Lo Fūfu: Bold Italian pairs happily with Japanese precision in this sleek open kitchen. *6-10pm Mon, Thu & Fri, from 1pm Sat & Sun €€*

893 Ryōtei: Glam Japanese den behind a graffiti facade, serving aroma-rich bites with Nikkei influences. Bookings a must. *6-11pm Tue-Sat €€€*

Madame Ngo: This Hanoi-style brasserie makes pho-nomenal soups but also plays with French colonial influences. *noon-10pm €€*

Good Friends: Old-school Chinese-community darling has a long Cantonese menu and great weekday lunch specials. *noon-10.45pm Fri-Wed €€*

KREUZBERG, FRIEDRICHSHAIN & EASTERN BERLIN

⭐ SIGHTS
1 Astronaut Mural
2 East Side Gallery
3 Jüdisches Museum
4 Karl-Marx-Allee
5 Nature Morte
6 Pink Man Mural
7 Rounded Heads Mural
8 Tempelhofer Feld
9 Yellow Man Mural

● SLEEPING
10 Kiez Hostel

● EATING
11 Aleppo Supper Club

12 Katerschmaus
13 Markthalle Neun
14 Michelberger

● DRINKING & NIGHTLIFE
15 Apotheken Bar
16 Bar Franzotti
17 Galander Kreuzberg
18 Limonadier

● SHOPPING
19 Flohmarkt Boxhagener Platz
20 Nowkoelln Flowmarkt

---

the launch of **Street Food Thursday** at **Markthalle Neun** *(marktthalleneun.de)*, a historic market hall that also hosts a popular farmers market on Friday and Saturday. The weekly Thursday snack-athon, which runs from 5pm to 10pm, remains a solid fixture on Berlin's culinary lineup and has also propelled numerous aspiring chefs to prominence.

Neukölln
MAP p128

Field of freedom

The airfield of **Tempelhofer Feld** *(tempelhoferfeld.de; free)* that so gloriously handled the Berlin Airlift of 1948–49 has been repurposed as one of the world's largest urban parks. In this steadily evolving open-sky adventure playground, cyclists

---

 DRINKING IN KREUZBERG: COCKTAIL BARS
MAP p128

Apothekenbar: Get your hands on a potent Penicillin at this charming cocktail bar in a retired 150-year-old pharmacy. *6pm-1am or later*

Limonadier: Top-shelf spirits make for a night of sophisticated drinking at this cocktail cavern with a sensuous 1920s vibe. *7pm-2am Tue-Sat*

Bar Franzotti: Overwhelmed by the 1000+ spirits at this vintage-style bar? Let the bartender whip up a cocktail tailored for you. *7pm-2am Mon-Sat*

Galander Kreuzberg: Leather armchairs and flattering lighting create an intimate ambience for the expert drinks at great prices. *6pm-1am Wed-Sun*

and bladers zip down old runways, while fun zones include barbecue areas, community gardens and basketball courts. In spring, Skudde sheep roll in to serve as natural lawnmowers.

Friedrichshain & Eastern Berlin   MAP p128

Political oppression in East Germany

Thousands of offices across 40 buildings served as the nerve centre of East Germany's most feared institution, the Ministry of State Security, better known as Stasi, until 1989. House 1 is now home to the **Stasimuseum** *(stasimuseum.de; adult/ student/under 12yr €12/6/free, tours additional €5)*, where exhibits unpack the organisation's origins, working methods and far-reaching grip on East German society and beyond.

Secrets, cells and fear

Victims of Stasi persecution often ended up at the infamous **Stasi Prison** *(stiftung-hsh.de; adult/concession €9/5)*, now a memorial site called Gedenkstätte Berlin-Hohenschönhausen. Between 1951 and 1989, over 11,000 suspected regime opponents were held in this vast remand facility, about 30 minutes' ride on tram M5 from Alexanderplatz.

Book a time slot online for a punch-in-the-gut tour through this claustrophobic warren, including peeks inside cells and interrogation rooms. Don't be shy to ask questions. For a deeper understanding of prison life and the Stasi surveillance machine, budget some time for the two on-site exhibitions.

Grim history, glorious art

Along Mühlenstrasse, a 1.3km stretch was saved from the Berlin Wall to become the **East Side Gallery** *(eastsidegall eryberlin.de; free)*. Featuring more than 100 paintings by international artists, the world's largest open-air gallery stands as a testament to the peaceful revolution unfurling German reunification.

The East Side Gallery runs between Ostbahnhof and the Oberbaumbrücke; kick off your stroll at either end. Each mural has a QR code you can scan to learn about the artwork and its creator. Also watch out for the shiny information stelae with historical bites. On many weekends, multilingual guides stand by to answer any burning Wall-related questions.

EAST BERLIN'S MONUMENTAL BOULEVARD

Friedrichshain brims with monumental architecture, but nothing quite matches the pomp and scale of **Karl-Marx-Allee**, a 2.3km stretch of socialist showmanship between Frankfurter Tor and Alexanderplatz. Stroll down this 90m-wide boulevard, known until 1961 as 'Stalinallee'. Bilingual information panels unpack the architecture and history. Restaurants, galleries and shops inject contemporary vibrancy.

Living in these monumental 'workers' palaces' was considered a privilege reserved for party loyalists. The apartments featured central heating, lifts, tiled baths and built-in kitchens – serious luxury for the time. The most impressive buildings, riffing on Moscow's wedding-cake style, were constructed from 1952 to 1960 between Strausberger Platz and Frankfurter Tor.

 EATING IN FRIEDRICHSHAIN: OUR PICKS   MAP p128

Michelberger: Locally adored all-day spot with upscale bistro fare made with ingredients from small producers and its own farm. *7am-11pm* €€	**Katerschmaus:** Light lunches and a meat-focused dinner menu, plus Spree views, at this spot below Holzmarkt. *noon-3pm & 6-10pm Mon-Sat* €€	**Aleppo Supper Club:** At his pint-sized cafe, Samer Hafez dishes up Syrian soul food enriched with 'secret' spices and made for sharing. *11.30am-11pm* €€	**Hafenküche:** Marina spot with self-service lunches, modern German dinners and Spreedeck beer-garden snacks. *noon-3pm Sat & Sun, 6-9.30pm Wed-Sun* €€

Potsdam

FAIRYTALE PALACE | COLD WAR HISTORY | LAKESIDE DELIGHTS

GETTING AROUND

Potsdam is about 35km southwest of Berlin. It can be reached in under an hour from central Berlin, on the S-Bahn (S1 or S7). The city lies within Berlin's C fare zone, so you'll need an ABC ticket.

Walking or cycling are the best ways to explore Potsdam; rent a bike from Pedales outside the Hauptbahnhof. Schloss Sanssouci is 3km from the train station and is served by buses 614 and 695.

☑ TOP TIP

The Potsdam tourist office maintains a branch at the Mobiagentur Potsdam in the Hauptbahnhof and another on Alter Markt in the historic centre near Museum Barberini. Sanssouci Park sits west of the Altstadt, while the Neuer Garten with Schloss Cecilienhof is north. Babelsberg is about 4km east of central Potsdam.

Potsdam, the state capital of Brandenburg, is home to magnificent palaces and gardens embraced by lakes and the Havel River. It's an essential stop if you're spending any time in the region at all. Leading the roll call of royal pads is Schloss Sanssouci, a charming mini-Versailles and summer refuge of Frederick the Great with a splendid park. No wonder UNESCO gave World Heritage Status to large parts of the city in 1990.

Most people visit on a day trip from Berlin, but you'll need more time if you don't want to miss out on its many other attractions. Find out why there's a Dutch Quarter, visit the palace that hosted the Potsdam Conference, peer behind the walls of a sinister KGB prison and soak up splendid vistas on a cruise along the tranquil lakes embracing this enticing city.

Stepping into Potsdam's Past

Restored historic centre

Potsdam's biggest stunner is **Schloss Sanssouci** *(Sanssouci Palace; spsg.de; adult/student/under 7yr €22/17/free)*. The rococo palace sits daintily above vine-draped terraces with Frederick the Great's grave nearby. Sanssouci's resplendent **park** *(free)*, Potsdam's oldest, is dotted with palaces reflecting the Italian obsession of successor Friedrich Wilhelm IV (1795–1861).

Although much of Potsdam's historic town centre fell victim to WWII bombing and socialist town planning, it's been nicely restored for exploring on foot. Potsdam's own **Brandenburger Tor** *(free)*, modelled after Rome's Arch of Constantine, is a gateway to the main shopping street, Brandenburger Strasse. The pedestrian drag links with the scenic **Holländisches Viertel** (Dutch Quarter).

Alter Markt, the old market square, is anchored by an obelisk and lorded over by the domed **St Nikolai-Kirche** *(nikolai-potsdam.de)*; clamber up 216 steps to the church's viewing **platform** *(€5)*. Finally, in **Altstadt**, don't miss exploring Impressionist masterpieces at the **Museum Barberini** *(museum-barberini.de; adult/child €18/free)*.

Cologne

GRAND CATHEDRAL | RHENISH JOIE DE VIVRE | ART MUSEUMS

Founded by the Romans, Cologne (Köln) offers a mother lode of attractions, led by its famous cathedral with filigree twin spires dominating the skyline. The museum scene is outstanding when it comes to art, but the city will also inspire fans of chocolate, sports and history.

Cologne's spirited locals are known for their liberal outlook and zest for life. Join them in the Pride celebration (one of Germany's biggest) in July, and in the beer halls of the Altstadt or bars in the student-centric Zülpicher Viertel, trendy Belgisches Viertel or gritty Ehrenfeld. Cologne also has an excellent electronic-music club scene.

Shopping is a popular pastime, with a fun mix of eclectic boutiques, and designer and vintage stores scattered throughout the neighbourhoods. For mainstream shopping, stroll along Hohe Strasse in the city centre, one of Germany's oldest pedestrianised shopping strips. Souvenir hunters should seek out the classic outlets selling the famous eau de cologne.

GETTING AROUND

Cologne is eminently walkable, and places further afield can easily be reached by public transport, bicycle or e-scooter. Radstation behind the Hauptbahnhof rents bikes.

Cologne's Pride & Joy

Uncover endless cathedral treasure

Cologne's geographical and spiritual heart is the magnificent, UNESCO-listed **Kölner Dom** *(koelner-dom.de; tower adult/child €8/4)*. It's a treasure-packed, centuries-long pilgrimage site, home to a powerful diocese centre.

Top billing inside belongs to the jewel-encrusted, gilded **Shrine of the Magi** (main altar). The basilica-shaped sarcophagus allegedly contains the remains of the three kings who followed the celestial star to Bethlehem. The bones were spirited out of Milan in 1164 by Emperor Barbarossa.

The Dom's newest stained-glass window, unveiled in 2007, is the **Richter Fenster** (south transept). The work of Germany's most important living artist, Cologne-based Gerhard Richter, it weaves together 11,500 square glass panes in 72 vibrant hues (a twist on Richter's 1974 work, *4096 Colors*).

☑ TOP TIP

The city's excellent website *(museenkoeln.de)* has information on most of Cologne's museums. The **MuseumsCard** *(individual/family €18/30)* is good for one-time admission to all municipal museums on two consecutive days and free public transport on the first day. Buy it online, at the tourist office opposite the cathedral or at participating museums.

HIGHLIGHTS
1 Kölner Dom
2 Schokoladenmuseum

SIGHTS
3 Kolumba
4 Museum Ludwig

5 Roman Arch
6 Römerturm
7 Römisch-Germanisches Museum

SLEEPING
8 Hostel die Wohngemeinschaft

9 Hotel Chelsea
10 Wasserturm Hotel Cologne

EATING
11 Bad Ape
12 Bei Oma Kleinmann
13 Chum Chay

14 Curry B
15 Freddy Schilling
16 Neobiota
17 Rievkoochebud

Take the 533 steps up the Dom's **south tower** that dwarfed all European buildings before the Eiffel Tower. En route to the 95m-high viewing platform, admire the 24-tonne **St Peter's Bell**, the world's largest free-swinging working bell.

From the Dom's heights, saunter into the vaulted medieval cellars of the **Domschatzkammer** (treasury), which practically spills over with precious reliquaries, robes, sculptures and liturgical objects.

A Romp Around Western Art

Visit a dazzling art museum

Museum Ludwig *(museum-ludwig.de; adult/child €12/free),* in a shed-roof building near the Dom, owes its reputation to a sublime collection of global modern art. In light-filled galleries you can binge on Picasso, pop art, Pollock and photography, or linger over German expressionists and the Russian avant-garde. Works rotate regularly because there's only room to show off one-third of the collection at a time, with the rest of the space reserved for temporary exhibitions. These dig into everything from post-colonial critique and identity politics to rising voices in global contemporary art and less well-known chapters of modernism.

Kölner Dom (p131)

Hail to the Ancient Romans

Tracking down Cologne's origins

Some 2000 years ago, Cologne was a thriving Roman city with temples, paved roads, an aqueduct and stone houses. Nobody knows how much of its ancient history still lurks beneath the modern city, but plenty of what's been dug up already can be admired in the **Römisch-Germanisches Museum** *(roemisch-germanisches-museum.de; adult/child €6/free).*

While its original 1970s home by the Dom is getting a serious facelift until at least 2030, highlights from its vast collection are on view in the Belgisches Haus near Neumarkt (closed Tuesdays). Standouts include a sculpture of Hercules mid-battle with a lion and a delicate marble torso dubbed the 'Kölsche Venus'. There's also remarkably well-preserved glassware and items from daily life like toys, tweezers, lamps and jewellery, the designs of which have changed little over time.

Ancient Roman ruins are scattered all over town. When checking out the dome, stop by the **Roman Arch** on the cathedral plaza, once part of the northern gateway to the Roman colony. Over at Zeughausstrasse 13 is the **Römerturm**

EXPLORING DOM DEEPER

Construction of Cologne's landmark cathedral began in 1248 in the French Gothic style but was suspended in 1560 for lack of money. The half-built church lingered for nearly three centuries and even served as a horse stable and prison during the Napoleonic occupation. A sizeable cash infusion from Prussian king Friedrich Wilhelm IV finally led to its completion in 1880. Miraculously, the cathedral got through WWII bombing raids with nary a shrapnel wound.

Kölner Dom has plenty of delights that must be experienced on guided tours (in English, upon request). Dive into the building's Roman-era roots on an archaeological tour, or climb to lofty heights to study its industrial-era filigree-iron roof truss or to get close-ups of its famous bells. Book on *domfuehrungen-koeln.de.*

EATING IN COLOGNE: OUR PICKS

Neobiota: Michelin-starred lair with breakfast until 3pm and innovative multicourse dinners in a casual setting. *10am-3pm & 7-11pm Tue-Sat* €€€

Bei Oma Kleinmann: Old-school, family-owned restaurant that has fed generations with schnitzel and other German fare. *5pm-midnight Mon-Sat* €€

Chum Chay: First-class plant-based Vietnamese at economy prices in Belgian Quarter; try the curry with rambutan and lychee. *noon-10pm Mon-Sat* €

Bad Ape: Cheerful lunch spot that doles out gourmet salads, low-gluten sandwiches and excellent coffee; lots of vegan options. *10am-6pm Tue-Sat* €

Schokoladenmuseum

KÖLSCH PRIMER

Cologne has its own style of beer, Kölsch, which is light, hoppy, slightly sweet and served cool in *Stangen* – skinny, straight glasses that only hold 0.2L. In traditional Cologne beer halls and pubs you don't order beer so much as subscribe; the constantly prowling servers, called *Köbes*, will ply you with another round until you indicate you've had enough by placing a beermat on top of your glass.

A ceaseless flow of *Stangen* filled with Kölsch, along with earthy humour and platters of meaty local foods, are the hallmarks of Cologne's famed beer halls. A local speciality served on select days is *Reibekuchen* (or *Rievkooche* in the local dialect), traditional potato pancakes.

(Roman Tower) that formed the northwest corner of the 4km-long Roman city wall.

Chocolate Paradise
Sweet museum treat

Cologne's **Schokoladenmuseum** (*schokoladenmuseum.de; adult/student/under 6yr Mon-Fri €15.50/9/free, Sat & Sun €17/10.50/free*) is a sleek, boat-shaped temple to the 'elixir of the gods' (as the Aztecs referred to chocolate), anchored at the tip of the old city port just south of the Altstadt. Its centrepiece is a walk-through **chocolate factory** that lifts the lid on the bean-to-bar process. Watch chocolatiers handcraft truffles and pralines, and find out how hollow bunnies are born. The interactive 'Cocoa's Journey Through Time' exhibition traces 5000 years of the cultural history of chocolate, from its pre-Columbian origins to its rise as a royal indulgence and the dawn of the chocolate vending machine. For an extra €3, you can cap your tour with a 30-minute **tasting session** (also offered in English). Or head straight to the glorious finale: dipping a wafer into the museum's famous 3m-high **fountain** flowing with 200kg of warm melted Lindt chocolate.

Dodge the crowds by visiting on a weekday, and save time by buying your time-slot ticket online.

Cologne's Creative Underbelly
Ehrenfeld street-art exploration

While Cologne is celebrated for its fine-arts scene, the city's streets are just as expressive. Murals, stencils, stickers, graffiti

– it's all out there, especially in Ehrenfeld, a former working-class *Veedel* (Cologne slang for 'neighbourhood') that's evolved into an eclectic cross-cultural cauldron of creativity.

Urban art royalty like Herakut, El Bocho, Stohead and M-City have splashed colour across once drab walls, often as part of the **CityLeaks Urban Art Festival** *(cityleaks-festival.de)*. The festival's been on hiatus since 2021 (a revival is planned) but the CityLeaks crew still runs street-art tours of Ehrenfeld and the Südstadt. Tours are also offered by **Alternative Cologne Tours** *(alternativecolognetours.com)*.

One of the most powerful pieces is right at Ehrenfeld train station: a tribute to local Nazi resistance group Edelweiss-piraten by hometown spraymeisters Captain Borderline. It's on Schönsteinstrasse, right under the railway arch where the SS publicly hanged 13 of the group's members in late 1944.

Christian Art Progressively Staged

Religious museum for the 21st century

Art, history, architecture and spirituality collide brilliantly at **Kolumba** *(kolumba.de; adult/child €8/free)*, the quietly striking art museum of the Archdiocese of Cologne. Designed by renowned Swiss architect Peter Zumthor, the minimalist structure encases the ruins of the late-Gothic church of St Kolumba, destroyed during WWII.

Start in the airy foyer, where an oversized steel door swings open into a cavernous, almost meditative space. A wooden walkway zigzags over exposed archaeological layers going back to Roman times, while soft daylight dancing through the perforated facade creates a sense of calm and mystery.

The actual galleries are up a steep staircase and are changed every September. However, the concept stays the same: modern art juxtaposed with sacral objects, creating a surprising dialogue between old and new. A wood-panelled library with leather chairs invites quiet reading or simply zoning out. Don't skip the **Madonna in the Ruins** chapel, an octagonal structure built from war debris in 1950; its separate entrance is on Brückenstrasse.

CARNIVAL: FOOLS, FLOATS & REVELRY

Called the 'fifth season', **Karneval** *(koelnerkarneval.de)* is one of Cologne's wildest parties, when the city collectively loses the plot over street parades, packed pubs and way too much Kölsch. Festivities peak in the week before Lent, kicking off on **Weiberfastnacht** (Thursday), when women playfully chop off ties and take charge. Over the weekend, parades featuring wacky homemade floats criss-cross the local neighbourhoods. By the time it all comes to a head with the big parade on **Rosenmontag** (Rose Monday), the entire city has come unglued. Swaying and drinking while crammed in a pub, or following other costumed fools behind a huge bass drum leading to who-knows-where, you'll be swept up in one of the world's most unhinged celebrations.

 EATING IN COLOGNE: FAST FOOD

Kebapland: Cologne's top kebab: marinated meat, charcoal-grilled and served with local flavour in Ehrenfeld. *11.30am-1am Sun-Thu, to 3am Fri & Sat* €

Freddy Schilling: Burgers in the Zülpicher Viertel student quarter: meaty or plant-based organic patties, home-made sauces, hand-cut fries. *noon-10pm* €

Rievkoochebud: Made-to-order local-style potato pancakes, a perfect preparation for an Altstadt drink-a-thon. *noon-8pm Wed-Sat, to 6pm Sun* €

Curry B: Join the queue for Cologne's *Currywurst* – fried bratwurst, slivered and slathered with house-made spicy curry ketchup. *11am-8pm Mon-Sat* €

Düsseldorf

ALTBIER BARS | AVANT-GARDE ART | BOLD ARCHITECTURE

GETTING AROUND

Rheinbahn *(rheinbahn. de)* operates an extensive network of U-Bahn trains, trams and buses throughout Düsseldorf. Tickets are available from bus drivers and vending machines at U-Bahn and tram stops, and must be validated upon boarding. Tickets bought inside vehicles are pre-validated.

Düsseldorf impresses with edgy architecture, nightlife that doesn't quit and an art scene to rival many flashier cities. At first, the capital of North Rhine–Westphalia may seem all buttoned-up business: banking, advertising, fashion and telecoms have helped make it one of Germany's wealthiest cities. Yet all it takes is a bar-hop around the Altstadt to realise that locals have no problem letting their hair down once they shed those Boss jackets. Nicknamed the 'longest bar in the world', this historic riverside quarter is packed with enough energy to keep things going well into the night. Down by the redeveloped harbour, Medienhafen is a parade of bold avant-garde architecture by international design-meisters. Urban explorers should check out creative and style-savvy neighbourhoods like Flingern and Unterbilk that offer fun shopping, laid-back cafes and good people-watching. For prime ramen and sushi, venture to Little Tokyo, the hub of Düsseldorf's huge Japanese community.

The Altstadt Beyond Beer

Hidden wonders, history, culinary delights

Düsseldorf's Altstadt is (in)famous for its 300-plus bars. Beyond partying, museums and historical gems make a case for visiting during daytime.

The **K20** *(kunstsammlung.de; adult/student/chld €9/5/ free)* is a powerhouse of modern art, from Klee, Picasso and Mondrian to seminal non-European heavyweights like Etel Adnan, Lygia Pape and Rasheed Arareen. Veer off Rheinuferpromenade to the **Hetjens Museum** *(duesseldorf.de/hetjens; adult/child €5/free),* covering 8000 years of world ceramic art.

On Burgplatz, the **Schlossturm** *(schifffahrtmuseum.de; adult/child €3/free)* is all that remains of Düsseldorf's old palace; it houses a small Rhine-focussed **museum**. The **Markt am Carlsplatz** *(carlsplatz-markt.de)* is a prime foodie playground.

☑ **TOP TIP**

The **Düsseldorf tourist office** *(duesseldorf-tourismus.de)* in the Altstadt has a wealth of printed information and staff eager to help with lodging, events tickets and the Düsseldorf Card. It also organises well-done city tours, including an Urban Art Walk, an Altstadt Beer Safari and a Sound of Düsseldorf music expedition.

DÜSSELDORF'S ARCHITECTURAL MARVELS

Kö-Bogen I & II: Daniel Libeskind's Kö-Bogen I caps the Königsallee with angular glass and limestone. Kö-Bogen II is practically a vertical park.

Basilika St Lambertus: The twisted spire of this Gothic church is not a design quirk – warped by a storm, it was deliberately left that way.

Tonhalle: An expressionist 1920s jewel, Düsseldorf's premier concert hall has a ribbed blue dome and started out as a planetarium.

Dreischeibenhaus: This 94m-high tower gets its name from the three offset slim slabs *(Scheiben);* it was a symbol of Germany's postwar economic recovery.

Neuer Zollhof: Stainless steel meets playful asymmetry in a trio of shimmering buildings that turned Medienhafen into a contemporary art piece.

★ HIGHLIGHTS
1 K20

● SIGHTS
2 Basilika St Lambertus
3 Dreischeibenhaus
4 Hetjens Museum
5 Kö-Bogen I & II
6 Schlossturm & SchifffahrtMuseum

● SLEEPING
7 Hotel Orangerie

8 Max Hotel Garni
9 Ruby Coco Hotel

● EATING
10 Brauerei im Füchschen
11 Markt am Carlsplatz
12 Münstermann Kontor
13 Naniwa
14 Pelican Fly
15 Takumi
16 Yabase

● DRINKING & NIGHTLIFE
17 Elephant Bar
18 Et Kabüffke
19 Melody
20 Sakura Bar
21 Uerige

● ENTERTAINMENT
22 Tonhalle

● INFORMATION
23 Tourist Office – Altstadt

Industrial Harbour Reimagined

Architectural port of call

Where dockworkers once hauled cargo, creative minds now forge ad campaigns and brainstorm headlines. The **Medienhafen** *(Media Harbour; medienhafen.de)* is Düsseldorf's boldest urban revitalisation project. The old commercial harbour is now a striking lineup of avant-garde buildings by top architects. Frank Gehry's **Neuer Zollhof** draws the most

---

 DRINKING IN DÜSSELDORF: ALTSTADT FAVES

Uerige: Traditional Altbier brewpub with hearty snacks, local colour aplenty and a merry crowd that often spills into the street. *10am–midnight*

Et Kabüffke: Chase your Altbier with a shot of Killepitsch (local liqueur blending 90 fruits, herbs and spices) served through the window. *11am–midnight*

Melody: Island of sophistication among the boisterous Altstadt bars, with quality cocktails and eggnog made by the owner. *10pm–late Wed-Sat*

Elephant Bar: Good drinks and good times at this James Bond–style '60s bar with complexion-friendly lighting and mellow sounds. *6pm–late Wed-Sat*

SAIKO3P/SHUTTERSTOCK

Medienhafen (p137)

camera clicks – a trio of warped towers sheathed in stainless steel, red brick and white plaster, respectively.

For a different selfie angle, head to the promontory below the Hyatt Regency Hotel, anchored by a silver-clad, egg-shaped bar that buzzes in summer. From this spot, the full sweep of Medienhafen with the Rheinturm TV tower is Insta-gold. There's also a two-hour **Media Harbour Tour** (*€20*) run by Düsseldorf Tourism.

Japanese Flavours & Culture

Tokyo on the Rhine

Düsseldorf's **Little Tokyo** is the commercial heart of the city's sizeable Japanese expat community. Centred on Immermannstrasse, just outside the Hauptbahnhof, this buzzing strip is chock-a-block with ramen joints, sushi bars, manga shops and Japanese supermarkets. Local faves for slurping ramen include **Takumi** and **Naniwa**, while **Yabase** is tops for sushi and **Sakura Bar** for cocktails.

 EATING IN DÜSSELDORF: OUR PICKS

Münstermann Kontor: Buzzy bistro with seasonal pan-European dishes that are both creative and down-to-earth. *noon-8pm Tue-Fri, from 11am Sat* €€€

Brauerei Im Füchschen: Boisterous and full of local colour – the 'Little Fox' is a true Rhenish beer hall. *11am-midnight Wed-Sun, from 3pm Mon & Tue* €€

Pelican Fly: 'Berlin-style *Imbiss*' (snack bar) reborn as a fries-and-wine bar in a retro-styled pavilion. *noon-3pm & 5pm-midnight Mon-Thu, noon-midnight Fri & Sat* €

Sattgrün: Cheerful vegan self-service buffet with international dishes in three sizes and two branches in the Medienhafen and Flingern. *noon-10pm* €

Hamburg

MARITIME HISTORY | INNOVATIVE ARCHITECTURE | NIGHTLIFE

Hamburg is one of Europe's coolest, most affluent cities, but most people don't know that – the vibe is just that unpretentious. Germany's largest port and second-largest city merits its historic label 'the gateway to the world'. It's been hustling since medieval times, especially in the late 19th and early 20th centuries, cultivating quiet wealth via global trade. Innovative architecture and sustainability shape a stylish, media-savvy modern city, yet Hamburg stays true to its maritime soul – embodied in endless, glimmering blues and squawking gulls. Today's zeniths include vibrant subcultures, lively neighbourhoods, and a performance scene defined by rising stars (which once included the Beatles). No, hamburgers weren't invented here (though patties are inspired by local cooks). And yes, the nightlife extends far beyond the notorious Reeperbahn red-light district. Rest assured, no matter where you drop anchor in Hamburg, it's a safe haven for letting the good times roll.

☑ **TOP TIP**

Undeterred by the infamous *Schmuddelwetter* (drizzly weather), Hamburgers have come up with inventive ways to enjoy the Elbe. No matter the weather, **StrandPauli** *(strandpauli. de)*, a sandy beach bar, is a lively favourite. If it's chilly, board the moored party boat **Frau Hedi** *(frauhedi. de)* where disco evenings get sweaty.

From Chambers to Courtyard

Uncover City Hall's hidden features

Hamburg's 1897 **Rathaus** *(hamburg-travel.com; tours adult/ child €5/free)* is a 647-room beehive full of fascinating, beautiful details. Currently the seat of Senate and Parliament, it's

 GETTING AROUND

Hamburg's excellent public-transport system (trains, buses, trams) will take you all around the city and into suburban neighbourhoods.

Bikes are free on public trains outside peak hours (6am to 9am and 4pm to 6pm). Download the **StadtRAD** *(stadtrad.hamburg. de)* app for cross-city bike-sharing. Driving is easy, but parking is a pain. Uber vehicles are limited and not worth long pickup waits; rely on taxis instead.

For an authentically local experience, board a **Hadag commuter ferry**. The **St Pauli Piers** is the key hub for seven Elbe lines used primarily by locals. The most important for sightseers is 62 – a seven-minute commute to the **Elbphilharmonie** (p141) pier.

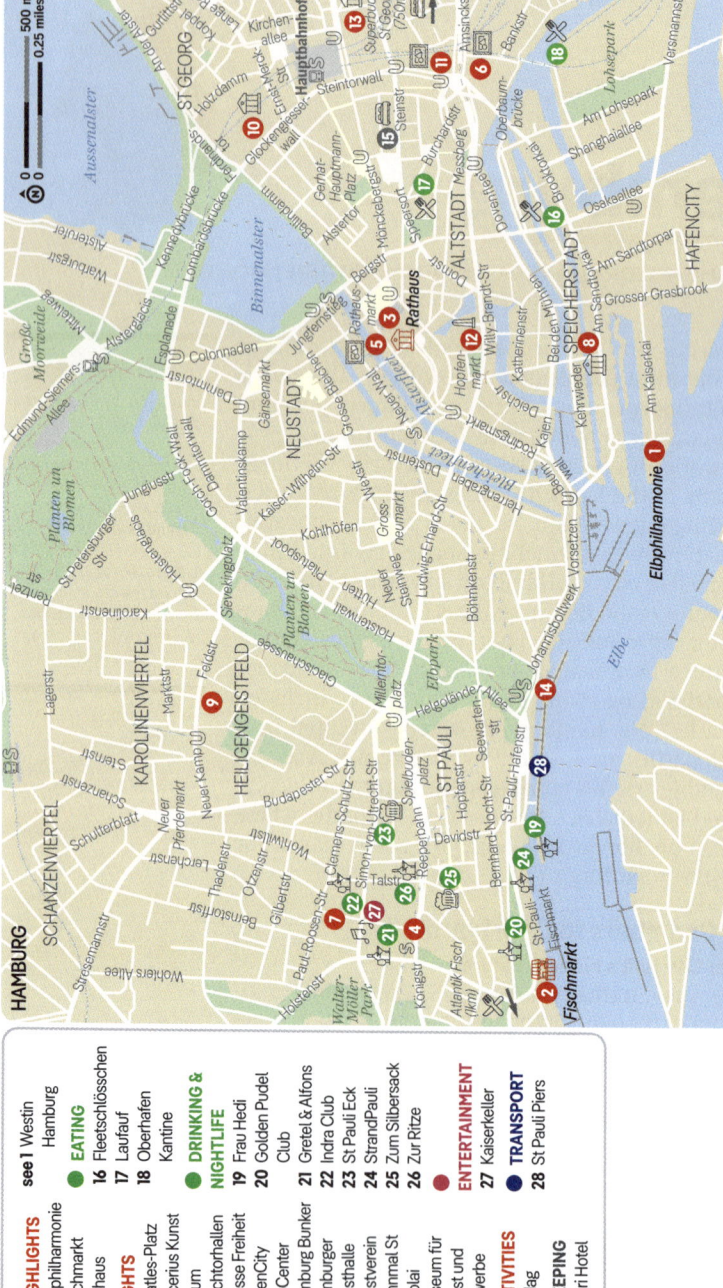

HAMBURG

● **HIGHLIGHTS**
1 Elbphilharmonie
2 Fischmarkt
3 Rathaus

● **SIGHTS**
4 Beatles-Platz
5 Bucerius Kunst Forum
6 Deichtorhallen
7 Grosse Freiheit
8 HafenCity InfoCenter
9 Hamburg Bunker
10 Hamburger Kunsthalle
11 Kunstverein
12 Mahnmal St Nikolai
13 Museum für Kunst und Gewerbe

● **ACTIVITIES**
14 Hadag

● **SLEEPING**
15 Henri Hotel

see 1 Westin Hamburg

● **EATING**
16 Fleetschlösschen
17 Laufauf
18 Oberhafen Kantine

● **DRINKING & NIGHTLIFE**
19 Frau Hedi
20 Golden Pudel Club
21 Gretel & Alfons
22 Indra Club
23 St Pauli Eck
24 StrandPauli
25 Zum Silbersack
26 Zur Ritze

● **ENTERTAINMENT**
27 Kaiserkeller

● **TRANSPORT**
28 St Pauli Piers

one of Europe's most opulent, still-functioning government buildings.

On a guided tour (see the website for booking information), you'll wind through a fraction of the building's maze of chambers. The most renowned are the **Kaisersaal** (Emperor's Hall), a lavish, neobaroque vision once designed to host Emperor Wilhelm II during visits, and the **Grosser Festsaal** (Great Hall) ceremonial room.

Tours aside, march through the Grand Entrance Hall during opening hours and take in its 'hidden' courtyard. Take breaks on comfy chairs with tables overlooking the eternally gorgeous Hygieia Fountain. The female bronze figure, the Greek goddess of health, commemorates Germany's last major cholera epidemic in 1892.

Historic Fish Sammies
Wake up early for the Fischmarkt

Wake up early on Sunday (or stay up Saturday night) to hit Hamburg's legendary **Fischmarkt** *(fischauktionshalle.com; free),* a port tradition since 1703. Over 70,000 people attend the weekly market, which is open from 5am to 9.30am April to October and from 7am November to March. Whether you're a morning person or not, the Fischmarkt is a truly energising, one-of-a-kind sunrise experience. Get caught up in its signature tidal wave of high-sensory shenanigans, from noisy vendors to smoky fish grilling.

The iconic specialities are the *fischbrötchen* (fish sandwiches) topped with decadent North Sea and Elber River delights. The assortment is incredible: pickled herring, smoked salmon, fried or grilled fish fillets, regional shrimp or crab, you name it.

Breakfast in hand, head to the historic **Fish Auction Hall**, inaugurated in 1896 and a testament to Hamburg's long-standing maritime heritage. While the building once hosted fish auctions, today it's a live-entertainment venue. Consider German *Schlager* (cheesy pop) and rock cover bands your 6am wake-up call.

Musical Heights & Iconic Architecture
Discover the Elbphilharmonie

Perched majestically over the Elbe River, the **Elbphilharmonie** *(elbphilharmonie.de; tickets €20-150)* is one of Europe's most exciting and recent architectural feats.

The landmark 2017-unveiled building harmonises old and new. Striking glass rises high above Hamburg's skyline, framing a

WELCOME TO THE WATERFRONT

The **Speicherstadt** is the largest warehouse district in the world, where the buildings stand on timber-pile foundations – oak logs, in this particular case. The seven-storey red-brick warehouses lining the Speicherstadt archipelago are a famous Hamburg symbol and they're increasingly filled with fine museums.

Meanwhile, the neighbouring **HafenCity** quarter, part of the port area where Speicherstadt is located, is a world seemingly being created before your eyes. Wander around and check out the Kesselhaus (Old Boiler House) where the **HafenCity InfoCenter** *(hafencity. com/infocenter)* is located; the information office is closed on Mondays. A room-sized scale model of Hamburg shows the full vision of HafenCity's expected completion in 2030 (it's only about 50% there).

 EATING IN HAMBURG: NORTHERN GERMAN SPECIALITIES

Fleetschlösschen: Overlook a Speicherstadt canal while eating Northern-style fish dishes with cucumber salad and remoulade. *11am-10pm* €€	**Laufauf:** North German dishes like *Bratheringe* (fried herring) in Altstadt. Well-priced lunch specials. *11.30am-10pm Mon-Fri, from 1pm Sat* €€	**Oberhafen Kantine:** Traditional Hamburg fare beneath a HafenCity train bridge. *5-9.30pm Tue, noon-9.30pm Wed-Sat, noon-5.30pm Sun* €€	**Atlantik Fisch:** Altona-based cafe run by a seafood vendor; offering 20 different *Fischbrötchen* (fish sandwiches). *6am-4pm Mon-Fri, from 7am Sat* €€

HAMBURG'S ART MILE

Enjoy Hamburg's five-pack of renowned art institutions, aka the Kunstmeile, with a three-day **Art Mile Pass** (kunstmeile-hamburg.de; €35).

Hamburger Kunsthalle: World-renowned museum with a treasure trove of period-spanning masterpieces.

Bucerius Kunst Forum: Private art museum with four annual exhibitions; multimedia links contemporary society and antiquity.

Museum für Kunst und Gewerbe: Europe's foremost, oldest applied arts institution: sculptures, jewellery, ceramics and more.

Deichtorhallen: Two industrial halls – one for modern/documentary photography, another for large-scale contemporary art.

Kunstverein: Long-established local art association for emerging contemporary and conceptual art.

Hamburg Bunker

restored historic brick warehouse. Inside, a one-of-a-kind concert hall has exceptional acoustics and a stunning auditorium orchestrating immersive symphony and musical experiences.

Architects allegedly drew inspiration from the Ancient Greek theatre at Delphi, sport stadiums and tents. The building's glass structure with its wave-like roof is meant to mimic the ethereal, floating quality of a hoisted sail, water wave, iceberg or quartz crystal. It provides contrast to the 1963-built heavy brick warehouse it sits atop.

Catching a concert in the state-of-the-art surrounds here is an unforgettable experience. Don't miss taking Europe's longest escalator up to the viewing platform, a 360-degree wrap-around balcony providing dizzying city and harbour perspectives.

Concrete Rooftop Garden

Scale the Hamburg Bunker

An anomaly on Hamburg's skyline, the brooding WWII concrete structure **Hamburg Bunker** (hamburgbunker.com;

DRINKING IN ST PAULI: PUB CRAWL

Zur Ritze: Pass between the painted legs of this Reeperbahn pub's entrance. Inside, it's a serious drinking den. *hours vary*

Golden Pudel Club: Tiny bar-club in a 19th-century bootleggers' jail. Programming prize underground bands and vinyl DJs. *10pm-6am*

Zum Silbersack: Diverse crowd and cheap drinks make for weird and wild evenings. Down an infamous caraway shot. *5pm-2am Mon-Thu, to 3am Fri & Sat, to 1am Sun*

St Pauli Eck: A quintessential German pub: jukebox, stiff pours and gruff staff behind a cluttered bar. *5pm-late Mon-Sat*

free) – a former air-raid shelter – was transformed in 2024 into a panoramic cultural attraction. Climb the cement-poured 'mountain path' up to a rooftop urban garden for unparalleled, 360-degree views across the city.

Though it's a gargantuan, painful reminder of the Nazi era, demolition was never realistic here. The amount of explosives required for demolition would likely raze the surrounding residential area. Today, it endures as a multi-purpose building holding everything from a hotel to a nightclub and cafe.

The highlight, however, is a 10,000-sq-metre rooftop garden with over 20,000 trees and more flora. Follow a spiralling staircase to get here; the ascent's 300-plus steps provide historical info along the way.

Finding the Fab Four
German Beatlemania

Long before forging rock-and-roll history, the Beatles paid their dues performing in Reeperbahn pubs. On the famous **Grosse Freiheit** party mile, the band set the stage for its meteoric rise. Stand atop the vinyl-record-shaped **Beatles-Platz** next to abstract steel sculptures of the Fab Four (including a hybrid of Ringo Starr and the band's original drummer during Hamburg days, Pete Best).

Down Grosse Freiheit, the band's name is featured outside the **Kaiserkeller** *(docksfreiheit36.de/kaiserkeller)*. Meanwhile, a small outside plaque commemorates the Beatles' inaugural German gig at the **Indra** *(indramusikclub.de)*. Another plaque at **Gretel & Alfons** claims this particular pub to be the boys' favourite haunt. Legend has it Paul McCartney ran up (and forgot) a considerable tab here. He eventually returned to pay up decades later.

Sacred War Memorial
Take in the views from Mahnmal St Nikolai

Mahnmal St Nikolai *(mahnmal-st-nikolai.de; observation deck & museum adult/child €5/3)* was the world's tallest building from 1874 to 1876, and it remains Hamburg's second-tallest structure (after the TV Tower). Today, the bombed-out remains of St Nikolai Church encompass a war memorial and **crypt history museum**. Take the elevator up to the church's 76.3m-high **observation tower** inside the surviving spire for awesome views. Down below, walk among church remnants in an open-air courtyard.

PATCHWORK CITYSCAPE

Harmonising surviving prewar structures, functionalist feats and seafaring motifs, Hamburg's architecture is a fascinating mishmash. During WWII, Hamburg's city centre – mostly Gothic and neo-Gothic architecture – was destroyed. The Rathaus remains as enduring style icon, while 19th-century Speicherstadt highlights the city's neo-Gothic-influenced era. Mid-20th-century functionalism saw classic architecture razed for unappealing, utilitarian structures. The period's 'high point' is the Fernsehturm (TV Tower), still Hamburg's tallest building. The exception to this architectural 'reset' was the indestructible WWII Hamburg Bunker. Now, city architects are incorporating maritime motifs along the harbour – the Elbphilharmonie and HafenCity are examples.

Lübeck

MEDIEVAL ARCHITECTURE | HANSEATIC HISTORY | MARZIPAN CAPITAL

GETTING AROUND

Lübeck's Altstadt is on an island encircled by the canalised Trave River. The Hauptbahnhof and central bus station are 500m west of the Holstentor. Walking around is easy; many streets are pedestrianised and off limits to all but the vehicles of hotel guests. Lübeck is an hour's drive from Hamburg or about 40 minutes by train.

Lübeck's global claim to fame is certainly its Christmas confections – but this Hanseatic city proves to be much sweeter than its marzipan. A 12th-century gem in Germany's northernmost state of Schleswig-Holstein, Lübeck has more than 1000 historic buildings. Picture-book streets are an enduring reminder of its role as the mighty Hanseatic League capital, a status that earned it the nickname 'the Queen of the Hanse'.

Designated a UNESCO World Heritage site in 1987, Lübeck's well-preserved Altstadt (old town) is abundant with delightful ornate facades and narrow cobblestone streets. It offers an alluring silhouette from its waterfront position on the Trave River, which leads towards the Baltic Sea and from there to Scandinavia. Beyond the medieval spires and red-brick buildings, Lübeck is a lively provincial city blending old-world character with urban impulses.

Hanseatic History & Medieval Gems

Tour Lübeck's museums

Lübeck's most impressive treasure, **Holstentor** (Holsten Gate) is among the best-known surviving medieval city gates in Germany. The **Museum Holstentor** *(museum-holstentor.de; adult/child €8/free)* sheds light on the city's mercantile glory days.

Essentially an open-air historical exhibit on Brick Gothic architecture, the cobblestoned **Museumsquartier St Annen** *(museumsquartier-st-annen.de; free)* comprises an old synagogue, church and several medieval buildings. The namesake **St Annen Museum** *(adult/child €8/free)* details the area's history tracing 700 years of art and culture; the adjoining **St Annen Kunsthalle** has ecclesiastical and contemporary art.

The **Europäisches Hansemuseum** *(European Hanseatic Museum; hansemuseum.eu; adult/child €16/free, incl guided tour €21)* offers fascinating accounts of Hanse's far-reaching network via high-tech audiovisuals and artefacts. The ticketing system 'personalises' tours according to your interests, bringing interactive experiences to another level. 'Choose your own adventure' across four thematic fields and one of 50 trading sites.

☑ TOP TIP

The **Lübeck Day Pass** *(1/2 days €12/16)* is excellent value. It offers access to all of Lübeck's museums; the **Day Pass Plus** *(1/2 days €18/22)* also includes the St Petri observation deck and St Marien churches.

Munich

WORLD-CLASS ART | BREWING TRADITIONS | METROPOLITAN VIBES

Munich isn't called Germany's secret capital for nothing. Nowhere else in the Bundesrepublik will you find such a lively blend of past and present, in a city that manages to combine Mediterranean flair with alpine flavours, traditional oompah culture with the freakishly modern, and horrible history with eco-tech.

And Munich's nickname isn't 'the City of Art and Beer' for nothing, either. Prepare for an art attack at the world-class museums in the Kunstareal, an entire quarter of the city centre given over to galleries and museums. There are also plenty more throughout the city. Then there's the beer, celebrated nightly in countless beer gardens and beer halls including the world's most famous, the Hofbräuhaus. It's so good that the annual Oktoberfest attracts over six million drinkers – and there are other beer festivals, such as the Starkbierzeit, that draw many an elbow-bender to the Bavarian metropolis.

The Altstadt & Residenz

Meet Munich on Marienplatz

The Altstadt's heart and soul, **Marienplatz** heaves from dawn till dusk and beyond with throngs of tourists, revellers and locals. Save for the 1638 **Mariensäule** (St Mary's Column) and the 1950s **Fischbrunnen** (Fish Fountain), the inventory of the square is limited. Completely dominating its northern side, the neo-Gothic **Neues Rathaus** *(New Town Hall; muenchen. travel; tower adult/child €7/3)* features gargoyles and other statuary. Pinpoint Munich's landmarks while catching the lift up the 85m-tall tower. Upcoming renovations here could last years. Arrive in front of the Neues Rathaus at 11am, noon or at 5pm (March to October) and see the famous Glockenspiel.

How Bavarian royalty lived

Munich's most visited sight, the **Residenz** *(residenz-muenchen. de; adult/child €20/free)* was the family home of the ruling Wittelsbach dynasty for over five centuries, from 1508 until WWI. Generations of big-egoed Bavarian royals shunned their

GETTING AROUND

The airport is around 30km northeast of the city centre. To reach the centre, take the S1 or S8 S-Bahn (around 40 minutes) to the Hauptbahnhof. An Uber costs €60 to €70.

Trams are good for getting around the centre and to the suburbs. The underground railway, the U-Bahn, serves the centre and the inner suburbs. There are eight lines; the main interchanges are at the Hauptbahnhof and the Sendlinger Tor. The S-Bahn lines go outside the city.

☑ **TOP TIP**

The Hauptbahnhof area has one of the highest concentrations of accommodation options in Munich. This location puts you within walking distance of many sights. However, during Oktoberfest bagging a room anywhere in Munich is almost impossible unless you book a year ahead.

predecessors' living quarters, preferring to commission their own, hence the sheer size and scale. Among several resplendent rococo and gilded rooms, the climax is Ludwig I's **Royal Palace**. The **Schatzkammer**, containing the Wittelsbachs' collections of jewel-encrusted priceless bling, is also not to be missed.

Mother of all Munich churches

Munich's top temple is the **Frauenkirche** (*muenchner-dom. de; south tower adult/child €7.50/5.50),* instantly recognisable on the city's skyline – no building in the Altstadt can stand taller than its 99m. Built in the 15th century but severely damaged during WWII and rebuilt, it has some interesting

Hofbräuhaus

SIGHTSEEING MADE EASY

Don't get your Pinakotheken in a twist while sightseeing in Munich. The city centre's bus route, the 100, aka **Museenlinie**, links over 20 museums and other interesting localities en route. The Königsplatz, Lenbachhaus, the Kunstareal and the English Garden are all linked by this ordinary *Stadtbus* (city bus). Leaving every 10 minutes in both directions (every 20 minutes on weekends), the 100 also serves as a kind of budget hop-on/hop-off route, especially with a day pass. The whole route takes around 25 minutes to complete, connecting to U-Bahn, S-Bahn and trams at both ends.

For the Kunstreal, the official website has an interactive stroll which eases some of the overwhelm here.

features including the tomb of Ludwig the Bavarian in the **crypt**. The highlight (though a rather pricey one) for most visitors is climbing the 98m **south tower** to peer out the small windows across all of Munich.

Check out the Hofbräuhaus

Even committed teetotallers should at least poke their heads around the door of the **Hofbräuhaus** *(hofbraeuhaus.de)*, Munich institution and the world's most celebrated beer hall. For those into Central European lager, a night on the Hofbräu is like the culmination of a hop-scented pilgrimage. It's a beer hall and tourist attraction rolled into one: take a seat in the main hall or in the horse-chestnut-shaded garden, order a *Mass* (1L tankard) and some Bavarian food and sway with the other tourists to the oompah band. The place is open every day of the year, even Christmas Day.

Feast at Munich's city-centre market

Bio *Weisswurst,* alpine cheese or pickled anything – **Viktualienmarkt** *(viktualienmarkt-muenchen.de)* has it all. Just steps from the Marienplatz, this 200-year-old, open-air market occupies 22,000 sq metres.

This is no ordinary farmers market. Over the past two decades it has become a dining hot spot, with countless stalls

 EATING IN THE ALTSTADT: FINE DINING

Alois – Dallmayr Fine Dining: Enjoy the double-Michelin-starred menu at this top-drawer Munich stalwart. *12.30-3pm Thu-Sat, 7pm-midnight Wed-Sat* €€€	**Les Deux:** The modern French cuisine at this restaurant near the Frauenkirche has earned it a Michelin twinkler. *noon-midnight Mon-Sat* €€€	**Tohru:** Minimalist Michelin Japanese cuisine in a retro dining room prepared by German-Japanese chef, Tohru Nakamura. *7pm-midnight Tue-Sat* €€€	**Le Stollberg:** Intimate little restaurant serving Bavarian food with Mediterranean touches. *11.30am-2.30pm & 6pm-midnight Wed-Fri, 4.30-11pm Sat* €€€

TOP EXPERIENCE

Kunstareal

The Kunstareal, Munich's cultural quarter, is made up of two areas. The heart and soul of Maxvorstadt is the Königsplatz, commissioned by Ludwig I as part of his 'German Athens' vision for Munich and resembling a city in the ancient world. The addition of the various Pinakotheken, the area's second focus, over the decades expanded the Kunstareal into today's starring attraction.

FOOTOO/SHUTTERSTOCK

Lenbachhaus

TOP TIPS

● On Sundays, try the €1 challenge (expect to be exhausted). Many institutions close Mondays.

● Main works from the closed Neue Pinakothek can be seen at the Sammlung Schack and the Alte Pinakothek.

● The lawns around the Alte Pinakothek are popular for picnics.

PRACTICALITIES

● kunstareal.de
● admission varies ● each institution has one late opening day

On Königsplatz

The **Lenbachhaus** (lenbachhaus.de; adult/child €10/free) specialises in members of the Munich-born modernist group *Der Blaue Reiter* (The Blue Rider) including Wassily Kandinsky and Paul Klee.

Meanwhile, the **State Museum of Egyptian Art** (smaek. de; adult/child €7/free) traces 5000 years of Egyptian and Sudanese history in one of Europe's finest collections.

Kunstareal Museums

With its vast collection of art from the 14th to the 18th centuries, the **Alte Pinakothek** (pinakothek.de; adult/child €9/free) is a world-class art museum. if you're going to choose just one gallery to visit in the Kunstareal, many would say this should be it. Da Vinci, Cranach the Elder, Dürer, Memling, Bruegel the Elder, Rubens, Botticelli, Rafael, Titian, Velázquez, Raphael...the list of big names and priceless masterpieces goes on room after room.

Germany's largest modern-art museum, the cavernous **Pinakothek der Moderne** (pinakothek.de; adult/child €10/free), comprises four museums in one – engaging (and often confusing), but there's something for everyone. The abstract, multihued **Museum Brandhorst** (museum-brandhorst.de; adult/child €9/free) showcases art from the 1960s onwards – Warhol, Hirst and co. Temporary exhibitions challenge the art world.

offering tasty gourmet (and not so gourmet) snacks. Put together a (very pricey) picnic or grab lunch. The market has its very own chestnut-shaded beer garden, the Altstadt's best and a Munich institution since 1807. All of Munich's main breweries take turns serving here, but in summer you'll have a long wait for a table.

Schwabing

Endlessly stroll an English Garden

Strolling through the vast meadows of the sprawling city park is how the good folk of Munich escape the stresses of the 21st century. The **Englischer Garten** *(English Garden; free)* is one of the world's largest urban parks. Dodge the joggers and high-speed cyclists to discover a tranquil world of woodland, birdsong and students swotting up in the sun.

In the park's middle, the **Monopteros** (1838) is a Greek temple with city-centre views. A short walk north lies the **Chinesischer Turm** *(Chinese Tower; chinaturm.de),* the unlikely setting for a classic beer garden.

Further north, the English Garden becomes wilder, despite two 'tamed' spots: **Kleinhesseloher See**, a lovely lake for boating around three little islands, and **Hirschau** *(hirschau-muenchen.de)* beer garden, one of Munich's best.

Theresienwiese & Olympiapark

Munich's best beer hall?

The vast, ear-shaped **Theresienwiese**, aka the *Wies'n* (meadow), is the home of Oktoberfest but it's a big, vacant, gravelly space the rest of the year. Just north, another lager-related attraction, the **Augustiner Bräustuben** *(braeustuben.de),* is a smarter stop. The oldest, second-largest of the 'big six', Augustiner is the last Munich brewery storing lager in oak barrels. The atmosphere in the evenings is slightly more authentic than its city-centre cousins.

Exploring Olympian levels

The **Olympiapark** *(olympiapark.de; free)* was the site of Munich's 1972 Summer Olympics – a chance to break with the past and the Nazi-era Berlin Olympics. It became better known for tragedy. Today, you can go up to the 190m-high viewing platform of the **Olympiaturm** *(adult/child €13/10).* The fast lift is nausea-inducing but these are Munich's best views bar none. Sometimes, the Alps are visible.

BEST MUNICH TOURS

Olympiapark Tour: Fascinating stadium experiences include a vertigo-inducing Stadium Roof Tour and zip-lining 35m above the pitch.

Radius Tours: Themed tours of Munich and beyond (Neuschwanstein, Salzburg). Its Third Reich tour is a classic.

Dark History Tours: Themed walks led by local-expert guides specialising in the Third Reich, WWII and medieval gore.

Munich Walk Tours: All kinds of walking tours in English including beer tours, the English Garden and cycling trips.

OzTour Munich: Award-winning city tours, Dachau trips and days out at Schloss Neuschwanstein.

Heart of Munich: Family-run agency offering city walking tours plus interesting Third Reich and Munich Suburbs tours.

EATING IN THE ALTSTADT: TRADITIONAL BAVARIAN PLACES

Augustiner Stammhaus: Monster beer hall with different rooms and a tranquil, old-world courtyard. *10am-midnight* €€

Fraunhofer: Wonderfully characterful, 19th-century Bavarian inn with a tiny theatre at the back. *5pm-1am* €€

Schneider Brauhaus: One of Munich's classic beer halls, with a rabble-rousing oompah band. *9am-10pm* €€

Bratwurstherzl: Sausages are the focus at this old Munich tavern with a Franconian twist. *10am-11pm Mon-Sat* €€

Bavaria

ALPS | STORYBOOK CASTLES | ROMANTIC FOREST

Bavaria packs a lot into its 70,000 sq km, from the glorious Alps and fertile Danube plain to the moody Bavarian Forest and the toytown-medieval Romantic Road. Devouring a vast chunk of Germany's south, Bavaria is like a country unto itself (many locals nostalgically dream it still is), with multilayered diversity and sophistication to match. If you came to Germany to see storybook castles and half-timbered towns, the Free State keeps its promises.

But incredibly varied Bavaria offers much more than the chocolate-box, felt-hat idyll. Descend from the Alps to learn about the rise and fall of the Nazis in Nuremberg, to follow the Wagner trail in Bayreuth or to sample a different local wine in every tavern in Würzburg. Destinations are often described as possessing 'something for everyone', but in Bavaria's case it just happens to be true. The Free State is no bargain, but it's worth every cent to see.

Ettal

Marvel at Ludwig II's alpine escape

A 45-minute drive from Garmisch-Partenkirchen, in a wide valley hemmed by peaks rising over 1700m in places, UNESCO-listed **Schloss Linderhof** *(schlosslinderhof.de; adult/child €10/free)* is the most remote and smallest of all Ludwig II's

 GETTING AROUND

Getting around Bavaria is simple, if slightly more expensive than it once was. With its smooth, fast and toll-free autobahn, Bavaria is best explored by car, though in big cities parking can be costly.

The vast majority of medium to large centres are linked by rail. The Bayern Ticket (aka Bayern Regional Day Pass) gives 24-hour access to all of Bavaria's rail system (except high-speed services).

There are no domestic flights within Bavaria.

castles and the only one he lived to see fully built. It's a bizarre yet unforgettable castle experience.

Explore a Benedictine monastery

The definite highlight of the famous, alpine-topped Benedictine monastery **Kloster Ettal** *(kloster-ettal.de; entry free, tour adult/child €5/free)* is a rococo basilica housing the monks' prized possession, a marble Madonna. On guided tours (German only), explore the monastery's architecture, beer brewery and liqueur factory.

Oberammergau

Admire Oberammergau's painted buildings

Any visit to this small town should begin with a wander around the centre to admire the numerous examples of *Lüftlmalerei*. These huge, decorative murals on house facades can be found throughout the Alps, but the style was invented here. Common motifs include biblical stories, and fairy tales are also popular. The **Little Red Riding Hood House** and **Hansel & Gretel House** depicts scenes from the Brothers Grimm's best-known tales.

☑ **TOP TIP**

Nuremberg's **Christkindlesmarkt** *(christkindlesmarkt.de)* in December is often touted as Germany's best. Fairy-lit stalls proffer Yuletide baubles, roasted chestnuts, toffee and mead bottles against medieval splendour. Famous local bratwurst and *Glühwein* (mulled wine) scent the air. Weekends get busy with locals and Czech tourists – visit on a weekday for a less shuffling experience.

CLIMBING THE NEUSCHWANSTEIN HILL

There are a number of ways to get up to Neuschwanstein. The cheapest is to walk – it costs nothing, but it's a long and relentless climb. If you want to visit Marienbrücke first, as we suggest you do, follow the signs as you near the top – there's a steep cut-through to the bridge. The other options are to take a horse-drawn carriage, but it takes you directly to the castle, which means you need to climb past Neuschwanstein and then back again. Unless you like the walk up, we recommend taking the shuttle bus up (it drops you at the start of the short trail to Marienbrücke), then walking down to the castle before following the road down on foot.

PHOTOGRAPHY IS ON/SHUTTERSTOCK

Zugspitze cable car station, Garmisch-Partenkirchen

Garmisch-Partenkirchen

Ascend Germany's tallest mountain

At 2962m, the **Zugspitze** (zugspitze.de; adult/child €75/37.50) is Germany's tallest mountain with the country's only (and shrinking) glacier. Going up is the most magical anywhere in the German Alps; dedicate at least half a day to the experience.

A cogwheel train called the **Zugspitzbahn** chugs up in a 75-minute, valley-viewing journey. At the **Zugspitzplatt**, a plateau below the summit, you can rent skis and snowboards (skiverleih-garmisch.com). A 10-minute cable car takes you up the final vertical metres to the top.

Füssen

A fairytale German castle

Rising amid the forested peaks like a fantasy vision, **Schloss Neuschwanstein** (neuschwanstein.de; adult/child €23.50/2.50) was the model for Disney's Sleeping Beauty castle. King Ludwig II's fairytale Schloss Neuschwanstein is Bavaria's most visited attraction, and as it comes into view from **Marienbrücke**, it's instantly obvious why.

You'll enjoy your visit more if you plan ahead. It can only be visited on guided tours (in German or English, about 35 minutes). Outside the peak summer season, tickets are available on-site, but reserving online is recommended – especially in summer.

 EATING IN FÜSSEN: OUR PICKS

Vinzenzmurr Metzgerai: Sample hearty food like *Leberkäse* (meatloaf) in a bun, goulash soup, bratwurst or schnitzel. *9am-6pm Mon-Fri, 8am-1pm Sat* €

Beim Olivenbauer: Tyrol meets the local Allgäu region at this fun eatery. Try the *Maultaschen* (pork and spinach ravioli) and a mug of local beer. *noon-11pm* €€

Zum Franziskaner: Specialises in *Schweinshaxe* (pork knuckle) and schnitzel as well as other meaty Bavarian and Allgäu staples. *11.30am-10pm Thu-Tue* €€

Zum Hechten: Füssen's best hotel restaurant keeps things regional with Allgäu favourites like schnitzel, noodles and venison goulash. *11am-10pm* €€

Ludwig's childhood palace

You get two for your money visiting Neuschwanstein. The 'other' castle, where King Ludwig II grew up, **Schloss Hohenschwangau** *(hohenschwangau.de; adult/child €26/14.50, incl Neuschwanstein €48.50/17)*, is just as interesting, if not as dreamily storybook-ish.

Climb high into the Alps

In summer, the cable car **Tegelbergbahn** *(tegelbergbahn.de; adult one-way/return €20.50/31, child €8.50/13)* ascends Tegelberg (1881m) to a mountain chalet. From the summit, and despite the relatively low altitude, the views seem to extend forever.

Augsburg

Pop into a Renaissance city

Ranking among Germany's oldest towns – its story dates back around 2000 years – Augsburg is worth as much time as you can give it. The city centre's offering is varied, from the fascinating **Fuggerei** *(fugger.de; adult/child €8/4)* settlement's social and architectural history, to memorable churches and great food. Its puppet or marionette theatre, **Augsburger Puppenkiste** *(puppenkiste.de; tickets from €10, museum adult/child €5/3.30)*, is one of southern Germany's most underrated museums.

Rothenburg ob der Tauber

Magical medieval streets

Few large villages or small towns in Germany are so impressively medieval as Rothenburg. Painstakingly preserved architecture makes the city centre a period piece of gables, turrets and half-timbered facades encircled by tower-dotted stone walls. A visit here is all about wandering around; the small square of **Plönlein** is a magical evocation of Rothenburg's charm. Arguably the best views are from the **Rathausturm** *(adult/child €4/2)*, the tower of the town hall.

Würzburg

Big, baroque and beautiful

The vast UNESCO World Heritage–listed **Residenz** *(residenz-wuerzburg.de; adult/child €10/free)*, once the home of local prince-bishops, is one of Germany's most beautiful baroque palaces. Commissioned in 1720 by prince-bishop Johann Philipp Franz von Schönborn, it took almost 60 years to complete. Today the 360 rooms are home to government institutions,

BAVARIA'S MEDIEVAL CITY WALLS

Rothenburg ob der Tauber: Extending over 2.5km, Rothenburg's ancient walls encircle the town – walk their length and admire them from afar.

Dinkelsbühl: Also 2.5km long, the walls at Dinkelsbühl are much quieter than Rothenburg's but just as beautiful.

Nördlingen: Dating back to the 14th century, Nördlingen's walls are almost perfectly circular.

Landsberg am Lech: One of Bavaria's least-known walled cities, Landsberg has fine, 15th-century fortified gates and imposing stone ramparts.

Nuremberg: Beginning opposite the Hauptbahnhof and extending around the Altstadt, Nuremberg's walls are a constant presence in the city.

EATING IN ROTHENBURG OB DER TAUBER: OUR PICKS

Zur Höll: Medieval wine tavern in Rothenburg's oldest building, offering regional specialities and Franconian wines. *5-11pm Mon-Sat* €€

Gasthof Butz: Family-run inn in a former brewery serving no-nonsense southern German dishes. *11.30am-2pm & 6-9pm Tue, Wed & Fri-Sun* €€

Mittermeier: Savour a finely crafted menu at one of Rothenburg's oldest fine-dining establishments. *6-9pm Tue-Sat* €€€

Weinstube zum Pulverer: Ancient spot serving classic German cooking in a tranquil ambience. *5-11pm Wed-Fri, noon-11pm Sat & Sun* €€€

The Romantic Road

From the vineyards of Würzburg to the foot of the Alps, the almost 400km-long Romantic Road (Romantische Strasse) is by far Germany's most popular tourist route. It passes through more than two dozen cities, towns and villages in a ribbon of half-timbered quaintness. This is the Germany many expect to see, with perfectly conserved towns delivering on all the promises seen pre-trip on Instagram.

KONSTANTIN YOLSHIN/SHUTTERSTOCK

Schloss Weikersheim, Weikersheim

VITAL STATS

Length 460km

Visitors Around 30 million annually

Year created 1950

Number of official stops 29

Number of castles and palaces 22

Number of UNESCO sites 4

Largest city Augsburg (population 301,000)

Smallest stop Röttingen (population 1681)

Number of autobahns 0

Most visited town Rothenburg ob der Tauber

PRACTICALITIES

● romantischestrasse.de

North to South

The Road is designed to be driven north to south. Leaving from Würzburg, the scenery becomes more magnificent. Getting to Würzburg is straightforward via regular trains from Munich (two hours), Bamberg, Frankfurt and Nuremberg (one hour from each). Spend a few days in Würzburg, including an afternoon at **Festung Marienberg** (schloesser.bayern.de; adult/child €4/free) with its 800-year-old bastions. The Romantic Road ends in Füssen, where **Schloss Neuschwanstein** (p152) is unmissable. From Füssen, Austria's Alps are nearby.

Romantic Road Coach

For those who aren't driving or cycling the Romantic Road, the **Romantic Road Coach** (romanticroadcoach.de) is a seasonal bus service (May to September) connecting towns not serviced by regular rail. The most popular routes are day trips (sometimes with wine tastings) from Würzburg or Frankfurt am Main to Rothenburg ob der Tauber. After Rothenburg, **Deutsche Bahn** (bahn.de) trains service 15 stations, including Dinkelsbühl, Harburg, Nördlingen, Donauwörth, Augsburg, Landsberg am Lech, Füssen and Munich. The coach route's midway stop is effectively in Weikersheim, a pretty small town straddling the Tauber River with the finest palace along the entire Road, **Schloss Weikersheim** (schloss-weikersheim.de; adult 60/80min tour €9/11).

university faculties and a museum, but the grandest 40 have been restored for visitors to admire.

Nuremberg

Revisit the Nuremberg trials

You can visit the courtroom where the Nazi leaders were tried for crimes against peace and humanity, now the **Memorium Nuremberg Trials** *(memorium-nuremberg.de; adult/child €7.50/2.50)*. Courtroom No 600 has been left pretty much as it was back then, and there's a multimedia exhibition telling the story of one of the world's most famous legal processes.

Regensburg

Explore religious Regensburg

The austere **Dom St Peter** *(bistum-regensburg.de; free),* dominating Regenburg's skyline, is a masterpiece of Gothic grandeur in Bavaria. Beyond incredible architectural features, the **Domspatzen** is a boys' choir that has been around for over 1000 years; they accompany the 10am Sunday service during the school year. Attached to the church, the **Domschatzmuseum** (Cathedral Treasury) overflows (and overwhelms) with lavish monstrances, tapestries and other treasures.

Bavarian Forest

Hiking and biking in the Bavarian Forest

Apart from the obvious attractions of the Bavarian Alps, there's no better place in the Free State to pull on hiking boots than the **Bavarian Forest National Park** *(nationalpark-bayerischer-wald.de)* and surrounding areas. The park extends for around 24,250 hectares along the Czech border, from Bayerisch Eisenstein in the north to Finsterau in the south. You'll encounter far fewer people on the trails here than in the Alps and there's also more wildlife to spot.

The European long-distance E6 hiking route cuts through the Bavarian Forest, but with over 350km of trails amid thick mountain spruce in the park, there are countless other routes to follow. Popular hikes include those to the summit of **Mt Lusen** (1373m), to the top of **Mt Grosser Arber** (1456m), the park's highest, and along the ridge that divides Bavaria from West Bohemia. Some paths in the national park are out of bounds from November to July.

Other activities include mountain biking, trail running, skiing and snowshoeing. The maps produced by Kompass – sheets 195, 196, 197 and 198 – are invaluable companions. They are available from tourist offices, some bookshops, the park visitor centre and online.

BASES FOR THE BAVARIAN FOREST

The German part of the Bavarian Forest is fringed by villages and small towns, all of which work as bases for exploring the national park. The more accessible ones can be reached via the Waldbahn railway line.

Zwiesel is the largest town just outside the park, with plenty of accommodation, places for eating and provisioning, a well-stocked, helpful **tourist office** *(zwiesel.de),* and a museum about local traditions. Another option for the south of the national park, **Grafenau** has shops, accommodation, a spa and a **tourist office** *(grafenau.de).* And if you're looking to combine the region's glass-making traditions with time spent exploring the park, **Frauenau**, very near the park's boundary, has the **Glasmuseum** *(glasmuseum-frauenau.de; adult/child €5/free, Sun €1).*

Stuttgart & the Black Forest

ENCHANTING WOODLAND | SPAS | INNOVATION

Places

 TOP TIP

The money-saving **SchwarzwaldCard** *(schwarzwaldcard.shop; adult/child from €51/35)* is good for three days of free or reduced entry to over 200 attractions, including cable cars, museums, adventure parks and swimming pools. Popular inclusions are the Triberger Wasserfälle and Europa-Park.

Welcome to the southwest, known as the sunniest region in Germany. You're in the state of Baden-Württemberg, where locals are renowned for their inventiveness, prosperity and work-hard, play-hard mentality. Stuttgart, the region's capital, has a proud history of engineering that has given the world the automobile, spark plugs and the pretzel. Freiburg, one of the world's greenest cities, is also a gateway to exploring the depths of the Schwarzwald.

The Black Forest (Schwarzwald), a sprawling mass of spruce trees, tight-knit villages and pocket-sized lakes, is a place that both adventure seekers and slow travellers will be captivated by. The name itself casts a mysterious spell over the region, and you wouldn't be blamed for expecting to see a wicked witch straight out of a Brothers Grimm fairy tale cackling in the sky. But with one step into the undergrowth, you'll soon discover the only mystery here is how they make such a delicious cake.

Stuttgart

Rev your engines

There's nothing more synonymous with Stuttgart than fast cars. At the **Porsche Museum** *(porsche.com; adult/child €12/6),* almost 100 Porsche vehicles are on display. There are kids' exhibits, a racing simulator and a comprehensive audio

---

GETTING AROUND

Covering Germany's southwest corner, the state of Baden-Württemberg is well connected by train, bus and autobahn. Trains run regularly and are your best option for getting around, though driving allows you to see and do more. Towns are best explored on foot.

Even the smallest of towns have dedicated bike paths. However, navigating long distances on two wheels may see you riding in the slip lane a fair bit. Bike routes such as the **Bodensee Radweg** *(bodensee-radweg.com)* are good options.

STUTTGART & THE BLACK FOREST

Map showing the Stuttgart and Black Forest region with locations including Homburg, Zweibrücken, Neustadt, Speyer, Heidelberg, Sinsheim, Rothenburg ob der Tauber, Landau, Bruchsal, Heilbronn, Schwäbisch Hall, Wissembourg, Karlsruhe, Pforzheim, Ludwigsburg, Schwäbisch Gmünd, Aalen, Haguenau, Rastatt, Baden-Baden, Stuttgart, Esslingen, Göppingen, Heidenheim an der Brenz, Bühl, Sindelfingen, FRANCE, Strasbourg, Kehl, Ruhestein, Black Forest National Park, Tübingen, Kirchheim unter Teck, Offenburg, Freudenstadt, Reutlingen, Günzburg, Nordschwarzwald, Ulm, Rust, Europa-Park, Hechingen, Balingen, Mittlerer Schwarzwald, Triberg, Rottweil, Colmar, Waldkirch, Villingen, Biberach, Tuttlingen, Bad Sulgau, Memmingen, Freiburg, Titisee, Messkirch, Bad Waldsee, Feldberg, Donaueschingen, Todtnau, Singen, Ravensburg, Leutkirch, Kempten, Südschwarzwald, Lörrach, Koblenz, Schaffhausen, Konstanz, Friedrichshafen, Wangen, Sonthofen, Basel, SWITZERLAND, Lake Constance, Lindau, Bregenz, AUSTRIA, Winterthur, Rhine, Neckar, Danube.

tour. You can even splash out and rent a Porsche for the day from the ticket desk.

Across town lies the 'competition'. The **Mercedes-Benz Museum** *(mercedes-benz.com; adult/child €16/8)* celebrates the evolution of the car over 135 years, contextualised through world history. From the first internal combustion engine to a history-making road trip in 1888 and the Silver Arrows sports-car hall of fame and the Popemobile, the collection is impressive and vast. The museum itself is an architectural marvel earning an entry in the Guinness World Records for the world's biggest artificial tornado – an atrium feature designed to extract smoke in case of fire.

 EATING IN FREIBURG: LOCAL CUISINE

Grosser Meyerhof: Altstadt tavern specialising in local Badish dishes such as *Maultaschen* (pork and spinach ravioli). *11.30am-11pm* €€

Heiliggeist Stüble: Dine on local specialities with the sound of church bells at this stylish tavern under the Münster. *11.30am-11pm* €€

Martin's Bräu: Home-brewed ales and meaty snacks like ox-tongue salad, bratwurst or pork knuckle. *11am-11pm Sun-Thu, to midnight Fri & Sat* €€

Schmidt: This is the best place to enjoy a fluffy, rich Black Forest cake and coffee. Big breakfast menu, too. *9am-6pm Mon-Sat* €

BLACK FOREST HAM

The tradition of smoking meat dates to the Middle Ages, and *Schwarzwälder Schinken* (Black Forest ham) still uses traditional methods today. This dry-cured, cold-smoked ham is known for its smoky aroma, dark outer crust and tender, salty-sweet interior. The process begins with pork leg, which is seasoned with salt, garlic, coriander, juniper and pepper, then cured for several weeks. It's smoked over fir and spruce wood before being air-dried at high altitudes, giving it its distinct character. Only ham made in the Black Forest region can carry this name, in efforts to ensure it's made using traditional methods and authentic regional ingredients. It's often enjoyed with thick slices of bread or added to *Flammkuchen* (Alsatian pizza).

Freiburg

Strolling the Altstadt

Spend a day walking the Altstadt, starting at the bustling farmers market (Monday to Saturday) on **Marktplatz**, where delicious produce and snacks abound. Work that off by climbing the 333 spiral steps up the spire of the 800-year-old **Freiburger Münster** *(freiburgermuenster.info; tower adult/child/under 7yr 5/3/free)* to be rewarded with Freiburg's best vistas. The cathedral is in constant need of maintenance, so expect to see some scaffolding (the only removal was for the Pope's 2011 visit). While wandering, look down at 19th-century, coloured stone mosaics (the stone came from the Rhine); they depict business emblems or cultural motifs – even pretzels.

Running along the Altstadt, the **Bächle water canals** (once medieval firefighting trenches) are as Freiburg-iconic as the Münster spire. Today, you'll likely find kids tugging sailboats along them, dogs taking a refreshing drink or locals dipping in. Local legend has it that if you set foot in a canal, you'll marry a local.

Europa-Park

Get your pulse racing

Europa-Park *(europapark.de; adult/child from €52/44)* is one of Europe's biggest and best theme parks. You can easily spend a whole day here and not see it all. Of 13 high-adrenaline roller-coasters, the standout Icelandic-themed **Blue Fire Megacoaster** blasts to 100km/h in just 2.5 seconds.

Black Forest National Park

A wild adventure

The **Nationalpark Schwarzwald** *(nationalpark-schwarzwald.de)* is a 10,000-hectare area best explored on foot. Magnificent flora and fauna abound. For a real adventure, you can even stay a night in the wilderness at a secret nature camp only accessible on foot. The visitors centre at Ruhestein offers maps and an exhibition on the project.

Triberg

Going cuckoo for a waterfall

The busy tourist town's claims to fame are cuckoo clocks and Germany's highest waterfall. **Triberger Wasserfälle** *(triberg. de; adult/child €8/7.50)* is impressive – winding boardwalks

DRINKING IN THE BLACK FOREST: LOCAL TIPPLES

Rothaus: Visit the Black Forest brewery in Grafenhausen to taste what makes its cult beer, the Tannenzapfle, so special. *11am-6pm*	**Alpirsbacher Klosterbrau:** Tour the family-owned brewery in Alpirsbach that has been crafting award-winning brews since 1880. *hours vary*	**Black Forest Distillers:** Pre-book a distillery tour in Lossburg to try Monkey 47, an award-winning dry gin made using 47 botanicals. *noon & 2pm Sat*	**Emil Scheibel Schwarzwald-Brennerei:** Learn to make great fruit schnapps at this distillery in Kappelrodeck. *9am-5pm Mon-Fri, 10am-1pm Sat*

and scenery-heavy trails abound – and cuckoo clocks less so, with many cheap imports. **Oli's Schnitzstube** *(olisschnitz stube.de)* still produces handcrafted clocks while **Rombach und Haas** *(black-forest-clock.de)* does ultra-modern ones.

Titisee
Make a splash
Titisee's scenic alpine lake is alive in summer with a quaint tourist village and plentiful water activites. The 7km shoreline has plenty of quieter swimming spots; in the town, there are good restaurants and souvenir boutiques. If weather isn't co-operating, the **Badeparadies Schwarzwald** *(badeparadies-schwarzwald.de; adult/child from €23/19)* indoor pool complex is a forest-hidden oasis.

Feldberg
'Tis the ski-son
Ski through the Black Forest mountains on **Feldberg**, the Black Forest's highest peak at 1493m. It's family-friendly and offers ski hire. Cross-country skiing is also popular, with 120km of marked trails winding through snowy enchantment – there's also snowshoeing, toboggan runs and hiking. Afterwards, hit the après-ski bars in small resort towns such as Todtnau and Feldberg.

Todtnau
Swing through the trees
From the **Blackforest Line suspension bridge** *(blackforest line.de; adult/child €12/9)*, get a bird's-eye view of the multi-tiered **Todtnauer Wasserfall** *(todtnauer-wasserfaelle.de; adult/child/under 6yr €2.50/1.50/free)*, one of the highest natural waterfalls in Germany. A combined ticket gets you entry to both the bridge and the waterfall, with a 2.4km circular walk connecting the two.

BEST SHORT HIKES IN THE BLACK FOREST

Uhrwaldpfad Rohrhardsberg: This 8km circular hike through dense forest features over 30 cuckoo clocks along the path from April to October.

Mummelsee to Hornisgrinde: From picturesque Mummelsee, this 4km loop ascends to Hornisgrinde, the highest peak in the northern Black Forest.

Allerheiligen Wasserfälle: This trail near Oppenau leads hikers 4.2km through a series of stunning waterfalls in a lush forest.

Gauchach Gorge Gourmet Trail: Challenging 5.6km trail through the wild Gauchach Gorge with its many waterfalls.

Muggenbrunn Barefoot Path: Feel spruce cones, bark mulch and fresh mountain water underfoot on this 600m-long trail. Great for kids.

WINTER FUN
Check out the ski resorts of **Garmisch-Partenkirchen** (p152) in Bavaria if you're keen on more winter adventures.

Bremen & Lower Saxony

ART MUSEUMS | WWII HISTORY | RICH GREENERY

Places

Lower Saxony, spilling northwards to the North Sea and in most parts flat as a pancake, is the largest German state after Bavaria. For the traveller, it's a low-key place with an understated character to its the landscape: wide-open spaces and heath, occasional hilly countryside, and tidal mudflats that submerge and reappear in daily cycles. Hanover, its capital, has several excellent museums, as well as large swathes of green space that invite a stroll. An hour's drive from Hanover, the Bergen-Belsen Memorial Site, a former concentration camp, reveals Lower Saxony's stark contrasts.

Meanwhile, Bremen is a city-state unto itself with its own port, Bremerhaven. Bremen brings together culture, particularly the fine arts, and plenty of nightlife in one small bundle. Within a short space of time, you can wind down medieval streets, duck into another gallery featuring unusual expressionism, stroll along the 'museum mile' and rest up in some great cafes and student places.

GETTING AROUND

Rail connections are excellent and often integrated with bus services. ICE fast trains service main hubs like Bremen and Hanover, and there's an extensive regional network.

To reach Bergen-Belsen Memorial Site, take an ICE or regional train to Celle. Take bus 900 from Schlossplatz and change to bus 110 at 'Küsterdamm, Winsen' stop. It's best to avoid Sunday, as only a *Rufbus* (call bus) completes the journey from Winsen and needs to be booked ahead.

Bremen

MAP p161

All about expressionism

Bremen's longstanding ties with expressionism are best reflected in the architecture along **Böttcherstrasse**. Red-brick houses sport unique facades; some are now artisan shops and art museums. The **Paula Modersohn-Becker Museum** *(museen-boettcherstrasse.de; adult/child €12/free)* showcases the early expressionist and member of movement-founding Worpswede artist colony. The adjoining **Roselius-Haus Museum** *(museen-boettcherstrasse.de; adult/child €12/free)*, in a 16th-century patrician house, primarily displays 16th- and 17th-century art. The standout is a section dedicated to Lucas Cranach the Elder.

Works of Gerhard Marcks

Next to Gerhard Marcks' **Town Musicians of Bremen Statue** on the Marktplatz, the same Brothers Grimm fairy tale it's

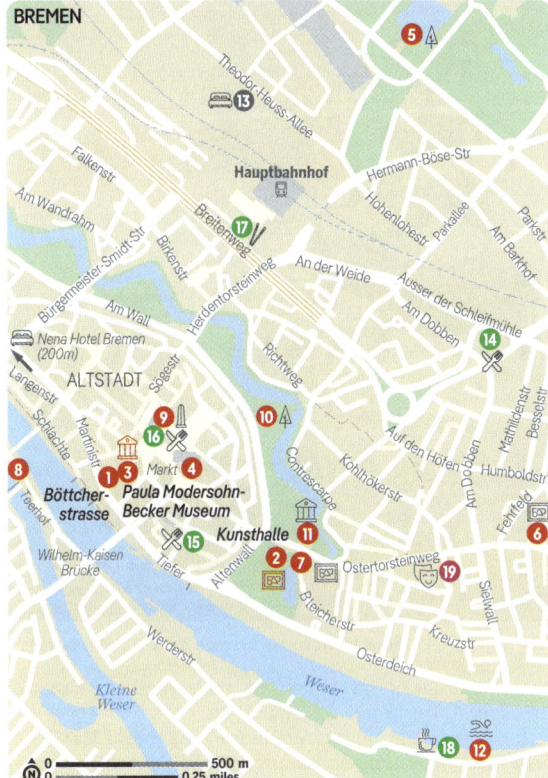

BREMEN

inspired by is charmingly re-enacted at noon from May to September. It's a beautiful, lighthearted performance honouring an artist condemned as 'degenerate' during Nazi times. The excellent **Gerhard Marcks Haus** *(marcks.de; adult/child €5/ free)* exhibits the artist's own donated works.

Bremen's cultural mile

The **Kunsthalle** *(kunsthalle-bremen.de; adult/child €15/ free)* is Bremen's premier art exhibition space with a large, permanent collection of paintings, sculpture and copperplate engravings, spanning medieval to present times. There's a

☑ **TOP TIP**

During trade fairs, hotels and private accommodation in Hanover and nearby towns are booked out, so it's important to always run a quick check online *(visit-hannover.com/ Messen-Kongresse)* before coming. As an alternative, visit Bremen first.

 EATING IN BREMEN: OUR PICKS ──────────────── MAP p161

Hanoi Deli: Sushi, Vietnamese dishes and some pan-Asian classics; large servings. *11.30am-10pm Mon & Wed-Fri, from noon Sat & Sun* €€

Bremer Ratskeller: Hearty traditional German cuisine beneath the Rathaus. Gorgeous vaulted ceilings. *noon-9.30pm Sun-Thu, to 10pm Fri & Sat* €€

Argana: Moroccan cooking in the Schnoor quarter. Lots of meat-based tajines, and veg offerings. *noon-3pm & 5.30-10pm Tue-Fri, 2.30-11pm Sat, 5.30-10pm Mon* €€

Al Pappagallo: Delicious Italian dishes prepared in an open kitchen and elegantly presented. *noon-2pm & 6-11pm Mon-Fri, 6-11pm Sat* €€€

BEST BREMEN PARKS & QUIET SPOTS

Wallanlagen: Bremen's town fortifications were converted into parkland in the 19th century, with ponds and meadows.

Teerhof: This quarter on the spit of land in the Weser River has a slightly abandoned feel, despite its gentrified housing. On the same peninsula but reached by ferry from Sielwall, the **Weser Strand** (Weser Beach) is a summer bathing spot, and **Café Sand** a popular retreat.

Bürgerpark Bremen: Northeast of the centre, an enormous stretch of parkland with lakes, trails, forests and meadows. It also has a small animal park, popular with kids.

Bibelgarten: The Bibel Garden is a tranquil yard at the entrance to the Bleikeller crypt.

ROSSHELEN/SHUTTERSTOCK

Town Musicians of Bremen Statue (p160), Bremen

beautiful range of the old masters, including Lucas Cranach the Elder, Dürer, Van Dyck and others.

Across from the gallery, **Wilhelm Wagenfeld Haus** *(wilhelm-wagenfeld-stiftung.de; adult/child €6/3.50)*, a former guardhouse and jail, now houses contemporary design from industrial to photography. It's named after a Bauhaus luminary.

Bremen's cultural mile gives way to great cultural venues in **Das Viertel**, such as the **Mensch, Puppe** *(menschpuppe.de; matinee adult/child €10/8, evening incl drink €25/15)* puppet theatre and a handful of galleries including the outstanding **Galerie Kramer** *(galeriekramer.de; free)*.

Hanover

Relax in royal parkland

Hanover's highlight is **Herrenhäuser Gärten** *(hannover.de/herrenhausen)*, a sprawling constellation of gardens. Start in the **Grosser Garten** *(incl museum & Berggarten adult/child €10/free)*, known for baroque golden sculptures, a maze and the beloved Niki de Saint Phalle Grotto. A path leads down to the Grosse Fontäne, one of Europe's tallest fountains jetting to 80m high. In summer, dancing fountain shows, **garden illuminations** *(adult/child €6/free)*, concerts and fireworks competitions delight.

Tthe **Museum Schloss Herrenhausen** *(incl Grosser Garten & Berggarten adult/child €10/free)* recounts the grounds' history from the 17th century to their Hanoverian royal creators.

Exploring the old town

Despite severe WWII damage, Hanover's small old town retains much historic character. The most interesting buildings on Am Markte, the central square, are the medieval **Altes Rathaus** *(Old Town Hall; altes-rathaus-events.de)* and the Gothic **Marktkirche** *(Market Church; marktkirche-hannover. de; free)*. **Leibnizhaus** on Holzmarkt was once the home of the renowned mathematician and philosopher Gottfried Wilhelm Leibniz (1646–1716) and has an attractive, reconstructed Renaissance facade. The nearby **Aegidienkirche** soberly recollects wartime horrors; the medieval church remains in bombed-out condition since 1943.

Not to be missed along the river are the voluptuous and fluorescent-coloured **Die Nanas** sculptures. These Venus figures are Hanover's beloved landmarks.

Into the sky, onto a lake

The **Neues Rathaus** *(adult/child €4/3.50)* has an unusually curved lift leading up to its green dome. A glass ceiling and floor make for an ascent that's nerve-tingling and claustrophobic (six-person capacity and busy in summer). Afterwards, stroll through parkland to **Maschsee** for endless splashy fun including rental pedalling and rowing boats. Ferries – some solar-powered – ply the lake from Easter to October (weather depending).

Bergen-Belsen

Visit a Holocaust memorial

Visiting the **Bergen-Belsen Memorial Site** *(bergen-belsen. stiftung-ng.de; free)*, a former concentration camp, takes you to where Anne Frank died in 1945. The modern **Documentation Centre** chronicles the fates of the people who passed through and the grounds' evolution from a forestry workers' barracks to a POW camp.

 DRINKING IN HANOVER: OUR PICKS

Waterloo: This beer garden is on the way to football club Hanover 96's home ground, with *Wurst* and more on the menu. *hours vary*

Brauhaus Ernst August: Sprawling brewpub with food, parties and live music, serving its own beers. *11am-11pm Mon-Thu, to late Fri & Sat*

Holländische Kakao-Stube: Historic (1895) Dutch coffeehouse with a great selection of pastries and a maritime ambience. *10am-6.30pm Mon-Sat*

Cafe Mezzo: Cafe and bar alongside the Pavillon cultural venue; the latter has live music and lots of events. *9am-midnight Mon-Sat, to 11pm Sun*

Dresden & Leipzig

BAROQUE | ROYAL TREASURES | ART

Places

Dresden p164
Leipzig p166

GETTING AROUND

Both cities are best explored on foot. In Dresden, trams connect the Altstadt and Neustadt and serve every corner of the centre. In Leipzig (1½ hours from Dresden by car or train), the distance between most attractions is walkable. For Plagwitz, KarLi and Connewitz, you'll need to catch a tram from the Hauptbahnhof or Augustusplatz. Install the Nextbike app on your phone to book municipal bicycles available in both cities.

With a colourful history as an independent entity, a quasi-empire at times, Saxony is the most distinctive East German region. It takes pride in speaking a dialect that other Germans – according to regular national opinion surveys – appear to dislike. This might be a secret strategy to keep others away from a land that is truly blessed.

Dresden's 18th-century cultural heyday is evident in the Altstadt's baroque wonders and their precious art collections. Across the river, Dresden's Neustadt has dozens of restaurants and shops and one of the liveliest nightlife scenes in Germany's east. In the north, Leipzig is an energetic and progressive metropolis that rivals Berlin as the country's hippest destination. Leipzig has nurtured some famous composers and scientists as well as important German painters, and has a plethora of fascinating museums and a world-class picture gallery. It's an all-round liveable city, half of which is covered by lakes and wood-like parks.

Dresden

A cityscape to die for

Before anything else, take in marvellous views from **Brühl's Terrace** (aka the Balcony Europe). Dark-green, untamed Neustadt banks juxtaposed against the blackened stones and baroque curves of Altstadt provide an intense visual experience.

Another marvel is the **Frauenkirche** *(frauenkirche-dresden.de),* a magnificent cathedral resurrected after being reduced to WWII rubble. Next, take in **Residenzschloss** *(skd.museum; adult/child €16/free),* a Renaissance palace home to Saxony's rulers for around 400 years. Its collections include the unmissable **Historisches Grünes Gewölbe** *(€16, incl other collections €28),* a real-life Aladdin's cave of precious ivory, silver, diamonds and jewels. Reconstruction on the bombed-out palace began in the 1960s and was finally completed in 2013.

Nearby, the **Albertinum** *(skd.museum; adult/child €14/free),* a former Renaissance-era arsenal, is the stunning home

Brühl's Terrace and Frauenkirche, Dresden

of the **Galerie Neue Meister** (New Masters Gallery), which has paintings by the likes of Caspar David Friedrich, Claude Monet and Marc Chagall.

Private Eden

At **Zwinger** *(der-dresdner-zwinger.de; adult/child €16/free)* palace, discover an Earthly version of paradise for the chosen – Saxon royals and their guests.

Inside, the **Gemäldegalerie Alte Meister** (Old Masters Gallery) is an astounding collection of 16th- to 18th-century European art including Raphael's famous *Sistine Madonna* (1513), and works by Titian and Cranach.

The extraordinary **Porzellansammlung** brings together 17th- and 18th-century porcelain from China and Meissen. The **Tiersaal** (Animal Hall) is the ultimate highlight with hundreds of porcelain animals. Lastly, the **Mathematisch-Physikalischer Salon**, a collection of scientific implements, will delight anyone interested in the Enlightenment.

Sounds of Dresden

Dresden's opera house, the **Semperoper** *(semperoper.de)*, is another architectural jewel in the Altstadt. Destroyed by Allied air raids, it was resurrected in 1945. Counting premieres of famous works by Strauss and Wagner, it still hosts world-class concerts today (buy tickets well ahead).

Dresden's other top venue for classical music is a strikingly different piece of GDR-era brutalism. The **Dresdner Philharmonie** *(dresdnerphilharmonie.de)* is home to one of Germany's best orchestras.

BEST DRESDEN FESTIVALS

Dixieland Fest: A May parade of Dixieland bands riding retro and steampunk vehicles; concerts are also held aboard steamships.

Filmfest Dresden: Held in April, the international short-film festival takes place in various city locations, including on giant screens in Altstadt.

Flottenparade: The full might of the Saxon navy is displayed in the 1 May parade, with Dresden's famous steamships floating past the Altstadt.

Louisenfest: 'Party, music, food' is the motto of this late-June festival celebrating the city's happening street. Visual arts are also on the menu.

Elbhangfest: A late-June festival organised by people living on the high bank of the Elbe between Pillnitz and Loschwitz.

EATING IN LEIPZIG & DRESDEN: OUR PICKS

Bayerische Bahnhof: Gose beer and stylish food in the intriguing setting of a defunct Leipzig railway station's waiting room. *noon-10pm* €€

Café Puschkin: KarLi's flagship hangout is well past its heyday, but it still draws a merry Leipzig crowd and has an eclectic menu. *9am-2am* €€

Lila Sosse: Intriguing vegan and meaty concoctions served in glass preserve jars inside Dresden's Kunsthof-passage courtyard complex. *4-11pm* €€

PlanWirtschaft: A quiet courtyard setting in the heart of Dresden's Neustadt and a menu alluding to GDR-era culinary standards. *5-11pm Tue-Sun* €€

☑ TOP TIP

Sold at tourist information centres, the Leipzig Card allows unlimited travel within one or three days and entitles you to discounts at most of the important museums.

Leipzig

You want a revolution?

Leipzig's **Nikolaikirche** *(nikolaikirche.de)* is famous for the 'peace prayers' held here every Monday at 5pm since 1982. Starting in September 1989, the prayers kicked off a chain reaction of events leading to East Germany's collapse and Germany's reunification.

The **Zeitgeschichtliches Forum** *(hdg.de; free)* further covers East German political history with an enormous exhibition, while the darker side of Communist times is chillingly documented by the **Stasi Museum** *(runde-ecke-leipzig.de; adult/student €5/4)*, located in the former secret police headquarters. English-language audio guides accompany displays (in German) on propaganda, surveillance devices, recruitment and other machinations.

Singing city

The 800-year-old boys' choir **Thomanerchor** still performs at its original base in the Gothic **Thomaskirche** *(thomaskirche. org)*. Bach repertoire honours the composer who led it for 27 years until his death. Bach's remains lie buried beneath a bronze plate afront the altar. The church hosts other musical events – some are free – including **Bachfest** *(bachfestleipzig.de)* in June.

Notes and notables

Walk the footsteps of Leipzig's famous composers along the 5km **Leipziger Notenspur** *(Leipzig Music Trail; notenspur-leipzig. de)*. Each of the 23 stops has information panels and phone numbers to call and listen for music or additional commentary. There are six museums along the route, most doubling as concert venues, including **Mendelssohn-Haus** *(mendelssohn-stiftung. de; adult/child €10/free)*, the house where Schumann composed the *Spring Symphony*, Wagner's former school, and apartments Edvard Grieg stayed in. At the interactive **Bach-Museum Leipzig** *(bachmuseumleipzig.de; adult/child €10/free)*, learn how to date a Bach manuscript, listen to baroque instruments or treat your ears to any of his compositions.

Treasures of knowledge

Leipzig University is one of the world's oldest, founded in 1409 by scholars fleeing the Hussite uprising in Prague. The list of alumni is stellar – from Goethe and Nietzsche to former German Chancellor Angela Merkel. Located in Augustusplatz, its contemporary home known as **Paulinum** looks like an airport terminal devouring a Gothic cathedral. It's a boldly postmodern tribute to the 13th-century university church, which stood here until East German authorities blew it up in 1968.

Thankfully, the university's treasure trove of scientific collections was left unscathed. The **Museen im Grassi** *(grassi-leipzig.de)* includes the **Musikinstrumenten-Museum** *(adult/child €6/free)* where you can discover five centuries' worth of music in an interactive sound laboratory. There's also the **Museum für Völkerkunde** *(free)* exploring global cultures and the **Museum für Angewandte Kunst** *(free)* flaunting Art Nouveau and Art Deco furniture, porcelain, glass and ceramics.

Central Germany

The map shows: Braunschweig, Hanover, BERLIN, Potsdam, Hildesheim, Magdeburg, Göttingen, Dessau, Wittenberg, Nordhausen, Halle, Kassel, Leipzig, Eisenach, Erfurt, Weimar, Dresden, Jena, Gera, Chemnitz, Suhl, Saalfeld, Coburg, Hof

HISTORY | ANCIENT BEECHWOOD | BROTHERS GRIMM

Central Germany is truly the heart of the country. Plenty of sites in Thuringia, Lower Saxony, Saxony-Anhalt and Hesse have a special historical resonance or even a mythic significance. And so much of the national story has unfolded here – key sites in intellectual, religious and political developments that have shaped modern Germany, Europe and beyond. Look no further for the seedbed of Germany's most revered artists, writers and thinkers from Goethe to Nietzsche and Bach.

Here, beyond the time-worn churches, half-timbered, 16th-century merchants' houses and grim fortresses of tourist brochures, you'll find glowing examples of the German rural ideal. Ancient swaths of beech and conifer forest, the low mountains and farmsteads of Brothers Grimm stories, and broad fields of corn and sunflowers are abundant. There's room to stretch your legs, to cycle, to swim and to get back to basics in some of the largest nature reserves in Central Europe.

Weimar

Discover Goethe's Weimar

Johann Wolfgang von Goethe (1749–1832), the colossus of German letters, spent much of his life in Weimar. He lived in the 18th-century *Wohnhaus* (residence) on Frauenplan square for more than 50 years. The house now houses the **Goethe-Nationalmuseum** *(klassik-stiftung.de; adult/student €10/4)*, the world's largest collection of Goethe manuscripts and artefacts.

Allow several hours to explore the residence and the superbly curated permanent exhibition, **Lebensfluten – Tatensturm** ('Floods of Life – Storm of Action') including where he wrote *Faust*. Meanwhile, the **Goethe Gartenhaus** *(klassik-stiftung. de; adult/student €7/3)* is where he lived prior to the *Wohnhaus*. The lovely cottage, surrounded by the garden that Goethe himself laid out, is within the 58-acre, UNESCO-listed **Park an der Ilm** *(free)*.

Places

Weimar p167
Kassel p168
Dessau p168
Wittenberg p168

GETTING AROUND

This region is most easily explored by car. In the towns, you can mostly get around on foot.
Deutsche Bahn *(bahn.de)* runs most services in Central Germany. The major rail hubs are Kassel and Halle, though there are regular connections throughout. Private operator **FlixTrain** *(flixtrain.com)* runs between Halle and Berlin but comfort is lacking. The region's bus network is efficient and much cheaper than rail.

Bauhaus beginnings

The **Bauhaus Museum Weimar** *(klassik-stiftung.de; adult/student €10/4)* commemorates the Bauhaus (literally 'building house') school founded in Weimar in 1919. The collection here focuses on the early days. To actually see Bauhaus architecture, **Haus Am Horn** *(adult/student €5/2)* is Weimar's only truly Bauhaus building.

The dark history of Buchenwald

Buchenwald concentration camp has been preserved almost untouched as a memorial, the **Gedenkstätte Buchenwald** *(buchenwald.de; tour adult/student €7/3, multimedia guide €5)*. Visitors are encouraged to wander quietly and freely around its numerous structures, including the crematorium.

Kassel

Deep dive into fairy tales

Kassel is an ideal launching pad for exploring the **Märchenstrasse** (Fairy Tale Road), one of Germany's most beguiling tourist routes. The 600km route stretches from Hanau, the birthplace of the Brothers Grimm, to Bremen. Of the 50-odd fairytale-associated stops, five are 'life stations' of the brothers: Hanau, Steinau, Marburg, Kassel and Göttingen. All make for excellent day trips or overnight destinations. Before heading off, discover the Brothers' legacy in Kassel at **Grimmwelt** *(grimmwelt.de; adult/student/under 3yr €10/7/free)*, the world's leading museum and archive on their work.

Dessau

The wonderful world of Bauhaus

Bauhaus, considered the most influential school of design and architecture of the 20th century, reached its creative peak in Dessau. The purpose-built **Bauhaus-Dessau Museum** *(bauhaus-dessau.de; adult/child €10/free)*, home to wonderful exhibitions curated from 49,000 pieces, is the world's second largest after Berlin. Also obligatory is the **Bauhausgebäude** *(adult/child €10/free)*. The iconic modernist building, designed by Gropius himself, is a teaching institution but permits audio guided tours inside.

Wittenberg

Lutheran churches and sights

The Lutherstadt-Wittenberg is UNESCO-recognised for its wealth of Reformation-related sites. Most important is the **Schlosskirche** *(schlosskirche-wittenberg.de; tower €3)* where Martin Luther nailed his *Ninety-Five Theses* to the door. There's also **Stadtkirche Wittenberg** *(stadtkirchengemeinde-wittenberg.de)*, where Luther conducted the world's first Protestant worship services in 1521.

Frankfurt am Main

SKYLINE VIEWS | APPLE WINE | ART MUSEUMS

Glinting with glass, steel and concrete skyscrapers, Frankfurt am Main (pronounced 'mine') is unlike any other German city. 'Mainhattan' is a high-powered finance and business hub, home to one of the world's largest stock exchanges and the gleaming headquarters of the European Central Bank, and it famously hosts some of the world's most important trade fairs, attracting thousands of business travellers. Yet, at its heart, Frankfurt is an unexpectedly traditional and charming city, with half-timbered buildings huddled in its quaint medieval Altstadt (old town), cosy applewine taverns serving hearty regional food, village-like neighbourhoods filled with outdoor cafes, boutiques and street art, and beautiful parks, gardens and riverside paths. The city's cache of museums is second in Germany only to Berlin's, and its nightlife and entertainment scenes are bolstered by a spirited student population. The area around the Hauptbahnhof is the red-light and drug district, and while it offers the cheapest accommodation, you should avoid it.

Frankfurt's Historic Heart

Roman market square

The **Römerberg** is Frankfurt's old central square, buzzing with tourists and street performers. Ornately gabled half-timbered buildings, reconstructed in the 1980s after WWII bombings, give an idea of how beautiful the city's medieval core once was. The photogenic **Rathaus** building, with its three step-gabled 15th-century houses, is one such example. In the time of the Holy Roman Empire, it was the site of celebrations during the election and coronation of emperors. Today, it houses the office of Frankfurt's mayor.

GETTING AROUND

Frankfurt is a surprisingly compact, small and navigable city. It is very walkable and the River Main acts as a primary landmark to guide your journey. To get a real feel for the city, try to take it in on foot as much as you can. Public transport is also robust and easy to use, with commuter trains, buses, trams and a subway system. If renting a car, parking can be a bit expensive, so prepare to pay €1 for every 20 minutes in most cases.

☑️ **TOP TIP**

The **Moselle Valley** is especially scenic walking country. Variants of the Mosel Erlebnis Route follow the entire Moselle Valley along both banks of the river. Expect some steep climbs if you venture away from the river, such as on the 185km-long Moselhöhenweg, which sticks to high ground but offers spectacular vistas.

BEST FESTIVALS IN FRANKFURT

Christopher Street Day: A colourful Pride parade in mid-July, as well as a *Strassenfest* (street festival) at Konstablerwache.

Rheingauer Weinmarkt: At this 10-day late-summer festival, enjoy a taste of over 600 wine varieties from the surrounding Rheingau region.

Apfelweinfestival: Frankfurt's famous *Apfelwein* is celebrated in August with tastings, music and storytelling in dialect.

Frankfurt Book Fair: The largest annual global book fair, Frankfurter Buchmesse, takes place at Frankfurt Messe in mid-October. Book early to get a hotel room.

Christmas Market: Every December, Frankfurt's Christmas market in the Altstadt brings cheer with choirs, *Glühwein*, stalls and traditional foods.

	HIGHLIGHTS		6 Historisches Museum Frankfurt		10 Steigenberger Frankfurter Hof
1	Kaiserdom	7	Museum für Kommunikation		
2	Römerberg				EATING
3	Städel Museum		ACTIVITIES	11	Im Herzen Afrikas
	SIGHTS	8	Primus Linie	12	Kleinmarkthalle
4	Deutsches Filmmuseum		SLEEPING	13	Occhio D'Oro
		9	Ruby Louise Hotel	14	Pizzeria Montana
5	Deutsches Romantik-Museum			15	Ramen Muku
				16	Zu den 12 Aposteln

Regal History
Climb the Kaiserdom

The red-sandstone Imperial Cathedral of St Bartholomew, aka **Kaiserdom** *(dom-frankfurt.de; tower adult/child €3/1.50)* or Frankfurt Cathedral, is located in the heart of the Altstadt. An unmatched view of the city is your reward if you climb the 328 steps up the cathedral's Gothic tower to the viewing platform at an impressive 66m. The cathedral itself, the construction of which began in the 13th century, houses many regal memories as the German emperors and kings of the Holy Roman Empire were either crowned or elected here. The original chapel where the elections took place is now used only for silent prayer. The cathedral was rebuilt after an 1867 fire and again after the bombings of 1944, which left it a burnt-out shell.

A Soaring Romantic Journey
Learn about German Romanticism

The **Deutsches Romantik-Museum** *(German Romanticism Museum; deutsches-romantik-museum.de; adult/child €12/3)*

SVEN HANSCHE/SHUTTERSTOCK

Kaiserdom

is the very first of its kind in the world, deep-diving into the art and ethos of the German Romantic movement.

The first-level Goethe gallery contains over 5000 paintings from 1750 to 1850. The 2nd-floor gallery broadens the scope to explore Romanticism as a whole, focusing heavily on the literary works from the era. Weave through a maze of mirrors and standing panes with varying definitions of Romanticism imprinted on them; you can even type out your very own ode to love. The 3rd-floor gallery brings the intense feelings of the German Romantics to life. Learn how philosophers, poets, novelists, painters and fine artists throughout Europe began to gain inspiration from the German Romantics.

Down the Main

Relax on a river cruise

The Main River divides the city, with Frankfurt proper on the northern bank, and Sachsenhausen on the southern. You can appreciate the city's many charms while bobbing down the river on a boat. Hour-long sightseeing cruises with **Primus Linie**

 EATING IN FRANKFURT: CHEAP EATS

| **Kleinmarkthalle:** Traditional market hall with stalls selling artisan smoked sausages, cheese and pastries, plus espresso bar. *8am-6pm Mon-Fri, to 4pm Sat* € | **Pizzeria Montana:** Thin-crust pizzas with premium ingredients prepared fresh and cooked in a wood-fired oven. *11.30am-10pm Mon-Fri, from noon Sat & Sun* € | **Ramen Muku:** One of Frankfurt's excellent Japanese restaurants serves homemade ramen noodles and sashimi. *noon-1.30pm & 6-9.30pm Wed-Sun* € | **Startorante:** Social enterprise offering hospitality training and apprenticeships to young women; it serves three-course lunches. *11.30am-2pm Tue-Fri* € |

THE TASTE OF FRANKFURT

Handkäs mit Musik: A tangy, sour-milk cheese topped with onions, vinegar, oil and sometimes caraway seeds. *Musik* refers to the onions' after-effect!

Apfelwein (Ebbelwoi): Frankfurt's famous apple-wine cider, served tart and dry, always in a diamond ribbed glass known as a *Gerippte*.

Grüne Sosse: A green sauce made from seven fresh herbs – chives, parsley, chervil, borage, sorrel, burnet and cress – served with boiled eggs, potatoes or schnitzel.

Frankfurter sausages: Slim, lightly smoked sausages, often served in pairs with mustard horseradish.

Frankfurter Kranz: A thick buttercream cake shaped like a crown, covered in crunchy caramelised nuts and topped with cherries.

(primus-linie.de) leave hourly from Eiserner Steg, or catch an evening cruise to see the city's glittering skyline as dusk falls.

Longer full-day and multi-day cruises often begin in Frankfurt and float onwards to Mainz where the river meets the Rhine. At the Rhine–Main junction, you can continue on through the spectacular Rhine Valley.

Get Your Culture Fix

Explore Museum Embankment

On the southern bank of the Main River, nine world-class museums line up like dominoes. A further three jostle for position on the opposite side under the name **Museumufer** (Museum Embankment). You'd need weeks to visit them all, so focus on the heavy hitters.

Founded in 1815, **Städel Museum** *(staedelmuseum.de; adult/child €16/free)* is a world-renowned art gallery with an outstanding collection of European art from masters like Rembrandt, Rubens and Cézanne. It also features temporary photography exhibits, included in the ticket price.

Next door is the **Museum für Kommunication** *(mfk-frankfurt.de; adult/child/under 5yr €8/2/free),* which promises to revive some nostalgia as you trace the history of communication from Mesopotamian writing stones through to today's ultra-connected tech, with engaging, hands-on exhibitions.

Movie buffs will love the **Deutsches Filmmuseum** *(German Film Museum; dff.film; adult/child/under 6yr €8/4/free),* where you can try your hand at editing, play around with green screens and explore iconic props, costumes and film posters.

Jump back across the river to visit the **Historisches Museum Frankfurt** *(historisches-museum-frankfurt.de; adult/child €8/free).* This museum focuses specifically on the long and storied history of Frankfurt. Don't miss the giant snow globe on the bottom floor.

EATING IN FRANKFURT: OUR PICKS

Zu den 12 Aposteln: German food such as Frankfurter schnitzel with *Grüne Sosse* and *Käsespätzle* under dim lamplight. *noon-11pm* €€

Druckwasserwerk: German cuisine in a beautiful building from 1899. Outside, there's an umbrella-shaded terrace. *5pm-midnight Mon-Sat* €€€

Occhio D'Oro: On the rooftop of the Flemings Hotel, this Italian restaurant with stunning city views serves regional cuisine. *6pm-midnight Mon-Sat* €€

Im Herzen Afrikas: Eritrean cuisine at a rustic tavern with a sandy floor and colourful murals transporting you to Africa. *4-11pm Mon-Fri, from 1pm Sat* €€

Beyond Frankfurt

Leave behind Frankfurt's towering cityscape to discover quiet charm, Gutenberg's legacy, medieval castles...and, of course, Riesling after Riesling.

Straddling the Rhine, Mainz offers a chance to explore the region's quieter side. The hometown of Johannes Gutenberg, the inventor of the printing press, Mainz has a sizeable university and a rich wine culture. Strolling along the Rhine and sampling local wines in a half-timbered tavern is as much a part of any Mainz visit as its fabulous sightseeing.

Between Rüdesheim and Koblenz, the Rhine cuts deeply through the Rhenish Slate Mountains, meandering between hillside castles and steep fields of wine-producing grapes. This is Germany's landscape at its most dramatic – forested hillsides alternate with craggy cliffs and near-vertical terraced vineyards. Idyllic villages appear around each bend, their half-timbered houses and Gothic church steeples seemingly plucked from the world of fairy tales.

Places

Mainz

TIME FROM FRANKFURT: **50MIN** 🚆

Birthplace of the printing press

The **Gutenberg-Museum Mainz** *(mainz.de; adult/child €10/4)* is a proud homage to the history of the printed word and the 15th-century Mainz native who invented it – Johannes Gutenberg. The museum's most incredible exhibits, kept under dim light, are the two copies of the 42-line **Gutenberg Bible**, printed in 1455 and hand-decorated. Don't miss the 20-minute

---

 GETTING AROUND

ICE trains run frequently from Frankfurt's Hauptbahnhof via the airport and are the easiest and quickest way to reach Mainz. All main attractions are within walking distance from the train station. The public bus and tram systems are easy to use.

Navigate the Romantic Rhine Valley by renting a car. Only two train lines run along this section of the Rhine. The Linke Rheinstrecke (Left Rhine Line) runs along the west bank from Cologne to Mainz, passing through Boppard, St Goar, Oberwesel and Bacharach. The Rechte Rheinstrecke (Right Rhine Line) runs along the east bank and passes through Braubach, Kaub, Assmannshausen and Rüdesheim.

KD runs cruises and scheduled services up and down the river between Cologne and Mainz. Travelling end to end takes over 11 hours, or you can opt for shorter sections such as St Goar to Bingen.

SADMAN/SHUTTERSTOCK

Drosselgasse, Rüdesheim am Rhein

demonstrations of Gutenberg's printing press to understand the ingenuity of his invention.

Chagall's blue-hued church

Around 200,000 pilgrims make their way to the **St-Stephan-Kirche** *(bistummainz.de/pfarrei/mainz-st-stephan)* every year. This would be just another Gothic church rebuilt after WWII were it not for the nine brilliant-blue stained-glass windows created by the Jewish artist Marc Chagall in the final years of his life, which serve as a symbol of Jewish–Christian reconciliation. Pick up an audio guide inside the church to learn more about each individual artwork.

Marvel at the Mainz markets

Three times a week year-round, open-air markets fill the pretty squares around **Mainzer Dom** *(bistummainz.de/mainzer-dom),* the city's immense 12th-century cathedral built from deep-red sandstone blocks. Many of the stall-holders have been selling local produce, smoked meats and more at these markets for generations. On Saturdays from March to November, you can enjoy the **Market Breakfast** with Mainz winegrowers. In front of the cathedral, treat yourself to a *Worscht un Woi,* a sausage served with a roll and wine. In December, these markets become even more festive, with Christmas shopping, holiday-themed stalls and carol music.

Heidelberg

TIME FROM FRANKFURT: 1HR

A majestic hilltop castle

Hit the Romantic Road for Heidelberg's Altstadt and the ruined Renaissance **Schloss Heidelberg** *(schloss-heidelberg.de; adult/child €11/5.50)*. The castle gardens are worth strolling for views of the Neckar River and the Altstadt rooftop. The castle cellar is also home to the **Heidelberg Tun (Großes Fass)**, the world's biggest wine barrel. The Schlossticket combines entrance to the castle and a ride on the **Bergbahn** funicular railway (a steep walk up is also an option).

Rüdesheim am Rhein

TIME FROM FRANKFURT: 1HR

It's wine o'clock

Although Rüdesheim is an unofficial starting point on a journey up the Rhine (day-tripping coach tourists abound), it stays surprisingly small and maintains its old medieval charms. Explore the kitschy, colourful town centre and, especially, the famously narrow medieval alley **Drosselgasse**.

Rüdesheim is primarily a winemaking town and its vineyards are UNESCO-listed. The town has its own delicious white variety, called the Rheingauer Riesling, which you can sample at **RheinWeinWelt** *(rheinweinwelt.de)*.

Koblenz

TIME FROM FRANKFURT: 1½HR

Fall in love with Festung Ehrenbreitstein

Perched 118m above the Rhine, the **Festung Ehrenbreitstein** *(Ehrenbreitstein Fortress; tor-zum-welterbe.de/festung-ehrenbreitstein; adult/child €10/5.50)* was indestructible for decades until Napoleonic troops arrived. To prove a point, the Prussians rebuilt it as one of Europe's mightiest fortifications. Inside, there are several museums and fabulous views from its ramparts and viewing platform, from where you can see the confluence of the Rhine and Moselle rivers. The most fun way to travel up is the **Seilbahn** *(seilbahn-koblenz.de; one-way adult/child €12/6)* cable car.

Where the rivers meet

At the point of confluence of the Moselle and the Rhine, the **Deutsches Eck** (German Corner) is a testament to German unity lost and found. The stone pedestal links up to a grassy promenade for the most perfect riverside stroll.

TASTE THE WINE ROUTE

One of Germany's oldest tour routes, the **Deutsche Weinstrasse** (German Wine Route) traverses the heart of the Palatinate (Pfalz) – a region of vine-covered hillsides, rambling forests, ruined castles, 35 picturesque hamlets and thriving fruit orchards. The drive is especially pretty during spring (March to mid-May) and harvest (September to October). Starting in Schweigen-Rechtenbach, on the French border, the route winds north for 85km to Bockenheim an der Weinstrasse, although it can be driven in either direction. Key stops along the way include the postcard-perfect medieval Riesling villages of **Bacharach** and **Oberwesel**, as well as fairytale landmarks in **St Goar**.

Places We Love to Stay

€ Budget €€ Midrange €€€ Top End

Berlin
MAP p119, p125 & p128

Generator Berlin Alexanderplatz € Huge and high-energy, this modern designer hostel has cheerfully painted private rooms and dorms, plus industrial-chic public areas.

Kiez Hostel € Central, squeaky-clean base with a welcoming homey vibe and imaginatively designed dorms, but limited check-in hours.

Cosmo Hotel €€ The lobby's extravagant lamps and armchairs set the tone for crisply angular rooms with silvery design accents and floor-to-ceiling windows.

Park Inn by Radisson Berlin Alexanderplatz €€ This sleek tower is honeycombed with 1029 generic but comfy rooms featuring panoramic windows, wooden floors and noiseless air-con.

Myer's Hotel Berlin €€ Feeling like your rich uncle's manor, this 56-room boutique hotel has antique-style rooms, a clubby bar and a cosy cellar spa.

Sly Berlin €€ Modern luxury meets local flair across four revamped factory-era buildings, anchored by a lush atrium and crowned with a rooftop sauna.

Hotel Château Royal €€€ Hip and haute boutique hotel in two listed buildings and a Chipperfield-designed annex features elegant rooms and site-specific art throughout.

Soho House Berlin €€€ This celeb-fave offers vintage-styled rooms in multiple sizes and access to members-only areas like the spa and rooftop pool.

Cologne
MAP p132

Hostel die Wohngemeinschaft € This next-gen hostel turned creative space has smartly designed rooms with themes from spaceship to Bollywood.

Hotel Chelsea €€ Originals created by international artists, in exchange for lodging, grace the public areas and 39 rooms, including the eye-catching deconstructivist top floor.

Wasserturm Hotel Cologne €€€ A-list sanctuary in a landmark water tower with quirky-luxe design, top gym and rooftop bar.

Düsseldorf
MAP p137

Max Hotel Garni € Modern self-check-in hotel near the Hauptbahnhof is a solid bargain base, with 11 snug but comfortable and quiet rooms.

Ruby Coco Hotel €€ 'Lean luxury' hotel with rooftop terrace, channeling Coco Chanel in rooms with glass-fronted shower cubicles.

Hotel Orangerie €€€ Stylish refuge in a neoclassical mansion in a quiet corner of the Altstadt within staggering distance of pubs, the river and museums.

Hamburg
MAP p140

Superbude St Georg € Design hotel-hostel combo with comfy beds, sleek private bathrooms and a 'rock star suite' – another location in St Georg near Central Station.

Henri Hotel €€ Kidney-shaped tables, plush armchairs, vintage typewriters – 1950s chic à la Don Draper. Rooms and studios for urban lifestyle junkies.

Westin Hamburg €€€ Hamburg's premier address, inside the lower half of the Elbphilharmonie. Rooms are stylish and minimalist. Splurge on an upper-floor room with city or harbour views.

Munich
MAP p146

Flushing Meadows €€ Up-to-the-minute minimalist design on the top two floors of an industrial building in the hip Glockenbachviertel. There are views, designer styling and a restaurant to enjoy.

Gästehaus Englischer Garten €€ Occupying a 200-year-old ivy-clad mill, this small guesthouse on the edge of the English Garden offers an intimate, pre-millennium experience in individually done-out, antique-speckled rooms.

Das Kleine Hotel in München €€ There's a dearth of accommodation in Maxvorstadt, so this 'little hotel in Munich' with its parquet floors, slightly dated fabrics and art sprinkled throughout is a well-used but welcome place to unpack.

Bayerischer Hof €€€ In a super-central location since 1841, this is one of the grandes dames of the Munich hotel world. Elegant rooms, impeccably regimented staff, antique-dotted public spaces and five fabulous restaurants.

Garmisch-Partenkirchen

Reindl's Partenkirchner Hof €€ Five-star everything here includes wine bar, gourmet restaurant and folk-themed rooms.

Gasthof zum Rassen €€
Behind a 14th-century frescoed facade, this guesthouse has modern rooms, antique public areas and Bavaria's oldest folk theatre.

Rothenburg ob der Tauber

Hotel Herrnschlösschen €€€
Occupying a 900-year-old Rothenburg mansion, this top-class hotel is a blend of ancient and new, Gothic and faux-retro.

Altfränkische Weinstube €€€
This 650-year-old Rothenburg inn has heaps of medieval character and an excellent restaurant.

Würzburg

Hotel Zum Winzermännle €€
Family-run converted winery in the heart of Würzburg with old-fashioned rooms, some with balconies.

Hotel Rebstock €€€
Würzburg's best hotel inhabits a renovated rococo town house, with great facilities, service and Altstadt location.

Bremen

MAP p161

Prizeotel Bremen City €
Good-value hotel, with large rooms in fluorescent colours and soundproofed windows close to the station. Prices vary, but it's great value during quiet times.

Nena Hotel Bremen €€€
Design hotel on the river in the centre, with indoor pool and wellness area.

Dresden

Hostel Mondpalast € Each playful room is designed to reflect a sign of the zodiac in this out-of-this-world hostel-bar-cafe in Neustadt.

Hotel am Terrassenufer €€
This brutalist GDR-era block looming over Altstadt features large rooms with panoramic views of the river.

Gewandhaus Hotel €€€ In Altstadt, the 18th-century trading house has sleek public areas plus beautiful and bright rooms.

Leipzig

Hostel Five Elements € Super-central and well-equipped hostel featuring dorms, cheap private rooms, comfy common spaces and cooking facilities.

Gwuni Mopera €€ No-nonsense rooms and an on-site restaurant-bar in a quiet courtyard across the ring road from Altstadt.

Townhouse €€€ Boutique gem with sound-sculpture lamps, Bach manuscript wallpaper and views of the Thomaskirche.

Weimar

Labyrinth Hostel € Artist-designed rooms in an extremely friendly and well-run hostel, close to the Weimarhallen Park.

Hotel Alt Weimar €€ Good-value rooms in the former home of 19th-century occultist, archivist and architect Rudolf Steiner.

Frankfurt am Main

MAP p170

25hours Goldman € Artfully decorated rooms in the east end, a 10-minute tram ride from Römer. Score the best deals and early check-in by booking directly. Paid parking.

Ruby Louise Hotel €€ Find a super-trendy vibe at this designer hotel featuring a rooftop terrace and reception on level 6.

Steigenberger Frankfurter Hof €€€ Luxurious rooms, full spa, bar and restaurant with outdoor dining. Perfect location-wise for exploring the city.

HELGA KING/SHUTTERSTOCK

Bayerischer Hof, Munich

Practicalities

HEALTH

Health care in Germany is of a high standard. German *Drogerien* (chemists) do not sell any kind of medication, not even aspirin. Even *rezeptfrei* (over-the-counter) medications for minor health concerns are only available at an *Apotheke* (pharmacy), so bring what you need along with you. Tap water is drinkable.

BALKANSCAT/SHUTTERSTOCK

ELECTRICITY

Germany's electricity supply is 230V, and plugs are of the European two-round-pin type (Type C and Type F). Most sockets accept both. Three-pin sockets are not used, so you'll only need standard European adapters.

PRIVACY

Photographing individuals in public places is not allowed in Germany unless you check with the person first. This is taken very seriously. Do not take photos of children. Many nightlife establishments ban photography completely.

SMOKING

Smoking is legislated differently in every state. Some bars, pubs and cafes allow smoking. Bavaria bans it practically everywhere, while in Berlin and Hamburg smoker-friendly bars abound. Look for a sign out front reading *Raucherkneipe* (smoking bar) to indicate such establishments.

DAYS OF CLOSURE

On Sundays, Germany observes *Ruhetag* (day of rest) when supermarkets, malls and individual retailers are closed. Don't expect to get any shopping done on these days. Some supermarkets are open in major train stations – these are helpful in a pinch, though expect long queues. Museums and restaurants stay open on Sundays but they might close on a Monday and/or Tuesday (check ahead).

OPENING HOURS

Opening hours vary seasonally and between cities and villages.
Banks 9am–4pm weekdays
Bars 8pm–2am
Cafes 10am–6pm
Restaurants 11am–10pm (food until 9pm)
Shops 10am–6pm Monday to Saturday
Supermarkets 8am–8pm Monday to Saturday (earlier in rural areas)

PUBLIC HOLIDAYS

Germany observes 11 national public holidays. Additional holidays vary between states.
New Year's Day 1 January
Easter March/April; Good Friday, Easter Sunday and Easter Monday
Ascension Day 40 days after Easter
Labour Day 1 May
Whit/Pentecost Sunday and Monday 50 days after Easter
Veteran's Day 15 June
German Unity Day 3 October
Christmas Day 25 December
Boxing Day 26 December

Language

German belongs to the West Germanic language family, with English and Dutch as close relatives.

Basics

Hello. Servus. *ser*-vus
Hello. Grüss Gott. grewss-got
Good morning. Guten Morgen. goo-ten *mor*-gen
Goodbye. Auf Wiedersehen. owf *vee*-der-zay-en
Bye. Tschüss./ Tschau. chüs/chow
Yes. Ja. yah
No. Nein. nain
Please. Bitte. *bi*-te
Thank you. Danke. *dang*-ke
Excuse me. Entschuldigung. ent-*shul*-di-gung
Sorry. Entschuldigung. ent-*shul*-di-gung

What's your name?
Wie ist Ihr Name? (pol) vee ist eer *nah*-me
Wie heißt du? (inf) *vee* haist doo

My name is ...
Mein Name ist ... (pol) main *nah*-me ist ...
Ich heiße ... (inf) ikh *hai*-se ...

Do you speak English?
Sprechen Sie Englisch? (pol) *shpre*-khen zee *eng*-lish
Sprichst du Englisch? (inf) shprikhst doo *eng*-lish

I don't understand. Ich verstehe nicht. ikh fer-*shtay*-e nikht

Directions

Where's (the station)?
Wo ist (der Bahnhof). vor ist (der *bahn*-hawf)

What's the address?
Wie ist die Adresse? vee ist dee a-*dre*-se

Could you please write it down?
Könnten Sie das bitte aufschreiben? *kern*-ten zee das *bi*-te owf-shrai-ben

Can you show me (on the map)?
Können Sie es mir (auf der Karte) zeige *ker*-nen zee es meer (owf dair *kar*-te) *tsai*-gen

Signs

Ausgang Exit
Eingang Entrance
Damen Women
Herren Men
Heiß Hot
Kalt Cold
Offen Open
Geschlossen Closed
Kein Zutritt No Entry
Rauchen Verboten No Smoking
Verboten Prohibited

Time

What time is it? Wie spät ist es? vee shpayt ist es
It's (10) o'clock. Es ist (zehn) Uhr. es ist (tsayn) oor
morning Morgen *mor*-gen
afternoon Nachmittag *nahkh*-mi-tahk
evening Abend *ah*-bent
yesterday Gestern *ges*-tern
today Heute *hoy*-te
tomorrow Morgen *mor*-gen

Emergencies

Help! Hilfe! *hil*-fe
Go away! Gehen Sie weg! *gay*-en zee vek
I'm ill. Ich bin krank. ikh bin krangk
Call the police! Rufen Sie die Polizei! *roo*-fen zee dee po-li-*tsai*
Call a doctor! Rufen Sie einen Arzt! *roo*-fen zee *ai*-nen artst

NUMBERS	
1	eins *ains*
2	zwei *tsvai*
3	drei *drai*
4	vier *feer*
5	fünf *fünf*
6	sechs *zeks*
7	sieben *zee*-ben
8	acht *akht*
9	neun *noyn*
10	zehn *tsayn*

NIKADA/GETTY IMAGES

Frankfurt International Airport

Arriving

Most travellers arrive in Germany by air or by rail and road from neighbouring countries. Frankfurt International is Germany's busiest airport (and one of Europe's largest), servicing some 300 destinations; it's the headquarters for Germany's flag carrier, Lufthansa. Non-EU visitors will probably enter into Europe and go through customs here, even if their final stop is elsewhere.

By Air

Most large and many smaller German cities have their own airports, and numerous carriers operate domestic flights within Germany. However, unless you're flying from one end of the country to the other, planes are only marginally quicker than trains.

By Rail

Rail services link Germany with virtually every country in Europe. **Deutsche Bahn** *(bahn.de)* handles ticketing. In the EU's Schengen (free-movement zone) crossing borders is visa-less; there are no passport controls entering from the Netherlands, Belgium, Austria and Switzerland, among others.

MONEY

Currency: Euro (€)

CASH

Cash is king in Germany. Always carry some and plan to pay cash at places like cafes and pubs. Since the pandemic, e-payments are catching on, but setting aside smaller bills for tips and emergencies is always a good idea. Barkeepers and kiosks may gripe about big notes.

CREDIT CARDS

Plastic is essential for booking hotels and sometimes for reserving tables at high-end restaurants. In Berlin, a small yet rising number of coffee and nightlife joints only take electronic payments, too. Usually Visa and Mastercard are accepted (not American Express or Diners Club). Kiosks usually require a minimum purchase of €10.

TIPPING

Quality of service and setting dictate how Germans tip. Say either the amount you want to pay, or *'Stimmt so'* for no change.

Hotels €1 to €2 per bag/cleaning day.

Restaurants Most Germans will tip 5% to 10%.

Cafes and bars Simply round up to the nearest euro.

Getting Around

For speedsters on tight schedules, driving a car on the autobahn's limitless stretches will be deeply satisfying, but parking in cities is a pain. Germany's excellent train system makes for efficient travel too – it's stress-free, you can stretch your legs and mind your carbon footprint. Last-minute bookings can be expensive during busy periods (weekends and holidays).

WERNER SPREMBERG/SHUTTERSTOCK

Public Transport
Germany's cities and larger towns have efficient public transport systems. Bigger cities such as Berlin and Munich integrate buses, trams, U-Bahn (underground) trains and S-Bahn (suburban) trains in one network. Fares are determined by zones or time travelled (sometimes both).

Car
German roads are excellent and no tolls are charged on any public roads. The country's pride and joy is its 13,000km network of autobahns (motorways). Every 40km to 60km, you'll find elaborate service areas with 24-hour petrol stations, toilets and restaurants.

Ridesharing
In cities, car-share apps like **Miles Mobility** *(miles-mobility. com)* offer renting cars by short duration or distance. Check out long-distance carpooling (travel in someone's private car in exchange for some petrol money) via **BlaBlaCar** *(blablacar.com)* and **Mitfahrzentrale** *(mifaz.de)*.

DRIVING ESSENTIALS

Drive on the right

No general speed limits – usually 50km/h in urban areas, 80km/h on secondary roads, 130km/h recommended on motorways

0.05%

Blood alcohol limit is 0.05%

Train
Intercity Express (ICE) trains are high-speed sprinters, and Regional Express (RE) are slower but more affordable public trains. Some private operators offer significantly cheaper fares, though on slower, older (and less comfortable) trains. Reserving seats is always smart.

Ferry
Ferries connect Germany's two seas, and provide convenient transport in its lake- and river-filled interior. Frequent ferries connect popular North and Baltic Sea islands; short-distance ferries shuttle passengers and vehicles along the Rhine and Elbe River.

Curated by
Kata Fári

Hungary

STUNNING ARCHITECTURE AND THERMAL SPAS

Hungary is home to one of Europe's most stunning capitals, thermal waters galore and people whose language you'll probably never speak, but who you'll definitely want to meet.

Hungary might be small, but it packs quite a punch. The country is steeped in history and tradition, its bounty of Art Nouveau architecture is astonishing, its thermal waters are restorative and its cuisine is as delicious as it is hearty. Budapest lays claim to the crown of most stunning capital in Europe, but it's so much more than a pretty face. With parks brimming with activity, museums filled with treasures, pleasure boats on the Danube and Turkish-era thermal baths belching steam, the Hungarian capital is a delight both by day and night.

In a country as flat as a *palacsinta* (pancake), Northern Hungary is as hilly as it gets, with towns rich in culture, vineyards renowned the world over and villages that cherish their traditions. Northwest of Budapest, the Danube Bend is a region of low peaks and attractive river towns steeped in history and the cultures of those who settled here. Southwest is Central Europe's largest lake, Lake Balaton (aka the Hungarian Sea), the favourite summer destination of locals, where sailing, soaking and stand-up paddleboarding is a way of life.

To the south and east is Hungary's heartland, the Great Plain, an intoxicating cocktail of countryside imbued with moody romance, splendid architecture and national parks.

BUDAPEST SPAS

THE MAIN AREAS

BUDAPEST
Scenic beauty, high culture, hot nightlife. **p186**

DANUBE BEND
Historical river towns vie for visitors' attention. **p198**

LAKE BALATON
Warm days at Central Europe's largest lake. **p201**

THE GREAT PLAIN
Horse shows and charming countryside. **p201**

NORTHERN HUNGARY
Wine, baroque architecture, folklore and forests. **p202**

For places to stay in Hungary, see p204

MARAKO85/SHUTTERSTOCK

Above: Széchenyi Chain Bridge (p191), Budapest; Left: Lukács Baths (p186), Budapest

Find Your Way

Hungary has no domestic flights as the country is small enough to get around by train, bus or boat. The public transport system is reliable and the roads are good. A car is only needed for rural Hungary.

TRAINS & BUSES

MÁV (*mavcsoport.hu*) operates reliable services to Hungary's major towns. Volánbusz runs an extensive bus network. The **Hungary Pass** (18,900Ft) provides unlimited travel throughout Hungary (available via the BudapestGO and MÁV apps or BKK, MÁV and Volánbusz ticket offices).

BOAT

Mahart PassNave (*mahartpassnave.hu*) runs excursion boats and hydrofoils on the Danube River from Budapest to places like Szentendre, Visegrád and Esztergom from April to September. **Balaton Shipping Company** (*bahart.hu*) passenger ferries serve about 20 ports on Lake Balaton.

Danube Bend, p198
Flanked by attractive towns, the Danube makes its bend 50km north of Budapest, flowing west towards Western Trans-danubia.

Northern Hungary, p202
Comparatively hilly, with main attractions that can be found around Eger and, 130km to the east, Tokaj.

Budapest, p186
The Queen of the Danube awaits with astonishing architecture, healing thermal baths and an unforgettable nightlife scene.

Lake Balaton, p201
Hungary's largest body of water. The 235km shoreline is dotted with villages a few minutes' drive from one another.

SLOVAKIA
AUSTRIA
ROMANIA
SERBIA
CROATIA

Eisenstadt
Mosonmagyaróvár
Esztergom
Győr Tatabánya
Kisbér
Szombathely
Jánosháza
Székesfehérvár
Hévíz
Nagykanizsa
Kaposvár
Tamási
Szekszárd
Pécs
Baja
Osijek
Dunaföldvár
Dunaújváros
Veszprém
Balatonfüred
Tihany
Kunszentmárton
Kiskunfélegyháza
Kecskemét
Szolnok
Kiskunhalas
Bugac
Szeged
Békéscsaba
Oradea
Debrecen
Püspökladány
Berettyóújfalu
Nyíregyháza
Kisvárda
Rakamaz
Tokaj
Szerencs
Miskolc
Eger
Füzesabony
Polgár
Salgótarján
Pásztó
Gyömrő
Gödöllő
Visegrád
Szentendre

BUDAPEST
Parliament
Liberty Monument
Ethnographical Museum
Open-Air Ethnographical Museum
Beautiful Women
Valley of the Beautiful Women

Lake Tisza
Great Plain
Hortobágy National Park
Körös-Maros National Park
Kiskunság National Park
Bükk National Park
Duna-Ipoly National Park
Bükk National Park
Dráva River
Duna-Dráva National Park
Zselic Region
Balaton Uplands National Park
Ormánság Region
Őrség Region
Fertő-Hanság National Park

Lake Balaton
Danube River

Setu Mare
BRATISLAVA

0   100 km
0   50 miles

CLARI MASSIMILIANO/SHUTTERSTOCK

Royal Palace (p190), Budapest

Plan Your Time

Hungary holds so much to see and do that you could easily fill a fortnight, but if you have less time, follow your interests to create your own curated trip.

Pressed for Time

● If you only have a day or two, focus on beautiful Budapest and explore both sides. Head up to the historic Castle District on the **funicular** (p190) and take in the views from the **Royal Palace** (p190) and **Fisherman's Bastion** (p190). Spend the afternoon soaking at **Széchenyi** (p186) or **Gellért Baths** (p186); in the evening take a river cruise offered byone of the various boat companies downtown.

A Week-Long Stay

● A week is enough to balance culture, nature and relaxation. After exploring **Budapest** (p186), you can day-trip to the **Danube Bend** (p198) to see charming local towns. In summer, **Lake Balaton** (p201), Central Europe's largest lake, is a must for sailing, stand-up paddleboarding and soaking. In autumn, **Northern Hungary** (p202) is best for hikes and discovering Hungary's world-renowned wine culture.

SEASONAL HIGHLIGHTS

SPRING
From March to June, Hungary is in full bloom, and Easter traditions are in full swing in historic Hollókő.

SUMMER
Scorching summer begins with Tihany's **Lavender Festival** (p201) in late June. The perfect time to relax at scenic Lake Balaton.

AUTUMN
Hungary's forests turn a riot of red and brown; it's a great time for hiking and touring the wine regions, particularly Tokaj-Hegyalja.

WINTER
Winter may be mighty cold, but it's the perfect time to relax in thermal baths and enjoy marvellous Christmas markets.

Budapest

SCENIC BEAUTY | HISTORIC SPAS | NIGHTLIFE

GETTING AROUND

Budapest is easy to navigate. The Danube clearly defines west and east: Buda and Pest. The public transport system is safe, efficient and inexpensive, and taxis are reasonably priced. You can also get around by bicycle, electric scooter or on foot. The BudapestGO app for public transport in the city offers several key features, including ticket and pass purchases, real-time route planning, a map, timetables and service updates. The city's official bike-sharing scheme is with the green MOL Bubi bikes.

☑ TOP TIP

Public transport tickets not only have to be purchased but also validated. Digital tickets come with a QR code scanner that you can use on machines at stations or the side of buses and trams before boarding, and passes have a QR code for inspection.

Budapest is a dazzling gem of a city, but its beauty is not all God-given: humankind has also played a role in shaping its pretty face. The city is an architectural treasure trove, with enough baroque, neoclassical, eclectic and Art Nouveau buildings to satisfy everyone. Overall, Budapest has a fin-de-siècle feel, for it was in the late 19th century, during the capital's golden age, that much of what you see today was built.

With parks brimming with activity, museums filled with treasures, pleasure boats on the Danube and Turkish-era thermal baths belching steam, the Hungarian capital is a delight both by day and night. Stroll along the Duna korzó, Pest's riverside embankment walkway, or cross any of the Danube bridges, and you'll pass young couples embracing passionately. It's then that you'll feel the romance of a place that, despite all the attempts from both within and without to destroy it, has never died.

Soak Away Your Worries

Take the plunge in a thermal bath

Hardly anything feels more relaxing in Budapest than plunging into a thermal pool and soaking away your stress in muscle-melting mineral-rich waters. Taking the waters is a way of life here, and the country – especially its capital – is a paradise for those seeking relaxation, healing and a bit of quirky local culture. Budapest lies on a geological fault line separating the Buda Hills from the Great Plain, and some 40,000 cubic metres of warm, mineral-rich water spurt forth each day. Hence the sobriquet, the 'City of Spas' – find the perfect combination of relaxation and restoration at one of several bathhouses in town. The most notable are Gellért Baths (unfortunately closed for renovations until 2028), the most beautiful bathhouse of all; **Széchenyi Baths** (*szechenyibath.hu; 10,000-17,000Ft)*, Europe's largest spa complex in a wedding-cake-like building; **Lukács Baths** (*lukacsfurdo.hu; 3600-8300Ft)*, a more local, health-oriented

Széchenyi Baths

WINE WITH A VIEW

Every September, the Royal Palace becomes a magnificent backdrop for the **Budapest Wine Festival**, when wooden kiosks are set up side-by-side at this historic venue to serve the country's finest red, white and sparkling wines from various regions, as well as a plethora of foreign bottles. A wide range of gastronomic delights is also available – many are prepared especially for the occasion and pair perfectly with the wines on offer. Various events, wine-focused workshops and concerts also take place in the gorgeous setting. This is one of the most elegant wine festivals in the country, and a perfect place to get familiar with lesser known but highly praised wines from all over the country. Tasting is by the glass, but bottles are also available.

destination; **Rudas Baths** *(rudasfurdo.hu; 9800-15,800Ft),* an original Turkish baths with a contemporary touch and a rooftop hot tub; and **Veli Bej Baths** *(irgalmasrend.hu/site/velibej/home; 4500-6000Ft),* a traditional Turkish bath with a modern twist.

Walk Down Memory Lane

Explore the Castle District on foot

The World Heritage–listed Castle District is home to historic sights, charming cobblestone streets, fascinating museums and stunning viewpoints that set the stage for a journey back in time. With a majestic monument on practically every corner, it's unparalleled when it comes to sightseeing. There's hardly another neighbourhood in the city with so many heavyweight sights crammed into such a compact space: the Royal Palace (p190), Fisherman's Bastion (p190) and neo-Gothic Matthias Church (p190) are all steps away from one another. Wear comfortable shoes for the cobblestone streets.

EATING & DRINKING IN THE CASTLE DISTRICT: OUR PICKS

White Raven Skybar & Lounge: Atop the Hilton Budapest, the city's highest sky bar offers jaw-dropping views and delicious drinks and finger food. *noon-10pm* €€€

Royal Guard Restaurant & Cafe: With a facade adorned with intriguing statues and weaponry, the Royal Guard houses a lovely cafe-restaurant. *11.30am-9.30pm* €€

Savoyai Terasz: Delicious coffee and dazzling views right at the foot of the Royal Palace. Plenty of musical events in the warmer months. *10.30am-8pm* €€

4 perc és kávé: This bite-sized cafe is fully vegan, making java mostly from oat milk. *8.30am-6pm Mon-Fri, from 9am Sat & Sun* €

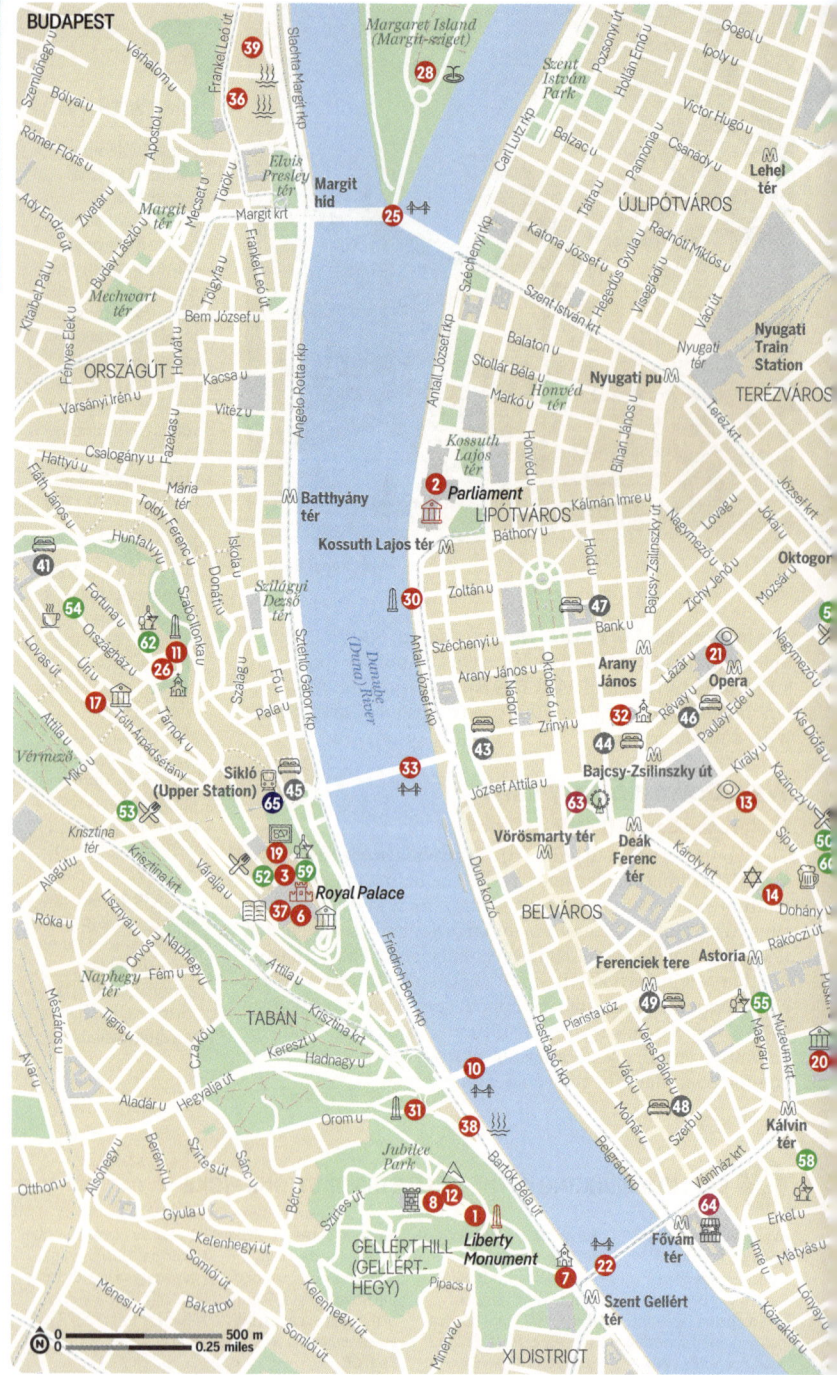

BUDAPEST

Margaret Island
(Margit-sziget)

Szent
István
Park

ÚJLIPÓTVÁROS

Lehel
tér

Elvis
Presley
tér

Margit
hid

Nyugati
Train
Station

ORSZÁGÚT

Nyugati
tér

Nyugati pu

TERÉZVÁROS

Kossuth
Lajos
tér

Batthyány
tér

Parliament

LIPÓTVÁROS

Oktogor

Kossuth Lajos tér

Arany
János

Opera

Bank u

Siklō
(Upper Station)

Danube
(Duna) River

Bajcsy-Zsilinszky út

Vörösmarty tér

Deák
Ferenc
tér

Royal Palace

BELVÁROS

Ferenciek tere   Astoria

TABÁN

Kálvin
tér

Naphegy
tér

Liberty
Monument

GELLÉRT HILL
(GELLÉRT-
HEGY)

Fővám
tér

Szent Gellért
tér

Jubilee
Park

0   500 m
0   0.25 miles

XI DISTRICT

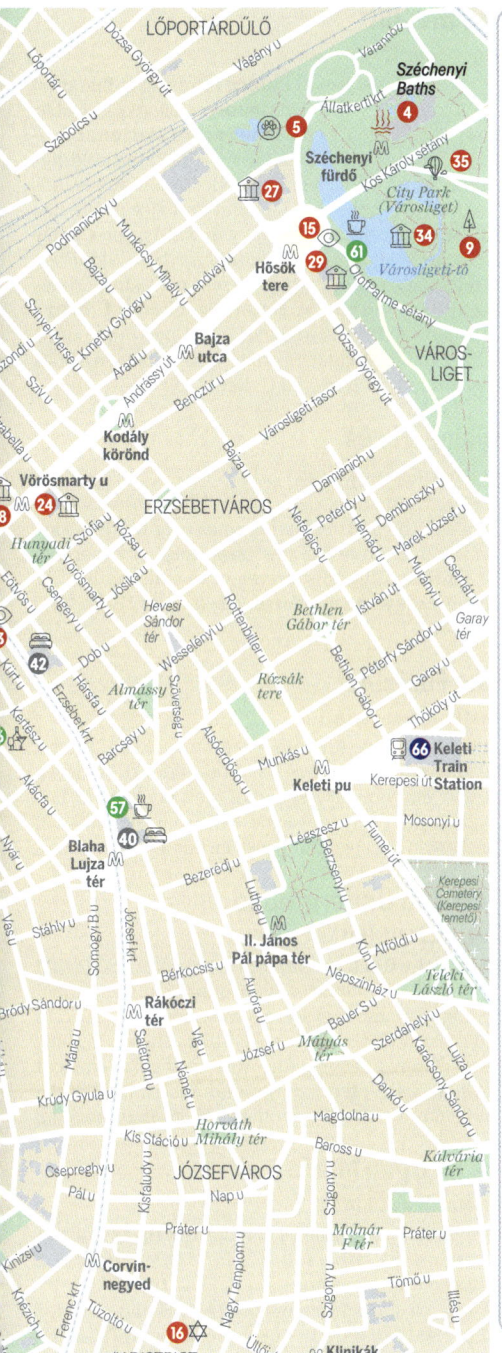

★ HIGHLIGHTS

1 Liberty Monument
2 Parliament
3 Royal Palace
4 Széchenyi Baths

● SIGHTS

5 Budapest Zoo
6 Castle Museum
7 Cave Church
8 Citadel
9 City Park
10 Elizabeth Bridge
11 Fisherman's Bastion
12 Gellért Hill
13 Gozsdu udvar
14 Great Synagogue
15 Heroes' Square
16 Holocaust Memorial Centre
17 Hospital in the Rock Nuclear Bunker Museum
18 House of Terror
19 Hungarian National Gallery
20 Hungarian National Museum
21 Hungarian State Opera House
22 Liberty Bridge
23 Liszt Ferenc Academy of Music
24 Liszt Ferenc Memorial Museum
25 Margaret Bridge
26 Matthias Church
27 Museum of Fine Arts
28 Musical Fountain
29 Palace of Art
30 Shoes on the Danube
31 St Gellért Monument
32 St Stephen's Basilica
33 Széchenyi Chain Bridge
34 Vajdahunyad Castle

● ACTIVITIES

35 BalloonFly

36 Lukács Baths
37 National Széchenyi Library
38 Rudas Baths
39 Veli Bej Baths

● SLEEPING

40 Anantara New York Palace Hotel
41 Baltazár
42 Corinthia Hotel Budapest
43 Four Seasons Gresham Palace Hotel
44 Hotel Central Basilica
45 Hotel Clark Budapest
46 Hotel Moments Budapest
47 Hotel President Budapest
48 Loft Hostel
49 Párisi Udvar Hotel

● EATING

50 Gettó Gulyás
51 Menza
52 Royal Guard Restaurant & Cafe
53 Stand25

● DRINKING & NIGHTLIFE

54 4 perc és kávé
55 Csendes Létterem
56 Instant-Fogas
57 New York Café
58 Púder Bárszínház
59 Savoyai Terasz
60 Szimpla Kert
61 Városliget Café
62 White Raven Skybar & Lounge

● ENTERTAINMENT

63 Ferris Wheel of Budapest

● SHOPPING

64 Nagycsarnok

● TRANSPORT

65 Funicular
66 Keleti (Eastern) Train Station

Castle on the Hill

Visit the enormous Royal Palace

Crowning Castle Hill, the **Royal Palace** towers over Budapest with a commanding presence. This immediately recognisable, emblematic attraction houses the **Hungarian National Gallery** *(mng.hu; entry adult/child 5400/2700Ft)* in buildings A to D, containing an overwhelming collection of thousands of artefacts presenting the development and rise of the fine arts in Hungary from the 11th century onwards; the **Castle Museum** *(varmuzeum.hu; entry adult/child 3800/1900Ft)* in building E tells the story of Budapest from prehistoric times to the present day; and the **National Széchenyi Library** *(oszk.hu; day pass 1200Ft)* is in building F. Don't miss out on the view from the Royal Palace's dome, accessible with your ticket to the Hungarian National Gallery.

Mesmerising Views

Marvel at Fisherman's Bastion

The bone-white, 140m-long neo-Gothic **Fisherman's Bastion** offers one of the prettiest panoramas over the Pest skyline. Its name comes from the medieval guild of fishermen responsible for defending this stretch of the old castle wall. Only the upstairs **viewing platform** *(adult/child 1500/750Ft)* requires a ticket.

Fun on the Funicular

Ascend Castle Hill in style

If you want to sneak some fun into reaching the Royal Palace, hop on the **funicular** *(adult/child 5000/2000Ft)*. Its steep 95m-long track, climbing at a speed of 1.5m per second, is a quick and convenient way up Castle Hill from the banks of the Danube, providing splendid views en route.

An Eerie World Underground

Venture below Castle Hill

The **Hospital in the Rock** *(sziklakorhaz.eu; entry adult/child 9500/4800Ft)* is a real underground hospital that was turned into a nuclear bunker and kept secret for decades – the government only declassified its existence in 2002. There are some 200 lifelike wax figures, original furniture, medical equipment and even a whole helicopter underground. Visit on one of the one-hour guided tours that depart hourly from 10am to 6pm.

Frescoes & Organ Music

Admire the Matthias Church

Perched high above Szentháromság tér, the **Matthias Church** *(matyas-templom.hu; entry adult/child 3100/2500Ft)* is a neo-Gothic confection. The interior features a beautiful combination of wooden statuary, colourful frescoes and gold-leaf detail. One of the best ways to enjoy the cathedral's interior is to attend one of the many classical concerts held here.

Fisherman's Bastion

All Aboard the Cutest Ride

Take a trip on the Children's Railway

One of the best ways to explore the Buda Hills, a favourite hiking spot of locals, is by riding the **Children's Railway** *(gyermekvasut.hu; entry adult/ child 1000/500Ft),* which is operated almost entirely by kids. The staff, aged 10 to 14 and dressed in smart uniforms, hold all the positions on the railway, from conductors to signallers, while a little adult supervision keeps things on track (the engineers, thankfully, are grown-ups). The Children's Railway operates year-round, giving you a different view of the Buda Hills each season.

An Island in the Middle of the City?

Walk around Margaret Island

Neither Buda nor Pest, Margaret Island (Margit-sziget) sits in the middle of the Danube. Just 2.5km long, it's not graced with many significant sights, but you can easily spend half a day exploring its swimming complexes, thermal spa, gardens and centuries-old ruins; on a hot summer afternoon, it makes for a lovely escape. The main attraction is the **Musical Fountain** that puts on a dramatic display five times a day, with jets 'dancing' to music and shooting up to 10m in the air. Catch the last show at 9pm, when the fountain is illuminated by hundreds of coloured lights.

Strenuous Climb for Splendid Views

Climb Gellért Hill

You can climb one of Budapest's most iconic landmarks, the 235m-high, tree-dotted **Gellért Hill**, surmounted by the **Citadel** and the **Liberty Monument**, a proud lady watching over Budapest with the symbol of peace, a palm branch, in her hands.

KNOW YOUR BRIDGES

While there are over a dozen bridges in Budapest, you'll spend most of your time photographing or crossing only a handful of them. One of the most striking and the star of many a photograph is the **Széchenyi Chain Bridge**, which was the first permanent bridge connecting Buda and Pest when it was inaugurated in 1849. The second was **Margaret Bridge**, which doglegs in the middle allowing it to stand at right angles to the Danube where it converges at the southern tip of Margaret Island. Sage-green **Liberty Bridge** is the locals' favourite, while slender and elegant gleaming-white **Elizabeth Bridge** connects the city centre with Gellért Hill. In WWII all of Budapest's bridges were blown up, though later rebuilt.

FRANK WAGNER/SHUTTERSTOCK

Parliament

From the top, the views of Buda, the Pest skyline and the gently curving Danube River are unbeatable. On the way, expect peaceful rest stops, a playground and slide park, and even the **Cave Church** *(sziklatemplom.hu; entry adult/child 1200/1000Ft)*, a functioning church set inside a cave – a real sight to behold.

Ghosts of Communism Past

Explore this huge open-air park

Memento Park *(mementopark.hu; entry adult/child 3000/1200Ft)* provides a sneak peek behind the Iron Curtain, guarding the gigantic statues of Lenin, Marx, Engels, homegrown heroes and other types of communist propaganda that were removed from the streets of Budapest after the fall of the Berlin Wall in 1989. You can opt for a guided tour or wander around on your own, but don't miss the park's top attraction, a pair of gigantic boots. It's a replica of the original 8m-high bronze statue of Stalin that was pulled down from its plinth on Dózsa György út in City Park during the 1956 Uprising and sawed apart until only the boots remained.

 EATING IN BUDAPEST: HUNGARIAN FOOD

Városliget Café: A long-standing restaurant serving tasty local fare, from traditional bean soup to schnitzel, along with lake views. *noon-10pm* €€

Menza: Retro-chic place with a modern take on Hungarian cuisine plus international favourites; try the red-wine beef stew. *11am-11pm* €€

Gettó Gulyás: The best place to try *pörkölt* (traditional beef stew) and *gulyás*, Hungary's favourite soup. *noon-11pm* €€

Stand25: Hungarian classics like goulash and *somlói* cake by Bocuse d'Or Europe winner Tamás Széll. *noon-4pm & 6pm-midnight Mon-Sat* €€

Hungary's Largest Building

Tour the Parliament

The **Parliament** (*parlament.hu; entry adult/child from 4500Ft*) stretches for 268m along the left bank of the Danube in Pest. It's a vast, stately building and repository of national treasures, a symbolic counterweight to the Royal Palace on Castle Hill across the river. The building is a blend of many architectural styles (neo-Romanesque, neo-baroque). You can take a 45-minute tour by audio guide of the North Wing; be sure to see one of the country's most important national symbols, the Holy Crown of Hungary.

History's Dark Side

A moving Holocaust memorial

On the Danube embankment south of the Parliament is a monument to Hungarian Jews shot and thrown into the river by members of the fascist Arrow Cross Party in 1944. Called **Shoes on the Danube**, it's a simple but poignant display of 60 pairs of old-style boots and shoes in cast iron along the riverbank.

The Country's Most Sacred Catholic Church

Visit the Basilica of St Stephen

The neoclassical cathedral, the largest in Budapest, is in the form of a Greek cross and can accommodate 8000 worshippers. The interior of **St Stephen's Basilica** glimmers in low-lit splendour, with Károly Lotz' golden mosaics on the inside of the dome seeming to produce a light all of their own. Its major drawcard is the Holy Dexter (or Holy Right), the mummified right hand of St Stephen, first king of Hungary, who was credited with establishing the Kingdom of Hungary and introducing Christianity as the state religion. The top of the dome, which offers fantastic views, can be reached on foot or via lifts. There are three ticket types: for the basilica, the treasury and the dome.

A Quick Spin

Short but sweet Ferris wheel flight

Dominating Erzsébet tér, the **Ferris Wheel of Budapest** (*oriaskerek.com; entry adult/child from 4300/2300Ft*) offers stunning panoramic views of Pest and across the Danube to Buda, and it's an easy way to get a view of the capital. Board after dark; the flight is particularly impressive at night.

A Night at the Opera

Music, laughter and a beautiful building

The neo-Renaissance **Hungarian State Opera House** (*opera.hu*) was completed in 1884 and is among the most beautiful buildings in Budapest. It's worth a visit as much to admire the incredibly rich decoration inside as to view a performance and hear the perfect acoustics. Tickets range from affordable to astronomical, but standing room costs next to nothing – or join one of the three one-hour daily **tours** (*9000Ft*) in English, which include a 10-minute performance at the end.

WHO WAS ST GELLÉRT?

A hill, a bath, a hotel, a city square and a metro station are all named after one man: St Gellért. But who was this guy? St Gellért was an Italian missionary who ended up in Hungary around 1020, after a storm disrupted his pilgrimage. King Stephen convinced him to stay, tutor his son and convert the masses to Christianity. After being named a bishop, he went on to live the life of a hermit. Unfortunately, legend has it that after the king died in 1038, the pagan Magyars hurled the bishop to his death in a spiked barrel. His **statue** now stands on the spot of his martyrdom, gazing peacefully down over the city.

Screaming young fans at concerts of their musical idols is nothing new under the sun. But would you have thought that this phenomenon started in the classical concert halls of 19th-century Europe? 'Lisztomania' was a term first coined by German poet and Franz Liszt's contemporary, Heinrich Heine. Biographer Oliver Hilmes wrote in his work *Franz Liszt: Musician, Celebrity, Superstar* that 'women tore at each other's hair in trying to lay hands on a glass or handkerchief that Liszt had used'. One of the greatest pianists that has ever lived was a true performer – he would toss his hair and sway over the keyboard, completely captivating his often hysterical audiences.

In the Footsteps of Franz Liszt
Music academy and museum

Opened in 1875, the **Liszt Ferenc Academy of Music** *(zeneakademia.hu)* is today housed in a newer Art Nouveau building built in 1907 and is both a university and Budapest's top classical-music venue. The renovated interior is worth visiting on a **guided tour** *(5300Ft)* if you're not attending a performance. The wonderful little **Liszt Ferenc Memorial Museum** *(lisztmuseum.hu; entry adult/child 3000/1500Ft)*, housed in the Old Music Academy, is where the great composer lived in a 1st-floor apartment for five years until his death in 1886. The rooms are filled with his instruments, furniture, books, portraits and personal effects.

The Continent's First Metro
Take a ride on the historic underground

One of Budapest's four metro lines, the **Millennium Underground Railway** is by far the oldest. Indeed, it was the first underground railway to open in continental Europe, preceding the Paris metro by 14 years. Today it runs for 4.4km below Andrássy út, serving 11 stations; to change direction, you must exit and cross the street.

Descend into Darkness
See the House of Terror

The **House of Terror** *(terrorhaza.hu; entry adult/child 4000-2000Ft)* is a moving museum focusing on the atrocities of Hungary's fascist and Stalinist regimes and commemorates their victims. It's set up in the former headquarters of both the Arrow Cross Party (Hungarian Nazis), and, later, the Communist Secret Police, used for interrogating and torturing 'enemies of the state'. The walls were allegedly extra thick to muffle the screams.

A Trip Back to the Belle Époque
The most beautiful cafe in the world

An ever-present queue outside the **New York Café** *(newyorkcafe. hu)*, once voted the most beautiful coffee house in the world, will certainly catch your eye in Erzsébetváros. Inside, you can immerse yourself in authentic 19th-century coffee-house culture amid gilded and marble surfaces, etched glass and frescoes, and live Hungarian music. During Hungary's belle époque, renowned writers were often seen putting pen to paper here.

Europe's Largest Synagogue
Explore the Great Synagogue

With its crenellated red-and-yellow glazed-brick facade and two enormous Moorish-style towers, Budapest's stunning **Great Synagogue** *(jewishtourhungary.com; entry adult/ child 13,000/10,500Ft)*, also called the 'Dohány utca Synagogue', is the largest Jewish house of worship in Europe, seating 3000 people. Visit for its majestic architecture, the Hungarian Jewish Museum and Archives, and the Holocaust Tree of

Gozsdu udvar

THE SPIRITS OF HUNGARY

Hungary's two most famous spirits are *pálinka* and Unicum. *Pálinka* is distilled from a variety of fruits and is akin to a strong brandy or eau de vie. It kicks like a mule and is served in most bars, some of which carry an enormous range – and almost all Hungarian households have suspicious mineral water bottles filled with homemade *pálinka*. Unicum's medicinal-looking bottle is instantly recognisable. The bitter aperitif has been around since 1790 – prepared according to a secret formula and aged in oak casks, it's available in four different tastes. The liqueur was apparently baptised by Austro-Hungarian Emperor Joseph II; when tasting it for the first time, he exclaimed, *'Das ist ein Unikum!'* (This is unique!).

Life Memorial. Admission includes an informative 45-minute tour in eight languages – tours start every 30 to 60 minutes.

Let the Party Begin

One long courtyard, lots of fun

Erzsébetváros has Budapest's most exciting nightlife, and **Gozsdu udvar** is its heart. It's a continuous 'courtyard' running a few hundred metres between Király utca 13 and Dob utca 16. A residential complex of seven blocks and six interconnecting courtyards when it was built in 1901, and part of the Jewish Ghetto during WWII, it's now lined with bars, clubs, cafes and restaurants, and pulses with music from dusk to dawn.

Harrowing History

Reminisce at the Holocaust Memorial Centre

The **Holocaust Memorial Centre** *(hdke.hu; entry adult/child 3600/1600Ft)* is the only public collection in the country that deals exclusively with the history of the Holocaust. Housed in a striking modern building that opened in 2002, the thematic permanent exhibition traces the rise of anti-Semitism in Hungary and follows the path to the genocide of the country's Jewish and Roma communities. A sublimely restored synagogue in the central courtyard, designed by Leopold Baumhorn and completed in 1924, hosts temporary exhibitions on the mezzanine level.

Romkocsma Is Where It's At

Boozing at ruin bars

Throwing back drinks at a ruin bar *(romkocsma)* filled with the most random knick-knacks is a real Budapest experience. The granddaddy of them all is **Szimpla Kert** *(szimpla.hu)*

HUNGARIKUMS

The culinary heritage of Károly Gundel (founder of City Park's famed Gundel Restaurant) is a Hungaricum, alongside many other wonderful things such as *lángos* (deep-fried dough with toppings), *pálinka* (fruit brandy), Herend porcelain, *teqball* and PICK salami. But what is a Hungarikum? The term refers to a collection of unique, culturally significant and nationally recognised products, practices or values from Hungary that embody the essence of the country's heritage. These can include food and beverages, agricultural practices, folk art, traditions, inventions and even natural phenomena. Being recognised as a Hungarikum is a mark of prestige and a point of national pride, signifying the importance of these products or practices to Hungarian identity and heritage.

Nagycsarnok

in Erzsébetváros, and some say it's still the best. **Instant-Fogas** *(instant-fogas.com)* is where two ruin bars merged to form the biggest in town. The quirkiest one is **Csendes Létterem** *(facebook.com/csendesvintagebar)* in Belváros and a slightly more upscale one is **Púder Bárszínház** *(puderbar.hu)* in Southern Pest.

The History of Hungary

Visit the Hungarian National Museum

The **Hungarian National Museum** *(mnm.hu; entry adult/ child 3500/1750Ft)* houses the nation's most important collection of historical relics. It traces the history of the Carpathian Basin from the Stone Age and that of the Magyar people and Hungary from the 9th-century conquest to the fall of communism. If you visit just one museum in Budapest, make it this treasure trove.

The Biggest Deal in Town

Shop and eat at Nagycsarnok

Nagycsarnok *(piaconline.hu)* or the 'Great Market Hall', opened in 1897 and is the city's biggest market. Gourmets will appreciate the variety of treats available here for less than you'd pay in the shops on nearby Váci utca. Head up to the 1st floor for Hungarian folk costumes, dolls, painted eggs, embroidered tablecloths, leather goods, carved hunting knives and other souvenirs, as well as cooked foods like *kolbász* (sausage), *pörkölt* (stew) and *lángos* (deep-fried dough with toppings).

Diamonds & Rust on Sale

Flea-market finds

One of the biggest flea markets in Central Europe, **Ecseri Piac** *(piaconline.hu)* sells everything from antique jewellery and Soviet army watches to top hats (and a fair amount of stolen antique goods too, it's said). Early Saturday is the best time to go for treasures. To get here, take bus 54 from Pest's Boráros tér, or for a quicker journey, express bus 84E, 89E or 94E from the Határ út stop on the M3 metro line.

A Park with Pizzazz

Spend an afternoon in City Park

Serene **City Park** (Városliget) is the Pest side's green lung and Budapest's favourite recreational space. But don't just think plentiful picnic spots and groomed gardens; City Park is home to major landmarks such as the world-renowned Széchenyi Baths (p186); the city's most famous plaza, Heroes' Square; the faux-historic but fairytale **Vajdahunyad Castle**; the enormous **Budapest Zoo and Botanical Garden**; a lovely lake (and ice-skating rink in winter), and a handful of outstanding museums. And all of this within just 15 minutes of the city centre.

Meet Hungary's Heroes

Awe at Heroes' Square

This picture-perfect plaza concluding tree-lined Andrássy út is Budapest's largest and most symbolic square, serving as an elegant gateway to City Park. Framed by monumental statues narrating the tale of Hungary's formation and resilience and flanked by two major museums, the **Museum of Fine Arts** and the **Palace of Art** (Kunsthalle), **Heroes' Square** offers a blend of culture, striking architecture and history. It's especially majestic at night.

Take Flight in a Hot-Air Balloon

Have a go at BalloonFly

If you observe Budapest's cityscape, you'll likely spot a hot-air balloon adding a dash of red and white to the Pest skyline. This is **BalloonFly** *(balloonfly.hu; entry adult/child 10,000/5000Ft),* which takes visitors for a flight up to 150m above City Park, providing a stunning bird's-eye view, with landmarks like Széchenyi Baths, Vajdahunyad Castle and Heroes' Square en route.

WHY I LOVE BUDAPEST

Kata Fári, Lonely Planet writer
You know that sudden gush of love you get when you look at somebody you've known forever but for a split second realise again just how beautiful they are? For me, this happens every time I cross a bridge in Budapest. My love story with the city has seen splashes at stunning spas, nights lost at random ruin bars, hikes through the Buda Hills, laps around Margaret Island, books read at century-old coffee houses, romantic boat trips on the Danube, and daily dog walks in a park centred by a castle. I love Budapest because it's elegant, historic, romantic, bohemian and random all at once, and even though I know it like the back of my hand, it still manages to surprise me time and again.

Beyond Budapest

WINE | LAKES | THE DANUBE

Places

Danube Bend p198
Lake Balaton p201
The Great Plain p201
Northern Hungary p202

☑ TOP TIP

The best time to visit Hungary is during the shoulder seasons of spring (March–May) and autumn (September–November), which have pleasant weather and generally fewer crowds. Lake Balaton is at its best but busiest in summer, while the country is a winter wonderland during the Christmas holidays.

Though Budapest is a superstar city and the main reason why most travellers visit Hungary, the country has much more to offer, from vineyards to tranquil countryside. Central Europe's largest lake, Lake Balaton, is the favourite summer destination of locals, where beaching and boating is a way of life. The wine regions in Northern Hungary grow grape varieties you may have never heard of but will end up gushing about. The Danube Bend's romantic towns are perfect for a quick spring getaway, while in the colder months, the hiking trails and the Great Plain's rural romance are ready to steal your heart.

Danube Bend

TIME FROM BUDAPEST: **1HR**

The Danube Bend is lined with romantic riverside towns that vie for visitors' attention. Travelling upriver from Budapest, the Danube draws you deeper into its spell as you leave the day-trippers behind in the arts-focused town of Szentendre (St Andrew), round the eponymous bend and pass the impressive citadel of Visegrád. Beyond that, the Danube swirls past Esztergom, which, like Visegrád, was once a royal seat of sorts but in contrast, Esztergom is a religious centre dominated by a vast hilltop basilica, which is Hungary's largest church. Due to its close proximity and easy accessibility, the Danube Bend makes a perfect getaway from Budapest.

Szentendre's open-air ethnographical museum

Situated 5km from **Szentendre** (take bus 878), this **ethnographical museum** *(skanzen.hu; entry adult/child 4000/2000Ft)* is an unusual plunge into a fascinating 'alternative village reality'. As you wander or ride on a hire bike through the grounds, you'll find yourself transported into a picturesque setting of immaculately reconstructed Hungarian rural architecture and

---

GETTING AROUND

Travelling around the country is easy and affordable, and Hungary is also a manageable size, with most inland journeys from Budapest only taking a couple of hours. Trains take you most places, while buses take care of the rest.

Sailing up the Danube Bend or cycling are fun alternatives. Driving is only necessary if you're planning to see the country's remote corners. For those travelling extensively, the Hungary Pass provides unlimited public transport.

AUSTRIA

VIENNA

Eisenstadt

BRATISLAVA

SLOVAKIA

Mosonmagyaróvár

Győr

Tatabánya

Esztergom

Szombathely

Zalaegerszeg

Őrség National Park

Hévíz

Nagykanizsa

Kaposvár

Balatonfüred

Balaton Uplands National Park

Tihany

Lake Balaton

Veszprém

Székesfehérvár

Érd

BUDAPEST

Gödöllő

Gyömrő

Szentendre

Visegrád

Hollókő

Pilis Park Forest

Salgótarján

Eger

Bükk National Park

Miskolc

Mezőkövesd

Lake Tisza

Tokaj

Nyíregyháza

Hajdúnánás

Debrecen

Hajdúböszörmény

Berettyóújfalu

Great Plain

Szolnok

Cegléd

Nagykőrös

Kecskemét

Kiskunfélegyháza

Bugacpuszta

Dunaújváros

Szekszárd

Pécs

Baja

Szeged

Hódmezővásárhely

ROMANIA

CROATIA

Mosonmagyaróvár

50 miles

100 km

199

Esztergom Basilica

PERFECTION IS SHALLOW

What makes Lake Balaton so beloved for outdoor recreation? According to the Balaton Limnological Research Institute, the shallowness and high water quality create possibilities for so many activities.

Central Europe's largest freshwater body (594 sq km) is incredibly shallow, with an average depth of about 3m. This promises delightful summer temperatures since waters don't take long to warm up; it also creates calm tides for enjoying water sports and plentiful recreation.

Shallowness does, however, make Lake Balaton sensitive to environmental disturbances, especially heat waves and algae blooms. That's why local conservation efforts are so important – particularly in recent years, with increasingly unpredictable conditions due to climate change.

villages and lured into a sense of actually being there. As you move through the different sections, you encounter hired extras in costume going about village life: artisans, craftspeople and peasants sitting on church steps, picking flowers or simply acting in character. A highlight is crossing the remote border post into 'Romania' and reaching a reconstructed town square in Transylvania with a pharmacy, working cafe and more. The museum is open from April to October.

Visegrád's magnificent hilltop castle

In **Visegrád**, it's an invigorating hike to the **Citadel** (wear decent shoes), and once you reach the top you'll have some of the region's finest views over the Danube. The exhibits inside the citadel are unlikely to knock your sweaty socks off, but they include a bit of armoury and a large waxwork of the Congress of Visegrád in 1335. Enjoy the view and the walk around the walls, and feel the wind whistling around you from the crown of this 330m hilltop. A spectacular 180-degree panorama opens up over the Danube and the hills beyond. The scene becomes a 360-degree view as you walk along the walls.

See Hungary's largest church

Perched on top of Castle Hill, **Esztergom Basilica** is Hungary's largest church and is famous for its distinctive 72m-high central dome (100m from the crypt to the top), making this basilica visible in all its monumental glory for kilometres around. By far the most strenuous but attractive approach to Castle Hill is via the so-called Cat's Stairs (Macskalépcső). These well-hidden and unmarked stone steps off Berényi Zsigmond utca zigzag relentlessly to the top of the hill. Benches to rest on become more plentiful the higher you climb, with a spectacular view over the Danube River making the effort worthwhile. Entry to the basilica is through a side door. While the church itself is free, there are admission fees for the treasury, the crypt and to climb the dome.

Lake Balaton

TIME FROM BUDAPEST: 2½HR

Historical wonders, impressive food and wine, and an unparalleled spa scene: Lake Balaton is where Hungarians relish
the good life. During the dog days, resorts and guesthouses are packed with holidaymakers beaching and boating in
opaque, turquoise-hued waters. Beyond the postcard-perfect
marinas and famously shallow swimming waters, Central
Europe's biggest lake has a wealth of attractions that may be
surprising – Balaton is equal parts quaint and chic. Thermal
spas, wellness centres and campsites reel visitors in, but it's
Balaton's hearty 'everything stew' of outdoorsy experiences
that makes the destination highly memorable: sipping wines
overlooking handsome vineyards, cycling adventures passing
dreamy coasts and lavender fields, and tiny towns packed
with historical treasures.

Catch lavender fever in Tihany

No visit to Lake Balaton is complete without seeing **Tihany**.
The town's famous lavender fields traditionally blossom from
mid-June to early July. During this time, aromatic purple fields
explode around the peninsula and coincide with activities and
events for the annual **Lavender Festival** *(welovebalaton.hu)*.
Lavender picking is only allowed in public areas, for example
on the so-called **Lavender Trail**.

Swimming and shoreside fun in Balatonfüred

There's no better spot to wade into Lake Balaton's famously
comfortable waters than from the two main beaches at **Balatonfüred**, **Esterházy Strand** *(balatonfuredistrandok.
hu)* and **Kisfaludy Strand**. Unfolding along the row of bars
and restaurants of the **Tagore Sétány** (the lake-hugging
promenade), both beaches (walking from the marina, Esterházy comes first, followed by Kisfaludy) are known for
their lively atmosphere. Lots of water activities are on offer
at both, from paddleboating to SUP rentals, as well as shady
spots for relaxing between dips and good toilet and changing facilities.

Soak in miracle waters in Hévíz

Just under 9km from Keszthely at the western tip of Lake
Balaton, the village of **Hévíz** lays claim to the world's largest swimmable thermal lake, which is fed by 80 million L of
thermal water daily. **Hévízi-tó** *(heviz.hu/en/lake-heviz)* is
an incredible sight. The temperature averages 33°C and never
drops below 22°C, even in winter, allowing you to bathe when
the surrounding fir trees have turned icy.

The Great Plain

TIME FROM BUDAPEST: 2HR

What the Outback is for Australians or the Wild West for
Americans, the Great Plain is for Hungarians. The Hortobágy region is the home of Hungarian cowboys and amazing horse shows, while Kecskemét and Szeged are cities to
explore for culture, architecture and that charming countryside feel.

VISEGRÁD GROUP

The centrepiece
of the citadel is
a waxwork that
graphically depicts
how the Visegrád
Group began. The
year was 1335
and the kings of
Bohemia, Hungary
and Poland came
together in Visegrád
to make deals, form
an anti-Habsburg
alliance, resolve
disputes and eat well,
judging by this waxy
portrayal. This was
the first diplomatic
cooperation between
the so-called
'Visegrád countries'.
In 1991, the Visegrád
Group was formed
between Hungary,
Czechoslovakia and
Poland to promote
cooperation and
mutual interests. It
later became the
Visegrád 4 when
Slovakia became
an independent
country. Friction
over approaches to
the war in Ukraine
have tested the glue
holding the group
together, but so far
their shared interests
have prevailed over
their differences.

Paintings, peacocks and majolica in Kecskemét

Lying halfway between the Danube and Tisza Rivers in the southern Great Plain, **Kecskemét** boasts some of the finest architecture of any small city in Hungary. Along with colourful Art Nouveau and Secessionist buildings, its museums and the region's excellent *barackpálinka* (apricot brandy) are major draws as well. An Art Nouveau masterpiece, **Cifrapalota** *(kkjm.hu; entry adult/child 1800/900Ft)* was built in 1902–03 by Géza Márkus. The grand townhouse is a visual feast with a whimsical majolica facade, a grand hall flaunting peacock motifs and a courtyard with fairytale flair. Exhibits inside include 19th- and early-20th-century Hungarian art as well as artefacts from Avar graves – mystical remnants from 6th-century Central Asian warriors.

Horse tricks and sand steppes

About 35km south of Kecskemét, **Bugacpuszta** *(bugacpuszta. hu)* is the easiest gateway to the rambling and disjointed Kiskunság National Park. Steer straight to the **Karikás Csárda**, a traditional inn, to buy tickets to the park and the popular Horse Show offered on Wednesdays, Fridays, Saturdays and Sundays between May and September. During this tightly choreographed 40-minute spectacle, horse herders crack their bullwhips and ride five horses at full tilt while standing on the rear two.

Flowers, leaves and waves in Szeged

The cultural capital of the Great Plain and Hungary's third-largest city, **Szeged** is an embracing town that's easy to love. A romantic symphony of lily-and-ivy motifs dancing across an undulating facade that juts out like a ship's bow, **Reök Palace** (1907) is an architectural showstopper and the crown jewel of Szeged's rich Art Nouveau scene. Step inside and you'll be just as wowed by the interior, especially the frilly wrought-iron staircase. Afterwards, pop into the street-level cafe **Reök Kézműves Cukrászda** for artisanal French pastries crafted by a two-time national cake champion.

Northern Hungary

TIME FROM BUDAPEST: 3HR

Northern Hungary is as hilly as the country gets. Hike on forested trails amid lovely rolling hills and scout castle ruins. Towns rich in culture, world-famous vineyards and villages that cherish their traditions make Northern Hungary an excellent place to connect with the country's spirit and history.

Eger's valley of the wine cellars

Cradled by vineyards and brimming with ornate baroque buildings, **Eger** (pronounced 'egg-air') is a jewellery box of a town with loads to see and do. A wine lover's fantasy come true, the famed **Valley of the Beautiful Women** *(Szépasszony-völgy; szepasszonyvolgy.info),* about 2km southeast of Eger's city centre, is home to several dozen wine cellars that welcome visitors who'd like to sample local vintages. Most open from 10am or noon to 6pm, until 8pm or later June to September,

Hollókő Castle

and some close on Mondays. Carved into volcanic rock, they're arrayed along a horseshoe-shaped road with a park in the middle, with a row of restaurants on the side.

Quick trip to centuries past

Long the home of the minority Palóc people, **Hollókő** *(holloko.hu)* is famous for the folk architecture of its **Old Village** (Ófalu), a UNESCO World Heritage Site since 1987. Unchanged for well over a century, its whitewashed wattle-and-daub houses – with carved balconies and overhanging porch roofs, bedecked with flowers in summer – are arrayed along a single main street, Kossuth utca. Although geared towards tourists (almost all domestic), Hollókő still manages to feel like a living, breathing village. The Old Village can be visited year-round but not much is open from November to March. Many visitors begin by walking from the tourist office through the woods to the hilltop **Hollókő Castle** *(Hollókői Vár; 3000Ft),* a distance of 1km. Built in the 13th century, the imposing stone structure looks like the setting for a fairy tale.

Taste Tokaj's liquid gold

At the confluence of the Bodrog and Tisza Rivers, the town of **Tokaj** is the commercial and touristic hub of the 27-village Tokaj-Hegyalja wine region. To sample the Tokaj region's extraordinary wines, head to a wine cellar *(pince),* cafe or restaurant that offers wine by the glass – they're dotted around the town centre.

THE BETYÁRS: BANDITS OF THE PUSZTA

The Great Plain highwaymen were infamous outlaws who ruled the vast, wild spaces of the *puszta* (Great Plain) in the 19th century. Many were landless farmers, seasonal workers, former soldiers or unemployed herders who turned to ambushing travellers and horse carriages to make ends meet. Operating in small, tight-knit gangs, these bandits struck fear into the hearts of travellers and traders passing through the unpatrolled, remote areas. Their daring heists and narrow escapes became the stuff of legend, with tales spreading far and wide. While they were definitely criminals, some saw them as Robin Hood–like folk heroes rebelling against social injustice. Eventually the law caught up with them, leading to their decline by the late 1800s.

Places We Love to Stay

€ Budget €€ Midrange €€€ Top End

Budapest

MAP p188

Shantee House € Share a yurt with your friends or that special someone in the Zen-like garden of Budapest's first hostel.

Loft Hostel € Friendly backpacker magnet with great kitchen, TV room with skylight, funny artwork and super-helpful staff.

Hotel President Budapest €€ Welcoming 150-room hotel on a beautiful street, with a stunning rooftop bar and a huge jadeite *turul* (falcon-like totem of the ancient Magyars and now a national symbol) in the lobby.

Baltazár €€ Family-owned boutique hotel offering individually decorated rooms with vintage furniture.

Hotel Central Basilica €€ The name says it all at this very central hotel opposite the basilica with 47 rooms, 10 of which face it.

Four Seasons Gresham Palace Hotel €€€ This one-of-a-kind luxury 179-room hotel was created out of the stunning Art Nouveau Gresham Palace (1906).

Párisi Udvar Hotel €€€ This stunner of a 110-room hotel is in the heart of one of the most beautiful buildings in Pest.

Anantara New York Palace Hotel €€€ Blends grandeur and comfort with luxurious rooms, an excellent spa and the historic New York Café next door.

Hotel Clark Budapest €€€ Stay at adults-only Hotel Clark for relaxation by the foot of the Chain Bridge and head up to the rooftop bar for lovely views.

Hotel Moments Budapest €€€ Stunning Art Deco hotel with 99 large rooms, an impressive lobby and an enviable location on UNESCO-listed Andrássy út.

Corinthia Hotel Budapest €€€ The hotel's lobby – a double atrium with a massive marble staircase – is among the most impressive in the city.

Szentendre

Bükkös Hotel & Spa €€€ Adults-only hotel pitching especially to couples on romantic breaks, with spa and massages. Central location, contemporary atmosphere and good breakfasts.

Visegrád

Hotel Silvanus €€€ On a forested hillside near the citadel, this large hotel has great views, an outdoor pool and spa. It was given a makeover in 2024.

Esztergom

Alabárdos Panzió és Apartmanház €€ Immaculate, quiet and very professionally run pension at the foot of the basilica and close to the museums. It also has apartments.

Tihany

Houses of History €€€ Charming B&B rooms set in 19th-century thatched-roof buildings formerly belonging to an abbey. Boasts a pool and also public beach access.

Balatonfüred

Füred Camping € Bungalows and caravans, plus a pool and direct lake access, offer relaxation on a budget. One of the largest camping grounds on the lake.

Anna Grand Hotel €€€ Once a sanatorium, today it's Balatonfüred's most historic grand hotel. Period antiques alongside modern furnishings abound; views of the hotel's courtyard and Gyógy tér square.

Kecskemét

Boutique Hotel Center €€ Slicked up in 2020, this pet-friendly outpost in the heart of town sports modern designer rooms accented with abstract art. Rates include a breakfast buffet.

Szeged

Noir Hotel €€ Superb, central pad marries high style with affordability and has spacious studios with sleek black-surface kitchens, ultra-comfy beds and terraces or balconies.

Eger

Hotel Estella €€ Half a block south of the Old Town, on the upper floors of a late-communist-era university building. Rooms are modern and well kept. Excellent value.

Hollókő

Tugári Vendégház €€ Old cottage in Hollókő with four charmingly furnished rooms and a communal kitchen for making food and friends.

Tokaj

Toldi Fogadó €€ Eclectic art adds a contemporary touch to this town-centre inn with good-sized rooms, a 15m pool, Jacuzzi and sauna.

Practicalities

LGBTIQ+ Travellers

While Budapest has a solid gay scene and gay visitors generally have a good time in Hungary, the country's stance on LGBTIQ+ issues is out of step with many other parts of Europe. The Hungarian government strongly promotes a conservative Christian agenda and still imposes laws against the local LGBTIQ+ community. While travellers aren't generally affected, be aware that PDA may attract unwanted attention.

Health

Hungary doesn't have any serious health risks, but it's still wise to make predeparture preparations. The European Health Insurance Card (EHIC) allows EU citizens to receive emergency state-provided healthcare.

ALLA SIMACHEVA/SHUTTERSTOCK

Funicular (p190), Budapest

Scams to Avoid

Dodgy restaurants and clubs in Budapest's party district (inner District VII) may overcharge foreigners, so check prices before you order. Don't hail taxis off the street and avoid the seemingly friendly touts waiting outside popular places – call a reputable company instead.

Solo Travel

Hungary is a popular and generally safe destination for solo travellers. Budapest has a massive array of budget-friendly and social accommodation options, including hostels that organise pub crawls and other outings. Women travelling alone should not encounter any particular problems besides some mild local machismo.

Bottled Drinks

When buying bottled or canned drinks in Hungary, you'll pay an additional 50Ft deposit per bottle, refundable when you return your empty bottles to any of the designated redemption machines inside bigger supermarkets.

Public Holidays

New Year's Day 1 January
Memorial Day of the 1848 Revolution 15 March
Easter March/April
Labour Day 1 May
Whit Monday May/June
Foundation of the State 20 August
Memorial Day of the 1956 Revolution 23 October
All Saints' Day 1 November
Christmas Day 25 December

Language

A symbol over a vowel in written Hungarian indicates it's pronounced as a long sound. Double consonants should be drawn out a little longer than in English. Note also that aw is pronounced as in 'law', eu as the 'u' in 'nurse', ew as 'ee' with rounded lips, and zh as the 's' in 'pleasure'. Finally, keep in mind that r is rolled in Hungarian and that the apostrophe (') indicates a slight y sound.

Basics

Hello. Szervusz/Szervusztok. (sg/pl) *ser·vus/ser·vus·tawk*

Goodbye. Viszlát. *vis·lat*

Excuse me. Elnézést kérek. *el·ney·zeysht key·rek*

Sorry. Sajnálom. *shoy·na·lawm*

Please. Kérem/Kérlek (inf/pol) *key·rem/keyr·lek*

Thank you. Köszönöm. *keu·seu·neum*

Yes. Igen. *i·gen*

No. Nem. *nem*

What's your name? Mi a neve/neved? (pol/inf) *mi o ne·ve/ne·ved*

My name is ... A nevem ... *o ne·vem ...*

Do you speak English? Beszél/Beszélsz angolul? (pol/inf) *be·seyl/be·seyls on·gaw·lul*

I don't understand. Nem értem. *nem eyr·tem*

Transport

bus busz *bus*

plane repülőgép *re·pew·lēū·geyp*

train vonat *vaw·not*

One ... ticket to (Eger), Egy ... jegy (Eger)be. *ej ... yej (e·ger)·be*

one-way csak oda *chok aw·do*

return oda-vissza *aw·do·vis·so*

Emergencies

Help! Segítség! *she·geet·sheyg*

Go away! Menjen innen! *men·yen in·nen*

Call the doctor! Hívjon orvost! *heev·yawn awr·vawsht*

Call the police! Hívja a rendőrséget! *heev·yo o rend·ēūr·shey·get*

I'm lost. Eltévedtem. *el·tey·ved·tem*

I'm ill. Rosszul vagyok. *raws·sul vo·dyawk*

Where are the toilets? Hol a vécé? *hawl o vey·tsey*

Eating & Drinking

What would you recommend? Mit ajánlana? *mit o·yan·lo·no*

Do you have vegetarian food? Vannak Önöknél vegetáriánus ételek? *von·nok eu·neuk·neyl ve·ge·ta·ri·a·nush ey·te·lek*

I'll have ... ... kérek. *... key·rek*

Cheers! Egészségetekre! *e·geys·shey·ge·tek·re*

I'd like the ... ... szeretném. *... se·ret·neym*

  bill A számlát *o sam·lat*

  menu Az étlapot *oz eyt·lo·pawt*

Shopping & Services

I'm looking for ... Keresem a ... *ke·re·shem o ...*

How much is it? Mennyibe kerül? *men'·nyi·be ke·rewl*

That's too expensive. Ez túl drága. *ez tül dra·go*

market piac *pi·ots*

post office postahivatal *paw·sh·to·hi·vo·tol*

NUMBERS

1
egy *ej*

2
kettő *ket·tēū*

3
három *ha·rawm*

4
négy *neyj*

5
öt *eut*

6
hat *hot*

7
hét *heyt*

8
nyolc *nyawlts*

9
kilenc *ki·lents*

10
tíz *teeze*

Tram, Budapest (p186)

Arriving & Getting Around

For most travellers visiting Hungary, Budapest is the main point of entry. Ferenc Liszt International Airport is about 16km southeast of the city centre. The main international train station in Budapest is Keleti railway station.

From the Airport
Shuttle bus 100E to/from central Pest (stop: Deák Ferenc tér) runs daily round the clock. A combination bus (200E) and metro is a bit cheaper but slower. Taxis are the fastest way to get to/from the airport.

Hungary Pass
If you're planning on travelling around the country, consider buying a Hungary Pass, good for unlimited travel throughout Hungary. It's valid for almost all services with **Budapest Public Transport** *(BKK; bkk.hu)*, suburban and regional buses, HÉV suburban railways and regional trains.

Validating Tickets
Budapest public transport tickets have to be validated after purchase. Digital tickets have a QR-code scanner (codes are on the sides of buses, trams and on ticket machines) and passes have their own QR codes that controllers check.

BudapestGO
The BudapestGO mobile app for public transport has several key features. You can buy and store digital tickets and passes directly on the app (don't forget to validate tickets with QR codes and show passes to inspectors). It also provides route planning and a map, timetables, and information on routes, connections and travel times, as well as updates on potential delays and other relevant information.

MONEY
Currency: Hungarian Forint (Ft)

CASHLESS PAYMENTS
Most restaurants, hotels, shops, car-hire companies and petrol stations across Hungary accept credit cards, especially Visa and MasterCard. American Express isn't always accepted.

CASH
When travelling outside Budapest, it's wise to carry cash in case it's not possible to pay by card. Smaller shops and ice-cream parlours appreciate coins and might struggle to break larger banknotes.

TIPPING
Add at least 10% for table service at restaurants. Instead of leaving money on the table, tell the server how much you want to pay in total, including the tip. Many restaurants already add a service fee of about 12% to 15% – check the receipt or ask before paying.

For places to stay
in Poland, see
p234

CINEMATOGRAPHER/SHUTTERSTOCK

Above: Old Town Market Square , Warsaw (p215); Right:Złota Brama, Gdańsk (p230)

Curated by
Marc Di Duca

Poland

A WARM, WELCOMING AND RESILIENT NATION

Poland is all about history: its millennium-long tale is set against centuries of European power struggles and features a cast of millions.

If you were to put together a list of countries with 'most eventful pasts', Poland would be high up in the rankings. The Slavic nation has spent centuries at the pointy end of history, grappling with war, invasion and meddling neighbours. 'Poland has not yet perished' goes the rather pessimistic first line of the national anthem, and indeed, no Russian tsar or German dictator ever managed to suppress the Poles' strong sense of nationhood and cultural identity.

In fact, Poland is thriving. The country's economic revival from one of the world's poorest nations, where petrol and food were once rationed, to a modern, vibrant economy has been remarkable. Its cities are modernising, its infrastructure is expanding and it occupies a strategic, central location within the EU and NATO. As a result, bustling Warsaw and Kraków exude a sophisticated energy that's a heady mix of old and new.

Away from the cities, Poland is geographically diverse, from its northern beaches to the long chain of mountains on its southern border. In between, towns and cities are dotted with ruined castles, market squares and medieval churches.

Although prices have skyrocketed in recent years, Poland is still good value. And as the Poles continue to reconcile their distinctive national identity with their location at the heart of a troubled Europe, it's become a fascinating time to visit.

LIYA_BLUMESSER/SHUTTERSTOCK

THE MAIN AREAS

WARSAW
Nation's capital with bags of history. **p212**

KRAKÓW
Poland's best-preserved city. **p218**

WESTERN POLAND
Vibrant, off-the-beaten-path destination. **p225**

POMERANIA
Beaches, castles and 20th-century history. **p229**

Find Your Way

Poland is big: it's the ninth-largest country in Europe. Journey times can be longer than you expected, but infrastructure is improving. Apart from the southern mountains, the country is largely flat.

Pomerania, p229

The capital of the north is Gdańsk, where you'll find great museums, the country's best beaches and the story of the Solidarity movement.

Warsaw, p212

An intriguing mix of royal palaces, communist-era architecture and compelling museums. Low-key and refreshingly few tourists.

Kraków, p218

Explore museums that unravel the city's complicated history and enjoy Poland's most sophisticated dining and entertainment.

Western Poland, p225

Two of Poland's most happening cities are Poznań and Wrocław. The first is a confident business centre; the second is a student town.

TRAIN

Rail is the most convenient way to travel. The network is relatively cheap and there are some high-speed rail services. Some of the old tracks and rolling stock remain in service, however.

AIR

Domestic flights are operated by LOT with a hub in Warsaw. There are few direct flights between other cities. Flying can save you hours on the trains.

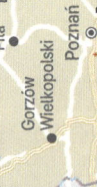

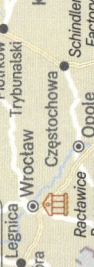

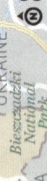

LITHUANIA

BELARUS

UKRAINE

SLOVAKIA

CZECHIA

GERMANY

Baltic Sea

Rostock

Schwerin

BERLIN

Szczecin
Stargard
Szczeciński

Koszalin
Słupsk
Kołobrzeg

Słowiński
National Park

Łeba

Hel

Gdańsk

European
Solidarity Centre

Museum of WWII

Malbork
Castle

Grudziądz

Bydgoszcz

Toruń

Piła

Gorzów
Wielkopolski

Poznań

Porta Posnania
Interactive
Heritage Centre

Poznań Cathedral

Zielona
Góra

Leszno

Głogów

Legnica

Jelena Góra

Karpacz

Wrocław

Racławice
Panorama

Opole

Ostrava

Brno

Częstochowa

Katowice

Oświęcim

Schindler's
Factory

Kraków

St Mary's
Basilica

Wieliczka
Salt Mine

Tarnobrzeg

Rzeszów

Lviv

Bieszczadzki
National
Park

Roztocze
National
Park

Zamość

Lublin

Chełm

Radom

Kielce

Piotrków
Trybunalski

Łódź

WARSAW

Warsaw
Rising
Museum

POLIN Museum of the
History of Polish Jews

Wilanów
Palace

Vistula

Biała
Podlaska

Terespol

Białystok

Biebrza
National Park

Łomża

Ostrołęka

Ostróda

Olsztyn

Lake
Śniardwy

Lake
Mamry

Suwałki

Ełk

Odra

Stargard

Stettin

Odra

200 km

100 miles

SEQOYA/SHUTTERSTOCK

Market square, Kraków (p218)

Plan Your Time

Poland could easily fill up a month of travels, so choose your destinations carefully to create an itinerary that's best suited to your availability.

Pressed for Time

● If you can only visit one place in Poland, then it should be **Kraków** (p218), Poland's tourist epicentre – it's a bit like Prague but with a more authentically Eastern European feel. There are museums galore as well as lots of Jewish and WWII heritage; when the sightseeing is over, there are many excellent, cosy taverns to retreat to.

A Week in Poland

● Start in **Kraków** (p218) with its royal sights, Jewish culture and WWII heritage, before taking a train to **Warsaw** (p212) to climb the PKiN Tower, feast in milk bars and ramble through royal gardens and palaces. From there, hop aboard a short flight to **Gdańsk** (p229), where beaches and museums dedicated to amber, WWII and the Solidarity trade union await.

SEASONAL HIGHLIGHTS

SPRING
The first flowers appear on the plains, but in April the sleet is still falling by the Baltic.

SUMMER
Poland can surprise with sweltering temperatures and high humidity. Ideal for Baltic beach days.

AUTUMN
The forests of southern and eastern Poland put on a fiery show and the cities are at their busiest.

WINTER
Snow can fall everywhere in Poland, but it's heaviest in the mountains. Sub-zero temps prevail for months.

Warsaw

MUSEUMS | ARCHITECTURE | HISTORY

☑ **TOP TIP**

On the right bank of the Vistula, the Praga neighbourhood has two beaches: Rusałka is near the zoo and has views of the Old Town skyline; Poniatówka is near the National Stadium and Saska Kępa. Borrow deck chairs, towels and other beach gear for free in summer.

By the end of 1945, the Polish capital of Warsaw lay in ruins. Rebuilding began almost immediately and it's a process that continues to this day. You'll encounter restored baroque, Gothic, neoclassical and Renaissance buildings in the Old and New Towns; gems of the post-WWII socialist-realist period, such as the grandiose Palace of Culture & Science; and innovative 21st-century revamps of old factories and other industrial sites.

Original fragments and treasures from Poland's turbulent past are preserved in a superb selection of museums. The exhibitions at the huge Warsaw Rising Museum, the even bigger POLIN Museum of the History of Polish Jews and the intriguingly cu-rated Museum of Warsaw leave no stone unturned.

This is also a city blessed with plenty of greenery. Enjoy the parklands at Wilanów, aptly described as Poland's Versailles, and stroll the shady paths of Ła-zienki Park to encounter petite royal palaces and an ornamental lake.

Take a Tour of the Royal Castle

History rebuilt

Warsaw's **Royal Castle** *(zamek-krolewski.pl; entry adult/ concession 60/45zł)* began life in the 14th century as a wood-en stronghold and evolved into one of Europe's most splendid

 GETTING AROUND

Warsaw Chopin Airport *(lotnisko-chopina. pl)*, 9km south of the city centre, has frequent buses and less-frequent trains to central Warsaw (30 minutes). From **Warsaw Modlin Airport** *(modlinairport.pl)* 39km north of the city, there's a bus connection to central Warsaw (one hour). Two efficient train lines provide access across much of Warsaw, but the distance between stations can be long. Local trains can also be used for crossing the city, most handily between the two sides of the Vistula River. Warsaw's extensive network of buses and trams is the fastest way to get around. Bolt and Uber are best for taxis.

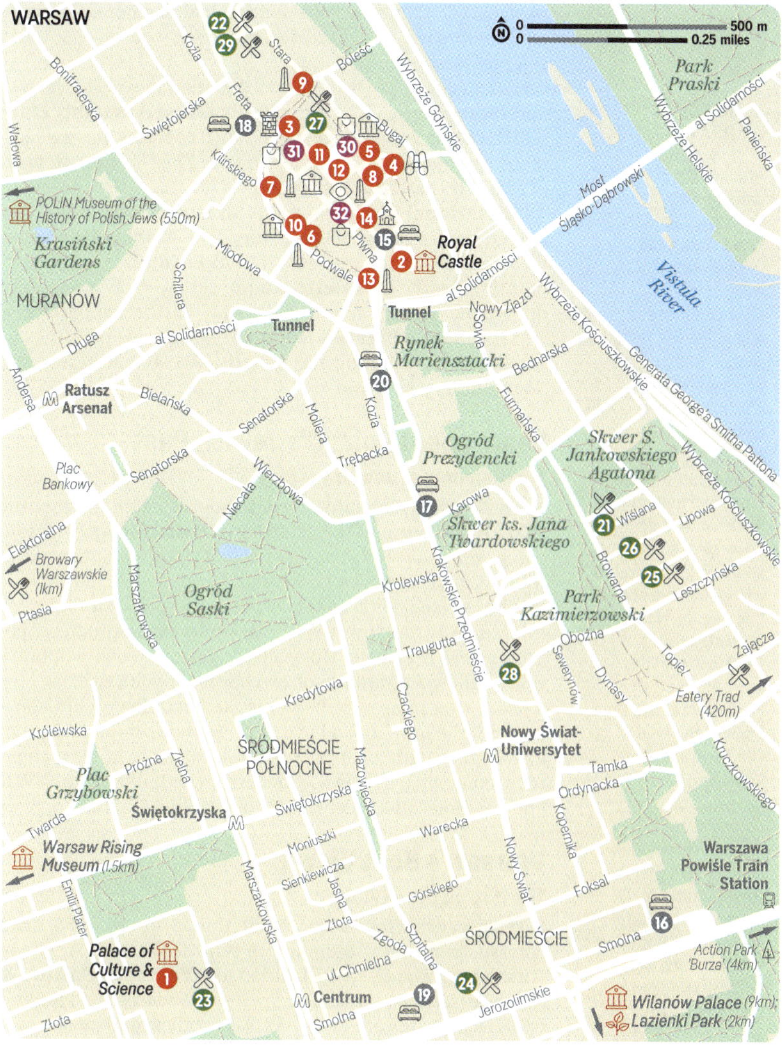
WARSAW
0 500 m
0 0.25 miles
Park Praski
Vistula River
Royal Castle
Krasiński Gardens
MURANÓW
POLIN Museum of the History of Polish Jews (550m)
Rynek Mariensztacki
Tunnel
Tunnel
Ratusz Arsenał
Plac Bankowy
Ogród Prezydencki
Skwer S. Jankowskiego Agatona
Skwer ks. Jana Twardowskiego
Browary Warszawskie (1km)
Ogród Saski
Park Kazimierzowski
Eatery Trad (420m)
Nowy Świat-Uniwersytet
ŚRÓDMIEŚCIE PÓŁNOCNE
Plac Grzybowski
Świętokrzyska
Warsaw Rising Museum (1.5km)
Warszawa Powiśle Train Station
ŚRÓDMIEŚCIE
Action Park 'Burza' (4km)
Palace of Culture & Science
Centrum
Wilanów Palace (9km); Lazienki Park (2km)
Kozia
Stara
Bolesć
Wybrzeże Gdyńskie
Wybrzeże Helskie
al Solidarności
Panieńska
Bonifraterska
Freta
Świętojerska
Wałowa
Bugaj
Kilińskiego
Most Śląsko-Dąbrowski
Miodowa
Piwna
Podwale
Schillera
al Solidarności
Nowy Zjazd
Sowia
Wybrzeże Kościuszkowskie
Generała George'a Smitha Pattona
Długa
Bednarska
Andersa
Bielańska
Senatorska
Moliera
Kozia
Furmańska
Trębacka
Senatorska
Wierzbowa
Karowa
Wybrzeże Kościuszkowskie
Niecała
Wiślana
Lipowa
Elektoralna
Browarna
Leszczyńska
Marszałkowska
Królewska
Krakowskie Przedmieście
Ptasia
Traugutta
Oboźna
Zajęcza
Sewerynów
Topiel
Dynasy
Kredytowa
Czackiego
Królewska
Kruczkowskiego
Próżna
Zielna
Mazowiecka
Tamka
Ordynacka
Twarda
Świętokrzyska
Kopernika
Warecka
Moniuszki
Sienkiewicza
Nowy Świat
Emilii Plater
Marszałkowska
Jasna
Foksal
Złota
Górskiego
Zgoda
Szpitalna
Smolna
ul Chmielna
Jerozolimskie
Złota
Smolna

✪ **HIGHLIGHTS**
1 Palace of Culture & Science
2 Royal Castle

● **SIGHTS**
3 Barbican
4 Dung Hill Terrace
5 Heritage Interpretation Centre
6 Jan Kiliński Monument
7 Little Insurgent Monument
8 Mazovia
9 Mosaic House
10 Museum of Artistic and Precision Crafts
11 Museum of Warsaw
12 Old Town Market Square
13 Sigismund's Column
14 St John the Baptist Cathedral

● **SLEEPING**
15 Castle Inn
16 Chopin Boutique B&B
17 Hotel Bristol
18 Oki Doki Hostel Old Town
19 PURO Warsaw Downtown
20 Safestay Warsaw Old Town

● **EATING**
21 Bez Gwiazdek
22 Enoteca
23 Kulturalna
24 Między Nami
see 18 Mon Nom
25 Oma
26 SAM Powiśle
27 Sambal
28 Syrena Irena
29 Żyto

● **SHOPPING**
30 Dom Sztuki Lodowej
31 Lapidarium
32 Polish Poster Gallery

REBUILDING WARSAW

Around 70% of Warsaw was destroyed during WWII. After 1945, this presented an opportunity for a wholesale reimagining of public spaces so that more parks and modern housing estates could be created. But not everything was swept away. Rubble was reused so that original bricks and other decorative elements could be incorporated – to learn more about this visit the **Heritage Interpretation Centre** in the Old Town and **Action Park 'Burza'**. By 1953 much of the Old Town and the Royal Route had been meticulously reconstructed, although it wouldn't be until 1984 that the **Royal Castle** (p212) would be complete. The enormous efforts of Varsovians were acknowledged in 1980 when UNESCO inscribed the Old Town on its World Heritage list.

palaces. For a time the Polish parliament met here. The original building was destroyed during WWII; what you see today is a post-war rebuild.

The interiors have been restored to their heyday in the 17th and 18th centuries. The magnificent **Great Assembly Hall**, with dazzling gilded stucco and golden columns, has an enormous ceiling painting, a re-creation of *The Disentanglement of Chaos* by Marcello Bacciarelli.

The **National Hall** is hung with six huge canvases depicting pivotal scenes from Polish history. The **Marble Room** has trompe l'oeil paintwork and portraits of Polish kings. The 22 paintings in the **Canaletto Room** were used as a reference during the reconstruction of Warsaw's historic buildings.

In the **Crown Prince's Rooms** are epic-scale paintings by Jan Matekjo, including *The Constitution of 3 May 1791* and *Stefan Batory at Pskov*.

Learn about Poland's Jewish Past

A millennium of Jewish history

Housed in a huge chunk of contemporary architecture, the **POLIN Museum of the History of Polish Jews** *(polin.pl; entry adult/concession main exhibit 45/35zł)* documents over 1000 years of Polish Jewish history. The extensive multimedia exhibition includes accounts of the earliest Jewish traders in the region through waves of mass migration, progress, pogroms, WWII and the Holocaust, right up to contemporary times. Allow a minimum of two hours for your visit.

Room after room examines every aspect of Jewish life, starting with the Jews' arrival in central Europe a millennium ago and ending with a film featuring local Jews talking about their contemporary lives. Obviously, the build-up to WWII and the Holocaust receive much attention.

Warsaw's Best Views

Top dog on the skyline

Seven decades after its 1955 debut, this 237m-tall, 3288-room colossus continues to dominate central Warsaw. A 'gift of friendship' from the Soviet Union, the **Palace of Culture & Science** *(pkin.pl; viewing terrace adult/concession 28/23zł)*, or PKiN, remains one of the Warsaw's tallest and most iconic buildings. The highlight is the view from the 30th-floor viewing terrace, accessed via a superfast lift.

 EATING IN OLD TOWN & NEW TOWN: OUR PICKS

Mon Nom: Lovely bistro, with potted plants and quirky art on the walls; a great breakfast or lunch spot. *9am-10pm Mon-Fri, to 11pm Sat & Sun* €€	**Sambal:** Indonesian restaurant serving authentic dishes such as *rendang padang*, a beef and coconut milk stew. *noon-9pm Tue-Fri & Sun, to 10pm Sat* €€	**Żyto:** Facing New Town Square, this Ukrainian restaurant serves hearty bowls of borscht and other regional dishes. *noon-10pm* €€	**Enoteca** Classy choice overlooking attractive New Town Square; good for Polish and Italian food or a simple glass of wine. *noon-10pm* €€€

MONUMENTS OF THE OLD TOWN

If you know where to look, you'll find fascinating historical and artistic monuments dotted around the Old Town.

START	END	LENGTH
Castle Square	Museum of Artistic and Precision Crafts	1.5km; 1-2hr

Spend a moment in Castle Sq, overlooked by the 22m **1 Sigismund's Column**, and consider that in 1945 all around you would have been rubble. Walk along ul Świętojańska to **2 St John the Baptist Cathedral**, Warsaw's mother church. Continue ahead to the **3 Old Town Market Square**. The picturesque square's central statue is the symbol of the city: Syrenka, the fierce mermaid brandishing a sword. Head inside the **4 Museum of Warsaw** to see the original statue.

Exit the square along ul Celna – look through a gate to see the bas relief **5 Mazovia** created in 1966 by sculptor Edmund Majkowski. Nearby, in **6 Dung Hill Terrace** overlooking the Vistula,

is the *Strong Man* statue. Continue along ul Brzozowa to the stout fortress walls that partly encircle the Old Town. Look out to the New Town beyond, where you can see a striking socialist-realist **7 mosaic** covering the side of one building.

Check out the stalls of craftspeople and artists in the **8 Barbican** before continuing around the fortress to find the poignant **9 Little Insurgent Monument**. Further along the walls is the **10 Jan Kiliński Monument** and a clock with copper and gold-leaf zodiac signs on the side of the **11 Museum of Artistic and Precision Crafts**.

The **Little Insurgent Monument** commemorates the child soldiers who died during the 1944 Warsaw Uprising.

Atop **Sigismund's Column** is a statue of Sigismund III Vasa (1566–1632), the Swedish-born king of Poland.

Jan Kiliński was a colonel during the failed 1794 Kościuszko Uprising against Russian and Prussian influences in Poland.

0 ___ 200 m
0 ___ 0.1 miles

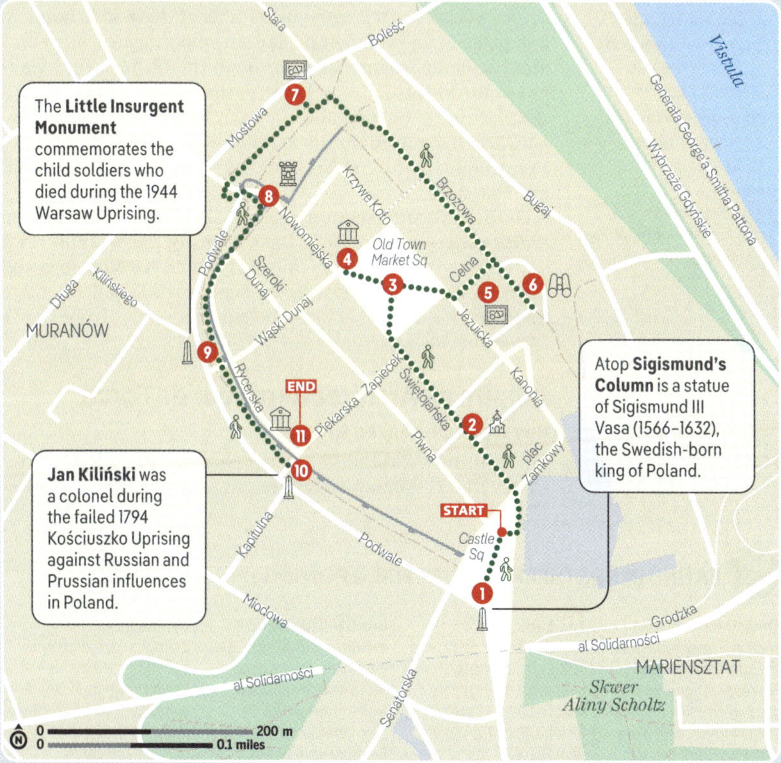

A Doomed Resistance

Warsaw in WWII

A former tram power station houses the **Warsaw Rising Museum** *(1944.pl; entry adult/concession 35/30zł)*, which covers in forensic detail Warsaw's heroic, doomed uprising against the German occupation in 1944. It's an immersive, dark and at times claustrophobic experience that evokes the horror of the times and the courage of the fighters.

The ground-floor exhibition begins with the division of Poland between Nazi Germany and the Soviet Union in 1939 and moves through the major events of WWII. An elevator then takes you to the mezzanine (2nd floor) and the start of the uprising in 1944 with day-by-day displays.

A life-size reproduction of the B-24J Liberator heavy bomber, used to drop supplies for insurgents, fills much of the ground-floor Liberator Hall. Here you can also watch newsreel films shot during the uprising, as well as a six-minute 3D film that re-creates the view from a flight over the devastated city in 1945.

Leafy Royal Grounds

Take a walk in Łazienki Park

Once a royal hunting ground, **Łazienki Park** *(lazienki-krolewskie.pl; entry free)* covers 76 hectares and is home to two palaces, an ornamental lake, an amphitheatre, museums and themed gardens. Stroll through the 18th-century Italianate Royal Garden, the 19th-century Romantic Garden, a small Chinese Garden and the early 20th-century Modernist Garden, centred on the art nouveau Chopin Monument. Free Chopin piano concerts (noon & 4pm Sun mid-May–Sep) are held here.

The park's centrepiece is the neoclassical **Palace on the Isle** *(adult/concession 60/30zł)*, incorporating the original royal bathing pavilion (*łazienki* in Polish). Some 140 paintings and art from King Stanisław August Poniatowski's collection are displayed here. Marble bas-reliefs depict scenes from Ovid's *Metamorphoses*.

Admire an Architectural Tour de Force

Royal palace packed with art

The **Wilanów Palace** *(wilanow-palac.pl; entry adult/concession 50/30zł)*, Warsaw's grandest, was commissioned by King

---

EATING IN NORTHERN ŚRÓDMIEŚCIE & POWIŚLE: POLISH CUISINE

Oma: Delish comfort food in a cosy room just like grandma's house. No reservations, so be prepared to line up. *noon-9pm Mon-Fri, 9am-9pm Sat, 9am-8pm Sun* €€

The Eatery Trad: Traditional dishes served with style in a retro ambience dining room next to the old Lotos Hotel. *1-11pm Tue-Sat, to 9pm Sun* €€

Bez Gwiazdek: Each month, artfully presented set menus at 'Without Stars' take inspiration from different Polish provinces. *5.30-10pm Tue-Fri, from 4pm Sat* €€€

Syrena Irena: Tasty pierogi, soups and other Polish staples at this stylish contemporary spin on a 'milk bar' budget diner. *11am-8pm Sun-Wed, to 10pm Thu-Sat* €

Łazienki Park

Jan III Sobieski in 1677. It changed hands several times over the centuries, with each new owner adding a bit of baroque here and a touch of neoclassical there. Miraculously, Wilanów survived WWII almost unscathed, and many of its furnishings and art were retrieved and reinstalled after the war.

The route through the palace involves some doubling back, but there are attendants to show the way. The tour starts with the **Princess Marshall Lubomirska's Apartments**, an immaculately restored salon dating from the late 18th century and including the magnificent Chinese and Hunting Rooms.

The **White Hall**, the palace's largest room, is hung with portraits of successive owners of Wilanów; the stairs here lead to the **Potocki Art Gallery**, displaying works of art gathered by the Potocki family, owners of Wilanów from 1799 to 1821.

Enveloping the palace is a splendid 45-hectare **park** *(adult/ concession 10/5zł)*, where the landscaping ranges from a fragrant lily and rose garden to the Orangery, dotted with contemporary sculptures.

WARSAW FIGHTS BACK

Every year on 19 April at noon and 1 August at 5pm sirens sound across Warsaw and people fall silent. This is in remembrance of the beginning, respectively, of the **Ghetto Uprising** (lasting 29 days) and **Warsaw Uprising** (lasting 63 days) in 1943 and 1944, and of those who fought bravely against the city's Nazi German occupiers.

In 1944, insurgents took control of large parts of Warsaw by creating barricades from ripped-up paving slabs and using the sewers as underground communication lines. Sadly, the hoped-for support from the Allies and the Soviets failed to arrive, even though the Red Army was camped just outside Warsaw. In both uprisings, well over 250,000 Poles lost their lives.

 EATING IN NORTHERN ŚRÓDMIEŚCIE & POWIŚLE: CASUAL SPOTS

SAM Powiśle: Relaxed bakery, cafe and deli with dishes made from organic produce. *8am-8pm* €€

Między Nami: Vibey cafe-bar serves delicious open sandwiches for breakfast. *4pm-midnight Mon, 10am-midnight Tue-Thu, 10am-1am Fri & Sat, 10am-8pm Sun* €€

Kulturalna: Great spot for something tasty in a spacious hall off the Teatr Dramatyczny in PKiN. *noon-midnight Sun-Thu, to 2am Fri & Sat* €€

Browary Warszawskie: Drink craft beer brewed on site and dig into culinary treats either from the brewery or the food hall. *noon-10pm Sun-Thu, to midnight Fri & Sat* €€

Kraków

HISTORY | ARCHITECTURE | CULTURE

☑ **TOP TIP**

Head to one of Kraków's communist-era bars *mleczny* (milk bars) for a trip down nostalgia lane to the 1980s and a wallet-friendly canteen meal of omelettes, pierogi, soup, mashed potatoes and other belly-fillers. Due to the increasing cost of living, they've seen a resurgence recently.

The southern metropolis of Kraków is the former capital of Poland and one of the finest medieval cities in all of Europe. The most quintessentially Polish destination, it's a place steeped in legends of dragons and kings. Its thousand years of history kicked off with plundering Tatar hordes and continued on through multiple royal dynasties, the waxing and waning of empires, the unfurling of Europe-wide trade routes in the Middle Ages, the decline that followed after the Polish capital was moved to Warsaw in the 16th century, the terror of the Nazi regime during WWII and decades of communist repression – all followed by its rejuvenation as a tourist magnet. Kraków's turbulent history bequeathed it layers of architecture, which survived WWII largely intact. And while the Holocaust casts a long shadow, Jewish culture is enjoying a renaissance in the rejuvenated Kazimierz district.

A Medieval Marketplace Unveiled

Explore an interactive subterranean museum

When Kraków's market square was undergoing renovations around two decades ago, the remains of the original millennium-old marketplace were found beneath the Cloth Hall. They have since been transformed into **Rynek Underground** *(muzeum krakowa.pl; entry adult/child 25/17zł),* a subterranean 'Middle Ages meets the 21st century' experience.

 GETTING AROUND

Trains and buses run from the airport to the central Kraków Główny train station and the adjacent bus station every 30 minutes (20 minutes, 4am to midnight). Thirty-minute taxi rides to the city centre cost 80 to 100zł with Kraków Airport Taxis and 40 to 75zł with Uber or Bolt.

The best way to explore the grid-like neighbourhoods is on foot. Kraków's integrated tram and bus system runs from 5am to 11pm, with less frequent night services after 11pm. Purchase tickets via the Jakdojade app or at the machines at tram stops and validate them on board.

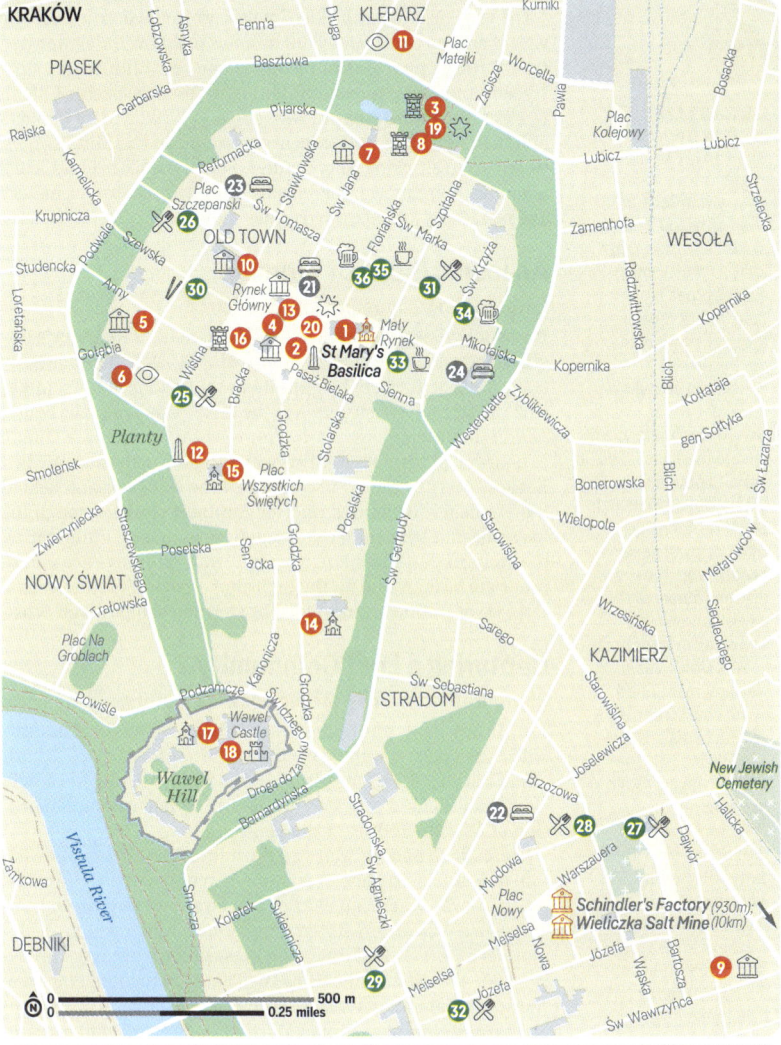

KRAKÓW

HIGHLIGHTS
1 St Mary's Basilica

SIGHTS
2 Adam Mickiewicz
3 Barbican
4 Cloth Hall
5 Collegium Maius
6 Collegium Novum
7 Czartoryski Museum
8 Florian Gate
9 Galicia Jewish Museum
10 Historical Museum of Kraków

11 Obwarzanek Museum
12 Papal Window
13 Rynek Underground
14 St Andrew's Church
15 St Francis' Basilica
16 Town Hall Tower
17 Wawel Cathedral
18 Wawel Royal Castle

ACTIVITIES
19 Free Walking Tour
20 Kraków Pub Crawl

SLEEPING
21 Bonerowski Palace

22 Dream Hostel
23 Globetrotter Guest House
24 Hotel Gródek

EATING
25 Antler Poutine & Burger
26 Charlotte Chleb i Wino
27 Dawno Temu Na Kazimierzu
28 Karakter
29 Kropka Kráków
30 Kuku Taiwanese
31 Milkbar Tomasza

32 Pierwszy Stopień

DRINKING & NIGHTLIFE
33 Bonobo
34 House of Beer
35 Pożegnanie z Afryką Cafe
36 Viva la Pinta

OBWARZANKI: A KRAKÓW SPECIALITY

As you wander around Old Town, you'll come across an *obwarzanki* stall on pretty much every corner. More than 200,000 of these chewy treats are baked and consumed in Kraków daily; get yours before lunchtime to ensure freshness. The braided dough rings are parboiled, baked and then sprinkled with poppy or sesame seeds – yup, these are the forefathers of the Jewish bagels that appeared in Kazimierz in 1610. *Obwarzanki* was first mentioned in the court records of King Ladislaus II Jagiello in 1394. The Kraków Bakers' Guild had a monopoly on *obwarzanek* production until the early 17th century, when rules were relaxed. Anyone can bake an *obwarzanek* now at the **Obwarzanek Museum** *(muzeummobwarzanka.com)*, including you.

The visit kicks off with video images projected onto a dramatic wall of smoke. Give yourself 90 minutes to follow the signposted trail through the ruins of medieval market stalls, with touch-screens and holograms highlighting different aspects of life in Kraków. Peer into a goldsmith's workshop, be wowed by women's and men's fashions and skincare practices in the Middle Ages, weigh yourself using long-defunct Polish measures and learn about 'vampire prevention burials' at an 11th-century cemetery and mercenary knights, hired by merchants to protect their wares.

An Iconic Place of Worship

Enter Kraków's most illustrious church

If you only visit one church in Old Town, make it **St Mary's Basilica** *(mariacki.com; entry adult/child 18/10zł)*. Dominated by two towers of different heights, it has undergone many changes since its original construction in the 1220s. Don't miss the hourly *hejnał* (bugle call) emanating from the taller tower – a tribute to a medieval trumpeter killed while sounding the alarm when Kraków was attacked. Enter through the side door and behold the exquisitely decorated interior. Sunlight passes through the magnificent 14th-century stained-glass windows, illuminating the chancel. Jan Matejko's colourful wall paintings are an appropriate background for the high altar – Poland's greatest masterpiece of Gothic art, designed by German sculptor Veit Stoss.

Capturing a Lost Community

Photographic journey through Jewish history

The innovative photographic **Galicia Jewish Museum** *(galiciajewishmuseum.org; entry adult/child 35/25zł)* is both a celebration of Jewish culture in the former region of Galicia (southeast Poland and western Ukraine) and a commemoration of Jewish victims of the Holocaust.

The main *Traces of Memory* exhibit takes you from 'Jewish Life in Ruins' – roofless remnants of synagogues, the shadow by a doorway where a mezuzah once was – to 'Jewish Culture That Once Was' (a devastated cemetery, a circular window). Memorials in forests and forgotten mass grave sites make up the Holocaust section, while 'How the Past Is Being Remembered' showcases images of a reconstructed slave labour camp, anti-Nazi graffiti and the empty chairs on Podgórze's main square. At the end, there's a hopeful note in the form of 'Revival of Jewish Life': images of Festival of Jewish Culture concerts and young Jews partaking in the March of the Living.

 EATING IN OLD TOWN: BUDGET BITES

Antler Poutine & Burger: This tongue-in-cheek Canadian burger joint also dishes up poutine (fries smothered in gravy and melted cheese). *noon-10pm* €

Milkbar Tomasza: A modern take on a traditional Polish *bar mleczny*, where panini sit proudly beside pierogi. *8am-6pm Mon-Sat, from 9am Sun* €

Kuku Taiwanese: Bowls of Taiwanese curry, dumplings with chilli sauce and sesame soup noodles are served with maximum efficiency. *11.30am-9.30pm* €

Charlotte Chleb i Wino: Warsaw restaurant outpost, known for croissants, croque monsieurs and sandwiches, along with French wine and coffee. *7am-midnight* €

Wawel Royal Castle

On any given day, Wawel Royal Castle – Poland's answer to Buckingham Palace and Westminster Abbey – teems with visitors. Its glorious mishmash of Romanesque, Renaissance and Gothic architecture – the product of conquests, fashion and multiple royal dynasties – plus glittering treasures, looming towers and verdant grounds demonstrates why Kraków is a world-class city.

Wawel Cathedral

The Royal Castle

In centuries past, the ground-floor **State Rooms** were where royals received guests, held court and entertained. Pass through the vast, individually styled halls, liberally sprinkled with oil paintings and 16th-century Flemish tapestries, including the ostentatious Throne Room.

The **Royal Private Apartments** are the 1st-floor bedchambers, with modestly proportioned beds that feature carved four-poster frames. The Renaissance furnishings of King Sigismund the Old, the painted ceiling beams of the royal guest room and the tiny bejewelled 'Hen's Foot' (Queen Jadwiga's chapel) in the 14th-century Belvedere Tower stand out.

Below, vaulted Gothic rooms hold the **Treasury's** sceptres and orbs, gold goblets, royal banners, textiles and exotic objects acquired by King Sigismund III.

Wawel Cathedral

Built on the orders of Władysław the Short (1306–33), the first king to be crowned here, the current incarnation of **Wawel Cathedral** (1364) is actually the third, with the 1020 CE original and its successor having burned down. Arguably the most important building in Poland, the cathedral has hosted the coronation of virtually every Polish king and queen. Poland's monarchs occupy tombs in the cathedral and the royal crypt.

TOP TIPS

● Book your visit to Wawel Royal Castle in advance.

● You can visit the castle grounds free of charge.

● You can either book tickets to Wawel Royal Castle's separate attractions or get a day pass that covers everything.

● Entry to Wawel Cathedral must be purchased separately.

PRACTICALITIES

● wawel.krakow.pl/en
● adult/child from 49/37zł
● 10am-4pm Mon, 9am-5pm Tue-Sun

PODGÓRZE'S UNLIKELY HERO

Podgórze was home to at least two prominent Gentiles who risked their lives to save Jews during the Holocaust. The best known is Oskar Schindler, the heavy-drinking profiteer and anti-hero, whose story was told to millions through Thomas Keneally's book *Schindler's Ark* (1982) and Steven Spielberg's *Schindler's List* (1993).

Schindler originally saved the lives of Jews because he needed their cheap labour at his enamelware factory, and he used his connections and paid bribes in order to keep his employees from being shipped off to concentration camps. As is movingly quoted at the end of Spielberg's film, in reference to a passage in the Talmud, 'Whoever saves one life, saves the world entire'.

KANUMAN/GETTY IMAGES

Wieliczka Salt Mine

Learn about Schindler & the Polish Resistance

Museum of German occupation

Covering the German occupation of Kraków during WWII, the interactive **Schindler's Factory** (*muzeumkrakowa.pl/en; entry adult/child 40/35zł*) – one of Kraków's most popular museums – is housed in the former enamel factory of Oskar Schindler, the Nazi industrialist immortalised in Steven Spielberg's 1993 film *Schindler's List*.

The 30-minute introductory film showcases ordinary Cracovians telling their (often horrific) stories of life under German occupation. You then pass through labyrinthine rooms, each revolving around a specific theme. Sepia photographs, original radio and video footage, period objects, multimedia installations and individual stories of the city's residents immerse you in the unsettling prewar years and the first days of the war. Move on to the German repression of the city's Jewish residents and members of the Polish resistance, and the outright horror of the deportations to the death camps.

Though abandoned after WWII, Oskar Schindler's former office survived intact. The room's centrepiece is a symbolic Survivors' Ark – a giant translucent cube filled made of thousands of enamel pots, similar to the ones made by Schindler's employees.

 EATING IN KAZIMIERZ: OUR PICKS

Karakter: Whole-animal dishes like tripe and sweetbreads, plus conventional offerings for the offal-averse. Three-course lunch (63zł) is a steal. *1-11pm* €€

Pierwszy Stopień: While the dishes at this plant-bedecked spot lean carnivore, the pearl barley kashotto with white asparagus is a thing of beauty. *1-10pm* €€

Kropka Kraków: Modern Polish joint with globally-tinged dishes (pierogi with Korean-style sauce) and natural wines. *4-10pm Tue-Fri, from 1pm Sat & Sun* €€

Dawno Temu Na Kazimierzu: Atmospheric Jewish-themed restaurant shows off hearty variations of lamb and duck in a tiny candlelit space. *10am-11pm* €€

Delve Deep into the Wieliczka Salt Mine

Three hundred kilometres of salt

Some 14km southeast of Kraków, the UNESCO-listed **Wieliczka Salt Mine** *(wieliczka-saltmine.com; entry adult/child 156/124zł)* has been welcoming tourists since 1722 and today is one of the area's most popular attractions. It's a subterranean labyrinth of tunnels and chambers – a whopping 300km distributed over nine levels, the deepest being 327m underground – dug out by miners over the centuries right up until 1996. A small part is open to the public via two guided tours: the **Tourist Route** and the **Miners' Route**. Highlights of the Tourist Route include the 17th-century Chapel of St Kinga, a subterranean church measuring 54m by 18m by 12m, and the enormous Stanisław Staszic Chamber, which measures 36m in height and has hosted a subterranean bungee jump and even an underground balloon flight.

The immersive three-hour Miners' Route gives you a deep appreciation for the demanding and perilous profession. Visitors dress in grey miners' coveralls and hard hats and are given a headlamp and emergency respirator. You then make your way through narrow workmanlike passages.

It is cool in the tunnels so bring a sweater. Buy tickets online in advance, particularly for the English-language tours, which sell out.

The Horror of Auschwitz-Birkenau

The Nazis' most infamous concentration camp

Many visitors combine a stay in Kraków with a visit to the **Auschwitz-Birkenau Memorial & Museum** *(auschwitz. org)*. Some 1.1 million people – mostly Jews – died at Auschwitz-Birkenau between 1941 and 1945: they were gassed, worked to death and mistreated. The scale of the place and the scope of the horror can be overwhelming. It is not a place to bring children.

Both sections of the camp – Auschwitz I and the much larger outlying Birkenau (Auschwitz II) – have been preserved and are open to visitors free of charge. It's essential to visit both to appreciate the extent and the inhumanity of the place.

Oświęcim (the Polish name for Auschwitz) has frequent train services from Kraków (65 to 100 minutes). Local buses run constantly between the station and the Auschwitz I entrance. Or you can walk the 1.5km in about 20 minutes. Frequent buses also link Auschwitz I with Birkenau; the walk is 3km.

KRAKÓW'S BEST TOURS

Free Walking Tour: Old Town tours depart four times daily from March to October (less frequently November to February). *(freewalkingtour.com)*

Kraków Pub Crawl: Classic drinking tour visits four venues and starts out from the Main Market Square. *(krawlthroughkrakow.com)*

Delicious Poland: Superb foodie tours of Kazimierz that involve sampling typical Polish food and drink until you're fit to burst. *(deliciouspoland.com)*

Jarden Tourist Agency: Personalised Jewish-themed tours, including two- and three-hour walking tours of Kraków's Kazimierz and Podgórze. *(jarden.pl)*

Cracow City Tours: Decent range of walking and bus tours, including a popular four-hour coach tour and excursions to the Wieliczka Salt Mine and Auschwitz-Birkenau. *(cracowcitytours.pl)*

DRINKING IN OLD TOWN: OUR PICKS

Pożegnanie z Afryką: Burlap sacks full of coffee, earth-coloured decor and nicely brewed espresso define this *Out of Africa*-themed coffee shop. *10am-8pm*

Bonobo: Linger over an espresso, cake or a glass of red wine at this well-stocked travel bookshop. *noon-11pm Mon-Fri, from 3pm Sat & Sun*

House of Beer: Sink into a leather sofa and choose from 21 draught beers and over 200 bottles from Poland, Germany, Lithuania and Belgium. *2pm-midnight*

Viva La Pinta: Award-winning microbrewery pouring a range of craft beers in a courtyard garden. Popular in summer. *4pm-midnight Sun-Thu, to 2am Fri & Sat*

THE ROUTE OF KINGS & QUEENS

This walk through the Old Town's cobbled streets follows the 400-year-old coronation route of Poland's kings and queens.

START	END	LENGTH
Florian Gate	Wawel Royal Castle	1.6km; 2½hr

Start at ❶ **Florian Gate**, the most important of Kraków's eight medieval gates. Together with the 15th-century ❷ **Barbican** – an impenetrable defence tower that withstood several sieges – the gate forms the City Defence Walls museum. Detour along ul Pijarska to ❸ **Czartoryski Palace**, then continue down ul Florianska to ❹ **St Mary's Basilica** (p220). Try to be here on the hour to hear the bugle call. Walk past the ❺ **monument to Adam Mickiewicz** (Poland's greatest literary hero) before cutting through the bustling ❻ **Cloth Hall**, a medieval shopping arcade in the middle of Rynek Główny, Europe's largest medieval town square. Head to its northwest corner to visit the ❼ **Historical**

Museum of Kraków inside the 17th-century Krzysztofory Palace. Proceed to the 14th-century ❽ **Town Hall Tower** for lofty Old Town views. Head to ul Jagiellonska and pass by ❾ **Collegium Maius**, followed by the neo-Gothic ❿ **Collegium Novum** (1873–87), then cut through the park that encircles Old Town to pass the ⓫ **Bishop's Palace** where former Pope John Paul II made appearances at the 'Papal Window'. Walk past ⓬ **St Francis' Basilica** and turn right onto busy ul Grodzka. You'll pass ⓭ **St Andrew's Church** – an 11th-century Romanesque fortress church – before turning down the cobbled ul Kanonicza that leads to ⓮ **Wawel Royal Castle** (p221).

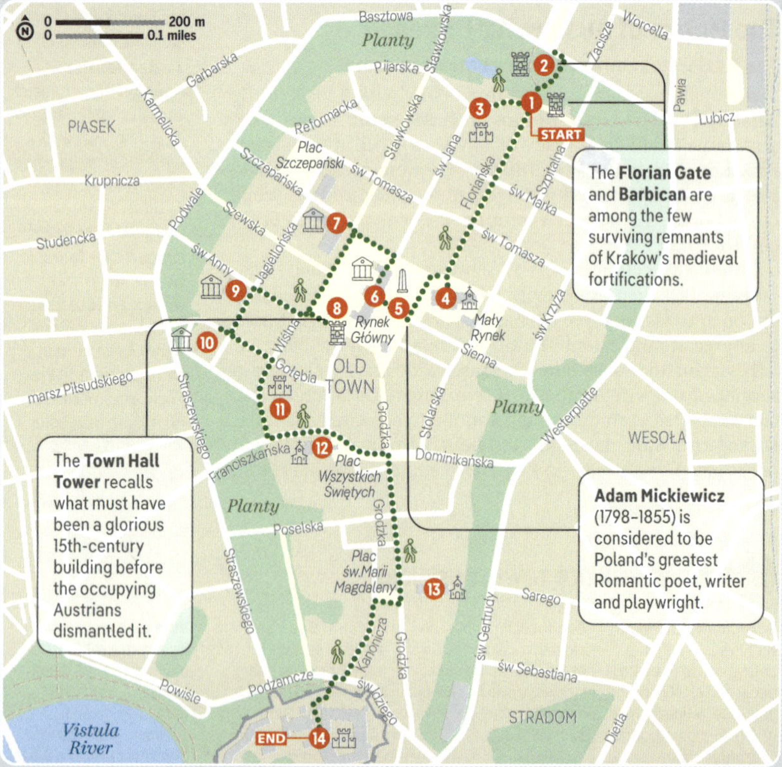

The **Florian Gate** and **Barbican** are among the few surviving remnants of Kraków's medieval fortifications.

The **Town Hall Tower** recalls what must have been a glorious 15th-century building before the occupying Austrians dismantled it.

Adam Mickiewicz (1798–1855) is considered to be Poland's greatest Romantic poet, writer and playwright.

Western Poland

ARCHITECTURE | HISTORY | NIGHTLIFE

The western Polish cities of Wrocław and Poznań are worthwhile stop-offs on a wider Poland tour. Slightly off the trodden path from Poland's main attractions, these two cities have a lot to offer travellers who make the effort to reach them.

Wrocław is the capital of Silesia and Poland's fourth-largest city, and its 12 islands, 130 bridges and verdant riverside parks on the Odra River are idyllic. The beautifully preserved ecclesiastic district on Cathedral Island is a treat for lovers of Gothic architecture.

Poznań's city centre buzzes and hums as locals head to its many restaurants, pubs and clubs. The city has bags of heritage, from medieval times to the mid-20th century, when Poznań rebelled in a big way against communist rule.

Wrocław

Everyone loves Wrocław (vrots-wahf) and it's easy to see why. The capital of Lower Silesia is a more manageable version of Kraków, with similar culture and entertainment offerings, plus an appealing character all its own.

Visit the old Town Hall

Poznań's Renaissance town hall, topped with a 61m-high tower, instantly attracts attention. Its graceful form replaced a 13th-century Gothic structure, which burned down in the early 16th century. Every day at noon two metal goats appear through a pair of small doors above the clock and butt their horns together 12 times, in deference to an old legend. These days, the town hall is home to the city's Historical Museum.

Wrocław's toughest climb and best view

Of the many towers you can climb in Wrocław, the most difficult – but most rewarding – is the 91m-high tower of the

Places
Wrocław p225
Poznań p226

GETTING AROUND

Wrocław is 3½ hours from Warsaw and three hours from Kraków by train. The city has an efficient network of trams and buses *(MPK; mpk. wroc.pl)* covering the city centre and suburbs; however, almost everything is within easy walking distance of the Rynek.

Poznań is relatively compact and the major museums are centrally located. The tram network is useful, but not all stops sell tickets.

☑ **TOP TIP**

Wrocław's helpful tourist office is centrally located at Rynek 14 and is open daily.

HERE COME THE DWARFS

Across Wrocław, you may (literally!) stumble upon **tiny bronze dwarfs** horse-riding, bellringing, singing, sleeping and much more. Measuring up to 30cm, the dwarfs pop up everywhere. Indeed, by 2025, there were more than 1100 and more continue to appear. The tourist office distributes a popular 'Find the Dwarf' map. There are also apps and a Dwarfs Festival in September, with a big weekend of games, culture and fun.

Wrocław's dwarf obsession began with Orange Alternative, a 1980s dissident group that used ridicule as a weapon during the humour-free days of communism. It painted pictures of orange-capped *krasnale* (dwarfs) on places where the authorities had painted over anti-government graffiti – cleverly drawing attention to the critical messages.

14th-century **Church of St Elizabeth** *(Kościół Św Elżbiety; elzbieta.archidiecezja.wroc.pl; tower adult/child 17/11zł)*, reached via a narrow set of 304 steps. What awaits is arguably the most expansive panorama in the city. Back on the ground, the 14th-century Gothic basilica has a triple nave reaching 30m and is lined by medieval chapels.

Wander the most evocative quarter

Cathedral Island (Ostrów Tumski) – which actually became connected to the mainland in the 19th century – was the cradle of Wrocław. It was here that the Ślężanie, a tribe of West Slavs, constructed their stronghold in the 7th or 8th century. In 1000, Wrocław's first church was built here.

The centrepiece of Cathedral Island, the **Cathedral of St John the Baptist** *(Archikatedra Św Jana Chrzciciela; katedra.wroclaw.pl; chapels & tower adult/child 35/25zł)* is a three-aisled Gothic basilica built between the 13th and 16th centuries with three beautiful **baroque chapels**. For views, climb 40 steps and a lift will then whisk you to the top of the 91m-high **tower**.

A wonder all around

A grand spectacle in its day, the **Racławice Panorama** *(Panorama Racławicka; mnwr.pl; entry adult/child 50/35zł)* still impresses. A giant cyclorama wrapped around the internal walls of a rotunda depicts the battle for Polish independence. It took place at Racławice, 40km northeast of Kraków, on 4 April 1794 between the Polish army and Russian troops. The Poles won, but it was all for nought: months later, the nationwide insurrection was crushed by the tsarist army and Poland ceased to exist as a nation until WWI.

Savouring the art of old

The **National Museum** *(Muzeum Narodowe; mnwr.pl; entry adult/child 20/15zł)* is a trove of fine art from across the ages, including medieval sculpture, Silesian paintings, ceramics, silverware and furnishings from the 16th to 19th centuries. The collection covers most of Poland's big names; be prepared for moody portraits and massive battle scenes.

Poznań

Poznań was founded in the 9th century on Ostrów Tumski (Cathedral Island) during the reign of Duke Mieszko I, Poland's first ruler, and became the seat of power along with Gniezno.

EATING IN WROCŁAW: TOP CHOICES

Restauracja Lwia Brama: Top-flight restaurant serves modern Polish fare in an inviting medieval cellar on Cathedral Island. Refined service. *noon-10pm €€€*

Baba: Much lauded upscale yet homestyle Polish bistro helmed by top chef Beata Śniechowska. Always buzzy, with a surprising local wine list. *4-8pm €€€*

Le Gosse Restauracja: Popular neighbourhood bistro with refined air aided by white tablecloths; it does a smashing breakfast. *9am-11pm €€*

Restauracja Wrocławska: Specialises in Silesian fare and great beer. Hearty dishes include seasoned pork, beef, mushroom and potato dishes. *noon-10pm €€*

LUKASZMALKIEWICZ.PL/SHUTTERSTOCK

Poznań Cathedral

In the Second Partition of Poland in 1793, the city fell under Prussian occupation and was later renamed Posen, a period that ended with the Wielkopolska Uprising in 1918. But the city is also famous for another rebellion: the massive June 1956 Uprising that led to calls for political change.

Explore Cathedral Island and Śródka

Located east of the Old Town across the Warta River, **Ostrów Tumski** (Cathedral Island) is where Poznań was founded. The original 9th-century settlement was gradually transformed into an oval stronghold surrounded by wood-and-earth ramparts, with an early stone palace. Mieszko I added a cathedral and further fortifications, and by the end of the 10th century, Poznań was the most powerful stronghold in the country. The best way to appreciate the double-towered Gothic **Poznań Cathedral** *(Katedra Poznańska; katedra.archpoznan.pl; entry free)*, its architecture and its historical background is by picking up an audio guide from the nearby **Porta Posnania Interactive Heritage Centre** *(Porta Poznania ICHOT; bramapoznania.pl; entry adult/child 28/22zł)*.

POZNAŃ'S FESTIVAL CALENDAR

Blues Express: Summer odyssey of blues concerts at train stations, starting in Poznań. *(bluesexpress.pl)*

Old Jazz Festival: Mid-September, with local and international jazz performers. *(oldjazzfestival.pl)*

Malta Festival Poznań: Late June, with alternative theatre and other arts. *(malta-festival.pl)*

St Martin's Day: On 11 November, with a parade from the Church of St Martin (Kościół św Marcina) to the Imperial Palace (Zamek).

Enter Enea Music Festival: Open-air jazz concerts in late May/June at Jezioro Strzeszyńskie, a lake 12km north of town. *(entereneafestival.pl)*

BitterSweet Festival: Top international music acts, held in Citadel Park in September. *(bittersweetfestival.pl)*

 DRINKING IN POZNAŃ'S CENTRE: OUR PICKS

SARP Social Club: Wednesday night jam sessions are a highlight at this bar, often with a jazz-funk flavour. *11-1am Tue-Thu & Sun, from 4pm Mon, 11-3am Fri & Sat*

Dragon Social Club: Eclectic pub and music venue with a relaxed vibe for a diverse, alternative crowd. *noon-1am Mon-Wed & Sun, to 3am Thu-Sat*

Blue Note Jazz Club: Opens for gigs; not all of them are jazz. Check the website at bluenote. poznan.pl. *hours vary*

Brovaria: Microbrewery serving its own Pilsner, honey, dark, wheat and seasonal beers. Also has a restaurant and hotel. *noon-11pm Mon-Sat, 11am-8pm Sun*

LONGFIN MEDIA/SHUTTERSTOCK

Monument to the Victims of June 1956

The June 1956 Uprising in Poznań

The June 1956 industrial strike in Poznań was the first mass protest in the Soviet Bloc, erupting just three years after Stalin's death. It originated in the city's largest industrial plant, the Cegielski Metalworks (then named after Stalin), when workers demanded a refund on an unfairly charged tax. A strike ensued, escalating into a full-scale protest when 100,000 people – one-quarter of Poznań's population at the time – gathered on Plac Mickiewicza, demanding 'bread and freedom' and improved working conditions. Ignored by city officials, an angry crowd stormed police headquarters and the Communist Party building, releasing 257 prisoners from jail. The uprising deteriorated into bloodshed after tanks and troops were brought in. Seventy-six people died and many more were wounded or arrested in this little-known struggle. Today, it is depicted at the **Museum of Poznań June 1956** (*Muzeum Poznańskiego Czerwca 1956; wmn.poznan. pl; entry adult/child 15/10zł*). The small museum is located downstairs in a neo-Romanesque castle, where you can take a fascinating step back into the events. English descriptions are limited. Across the road is the evocative **Monument to the Victims of June 1956**.

EATING IN POZNAŃ'S CENTRE: OUR PICKS

Pyra Bar: Lots of potato dishes, some of which are vegetarian and gluten-free. Or just hang out with a drink. *11am-9pm Sun-Thu, to 11pm Fri & Sat* €

Republika Róż by Andrzej Gołąbek: Menu of hearty, well-prepared Polish mains. Excellent soups, salads and burgers, too. *noon-10pm Tue-Sat, to 8pm Sun* €€

Fromażeria: Acclaimed restaurant with a cheese-tasting menu, combining Polish and French traditions. *5-10.30pm Mon-Thu, to midnight Fri & Sat, 2-10pm Sun* €€€

MUGA: Seasonal international dishes in this long-standing gourmet favourite, with an affiliated Casa de Vinos wine bar. *5-10pm Tue-Sat* €€€

Pomerania

Słowiński National Park
Łeba
RUSSIA
Hel
Gdańsk
Słupsk
Malbork
Olsztyn
Bydgoszcz Grudziądz
Toruń

CASTLES | HISTORY | BEACHES

History, amber, beaches and red bricks have shaped Poland's breezy northern province, one of Poland's most engaging regions.

Cream-hued beaches shelving into the nippy Baltic Sea, wind-crafted dunes vivid against leaden skies, stern red-brick churches and castles erected by a medieval order of pious knights and silenced shipyards that once seethed with anti-communist tumult – this is Pomerania, Poland's north, a land of many faces.

The epicentre of Pomerania is Gdańsk, northern Poland's metropolis, a rapidly modernising city with a photogenic historic centre. Like most of the region, Gdańsk has changed hands many times over the centuries, each invader bequeathing a layer of architecture and culture for today's visitors to enjoy.

South of Gdańsk, top billing goes to Malbork Castle, once the mothership of the Teutonic knights and still the world's largest brick building.

Gdańsk

Follow the Royal Way

Lined by the city's grandest facades, Gdańsk's **Royal Way** was the route Polish kings traditionally paraded down during their periodic visits. Of Poland's three Royal Ways (Warsaw, Kraków and Gdańsk), Gdańsk's is the shortest at just 500m long.

Places

Gdańsk p229
Malbork p232

☑ **TOP TIP**

Buy amber at Gdańsk's Amber Museum, Mariacka St and the amber market in the Foregate at the western end of Długa St.

 GETTING AROUND

Gdańsk has a comprehensive public transport network that's cheap and easy to use. Buses, trams and the SKM train service run to every corner of the city and beyond. Single tickets cost just 4.80zł, and a 24-hour pass is 22zł. The website of the public transport company (ztm.gda.pl) has a useful journey planner. This flat city can also be seen by bike and shared scooters. That said, the best way to see the old historical centre is on foot. Trains run regularly from Gdańsk to Malbork.

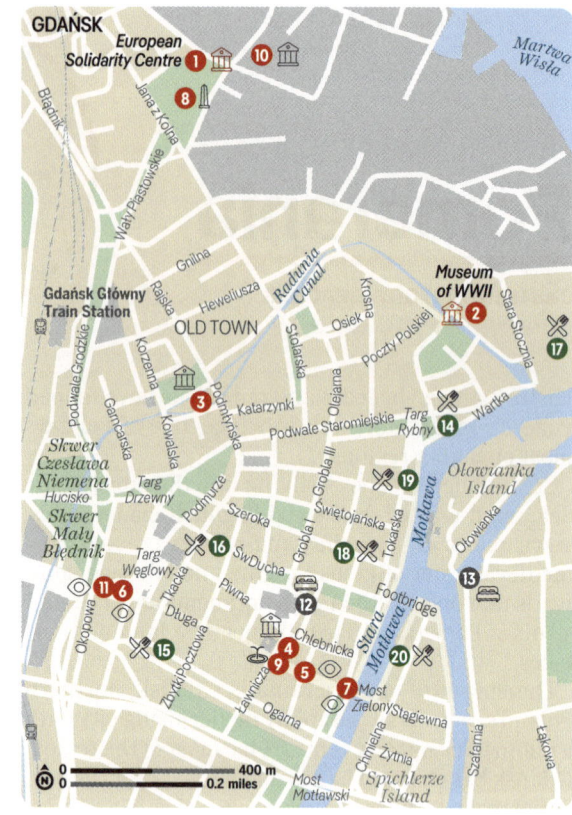

Starting at the western end, turn your back on rumbling Okopowa to face the **Upland Gate** (Brama Wyżynna), the traditional entry point for kings dating from 1574. It now houses the Pomerania Regional Tourist Office. A few steps east rises the **Foregate**, a large 15th-century construction that has served as an execution site, a jail, the city's amber museum and now an amber market. Just beyond the Foregate's hefty doors stands the 17th-century **Złota Brama** (Golden Gate), a triumphal arch. On the other side extends **ul Długa** (Long St) with its many rebuilt townhouse gables.

After 325m, ul Długa suddenly widens out into **Długi Targ**, Gdańsk's showpiece square. On your left gurgles the famous **Neptune Fountain**, behind which lurks the **Artus Court Museum**, part of the Historical Museum of Gdańsk. Also on the right, near the western end of the square, is the city's modest tourist office. Blocking the way to the riverfront is the Royal Way's exit, the 16th-century **Green Gate** (Brama Zielona). Meant as a residence for the king (who never stayed there), it once housed the office of Lech Wałęsa, leader of Poland's first independent trade union and Nobel Peace Prize winner, when he was president. It is now home to the National Museum's photographic exhibition.

Tour Gdańsk's must-see museum

Opened in 2016, the **Museum of WWII** *(muzeum1939.pl; entry adult/concession 32/22zł)* is a bold addition to the northern end of Gdańsk's waterfront. A must-visit attraction, it traces the fate of Poland during the world's greatest conflict, focusing on human suffering. Few leave unmoved. The museum covers 5000 sq m, so a minimum of three hours is needed to do the main exhibit justice.

Opened by local lad and Polish prime minister Donald Tusk in 2017, the museum occupies one of Gdańsk's most striking buildings. Outside, all you can see is a wedge of glass and steel, like a missile that has wedged itself into the earth without exploding. Most of the structure that houses the main exhibition is a bunkerish, brutalist grey concrete block, 14m underground.

The museum is divided chronologically into three sections with 18 individual spaces. The first section examines the causes of the war, tracing the rise of Hitler, the Nazis and other totalitarian regimes after WWI. Section two largely deals with the human suffering caused during WWII, from concentration camp prisoners and the persecuted Polish intelligentsia to soldiers on the front line and those subjected to forced labour. The third and final section looks at how WWII ended and its impact on Europe after 1945. The museum is free on Tuesdays.

A glimpse into prehistory at the Amber Museum

Gdańsk's **Amber Museum** *(muzeumgdansk.pl; entry adult/child 37/26zł)* has become an unmissable attraction since it opened in 2020. It's housed in dramatic style within the massive red-brick hulk of the Great Mill, a medieval structure that has long since ground its last grains.

The interior of the Great Mill has been blacked out to enhance the glow of the nuggets, blobs and small boulders of prehistoric tree sap that seem to be illuminated from within. The lower floor looks at amber in its natural form, with slabs containing insects and plants (inclusions) and lumps in all shapes, sizes and colours, as well as lots of information on how amber is formed and why there is so much of the stuff in the Baltic. The upper floor explores what people have used amber for over the millennia: from medicine to tools to crucifixes, chess sets and furniture. For those in the market for Baltic gold, the best is saved for last in the shape of a large amber jewellery shop.

TOP SOUVENIRS

Amber: Milky white, treacle gold and liver red hunks of fossilised resin wash up on Baltic beaches after winter storms.

Goldwasser: Spice-infused liqueur with flakes of 22-karat gold has been distilled in Gdańsk since 1598. Yes, you can drink it!

Kashubian handicrafts: The region south of Gdańsk produces some distinctively Slavic handicrafts, such as ceramics and linen.

Solidarność memorabilia: A Lech Wałęsa moustache, a 1980s pin badge or just about anything bearing the famous Solidarność logo: memorabilia celebrating the famous trade union makes for a unique souvenir.

Jopenbier: Made by the PG4 microbrewey near the train station, this is Gdańsk's traditional beer.

EATING IN GDAŃSK: BEST LOCAL FOOD

Pomelo Bistro Bar: Using ingredients from mostly local suppliers, the menu at this eclectic, colourful place features Kashubian dishes. *9am-10pm €€*

Restauracja Motlava: Almost gourmet versions of Polish and Kashubian dishes in an understated dining environment. *noon-10pm €€*

TYGLE: Finely crafted local dishes populate the refreshingly brief menu at this well-run restaurant with an upmarket feel. *9am-9pm Mon-Sun €€*

Stacja Food Hall: In the Galeria Metropolitana mall, this food hall has hard-to-find Kashubian options. *noon-10pm Mon-Thu, to midnight Fri & Sat, to 9pm Sun €*

GDAŃSK TOURIST CARD

The Gdańsk Tourist Card *(kartaturysty. visitgdansk.com)* grants free entry to many of the city's attractions, including the Amber Museum, the National Maritime Museum and the Historical Museum of Gdańsk, as well as discounts to other attractions and restaurants. The slightly over-complicated card comes in two versions: Explorer and Premium Explorer, the difference being that Premium gives you access to more attractions while the simple Explorer card is more focused on families. You also have the option of adding public transport tickets to your package. Cards are valid for 24/48/72 hours *(65/75/85zł)* and are available from the city's municipal tourist offices or online. Download the card to your phone to save 5zł.

Solidarity at the shipyard

North of the city centre, Gdańsk's former shipyard played a major role in bringing an end to communism in Eastern Europe. Led by shipyard electrician Lech Wałęsa, it was here that dockers punched a hole in the communist monolith, the resulting cracks spreading to the Berlin Wall and the Iron Curtain.

The first structure you'll see at the shipyard is the striking **Monument to the Fallen Shipyard Workers**, which commemorates those killed in the riots of 1970. This was the first monument in a communist country to commemorate the ideology's own victims.

Though the vast majority of production facilities have been cleared away, the original Lenin shipyard gates have been left untouched, the huge 'STOCZNIA GDAŃSKA' sign a great selfie spot.

The main attraction in the shipyard area is the excellent **European Solidarity Centre** *(ecs.gda.pl; entry adult/child 35/30zł)*, housed in a purposefully ugly example of 21st-century architecture. Its rusty steel plates were designed to evoke ships under construction. The extensive permanent exhibition examines Poland's post-war fight for freedom, from the Gdańsk shipyard strikes of the 1970s to the round-table negotiations of the late 1980s and beyond. The displays blend state-of-the-art multimedia with actual artefacts. Don't miss it.

A short stroll through the now-landscaped former shipyard brings you to the **Sala BHP**, the shipyard's former Health and Safety Building. This is where the dock workers' 21 demands were famously signed off; it has been left exactly as it was then.

Malbork

Visit the world's largest red-brick castle

Malbork Castle *(zamek.malbork.pl; entry adult/concession 80/60zł)* is the largest in Poland – and indeed in Europe. This massive, UNESCO-listed, red-brick complex on the banks of the Nogat River was begun by the Teutonic Knights in the 13th century and served as the order's headquarters for almost 150 years.

Visits are by a self-guided audio tour that ushers you through the complex at a reasonable pace. First up is the **Middle Castle** where the Grand Masters' Palace sports grand interiors, including the kitchen with its 6m-wide fireplace and the Great Refectory, the largest chamber in the castle. Opposite is an excellent amber museum, a highlight of the tour. The prescribed route then continues to **St Anne's Chapel**, where 12 of the Grand Masters are buried.

 EATING IN GDAŃSK: BEST TRADITIONAL RESTAURANTS

Restauracja Gdańska: Hearty traditional dishes amid antiques and model ships at Gdańsk's most famous restaurant. *noon-10pm* €€€	**Restauracja Pod Łososiem:** Founded in 1598 and famous for its fish dishes, this is one of Gdańsk's most highly regarded restaurants. *9am-9pm* €€€	**Kubicki:** Top Gdańsk restaurant dating from more than a century ago. It serves 100% local dishes. *1-10pm* €€€	**Tawerna Dominikańska:** Popular with tourists and locals, this contemporary restaurant by the river serves well-presented local favourites. *10am-1am* €€

EWG3D/GETTY IMAGES

Malbork Castle

Next comes the **High Castle** with its spectacular arcaded courtyard. This was the monastic part of the castle, where monks would sit in session in the Chapter House before heading for the refectory. The mock-up of the monks' medieval kitchen is an aromatic affair with nary a potato or tomato in sight.

One of the most striking interiors is **St Mary's Church**, accessed through a beautiful Gothic doorway known as the Golden Gate. Damaged during the bombardment of 1945, renovation ended in 2016 with the walls left as bare brick – a powerful reminder of the Red Army shells.

History of Malbork Castle

This immense castle took shape in stages. First came the so-called High Castle, the formidable central bastion begun around 1276. When Malbork became the Teutonic Knights' capital in 1309, the fortress expanded. The Middle Castle was built to the side of the high one, followed by the Lower Castle. The whole complex was encircled by three rings of defensive walls. The Polish army seized Malbork in 1457 during the Thirteen Years' War when the military power of the knights started to erode. Malbork then became the residence of Polish kings visiting Pomerania. After the First Partition in 1772, the Prussians turned it into barracks. Despite sustaining serious damage during WWII, the entire complex has been rebuilt.

Places We Love to Stay

€ Budget €€ Midrange €€€ Top End

Warsaw MAP p213

Oki Doki Hostel Old Town
€ Prime-location hostel with pleasant dorms and private rooms, a well-equipped kitchen and inviting social spaces.

Safestay Warsaw Old Town
€ Large and lively hostel with comfy beds, clean bathrooms, well-equipped kitchens, a choice of dorms (some women only) and private rooms, and a friendly on-site bar.

Castle Inn €€ Overlooking Castle Sq, this creatively designed 'art hotel' has quirkily themed rooms, including Jungle, Orient Express and Comic Book.

Chopin Boutique B&B €€ Vintage furniture lends each room a unique vibe. Superb breakfast buffet, free bicycles and nightly Chopin recitals. Also pet friendly.

PURO Warsaw Center €€ Polish brand of Scandi-style design hotels has a winner with its brand-new, perfectly located property. The Loreta bar has great skyline views.

Hotel Bristol €€€ Warsaw's most historic address where VIPs and celebs have stayed throughout the decades. Its neoclassical facade conceals original art nouveau features.

Kraków MAP p219

Globetrotter Guest House
€ Spacious, wallet-friendly private rooms (singles, doubles and quads) in a quiet Old Town corner. Has tea/coffee facilities, laundry service and guest fridge.

Dream Hostel € A mixture of 5-bed dorms and private en-suites with lime-green accents in a handy central location. A sound Kazimierz choice; the guest kitchen is a bonus.

PURO Kráków Kazimierz
€€ Stylish rooms, spot-on technology, a well-equipped gym and all-day brasserie attract millennial professionals.

Hotel Gródek €€ A tranquil cul-de-sac location, rooftop terrace overlooking the Old Town and a library with a cosy bar are perks at this intimate boutique hotel with individually-designed rooms.

Bonerowski Palace €€€ Luxe 14th-century palace featuring Europe's largest Swarovski chandelier, medieval portals and restored polychrome decor; the 16 antique-furnished rooms and suites come with marble bathrooms.

Wrocław

Babel Hostel € Close to the train station, pleasant budget accommodation, dorms and private rooms in renovated apartment rooms with pretty decor. Funky common room.

Wrocław Patio €€ Spread behind the Victorian facades of two adjoining tenements overlooking the Church of St Elizabeth and connected by a sunny courtyard. Has comfortable rooms in many styles.

Hotel Monopol €€€ Top hotel holds 120 luxurious rooms behind an elaborately sculpted facade. Bonuses include a panoramic rooftop restaurant and bar, pool, sauna and a breakfast buffet.

Poznań

Hotel Stare Miasto €€ Good value choice featuring a tastefully chandeliered foyer and spacious breakfast room. Bright, decent-sized rooms with some cheaper smaller singles.

Hotel Altus Poznań €€ Old Town high-rise hotel on Święty Marcin with stylish rooms and great views from the upper floors.

Puro Poznań Stare Miasto
€€€ Central location, underground car park, designer decor, comfortable lobby, helpful staff and sharply styled bedrooms flooded with light.

Gdańsk MAP p230

Camping Nr 218 Stogi € Gdańsk's best-known campsite at Stogi Beach. Good facilities, but it gets overcrowded in July and August.

Hotel Podewils €€€ Vintage guestrooms, elegant period furniture, carpet bags of old-world charm and an unrivalled view of the Old Town across the Motława River.

Gotyk House €€€ Gothic-themed guesthouse squeezed into Gdańsk's oldest building. Has a wonderful location next to St Mary's Church.

Practicalities

LGBTIQ+ Travellers

Poland isn't a place that welcomes overt displays of LGBTIQ+ sexual orientation. Since 1990, this deeply religious country has found LGBTIQ+ rights tough to handle. The populist Law and Justice Party openly encourages anti-gay sentiments.

Health

Poland has a good healthcare system. Urban hospitals are on par with Western Europe, but in rural areas this may not be the case. You'll need an EHIC (European Health Insurance Card) to access care for free. A UK GHIC (Global Health Insurance Card) will get you free emergency treatment.

Electricity

Polish current works on 230V/50Hz. Almost all sockets in Poland are the modern European two-prong type. If travelling from outside Europe you'll need an adapter.

Smoking

Poland has had a comprehensive smoking ban since 2010, and lighting up is prohibited in all public places. However, because of the relatively high number of smokers in the country, many ignore this rule, especially at public transport stations. Cheaper hotel rooms in Poland can still have a bit of a stale cigarette smell.

BBA PHOTOGRAPHY/SHUTTERSTOCK

Old Town Market Square (p215), Warsaw

Opening Hours

Banks 9am–5pm Monday to Friday, to 1pm Saturday
Offices 8am–4pm Monday to Friday
Post Offices 8am–8pm Monday to Friday, to 1pm Saturday
Restaurants 11am–11pm
Shops 8am–6pm Monday to Friday, 10am–8pm Saturday
Supermarkets 7am–10pm Monday to Saturday

Visas

Poland is part of the Schengen Area. Visitors from the UK, USA, Australia, New Zealand, Canada, Japan and many other countries do not need visas. Most visa-free nations outside the EU can stay for a maximum of 90 days out of 180.

Public Holidays

New Year's Day 1 January
Epiphany 6 January
Easter Sunday & Monday March/April
Labour Day 1 May
Constitution Day 3 May
Pentecost Sunday 7th Sunday after Easter
Corpus Christi 9th Thursday after Easter
Assumption Day 15 August
All Saints' Day 1 November
Independence Day 11 November
Christmas 25 and 26 December

Language

Polish vowels are generally pronounced short. Nasal vowels are pronounced as though you're trying to force the air through your nose, and are indicated with n or m following the vowel. Note that ow is pronounced as in 'how', kh as the 'ch' in the Scottish loch, and zh as the 's' in 'pleasure'. Also, r is rolled in Polish and the apostrophe (') indicates a slight y sound.

Basics

Hello. Cześć. *cheshch*
Goodbye. Do widzenia. *do vee·dze·nya*
Excuse me. Przepraszam. *ps·he·pra·sham*
Sorry. Przepraszam. *pshe·pra·sham*
Please. Proszę. *pro·she*
Thank you. Dziękuję. *jyen·koo·ye*
Yes. Tak. *tak*
No. Nie. *nye*
What's your name?
Jak się pan/pani nazywa? (m/f pol) *yak shye pan/pa·nee na·zi·va*
My name is ...
Nazywam się ... *na·zi·vam shye ...*
Do you speak English? Czy pan/pani mówi *chi pan/pa·nee moo·vee* po angielsku? (m/f) *po an·gyel·skoo*
I don't understand.
Nie rozumiem. *nye ro·zoo·myem*

Transport

boat łódź *wooj*
bus autobus *ow·to·boos*
plane samolot *sa·mo·lot*
train pociąg *po·chonk*
One ... ticket Proszę bilet *pro·she bee·let* **(to Katowice),** ... (do Katowic) *... (do ka·to·veets)* **please.**
one-way w jedną stronę *v yed·nom stro·ne*
return powrotny *po·vro·tni*

Emergencies

Help! Na pomoc! *na po·mots*

Go away! Odejdź! *o·deyj*
Call the doctor/police!
Zadzwoń po lekarza/policję! *zad·zvon' po le·ka·zha/po·lee·tsye*
I'm lost. Zgubiłem/Zgubiłam się. (m/f) *zgoo·bee·wem/zgoo·bee·wam shye*
I'm ill. Jestem chory/a. (m/f) *yes·tem kho·ri/a*
Where are the toilets?
Gdzie są toalety? *gjye som to·a·le·ti*

Eating & Drinking

What would you recommend? Co by pan polecił? (m)/Co by pani poleciła? (f) *tso bi pan po·le·cheew/tso bi pa·nee po·le·chee·wa*
Do you have vegetarian food? Czy jest żywność wegetariańska? *chi yest zhiv·noshch ve·ge·tar·yan'·ska*
I'd like the ..., please. Proszę o rachunek/jadłospis *pro·she o ra·k·hoo·nek/. ya·dwo·spees*
I'll have ... Proszę ... *pro·she ...*
Cheers! Na zdrowie! *na zdro·vye*

Shopping & Services

I'm looking for ... Szukam ... *shoo·kam*
How much is it? Ile to kosztuje? *ee·le to kosh·too·ye*
That's too expensive. To jest za drogie. *to yest za dro·gye*
market targ *tark*
post office urząd pocztowy *oo·zhond poch·to·vi*
tourist office biuro turystyczne *by·oo·ro too·ris·tich·ne*

NUMBERS

1
jeden *ye·den*

2
dwa *dva*

3
trzy *tshi*

4
cztery *chte·ri*

5
pięć *pyench*

6
sześć *sheshch*

7
siedem *shye·dem*

8
osiem *o·shyem*

9
dziewięć *jye·vyench*

10
dziesięć *jye·shence*

Tram, Kraków (p218)

MONEY
Currency: Złoty (zł)

CASH VERSUS CARDS
Even a mobile coffee machine on the back of a bike might take a credit or debit card. However, always carry some cash just in case.

EUROS
The common currency is not likely to make an appearance any time soon, but you can still pay with euros at major tourist sights and most city hotels, and even some restaurants.

ATMS
ATMs are ubiquitous in cities and towns, but villages rarely have one. Stick to banks and avoid free-standing Euronet ATMs in shops, which give a much poorer rate of exchange than other ATMs and charge a fee.

Arriving & Getting Around

Poland may be Eastern Europe's best served country by air, with flights from across the continent and overseas. Improving transport infrastructure means getting around is not the trial it once was.

City Transport
All Polish cities and large towns have bus, tram and even metro services that are cheap and efficient. Download the relevant transport app on your smartphone to avoid hassling with tickets.

Polish Trains
PKP *(Polskie Koleje Państwowe; pkp.pl)* is the main train operator. The system is undergoing extensive modernisation with new tracks and stations coming online every week. PKP also runs trains to other European cities.

Driving Essentials
Drive on the right and have headlights switched on day and night, year-round. The blood alcohol limit is 0.2g/L. Road conditions are improving, but watch out for bad surfaces and potholes in rural areas.

Arriving by Air
With over 20 million passengers annually, Warsaw's Chopin Airport (WAW) is the busiest in the country. Ryanair has its own airport: Modlin (WMI), 40km north of the capital. Kraków (KRK) and Gdańsk (GDN) also have busy airports with domestic and international connections. There are flights to Poland from around the world, including North America, the Middle East and Asia.

Curated by
Luke Waterson

Slovakia

MAJESTIC MOUNTAINS, CASTLES AND MEDIEVAL MARVELS

Close to tourist hotspots Vienna and Budapest, Slovakia will always be beautifully off-piste. This is its allure: ornate historic architecture and astounding mountainous terrain that remains perennially crowd free.

Nature defines Slovakia. The capital Bratislava has an Old Town full of arresting medieval and baroque buildings, but the forest-swaddled hills looming just behind it dominate the proceedings. These soon swoop into the serrated summits of the High Tatras, Europe's smallest alpine mountain range, yet still home to many of Eastern Europe's loftiest peaks and the Carpathians' very highest. Then there's the east's gorge-gouged national park Slovenský Raj; UNESCO-listed, cave-riddled Slovenský kras; and another UNESCO spectacle, the primeval beech forests of the Carpathians. In the south, the Danube River frames the landscape.

Consequently, the culture here is of a back-to-nature, down-to-earth sort: hiking, cross-country skiing, alfresco fire-pit grill-ups, overnight sojourns in middle-of-nowhere mountain houses, traditional costumed dances and brightly hued wooden architecture all showcase the countryside's extraordinarily vivid folklore.

Tradition is not lost here, as it can be in more urbanised nations. Surrounded by busier destinations like Austria (west), Czechia (northwest) and Hungary (south), this under-the-radar country may not receive the attention it deserves. But if you dig entire districts, villages and towns of seamlessly preserved medieval buildings, if you're entranced by the world's densest concentration of castles, if you yearn for thick forests and jagged mountains and prefer these places to be untrammeled and peaceful, Slovakia should be your next adventure.

KAYO/SHUTTERSTOCK

THE MAIN AREAS

BRATISLAVA
Slovakia's capital and castle-dotted surroundings. **p242**

WESTERN SLOVAKIA
More castles and national parks. **p248**

HIGH TATRAS & EASTERN SLOVAKIA
Mountains and medieval townscapes. **p251**

For places to stay in Slovakia, see p255

BEATRICAB/SHUTTERSTOCK

Above: Lomnický štít (p252), Tatranská Lomnica; Right: Blue Church (p246), Bratislava

Find Your Way

Slovakia's centre-of-Europe location extends from Austria and Czechia in the west, Hungary in the south, Poland in the north and Ukraine in the east.

High Tatras & Eastern Slovakia, p251

Come here for hiking, skiing and *chata* (mountain house) stays. Continue east for medieval towns and stunning landscapes.

Western Slovakia, p248

Steep forests and hidden fortresses enchant throughout the countrified Malé Karpaty (Small Carpathians).

Bratislava, p242

The medieval centre delights. Connoisseurs relish the museums while nature-lovers embrace the proximity of the river and tree-cloaked hills.

TRAIN

From Bratislava, the main cross-country line has hourly links to Trenčín (1¼ hours), Žilina (two hours; for Malá Fatra national park), Poprad (four hours; for the High Tatras) and Košice (5½ hours). Trains serve Vienna and Budapest, too.

CAR

It's 4½ hours' drive (437km) from Bratislava to Košice via Nitra and Poprad. This journey runs almost the entire west-to-east length of Slovakia. Cars help in remote rural areas and poorly connected destinations like Banská Štiavnica.

POLAND

UKRAINE

HUNGARY

CZECHIA

AUSTRIA

Vistula

Tisza

Danube

Bardejov
Prešov
Michalovce
Košice
Spiš Castle
Levoča
Slovenský Raj National Park
Kežmarok
Ždiar
Zakopane
Poprad
Popradské Pleso
Vrátna Valley
Liptovský Mikuláš
Ružomberok
Jasná
Vlkolínec
Banská Bystrica
Banská Štiavnica
Žilina
Martin
Čičmany
Prievidza
Trenčín
Trenčín Castle
Piešťany
Trnava
Nitra
BRATISLAVA
Bratislava Forest Park
St Martin's Cathedral
Hlavné námestie

50 miles
100 km

Hlavné námestie (p242), Bratislava

Plan Your Time

One week is sufficient for Slovakia's highlights. Use Bratislava or Košice as your base: the former for culture, the latter for mountain scenery.

A Weekend Break

● Begin in **Bratislava's** comely medieval Old Town, discovering knockout square **Hlavné námestie** (p242) and **Bratislava Castle** (p245) for city views. Visit some cafes: Bratislava's are special. Take an afternoon picnic to hilly **Bratislava Forest Park** (p246). On day two, head to icons like the **Blue Church** (p246), **City History Museum** (p243) or a half-day exploration of castle **Hrad Devín** (p248).

A Week or More

● Spend two to three days in Bratislava, and don't miss the **Danubiana Meulensteen Art Museum** (p246) and the fortress **Červený Kameň** (p249). Tour **Trenčín Castle** (p249), then proceed to Poprad to explore the **High Tatras** (p251) for two days. Wander medieval gems **Levoča** (p254) and **Bardejov** (p254), and finish in dignified Košice, arranged around **St Elizabeth's Cathedral** (p254).

SEASONAL HIGHLIGHTS

SPRING
Bratislava City Days enlivens the capital with street performances and openings of normally off-limits city spaces.

SUMMER
Bratislava Cultural Summer delivers two months of music. In July, check music fest Pohoda (Trenčin) or Východná Folk Festival (High Tatras).

AUTUMN
Western Slovak towns and the Tokaj wine region near Košice celebrate grape harvest; Pezinok has the biggest wine festival.

WINTER
Bratislava's **Christmas Markets** (p244), which begin in late November, brighten the city centre.

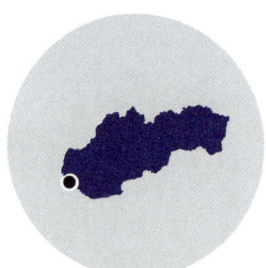

Bratislava

ARCHITECTURE | CAFES | COUNTRYSIDE EXCURSIONS

GETTING AROUND

Walking around the Old Town is best, though wheelchairs and prams may struggle with the cobbled streets. Trolleybuses run from Hlavná stanica train station to the Old Town and Koliba for Bratislava Forest Park. Take buses from Most SNP bus station to Hrad Devín or Danubiana Meulensteen Art Museum. Trains (from Hlavná stanica) or buses (from main bus station Mlynské nivy) link the capital with Western Slovakia. Seasonal boats connect Bratislava and Devín.

☑ **TOP TIP**

Bratislava's Old Town invites you to linger, but don't limit your time to just this area: Bratislava Forest Park, Danubiana Meulensteen Art Museum and stupendous castles like those at Devín are all a part of Bratislava's rich tapestry.

Bratislava is an ideal mid-sized city, big enough to have a swag bag of internationally significant sights yet sporting a centre small enough to stroll. Abutting dramatic nature – its suburbs ascend into the lonely foothills of the Malé Karpaty (Small Carpathians) and its Old Town brushes the Danube – it's also well-connected to major cities like Vienna, Budapest and Prague.

At the centre of Europe, Bratislava has always been prone to invasions. It fell to Roman, Hungarian and Austrian invaders, was briefly incorporated in early Slavic states, and spent time as a socialist country following WWII. This historical hotchpotch explains a cityscape that interweaves a stone castle built by the Slavic Great Moravian people, medieval Hungarian burghers' houses and baroque palaces, and some startling Soviet brutalism.

Yet, as you unwind in an elegant cafe-bar in the lively Old Town, with live music reverberating nearby, you'll likely opine that Bratislava – upheaval aside – has had the last laugh.

Meander the Old Town

Bratislava's iconic medieval heart

No matter how often you visit Bratislava, acquainting yourself with the city on foot always works wonders. Enter the Staré mesto (Old Town) through the only surviving city gate from Bratislava's 13th-century walls, **Michael's Gate** *(Michalská brána; muzeumbratislava.sk; adult/child €6/4)*. Buy tickets in nearby **Red Crayfish Pharmacy** and climb the small baroque tower for stunning panoramas. Afterwards, walk cobbled Michalská, Biela and Františkánske námestie to **Hlavné námestie**, the city's main square and the showcase for some of its most beloved historic buildings.

Among the architectural set-pieces, the standout is **Stará radnica** (Old Town Hall), a 14th-century clocktower-crested

BRATISLAVA

Tolstého

Slavín War Memorial
(600m)

Bratislava Forest Park (4km); 🏕
Loft Hotel Bratislava (200m)

Hotel Arcus (400m);
Roxor (1.1km)

OLD TOWN
(STARÉ MESTO)

Bistro St. Germain (1.1km);
Bike Bratislava (1.3km)

Blue
Church

Hlavné
námestie

City History
Museum

St Martin's
Cathedral

Bratislava
Castle

Eugena
Suchoňa
nám

Hviezdoslavovo
nám

Nám L
Štúra

Danube
River

Danubiana Meulensteen
Art Museum (2km)

0   500 m
0   0.25 miles

complex that's among Slovakia's oldest standing structures. This encompasses the excellent **City History Museum** *(Múzeum mesta Bratislavy; muzeumbratislava.sk; adult/child €8/4)* charting Bratislava's importance down the ages, from its role as monarchical crowning place to its guilds and crafts. Tickets include entry to the Apponyiho Palace, prime Bratislava views from the tower and a ground-floor exhibition on local viticulture (tastings cost extra).

SLOVAKIAN WINE

The vineyards carpeting Western Slovakia's Malé Karpaty are a somewhat surprising landscape feature. But winemaking traditions run deep: viticulture here predates Roman occupation. Southeast Slovakia's honey-like Tokaj wines, which King Louis XIV called 'the king of wines, wine of kings', are Slovakia's most distinctive; the Malé Karpaty region, meanwhile, produces wonderful whites. **Pezinok**, with its wine cellars, winemaking museum and mid-September **wine festival** (*visitbratislava.com*), makes an atmospheric spot to sample the local wines. Malá Tŕňa, southeast of Košice, is the Tokaj region hub. Several Bratislava bars and the City History Museum – which has an expert-selected collection featuring any year's 100 best wines – are the capital's best places to partake.

Bratislava Castle

SAIKO5P/SHUTTERSTOCK

In the square's centre, **Roland's Fountain** supposedly dates to 1572. It's topped by a knight who bears a likeness to ex-Hungarian king Maximilian II. According to local legend, he bows every New Year's Eve. Bratislava's fabled **Christmas Markets** present the square Hlavné námestie at its loveliest.

Marvel at St Martin's Cathedral

The crowning place of Hungarian monarchs

St Martin's Cathedral (*Dóm svätého Martina, dom.fara.sk; entry free*), with its terracotta roof and white walls sheering to an 85m-high spire, has a colourful history: it was the coronation place for 19 Hungarian kings and queens between 1563 and 1830, a time when Ottoman invasions made the previous monarch-making spot (Székesfehérvár) too dangerous. The interior of this 14th- and 15th-century Gothic sanctuary also has four chapels, a horseback statue of St Martin, extensive crypts and stained-glass windows to hold you in thrall.

Boat Trips along the Danube

Bratislava by water

Bratislava is the fourth-biggest city on the EU's longest river and Danube boat trips, conveniently departing from the Staré

 EATING IN BRATISLAVA: CAFES AND SNACKS

Black.: Coffee roasters concentrate on the exquisite coffee here, also tempting with cakes and vegan sandwiches. *9am-6pm* €

Emil: In the Mirbach Palace, Emil serves coffee and light bites in its vaulted interior and courtyard. *l0am-l0pm Tue-Sat, to 8pm Sun, to 6pm Mon* €

Bistro St Germain: This chic eatery concocts breakfasts, three-tier sandwiches, burgers and wraps. *llam-llpm Mon & Tue, from 8am Wed-Sat, 8am-9pm Sun* €

Soupa: Friendly to wallets, dietary restrictions and the environment, veggie- and vegan-friendly Soupa is a stalwart choice. *8am-6pm Mon-Fri* €

mesto's southern edge east of Most SNP, are a fun way to appreciate the city and its fetching surrounds. Trips with **LOD** *(lod.sk)* head upriver to Hrad Devín (p248), a crag-top castle on the Slovakia–Austria border *(€24 return; daily Apr-Sep, weekends Oct & Nov)*, and along Bratislava's stretch of the Danube *(€15 return; daily Apr-Sep)* to catch optimal Old Town vistas. **Twin City Liner** *(twincityliner.com; from €25 one-way; 1½ hours)* runs boats upriver to Vienna, also passing Hrad Devín and Donau-Auen National Park's tranquil forested riverbanks.

Climb to Bratislava Castle
A fortified settlement from the beginning

The capital's dominant landmark is the huge four-turreted **Bratislava Castle** *(snm.sk; grounds free, museum adult/child €14/7)*, standing on its own hilltop across the ring road west of the Staré mesto. The 9th-century remnants of the original Great Moravian castle are still on display and the 13th-century **Crown Tower** can be climbed for bird's-eye views. The current castle's white walls and terracotta roofs were mostly achieved in the 1760s under renowned Habsburg monarch Maria Theresa. Today, the Renaissance- and rococo-styled fortress can be explored through its **Museum of History**, which provides an overview of Slovakia from medieval times onward and serves as an access point to the castle's interior, including the Crown Tower. But the free-of-charge **grounds** are the highlight: the **baroque gardens** and zigzagging pathways afford beautiful views of the Danube-wrapped Staré mesto.

Stroll along the Hviezdoslavovo námestie
Home to performing arts and quirky statues

Long tree-lined **Hviezdoslavovo námestie** *(free)* is probably the most appealing city square for lingering. At the eastern end are the historic building of the 1886-built **Slovak National Theatre** (closed for repairs, with shows currently at the **New SND**, just southeast of the Staré mesto) and Reduta Palace housing the **Slovak Philharmonic** *(filharmonia.sk; tickets from €16)*. Prefer quirky to queen-like? Check much-loved statue **Watcher** *(Čumil; visitbratislava.com; free)*, a statue of a worker emerging from a manhole. It's north of the square along Rybárska brana.

INDEPENDENCE STRUGGLES

Short-lived Slavic kingdoms Samo's Empire (c 631–c 658 CE) and Great Moravia (c 833–c 927 CE) both encompassed parts of Slovakia. But Slovak history has largely taken place under the jurisdiction of foreign powers, in particular the Hungarians, who controlled Slovakia between 895 CE and 1918. After WWI, a temporary Slovak Socialist Republic was created in the southeast before Slovakia was incorporated into Czechoslovakia. Then came German (WWII) and Soviet (1947–91) control. Only in 1993, after the Velvet Divorce brought separation from Czechia, did Slovakia become permanently independent. Bratislava's Námestie SNP is the cradle of Slovak independence: this was where crowds gathered during the run-up to the fall of communism.

 EATING IN BRATISLAVA: BEST RESTAURANTS

| **Modrá Hviezda:** The 'Blue Star' specialises in glamorous Slovak dishes, like venison with caramel-cognac sauce. *5.30-10pm Wed-Fri, noon-10pm Sat & Sun* €€€ | **Bratislava Flagship:** Popular intro to Slovak cuisine in a vault-roofed former theatre. *11am-10pm Mon-Thu, 11am-11pm Fri, noon-11pm Sat, noon-10pm Sun* €€ | **Gatto Matto:** Out-of-this-world pizza is the driving force of this Italian restaurant within a smart townhouse near St Martin's Cathedral. *11am-10pm* €€ | **Roxor:** The journey to this standout near Račianské mýto park 2km north of the Staré mesto is repaid by Bratislava's best burger experience. *11am-9pm* €€ |

BUDGET-FRIENDLY TIPS

Slovakia is among Europe's cheapest countries to travel in. These tips will help you save even more. The Bratislava Card *(card.visitbratislava. com)*, starting at €30 for 24 hours, secures free entry or discounts to a number of the capital's attractions and eating and drinking spots. Many city experiences are free anyway, like the Bratislava Castle grounds and stellar viewpoints , including the Slavín War Memorial and Bratislava Forest Park.
  Meanwhile, a restaurant's set menu *(denné menu)* often gets you a substantial one- or two-course meal for a few euros. Heading across Slovakia, train travel is cheap, with a Bratislava–Košice fare costing under €20. Public transport, be it the train or bus, is affordable, reliable and reaches most key places.

Hike Around Bratislava Forest Park
Explore the Small Carpathians
The **Malé Karpaty** (Small Carpathians) forested massif sweeps northeast across Western Slovakia to Slovakia's best national parks in the Carpathians proper. Bratislava's northern suburbs rise into the foothills through **Bratislava Forest Park** *(visitbratislava.com; free)*. Amid these hilly, thickly wooded footpaths and biking trails is the **Kamzík TV mast** *(veza.sk; observation deck €7)*, its revolving restaurant and viewpoint marking the park's high point. From Hlavná stanica, take bus 145 or trolleybus 44 to final stop Koliba: Kamzík is then a 1.75km walk.

Bratislava's Blue Church
The city's prettiest building
Dedicated to St Elisabeth of Hungary, the early 20th-century **Blue Church** *(modrykostol.fara.sk; free)* is a powder-blue-and-cream vision. The edifice is an art nouveau masterpiece, from its undulating arches to cupola-crested clocktower tip (36.8m). See the website for its limited opening hours.

From Contemporary Art to White-Water Rafting
Danube-based delights in Čunovo
Countrified suburb Čunovo has two top-tier Bratislava attractions right on the Danube – although each is likely to attract a different type of person. The main draw is Slovakia's most spectacular art gallery. Atop a gorgeous river promontory, the **Danubiana Meulensteen Art Museum** *(danubiana. sk; adult/child €12/6)* impresses with its waterside location and outdoor sculpture garden. Inside, floor-to-ceiling gallery windows overlooking the Danube are the eye-catching accompaniment to contemporary art displays, including works by groundbreaking Slovak artists like Rudolf Sikora and Miroslav Cipár.

Practically adjacent to the museum is the world-class watersports complex **Divoka Voda** *(divokavoda.sk)*, its two churning channels offering Class II to IV rapids for instructor-guided white-water rafting *(from €35 per 1½ hours)* and kayaking *(from €10 per hour)*.

To get here, take bus 91 from Most SNP bus station to end-of-the-line Čunovo and walk (3km). Alternatively, hire bikes from **Bike Bratislava** *(bikebratislava.sk; €25 per day)* and cycle from the Staré mesto (19km via riverside cycleways).

Oddball Tours of the Soviet Era
Take in the city's brutalist landmarks
Slovakia was where the Eastern Bloc once met the West, and Soviet-era builders consequently made bold brutalist statements along the frontier in Bratislava. Most striking in the Staré mesto is **Most SNP** *(u-f-o.sk; adult €9.90)*, a

Slavín War Memorial

BEST MUSEUMS & GALLERIES

Bratislava City Gallery: The best bit about this nationally important art collection, spread across the Mirbach and Pálffy Palaces, is Pálffy Palace's 'Passage' exhibit featuring 15,000 books, arranged around mirrors, which creates the illusion of peering into a never-ending library.

Slovak National Gallery: Engaging riverside art space hosting the city centre's best contemporary art exhibits.

Museum of Jewish Culture: Compelling museum located in the city's former Jewish quarter, which was largely destroyed during the construction of the Bratislava ring road.

Nedbalka Gallery: Focuses on displays of 20th-century Slovak art and sculpture, impressively arranged around an atrium.

bridge outlandishly crowned by a 95m-high bar-restaurant and flying saucer-shaped observation deck. It rises above the ring road where it crosses the Danube. Across the bridge to the south is the super suburb **Petržalka**, Europe's largest Soviet-era housing estate.

Another exceptional viewpoint is the **Slavín War Memorial** *(visitbratislava.com; free)*, northwest of the Staré mesto on Slavín Hill. The monument, topped by a swastika-crushing soldier, honours the Soviet soldiers who died liberating Bratislava from German forces in 1945; it was built between 1957 and 1960.

Visit these and many other Soviet-era landmarks with the fun offbeat tours run by **Authentic Slovakia** *(authenticslovakia.com; per person in normal/Soviet-era vehicle €35/55)*.

 ## DRINKING IN BRATISLAVA: BEST BARS

KC Dunaj: Alternative cultural centre with a rooftop bar and eclectic performances from live music to comedy. *4pm-1am Thu-Sat, to midnight Sun-Wed*

Bratislavský Meštiansky Pivovar: This brewery serves its own beers along with traditional Slovak dishes. *11am-11pm Tue-Sat, to 10pm Sun & Mon*

Cafe Verne: Mingle with locals to sample buzzing Bratislava nightlife in this boho spot. *9am-midnight Mon-Thu, 9am-1am Fri, 10am-1am Sat, 10am-midnight Sun*

Sky Bar & Restaurant: Drinks, especially cocktails, and Spanish-influenced cuisine with stunning Staré mesto views. *5pm-midnight Tue-Sat*

Western Slovakia

CASTLES | ANCIENT MINING TOWN | NATIONAL PARK

Places

☑ TOP TIP

A great way to explore Western Slovakia is on foot in the Malé Karpaty hills. The beautiful 102km Štefánikova Magistrála trail runs across the region from Hrad Devín at the Slovakia–Austria border to Bradlo. The path is named after Slovak WWI hero Milan Štefánik.

Western Slovakia is an outdoor playground of bedazzling, forest-cloaked and castle-flanked mountains that increase in magnitude as they approach the peaks of the High Tatras to the east. And best of all? It's easily visited on day trips from Bratislava. In addition to splendid strongholds, like those at Devín, Červený Kameň and Trenčín, there's also the enchanting UNESCO-listed medieval mining settlement of Banská Štiavnica in the south and an explosion of greenery in the folklore-rich Malá Fatra National Park further east. The latter was once the stomping ground of Slovakia's real-life Robin Hood: Juraj Jánošík, a 17th-century bandit-turned-hero, and the topography befits that of an outlaw's lair, with bulky mountains tumbling into concealed forested ravines. Meanwhile, the Malé Karpaty (Small Carpathians) range of hills ramparts the region's north, presiding over the homonymous wine region that yield much of the country's best vino.

Devín

TIME FROM BRATISLAVA: **25MIN** 🚌

Embattled borderland bastions

Bratislava's suburbs stretch to the Austrian border, where clifftop castle **Hrad Devín** *(hraddevin.mmb.sk; €8)* guards the Danube's confluence with the Morava. First built in stone in the 13th century, it contains an archaeological exhibition

---

 GETTING AROUND

Regular trains head northeast from Bratislava to Trenčín (1¼ hours) and Žilina (two hours), the jumping-off point for Malá Fatra National Park. Buses connect Bratislava to the important castles of Devín, Červený Kameň and Bojnice. Buses are also best from Bratislava to Banská Štiavnica, though there are fewer services. And don't discount walking. Picturesque pathways, including the long-distance Štefánikova Magistrála, thread the entire region through its lovely forested hills.

Trenčín Castle

showcasing site finds from Neolithic times onwards and stages summertime events from kid-friendly medieval games to DJ sessions. Bus 29 links Devín to Bratislava's Most SNP bus station. Boats (p245) run here too.

Trenčín

TIME FROM BRATISLAVA: 1¼HR

Castle-topped medieval treasure

Trenčín, the 2026 European Capital of Culture, is a dashing, richly historic city built around a beguiling square. The cityscape's climax is cragtop **Trenčín Castle** *(muzeumtn.sk; adult/child €9/4, with tour €12/5)*, its storied walls dating to the 11th century. A famous Roman inscription from 179 CE on the cliff beneath the castle can be glimpsed from the Hotel Elizabeth.

Banská Štiavnica

TIME FROM BRATISLAVA: 3½HR

Magical mining tour

Sparkling like the silver once found in its hills, this UNESCO-listed 13th-century mining town is a trove of riches. Top sights include burghers' houses from the 16th to 18th century, the

CASTLES AND CRACKING VIEWPOINTS

Hrad Bojnice: This spellbinding, still-furnished turreted affair is the most fairytale-like fortress. It's 60km southeast of Trenčín and 177km northeast of Bratislava.

Hrad Beckov: A whopping fortress presiding over the Váh River valley from a 60m-high crag; 20km southwest of Trenčín.

Hrad Červený Kameň: Above Častá, 37km northeast of Bratislava, this furnished 16th-century castle stands out amid the green Malé Karpaty slopes.

Vrátna Valley: Climb by cable car through Malá Fatra National Park to access ridge hikes at 1500m.

Čičmany: This village, a 1¼-hour bus ride southwest of Žilina, is a cherished vestige of Slovak folklore.

Kalvaria: The best panoramas of Banská Štiavnica come from the baroque chapel complex.

EATING BEYOND BRATISLAVA: OUR PICKS

La Piazetta: Suave space in castle-crowned Trenčí n for some of Slovakia's finest Italian cuisine. *11am-10pm Mon-Thu, to 11pm Fri, noon-10pm Sat €€*

Gurmánsky Grob: Brilliant spot with an inviting garden 20km northeast of Bratislava. Sample traditional Slovak oven-roasted goose. *11am-10pm €€*

Terchovská Koliba Diery: Scenic restaurant near Terchová's Horné Diery gorge evokes a romanticised shepherd's hut, with traditional Slovak fare. *10am-9.30pm €€*

Elizabeth Cukráreň & Kaviareň: Pamper yourself in Piešt'any, then enjoy coffee, cake or local wine at this elegant spa complex. *9am-9pm €*

JAROMOND/SHUTTERSTOCK

Malá Fatra National Park

astounding hillside chapel complex **Kalvária** *(kalvaria.org; free)* and the dignified centrepiece **Old Castle** *(muzeumbs. sk; adult/child €8/4)*. Delve into the centuries-old mining heritage at the **Open-Air Mining Museum** *(muzeumbs.sk; adult/child €14/7)* 2km west of town, where 90-minute guided tours explore old mine passageways. Buses from Bratislava change at Zvolen; trains take longer.

Malá Fatra National Park

TIME FROM BRATISLAVA: **3HR** 🚌 + 🚍

Folklore, gorges and mountain magic

This tantalising 226-sq-km mountainous swathe is greener and less visited than the High Tatras. Yet it contains some serious summits, including high point **Velký Kriváň** (1708m), plus extensive hiking trails and a beautiful ski area.

Northern village Terchová makes the best base. It's crested by the **Juraj Jánošík Statue**, which honours the local folk hero and outlaw, whose birth and exploits in these parts imbue the peaks with added mystique. The must-do hike is **Horné Diery** *(slovakia.com; free)* a precipitous waterfall-splashed gorge reached via a three-hour out-and-back trail with ladder-and-chain sections. Access it from Hotel Diery, 2km east of Terchová. A photogenic road south of Terchová rises to Vrátna Výťah and the **Vratna Valley ski area** *(vratna.sk; day pass €25)*. Take **Vrátna Cable Car** *(€21 return)* for a spectacular 15-minute ascent to the Snilovské saddle (1524m) below Chleb Peak. Ski slopes (Dec-Mar) and more hiking trails beckon up top.

Buses connect Terchová to Žilina (45 minutes) and Vrátna Výťah (15 minutes).

High Tatras & Eastern Slovakia

MOUNTAINS | OUTDOOR ADVENTURE | MEDIEVAL TOWNS

Welcome to the 1.5-mile-high club: the jagged peaks of the High Tatras (Vysoké Tatry) have some 25 summits that surpass 2400m. These are Slovakia's highest mountains and some of the highest in Eastern Europe as well. The encompassing Tatras National Park (Tatranský národný park), accessed from Poprad by mountain railway, cable car and hiking trails, is Slovakia's top outdoor destination. It's home to skiing, phenomenal hiking – including the famous 72km-long Tatranská Magistrála, a rugged hike that traverses the whole range – and more eclectic activities such as dogsledding, river trips, bear-spotting and overnighting in high-altitude huts.

But don't forget to lower your gaze from the snowy summits and turn further east. Slovakia's second city Košice and a surfeit of UNESCO World Heritage Sites – from medieval towns Levoča and Bardejov to ornate wooden churches and cave-ridden karst – will make your moments in Eastern Slovakia as eye-catching as they are esoteric.

Places

Poprad p251

Tatranská Lomnica p251

Starý Smokovec p252

Štrbské Pleso p252

Košice p254

☑ TOP TIP

There is a great deal to see in this relatively small region. Love mountain scenery? Stick to the High Tatras for drama, Slovenský Raj for beauty or Slovenský kras for off-piste karst. Culture? Košice. History? Košice with journeys out to Levoča, Bardejov and around.

High Tatras
Head to the mountain resorts

If you crave proximity to the raw power of the mountains without sacrificing a cent of comfort, the High Tatras resorts are for you. **Tatranská Lomnica** is on the eastern side, the

---

 GETTING AROUND

The dependable Bratislava–Košice train line serves Poprad, Spišská Nová Ves (change for buses to Levoča and Slovenský Raj National Park), Presov (change for trains to Bardejov) and Košice, where you can get buses to the likes of caving hotspot Slovenský kras and the Tokaj wine region. The Tatras Electric Railway links Poprad to outdoor activity bases in the High Tatras, with cable cars ascending further into the mountains.

These are our favourite High Tatras day hikes, easily accessed via public transport.

Ždiar to Veľké Biele Pleso (4½hr): Climb from winsome Ždiar to the mountain tarn where the Tatranská Magistrala multi-day trail begins.

Štrbské Pleso to Popradské Pleso (1½hr): Link two alpine lakes, then replenish calories at Horské Hotel Popradské Pleso at trail's end.

Hrebienok & Studeny Potok Circuit (1½hr): Forest loop from the funicular top station passes by delightful waterfalls.

Štrbské Pleso to Kriváň (7hr): Out-and-back trek from Slovakia's prettiest mountain lake to its prettiest peak Kriváň (2494m).

Smokovec resorts of Starý (Old), Novy (New), Horný (High) and Dolný (Low) Smokovec are in the middle, and Štrbské pleso is to the west.

From **Tatranská Lomnica**, Slovakia's most hair-raising cable car ascends to **Lomnický štít** (*vt.sk; adult/child return to Skalnaté pleso €32/24, return Skalnaté pleso–Lomnický štít €59/51*), the nation's second-highest summit at 2634m. Take a six-seat chairlift to Štart, then the gondola to **Skalnaté Pleso** (*vt.sk; free*), a winter sports area and hiking trailhead beside a lake, which is poised infinity pool–style on the mountainside. A vertigo-inducing cable car then soars an additional 855m in under nine minutes to the mountaintop. Timeslots can sell out quickly; you get 50 minutes on the summit to take pictures and enjoy refreshments in the cafe. **Ski Resort Tatranská Lomnica** (*vt.sk; day pass €55/41*) has some dramatic pistes: the black run from Lomnické sedlo is Slovakia's steepest.

In the Smokovec area, the 19th-century resort **Starý Smokovec** makes the most atmospheric base. Learn how to climb the toughest summits and other extreme activities with the **Mountain Guide Society** (*tatraguide.sk; tours €400-500*). You can also climb to **Hrebienok**, complete with restaurant, gallery and trailheads, for some thrilling and demanding hikes. Access is via the **Hrebienok Funicular** (*vt.sk; return adult/child €15/12*).

The most dazzling resort, however, is **Štrbské Pleso**, set around a divine forest lake. Lakeside lodges here provide the High Tatras' best places to stay. Take out a **row boat** (*strbskepleso.sk; €23 per 40 minutes*), walk around the lake, or dine along its shores. The best hike is the 1½-hour climb through forest to wild-feeling **Popradské pleso** lake, from where bigger peaks rise up.

All resort areas are connected by mountain railway to Poprad.

Off-piste thrills

Ready for some outdoor adventure? Sign up for an excursion run by **Adventoura** (*adventoura.eu; per person from €130*). Search the High Tatras for brown bears on a bear-watching tour (Jun-Oct), try dog-sledding in winter or go rafting down the Dunajec River gorge in summer. Both white-water rafts and traditional wooden rafts are available.

Hut-to-hut hikes

If you've ever trekked in the Alps, then you're likely familiar with the hut-to-hut system that enables hikers to spend multiple nights in the backcountry without having to pitch a tent. Slovakia's mountain ranges, including the High Tatras,

EATING IN THE HIGH TATRAS: OUR PICKS

Vino & Tapas: In Poprad, this brick-walled place creates food art with great wine pairings. *11am-2.30pm & 6-9.30pm Tue-Fri, 6-9.30pm Sat* €€€

Felka Café & Brew Bar: Probably the High Tatras' best barista coffee, bagels and cakes, on the road to Poprad Airport. *8am-6pm Mon-Fri, from 9am Sat & Sun* €

Koliba Patria: On the Strbské pleso lakeshore, Slovak mountain dishes, like deer goulash or sheep's cheese dumplings, are exemplary. *11.30am-9pm* €€

Humno Tatry: Lively chalet-style restaurant, cocktail bar and club, by the Tatranská Lomnica cable-car base station. *11am-10pm Sun-Thu, to 3am Fri & Sat* €€

Štrbské pleso

have a similar network of mountain huts: this is the best way to experience the country's mountainous terrain. For a small fee, you can stay in the beautiful *chaty* (mountain huts) situated strategically across the range. The four-day traverse on the well-signposted **Tatranská Magistrala** trail, from Vel'ke biele pleso (east) to Podbanské (west), is a phenomenal hut-to-hut experience. Our favourite overnight huts? Lakeside **Chata pri zelenom plese** (p255) *(chataprizelenomplese.sk)* is a 30-minute hike from the trailhead, and wood-ensconced **Zamkovského chata** *(zamka.sk)* is perfect for night two. Accommodation is basic but dinner and breakfast are usually available and the mountain panoramas are unbeatable. Figure on €50 for a bed, breakfast and dinner, or €18 for just a bed.

Eastern Slovakia

Central Europe's greatest fortress

UNESCO-listed masterwork **Spiš Castle** *(Spišský hrad; spissky hrad.com; adult/child €8/4)* is one of Europe's largest fortifications. The 12th-century stronghold sprawls for four hectares through bulwarks and bulky defensive walls over a hilltop 1km east of village Spišské Podhradie. Views from the fortifications are fantastic and far-reaching. In summer, **night tours** *(adult/ child €10/8)* are atmospheric, crowd-beating ways to explore this prodigious ruin. From Poprad, it's an hour-long bus ride east to Spišské Podhradie's main square; the entrance to the castle, clearly visible from here, is 850m southeast.

Gorgeous hikes in Slovenský Raj

Discerning outdoor-lovers routinely cite **Slovenský Raj National Park** *(Slovak Paradise; npsr.sk; free)* and its forests, cliffs, ravines and waterfalls as harbouring the country's finest hiking. The standout stretch departs from **Podlesok**: it's a two-hour ascent up a precipitous ladder- and technical-assist trail through **Suchá Belá Gorge**. Return via Kláštorisko, and

---

SLOVAKIA'S SECRET PLACES

Brano Chrenka, founder of Authentic Slovakia *(authentic slovakia.com)*, recommends his favourite under-the-radar destinations. **Bradlo** This mountain above Košiarská village has a monument to Slovak WWI hero Milan Rastislav Štefánik. The atmosphere is special and the views over the Myjava region's hills is superb. **Slovenský Kras National Park** (p254) Come for plateaus, caves and gorges like Zádielska tiesňava. It's in between Košice and Rožňava. **Súľovské Skaly** My favourite rock formations in Slovakia: otherworldly shapes and a not-too-demanding hike. **Červený Kláštor** Stay in this monastery on the Dunajec River gorge: it's authentic and full of atmosphere.

UNMISSABLE UNESCO SITES

Levoča: This town, 40 minutes by bus from Poprad, is festooned with Gothic-Renaissance buildings like the Church of St Jacob, which has a wondrous altar.

Bardejov: Dazzlingly intact Middle Ages trading hub of bewitching, steep-roofed buildings. It's 1¾ hours north of Košice by train.

Hervartov Church: Finest of the nine wooden churches of the Slovak Carpathians, representing the crossroads between Roman Catholic and Greek Orthodox faiths. It's 19km southwest of Bardejov.

Poloniny National Park: Forested expanse that's part of UNESCO's Ancient and Primeval Beech Forests of the Carpathians. Access from Runina, 122km northeast of Košice.

descend to the Hornád River and riverbank paths to return to Podlesok. Altogether, it's a five-hour loop. From Hrabušice, 2km northeast of Podlesok, buses (or a 5km walk) reach Spišský Štvrtok and mainline trains.

Visit Košice, Slovakia's second city

Košice is Eastern Slovakia's biggest city, with a nexus of culture and historic architecture along **Hlavné námestie**. This long plaza of flower-bedecked gardens and cafes is in the running for the hotly contested title of 'Slovakia's prettiest town square'. The main feature is Slovakia's largest church, **St Elizabeth's Cathedral** (*domsvalzbety.sk; free, tower adult/child €3/2*), with gaudily elaborate roof decorations: climb the north tower's 160 stone steps for the city centre's finest views. Also on the square is Slovakia's first musical water feature, the **Singing Fountain** (*visitkosice.org; free*) and, two blocks east, the quaint thoroughfare of workshops known as **Hrnčiarska** (*visitkosice.org; free*), which showcase centuries-old trades such as blacksmithing and herbal medicine.

Go underground in Slovenský kras

Rožnava, 50 minutes by train from Košice, is the stop-off for delving into **Slovenský Kras National Park**, which comprises the Slovakian part of one of Europe's greatest cave systems. Of the many cavernous marvels, **Domica Cave** (*ssj.sk; tour adult/child €10/5*), one hour southwest of Rožnava by train and bus, is the largest, with tours that include an underground boat ride. The extraordinary **Dobšinská Ice Cave** (*ssj.sk; tour adult/child €12/6*), packed with ice and enthralling speleothems (mineral deposits), is one hour north by bus.

 EATING IN KOŠICE: OUR PICKS

San Domenico Caffe: Trailblazer for vegan food in Košice, with first-rate cakes a block off the main square. *7.30am-7.30pm Mon-Sat, from 9am Sun* €	**Republika Východu:** Superb bistro offering everything from fruit-and-granola bowls to succulent beef cheeks. *8am-10pm Mon-Thu, to 11pm Fri & Sat, to 8pm Sun* €	**Pub u Kohúta:** Atmospheric pub serving hearty Slovak fare alongside Hrnčiarska's traditional crafts workshops. *11am-2pm & 4-11pm Mon-Fri, noon-midnight Sat* €	**Slávia:** Art nouveau diamond with a glass-roofed restaurant on the main square and a Slovak-international menu. *8am-11pm Mon-Fri, 9am-11pm Sat, 9am-10pm Sun* €€€

Places We Love to Stay

€ Budget €€ Midrange €€€ Top End

SLOVAKIA PLACES WE LOVE TO STAY

Bratislava
MAP p243

CHORS Like a Hotel € Hostel or hotel? The small-but-smart 'capsule rooms' at this well-appointed place start cheap. Even the dorms are comprised of separate private cabins. Round-the-clock bar and all-you-can-eat breakfasts (€8).

Loft Hotel Bratislava €€ Retro industrial chic is the theme in the Loft's sleek 111 rooms, perfectly complementing the cool on-site brewery-restaurant Fabrika.

Hotel Arcus €€ Outside of the centre, near gorgeous Medická záhrada, these relaxed middleweight digs have high-ceilinged rooms either with balcony or overlooking the serene garden.

Marrol's Boutique Hotel €€€ The capital's most sophisticated accommodation is this neo-baroque boutique choice with an elegant restaurant, spa and fitness centre.

Roset Boutique Hotel €€€ With an art nouveau exterior, these generous, minimalist apartments on the Staré mesto's edge are both practical (safes; kitchenettes) and luxurious (towelling robes; turn-down service).

Hotel pri Mlyne €€€ Take the bus from Bratislava's Lamač train station to Lozorno (25 minutes) to reach this romantic oasis with a spa and landscaped grounds. Countryside peace and city proximity.

Pezinok

Palace Art Hotel €€€ Elegant, park-enfolded 800-year-old chateau in the wine town of Pezinok, with two beautiful restaurants.

Piešťany

Ensana Thermia Palace €€€ Flanked by gardens and resplendent with art nouveau design, this palatial complex is *the* place to experience Piešťany's fabled spa culture.

Trenčín

Hotel Elizabeth €€ Yellow-and-cream art nouveau beauty below Trenčín Castle crag that's a visitor attraction itself. Trenčín's Roman inscription, carved in 179 CE, can be seen from its terrace.

Banská Štiavnica

Divná Pani Luxury Gallery Rooms €€€ Plush, idiosyncratic central Banská Štiavnica burgher house. Each room is an art gallery; the cafe is a statue-dotted library.

Malá Fatra National Park

Hotel Diery €€ Whitewashed apartments and rooms have a wellness area, *koliba* (rustic Slovak restaurant) and, right outside, the trailhead for Malá Fatra's breathtaking Horné Diery gorge.

High Tatras

Chata pri zelenom plese € Our pick for a *chata* (mountain hut) stay: superlative High Tatras ridge views from the cosy bar-restaurant alongside Zelené pleso lake, a tough two-hour hike from the Skalnaté pleso cable-car station.

Horský Hotel Popradské Pleso € Epitomises Slovakia's 'Horský Hotel' tradition: basic but beautifully located hotels in remote mountain locales. This lake-fronting place has a restaurant and outdoor sauna/hot tub. It's a 90-minute hike up from Štrbské pleso.

Ginger Monkey Hostel € The High Tatras' eastern flanks, the Belá Tatras, have charming Ždiar as their base, and this brightly painted, wood-built hostel is the village's most atmospheric lodging.

Grand Hotel Kempinski €€€ The best address at the best High Tatras resort: lovely lakeside Štrbské pleso. Outstanding mountain luxury from the bathtubs and minibars in the rooms to the chandelier-hung pool. Exquisite peak-dotted panoramas.

Košice

Penzión Slovakia €€ The 11 rooms above the Rosta steakhouse, a stone's throw from Košice's main square, each represent a different Slovak city.

Ecohotel Dália €€ Excellent 37-room, lower-middle-range choice several blocks from the main square. Among Slovakia's first ecohotels.

Levoča

Hotel U Leva €€ Fronting Slovakia's most magnificent medieval townscape: Levoča's lovely main square. Rooms exude warm-hued colours and substantial polished wood. There's a prepossessing vaulted restaurant.

Practicalities

Tourist Information
Slovak Tourist Board *(slovakia.travel/en)* Slovakia's official tourist resource online.
Tourist Information Centre *(visitbratislava.com)* Bratislava's helpful main tourist office, near Hlavné námestie.
Visit Košice Infopoint *(visitkosice.org/en)* Košice's tourist office, on the main square Hlavné námestie.

Health & Safe Travel
The biggest risks in Slovakia come in the great outdoors. Bears reside in mountainous areas: stick to marked paths. Mountain exploration comes with other dangers: avalanches, rapidly changing weather and, of course, tumbling over sheer rock faces. Seek advice before attempting mountain hikes.

Etiquette
Greetings Start conversations politely: Slovaks are initially quite formal, but soon open up.
Privacy Respect personal space and don't ask intrusive questions until you get to know someone better.
Clothing Never wear revealing clothing in a church; always take off your shoes when entering someone's home.

Electricity
Type E sockets are most common here: two round holes plus the earth pin.

SHEVCHENKO ANDREY/SHUTTERSTOCK

Tatranská Lomnica (p252)

Opening Hours
Banks 8am–5pm Monday to Friday
Restaurants 11am–10pm
Museums 9am–4pm Tuesday to Sunday
Cable cars 9am–4pm

Entry & Exit Formalities
Slovakia is in the Schengen area, an EU territory that allows Schengen citizens, and many others, free movement across internal borders without checks. Non-EU passports should still have an expiry date of ideally six months or longer after the visitor's intended departure date. Most visitors don't need visas for stays of under 90 days.

Language
Hello. Ahoj.
Good morning. Dobré ráno.
Good day. Dobrý deň.
Good evening. Dobré večer.
Goodnight. Dobrú noc.
How are you? Ako sa maté (formal), Ako sa maš (informal)
Cheers! Na zdravie!
Bon apetit. Dobru chut.'
Do you understand? Rozumiete? (formal), Rozumieš? (informal)
I understand/don't understand. Rozumiem/Nerozumiem.
Do you speak English? Hovorité po anglicky?
Excuse me! Prepáčte!

Bratislava–Košice train (p251)

MONEY

Currency: Euro (€)

CASH OR CARD?
There are ATMs that accept international cards in nearly all towns and cities, and even many villages. Most hotels, restaurants and attractions countrywide take card payments. Nevertheless, carry cash as a back-up for purchases at markets, museum tickets and even accommodation in remoter locations – scenarios in which paying with a card may be impossible.

TIPPING
Slovaks don't tip consistently. However, tipping of up to 10% for main restaurant meals is becoming increasingly common in tourist hubs like Bratislava. Rounding up restaurant bills and taxi fares at least one or two euros as a minimum is common practice.

Arriving & Getting Around

The main visitor entry point is Bratislava's MR Štefánik Airport, which serves many European destinations. Getting around Slovakia is a breeze via its superb, regular and punctual train and bus network.

Arriving by Air
Besides Bratislava airport, there's a well-connected airport in Košice. Vienna (one hours' drive from Bratislava) has more flight options, especially for destinations outside Europe.

Arriving by Train
Bratislava makes a handy cross-Europe rail stop, with trains throughout the day regularly arriving from Vienna (one hour), Budapest (2¼ hours) and Prague (4¼ hours).

Arriving by Boat
The most stylish way to arrive is via boat along the Danube. Boats ply the Vienna–Bratislava route at least once daily from March to November, and less frequently in winter.

Getting Around
Within Slovakia, trains are best. From Bratislava, major destinations include Trenčín (change for some of Western Slovakia's best castles), Žilina (for Malá Fatra National Park), Poprad (for connections to the High Tatras, plus other places like Levoča), Prešov (for Bardejov) and Košice. Buses will get you to all other places.

For places to stay in Slovenia, see p272

NOSOVA ELIZAVETA/SHUTTERSTOCK

Above: Bled Island (p268), Lake Bled;
Left: Franciscan Church of the Annunciation (p266), Ljubljana;

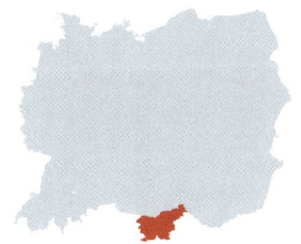

Slovenia

RELAXING TOWNS AND PRISTINE NATURE

Living proof that the best things really do come in small packages.

From the soaring peaks of the Julian Alps and the subterranean magic of the Postojna and Škocjan caves, to the sparkling emerald-green lakes and rivers and the short but sweet coastline along the Adriatic Sea, tiny Slovenia – with a surface area of just 20,000 sq km and a population of two million people – really does have it all. A welcoming mix of climates brings warm Mediterranean breezes up to the foothills of the Alps, where it can snow even in summer. And with more than half of its total surface still covered in forest, Slovenia does more than simply claim it's 'green', it really is one of the greenest countries on earth.

UNAPHOTO.COM/SHUTTERSTOCK

The country is first and foremost an outdoor destination. The list of activities on offer is endless, with the most popular pursuits being skiing, hiking and, increasingly, cycling. Fast rivers like the Soča cry out to be rafted and there are ample chances to try out more niche activities like horse riding, ballooning, caving and canyoning.

But don't sleep on Ljubljana. Slovenia's capital is a culturally rich city that values sustainability over unfettered growth. Enlivened by native-son Jože Plečnik's buildings and beautification projects and a pretty riverside location, Ljubljana is worth a couple of days of pleasant rambling. See the castle, museum-hop and enjoy Slovenia's best cafes and restaurants.

THE MAIN AREAS

LJUBLJANA
Slovenia's green, livable – and fun – capital city. **p262**

LAKE BLED & JULIAN ALPS
Mountain peaks, perfect lakes and blue-green rivers. **p268**

SLOVENIAN KARST & COAST
Stunning caves and a romantic Adriatic port city. **p270**

Find Your Way

The best of Slovenia includes sightseeing in Ljubljana, the highlights of the lakes and peaks of the Julian Alps, and the country's unique karst and coast region.

TRAINS & BUSES

Public transport is good and you won't necessarily need a car to get around. Trains and buses can take you to all the places covered here. We've noted, where appropriate, whether train or bus is the better option.

CAR

Cars are practical for moving around the country quickly. That said, don't use your own vehicle to get around Ljubljana. The centre is largely closed to car traffic, and walking and cycling are much more practical.

Ljubljana, p262

Enjoy low-stress strolling around Slovenia's immediately charming capital city.

Slovenian Karst & Coast, p270

Mix incredible caving with the sea breezes, sunsets and seafood along the Adriatic Coast.

Lake Bled & Julian Alps, p268

Take in the beauty of Lake Bled and then swim or paddle at Lake Bohinj and Bovec.

40 km
20 miles
0

HUNGARY

AUSTRIA

Hodoš
Murska Sobota
Beltinci

Maribor

Dravograd
Sloveni Gradec
Ravne na Koroškem
Celje
Žalec
Trbovlje Hrastnik
Zagorje ob Savi
Krško

Velenje

Klagenfurt

Kranjska Gora
Jesenice
Bled Castle
Bled
Lake Bled
Bled Island
Mt Triglav
Lake Bohinj
Most na Soči

Škofja Loka
Kamnik
Domžale
Kranj

LJUBLJANA
Vrhnika
Litija
Grosuplje
Trebnje
Novo Mesto

Ivančna Gorica
Ribnica
Kočevje

Sava

CROATIA

Cerknica
Logatec
Postojna Cave
Postojna
Pivka
Ilirska Bistrica

Idrija
Divača
Lokev
Škocjan Caves

Nova Gorica
Ajdovščina
Lipica
Koper
Izola

Soča

Trieste
Tartinijev Trg
Piran

ITALY

Adriatic Sea

Triple Bridge (p266), Ljubljana

Plan Your Time

Two to three days is sufficient for the major sights in Ljubljana. You can cover the country's highlights in a week.

A Weekend in Ljubljana

● Explore **Ljubljana Castle** (p262), then wind through the tiny squares of the **Old Town** (p264). Admire **Prešernov trg** (p266) and take in the perplexing geometry of Jože Plečnik's **Triple Bridge** (p266). Wander through the **Central Market** (p264) or float down the Ljubljanica River in a **historic boat** (p267). Spend day two touring Plečnik's **National & University Library** (p267) or the **City Museum of Ljubljana** (p267).

A Week's Sightseeing

● Begin in Ljubljana before heading up to Bled to see one of the world's prettiest **lakes** (p268). Check out the equally beautiful **Lake Bohinj** (p269) and then raft the rapids of the **Soča River** (p269). Head south to see two of Europe's most impressive caves: **Postojna** (p270) and **Škocjan** (p271). Finish up at the breathtaking port of **Piran** (p271).

SEASONAL HIGHLIGHTS

SPRING

Expect sunshine, warm temps and wildflowers in Alpine valleys. It's still too cold to swim in the Adriatic.

SUMMER

Coastal resorts like Piran fill to the brim. Lakes Bohinj and Bled are warm enough to swim in.

AUTUMN

Mountain air grows cooler and swimming winds down. Resorts like Bled and Bohinj hold their last big shindigs.

WINTER

It's ski season in the Julian Alps. Carnival celebrations are held around the country in February or early March.

Ljubljana

CITY FUN | MUSEUMS | ARCHITECTURE

GETTING AROUND

Central Ljubljana is closed to motor-vehicle traffic, so take public transport or walk, which is a delight. The main promenade follows the Ljubljanica River and is lined by restaurants and cafes. Ljubljana is also ideal for cyclists, and there are bike lanes and special traffic lights everywhere. Hire bikes from the popular **BicikeLJ** *(bicikelj. si)* bicycle-sharing system for a nominal fee. From April through October, the Slovenian Tourist Information Centre rents bikes and hands out bike maps.

☑ **TOP TIP**

Start at the **Ljubljana Tourist Information Centre**, where the enthusiastic staff dispense information, maps and useful literature. They can help book accommodation and also offer a range of interesting city tours.

Throughout history, Ljubljana (loo-BLI-ah-nuh) has always retained the relaxed ambience of a small town, rather than a sprawling metropolis. This is a feeling that continues to this day: Slovenia's capital is one of Europe's greenest and most liveable urban spaces. Car traffic is restricted in the centre, leaving the leafy banks of the emerald-green Ljubljanica River, which flows through the city's heart, free for pedestrians and cyclists to enjoy. In summer, cafes set up terrace seating along the river. Slovenia's master of mini-malist design, Jože Plečnik, graced the capital with beautiful bridges and buildings, as well as dozens of classical design elements such as pillars, pyramids and obelisks, which exist solely to make the city even prettier. Attractive cities are often described as 'jewel boxes', but here the name really fits.

Castle Hill

Ljubljana's stately castle has stood guard over the town since medieval times (12th century) and grew in importance in the 15th century under the Habsburg monarchy as a bulwark against Ottoman encroachment. These days, it's the first port of call for visitors wanting to know more about the origins of the city or simply to have some fun.

Explore Ljubljana Castle

Hike or ride a **funicular** up to lofty **Ljubljana Castle** *(ljubljanskigrad.si)*. There's tons of fun things to do up here, including many activities designed for families and small children. If you don't have much time or don't want to spend much money, the grounds are free to enter. Note, however, you'll have to pay to see the historic chambers, including the castle **Watchtower** and the **Chapel of St George**, and to visit the **Virtual Castle**, **Slovenian History Exhibition** and **Museum of Puppetry**. See the various options and admissions packages in the sidebar (p264).

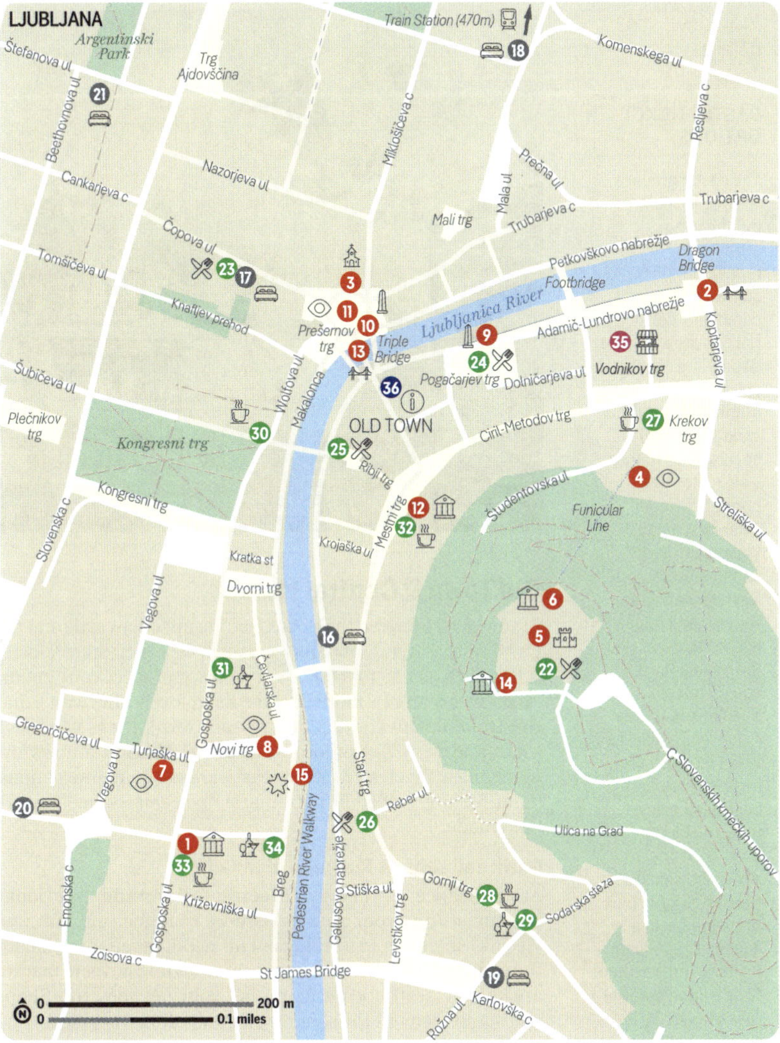

LJUBLJANA

Argentinski Park

Train Station (470m)

Štefanova ul

Beethovnova ul

Trg Ajdovščina

Komenskega ul

Cankarjeva c

Nazorjeva ul

Miklošičeva c

Prečna ul

Mala ul

Restljeva c

Tomšičeva ul

Čopova ul

Mali trg

Trubarjeva c

Trubarjeva c

23 **17**

3

Petkovškovo nabrežje

Dragon Bridge

2

Knafljev prehod

11 **10**

Prešernov trg

Footbridge

Ljubljanica River

Adamič-Lundrovo nabrežje

Kopitarjeva ul

Šubičeva c

13

Triple Bridge

9

Pogačarjev trg

24

Dolničarjeva ul

35

Vodnikov trg

Plečnikov trg

36

Makalonca

Wolfova ul

OLD TOWN

Ciril-Metodov trg

Krekov trg

27

4

Kongresni trg

30

25

Kongresni trg

Ribji trg

Mestni trg

12

32

Študentovska ul

Funicular Line

Str
iška ul

Slovenska c

Kratka st

Dvorni trg

Krojaška ul

6

Vegova ul

16

5

Gregorčičeva ul

31

Cankarjeva ul

Gosposka ul

Novi trg **8**

22

14

Vegova ul

Turjaška ul

7

15

Stari trg

20

Ribar ul

Ulica na Grad

C Slovenskih mladih upocov

1

33 **34**

26

Pedestrian River Walkway

Gallusovo nabrežje

Stiška ul

Gornji trg

28

29

Emonska c

Gosposka ul

Breg

Levstikov trg

Sodarska staza

Zoisova c

Križevniška ul

St James Bridge

19

Rožna ul

Karlovška c

0 ————— 200 m
0 ————— 0.1 miles

N

KIRK FISHER/SHUTTERSTOCK

Old Town & Central Market

Sandwiched between the slopes leading up to the castle and the Ljubljanica River, Ljubljana's narrow Old Town (Staro Mesto) is the city's oldest quarter. It's comprised of three contiguous, evocative squares – more like one long, lovely alleyway – that run from Mestni trg to Stari trg and Gornji trg as you move south and east. The adjoining **Central Market** follows the Ljubljanica River as it bends eastwards. The market's dominant feature is Plečnik's dramatic neo-Renaissance Plečnik Colonnade.

Gawk and shop at Plečnik Colonnade

At first glance, the massive **Plečnik Colonnade** *(free)* looks like something from classical Greece or Rome, and that was Plečnik's intention in working out his neo-Rennaisance plan for the complex. The colonnade and surrounding farmers market are not just aesthetic pleasures but gourmet ones, too. Shops and stands around the square sell everything from meats and cheeses to fresh fruit and veg – this is a great place to stock up on provisions. Most vendors open from 6am to 6pm on weekdays, with shorter hours on Saturday. Pogačarjev trg serves as

BEST FOR EATING IN LJUBLJANA: OUR PICKS

Gostilna Na Gradu: Treat yourself to Slovenian specialities at Ljubljana Castle at this Michelin Bib Gourmand winner. *noon-10pm Mon-Sat, to 5pm Sun €€*

Pop's Place: Centrally located craft beer and burger bar that's become a must-visit. Avoid traditional meal times: it gets busy. *noon-midnight €€*

JAZ by Ana Roš: Michelin-starred chef Ana Roš brings her inventive dishes using locally sourced ingredients to Ljubljana at prices that won't break the bank. *noon-midnight Mon-Sat €€€*

Vino & Ribe: This unassuming spot in the Old Town has a small but excellent menu of grilled fish, fried fish, sardines and carafes of house wine. *noon-10pm €€*

Dragon Bridge

DRAGON OBSESSIONS

With those scary-looking dragons on Dragon Bridge and a dragon prominent on the city's coat of arms, many visitors assume Ljubljana's dragon obsession goes back centuries. While dragon symbols have been floating around since medieval times, the city's fling with dragons is a relatively modern affair. Just before the turn of the 20th century, a wily mayor named Ivan Hribar apparently persuaded the authorities in Vienna that Ljubljana needed a new crossing over the Ljubljanica and submitted plans for a 'Jubilee Bridge' to mark 50 years of Franz Joseph's reign. The early designs for what's today Dragon Bridge envisaged winged lions, but these were swapped out at the last minute for dragons. The rest is history.

the setting for the weekly popular food fair **Odprta Kuhna** ('Open Kitchen') held on Fridays from March to October.

Look inside Ljubljana's Town Hall

Walk inside the city's striking Gothic **Town Hall** *(visit ljubljana.com; free),* the seat of the city's government since the late 15th century, to find a late Renaissance courtyard, arcaded on three levels, where theatrical performances once took place. Look above the south portal leading to a second courtyard to see a unique relief map of medieval Ljubljana as the city appeared in the second half of the 17th century.

Snap a photo of Dragon Bridge

The much-loved **Dragon Bridge**, topped with four scary-looking dragons, one on each corner, and adorned with 16 smaller dragons, is prime Instagram territory. Indeed, it's fair to say if you don't take a shot of one of those dragons, well, then you haven't actually been to Slovenia. Aside from dragon imagery, the bridge, built in Viennese Secession (art nouveau) style in 1901, is regarded as one of the most beautiful bridges of this particular style ever built.

BEST COFFEE IN LJUBLJANA: OUR PICKS

Cafe Čokl: This fair-trade place near the foot of the castle's funicular station roasts its java in-house; see the chalkboard for daily specials. *7am-6pm*

Kavarna Zvezda: Possibly the best cakes in Ljubljana, with pride of place going to the *gibanica* (layer cake of poppy seeds, walnut and curd cheese). *8am-9pm Mon-Sat, 10am-8pm Sun*

Stow Cafe: Fresh-roasted speciality coffee in the Ljubljana City Museum. Tell the museum ticket office you're going to the cafe to avoid the admission fee. *10am-6pm Tue-Sun*

Črno Zrno Specialty Coffee: In the Old Town, light-roasted coffee from Colombia as well as special 45-minute guided tastings (per person from €25). *11am-3.30pm Mon-Sat*

STEPH COUVRETTE/SHUTTERSTOCK

Prešernov Trg & Center

Tiny **Prešernov trg** serves as the centrepiece of Ljubljana's wonderful architectural aesthetic. The square, a public space of understated elegance, serves not only as the link between Center (the modern part of the city) and the historic Old Town but also as a favourite meet-up point. Taking pride of place is the **Prešeren Monument**, erected in honour of Slovenia's greatest poet, France Prešeren (1800–49).

Contemplate the Triple Bridge

The **Triple Bridge** *(free)* runs south from Prešernov trg to the Old Town. When it was built as a single span in 1842 it was nothing spectacular, but between 1929 and 1932 superstar architect Jože Plečnik added the two pedestrian side bridges and furnished all three with stone balustrades and lamps. The name was changed and, almost a century later, the bridge was added to the UNESCO World Heritage list, along with several sites recognised as 'Plečnik's Ljubljana'.

Explore the Franciscan Church

The 17th-century salmon-pink **Franciscan Church of the Annunciation** *(marijino-oznanjenje.si; entry €3),* could well

 BEST FOR DRINKS IN LJUBLJANA: OUR PICKS

Kolibri: Sip exquisitely crafted cocktails in a cosy nook on a hidden corner in Center. *7pm-midnight*	**Ferdinand:** Great cocktails, craft beers and cosy outdoor seating on a quiet stretch of the Old Town. *9am-midnight*	**Wine Bar Šuklje:** Welcoming wine bar for sampling highly rated wines from Bela Krajina in southeastern Slovenia. *9am-11pm*	**Pritličje:** By day, a popular cafe with convenient sidewalk terrace. By night, a lively bar and cultural centre. *9am-1am Sun-Wed, to 3am Thu-Sat*

Ljubljanica River

be the unofficial symbol of the city, and is just as striking inside as it on the outside. Enter through a small door to the left of the main entrance to find a riot of baroque design inside.

Learn about Roman-era Ljubljana

The excellent **City Museum of Ljubljana** *(mgml.si; adult/ child €8/6)* is strong on Ljubljana's Roman origins as the colony of 'Emona'. The museum highlights a reconstructed street that once linked the eastern gates of Emona to the Ljubljanica as well as a collection of well-preserved classical artefacts.

Tour Plečnik's masterpiece library

Among all the buildings the architect and urban planner Jože Plečnik designed for Ljubljana, the working **National & University Library** *(nuk.uni-lj.si; adult/child €5/free)* is widely considered his masterpiece. Art historians contend this is where the great man aligned his designs and materials with the larger purpose of the building itself: the acquisition of knowledge. The **Main Reading Room** sports huge glass walls and stunning lamps, which were also designed by Plečnik. The library is open to visitors from 10am to 6pm Monday to Friday and 2.30pm to 6pm on Saturday.

Sail the Ljubljanica River

Sailing along the Ljubljanica River is a relaxing and fun way to take in the city. Several companies run tours, but only the creatively named **Barka Ljubljanica** *(Ljubljanica Boat; barka-ljubljanica.si; tours adult/child €15/7)* operates a wooden vessel. It's 10m long and carries up to 48 people on a 50-minute tour. Boats depart hourly from the Breg embankment, just below **Novi trg**.

CITY PLANNER EXTRAORDINAIRE

Few architects have had as great an impact on their hometown as Jože Plečnik. Born in Ljubljana in 1872, Plečnik was educated in Graz and studied under architect Otto Wagner in Vienna. From 1911 he spent a decade in Prague teaching and helping renovate Prague Castle. Plečnik's list of Ljubljana creations is endless: from the National and University Library and colonnaded Central Market to the cemetery at Žale, where you can see his own simple headstone. He was also a city planner, and redesigned the banks of the Ljubljanica River, including the Triple Bridge, and Tivoli Park. His eclecticism alienated him from mainstream modern architecture during his lifetime, and he was relatively unknown outside his home country when he died in 1957.

Lake Bled & Julian Alps

OUTDOOR ADVENTURE | BLISSFUL VIEWS | HISTORIC CASTLES

Places

Lake Bled p268
Lake Bohinj p269
Soča Valley p269

☑ TOP TIP

Time your visit to avoid the summer high season (July and August) when tour buses descend upon the lake and camper vans clog the narrow streets. Winter snow can make roads impassable in these parts. Vršič Pass closes most years from November to April.

The Julian Alps region is the Slovenia of tourist posters: mountain peaks, mirror-like lakes and blue-green rivers. Prepare to be charmed by Lake Bled (with an island and a castle!) and surprised by Lake Bohinj (how does Bled score all that attention when down the road is Bohinj?). The lofty peak of Mt Triglav, at the centre of a national park of the same name, may dazzle you enough to prompt an ascent.

Lake Bled

TIME FROM LJUBLJANA: **1HR** 🚌

With its bluish-green lake, handsome church on an islet, a medieval castle clinging to a rocky cliff and some of the highest peaks of the Julian Alps as a backdrop, Bled has become Slovenia's most popular resort. It attracts everyone from honeymooners to backpackers, who come for the romantic setting, hiking, biking, water sports and canyoning.

Take in the castle, lake and island

Lake Bled is best explored on foot and by boat. Three footpaths signposted 'Grad' lead to **Bled Castle** *(blejski-grad. si; entry to castle & museum €17)* and if you start around the **Blejsko Srce** (Heart of Bled) it should take you between 15 and 25 minutes. Magical, tiny **Bled Island** sits in the middle of the lake and is just as picturesque up close. Board one of the *pletna* (a wooden boat that resembles a Venetian gondola) at **Gondolas Mlino** *(round trip €18)* for a short ride that feels like a time machine. Once you arrive, climb the 99 stairs into the **Church of the Assumption** *(blejskiotok.si; €12)*.

GETTING AROUND

Bus connections from Ljubljana to Bled and Bohinj are frequent and cheap. Buses are also good for moving between places within the region. Both lake areas are compact and walkable. The area is committed to sustainable travel so drivers can stow their cars and hit the foot or bike paths to move around. The Soča Valley is spread out and easiest to explore by car.

Lake Bohinj

TIME FROM LJUBLJANA: 1½HR

Lake Bohinj may lack Bled's glamour, but it's less crowded and in many ways more authentic. It's an ideal summer holiday destination. People come primarily to swim in the crystal-clear water, and to enjoy leisurely cycling and walking trails as well as outdoor pursuits like kayaking and horse riding. It's 26km southwest of Bled.

Go swimming, boating and paddleboarding

Lake Bohinj's chilly waters warm to a swimmable 22°C in July and August. You can enter the water from any point on shore, though the decent small beaches on both the northern and southern shores are most convenient. Some beaches on the northern shore are reserved for naturists. Adventure outfitters around the lake rent kayaks, canoes and SUP boards and provide guides for hiking and mountaineering. In winter you can go skiing, snowshoeing and ice climbing. We've listed our favourite excursions in the sidebar.

Soča Valley

TIME FROM LJUBLJANA: 2HR

The Soča Valley, particularly the arresting blue-green colour of the Soča River, is just as stunning as you've heard, and neither photos nor written descriptions do it justice. It's worth exploring slowly, from the frothy rapids to the placid streams. Thrill-seekers flock to the town of Bovec for outdoor fun.

Whitewater rafting on the Soča

Whitewater rafting on the **Soča River** is one of the most thrilling adventures Slovenia offers. Several outfitters run trips down the river from bases around Bovec. **Nature's Ways** *(econaturesways.com)* runs guided white-water rafting and canyoning adventures for small groups, with an emphasis on minimal environmental impact. And lots of screaming, of course. **Soča Rafting** *(socarafting.si)* was the first rafting company in Slovenia and is still at the top of its game, offering novelties such as hydrospeed, where you glide along the river and might get mistaken for a fish. For something different, **Adrenalin Park Bovec** *(ziplinesslovenia.si)* features more than 3km of ziplines over the Julian Alps. They also rent e-bikes, scooters and kayaks.

BEST OF BOHINJ OUTDOORS

Savica Waterfall: An easy(ish) stroll through lush forest leads to one of Slovenia's most magnificent waterfalls.

Mostnica Gorge: Spend the day listening to the sounds of the forest as you follow wooded paths towards a heavenly valley.

Hike & Bike: Organises nighttime walks by lantern around the lake and guided forest therapy meditation sessions.

Electric Boat Tours: Operates throughout the year between Ribčev Laz and Ukanc; there's no better way to take in the lake.

Vogel Ski Centre: The 22km of runs make this a top skiing destination. It's 1540m above the lake's southwestern corner and accessible by cable car from Ukanc.

 ## BEST FOR EATING IN BLED & BOHINJ: OUR PICKS

Park Restaurant & Cafe: The creator of Bled's trademark *kremšnita* (cream cake) recipe is still the best, according to almost everyone. *11am-10pm* €€

Bled Castle Restaurant: Recognised as one of the top sustainable restaurants in Europe, this elegant dining room overlooks Lake Bled. *noon-10pm* €€

Hotel Bohinj: The chic hotel restaurant near Lake Bohinj is open for lunch, snacks and dinner, with a wide range of main courses and desserts. *noon-10pm* €€

Majer'ca: Modern Alpine cuisine near Lake Bohinj, with multi-course tasting menus you can design yourself. *4-10pm Mon-Fri, 1-9pm Sat & Sun* €€

Slovenian Karst & Coast

CAVES | ADRIATIC SUNSETS | SEAFOOD

Places

Postojna Cave p270
Piran p271

☑ **TOP TIP**

Parking is tight along Slovenia's coast, particularly in Piran. Work out parking in advance with your hotel. For Piran, parking is only available at Garage Fornače, outside the Old Town. Shuttle buses (5am to 1am) connect the parking area and town centre.

The Karst region is a limestone plateau stretching from the Gulf of Trieste to the Vipava Valley. Rivers, ponds and lakes can disappear and then resurface in the Karst's porous limestone, often resulting in underground caverns like the fabulous caves at Postojna and Škocjan. To the southwest, Slovenia's short Adriatic Sea coastline (just 47km) features clean beaches, boats for rent and delicious seafood, with the highlight being the port of Piran.

Postojna Cave

TIME FROM LJUBLJANA: 1HR 🚗

The jaw-dropping Postojna Cave system, a series of caverns, halls and passages, extends underground for some 24km and is two million years old. Visits are by 1½-hour guided tours, with much of the distance covered by electric train. Note the cave has a constant temperature of 8°C to 10°C, so a warm jacket and decent shoes are advised.

Tour a subterranean wonderland

Stepping through the entrance of **Postojna Cave** (*postojnska-jama.eu; adult/student/child in high season €32.90/25.90/19.50; tours hourly 9am-6pm, daily Jul & Aug, fewer departures rest of year*) takes you from the clear light of the Mediterranean hinterland and into the darkness and then, as your eyes adjust, into another world. Few places in Slovenia have the power to dazzle quite like this. Guided tours unveil 5km of the expansive cave. Entering the **Great Mountain** cavern feels like stepping into the secret den of a James Bond villain or some kind of Hollywood special effects scene. From there, you pass through dry galleries adorned with delicate stalactites, needle-shaped formations and even translucent 'curtains'.

GETTING AROUND

Postojna lies 53km southwest of Ljubljana and is connected to the capital by regular buses and trains. Buses running between Ljubljana and the coast stop at Divača, from where a bus continues on to the Škocjan Caves. That said, a car is more practical for reaching these caves. Regular buses travel between Ljubljana and Piran. Once in town, the port area is small and walkable. Note that cars are restricted in Piran's Old Town.

See more jaw-dropping beauty at Škocjan Caves

The immense complex of **Škocjan Caves** *(park-skocjanske-jame.si; guided tour adult/concession/child €18/14/9)*, just 20km southwest of Postojna, is – for many travellers – a rival to Postojna Cave for the title of Slovenia's best cave experience. The Škocjan cave system was formed by the Reka River, which carves its way through a gorge beneath Škocjan village and then vanishes into the Dead Lake. Two-hour guided tours begin at 500m-long **Silent Cave**, which is filled with beautiful stalactites, stalagmites and flowstones that resemble snowdrifts. Silent Cave ends at the **Great Hall**, 120m wide and 30m high – it's a fantasy world of exotic dripstones, deposits and mighty stalagmites.

Piran

TIME FROM LJUBLJANA: **2HR** 🚗

Clustered in a tight huddle of stone and terracotta on a narrowing peninsula in the northern Adriatic, Piran (Pirano in Italian) sparkles as the crown jewel of Slovenia's 47km coastline. Wander the twisty alleyways of the impeccably preserved Old Town with its Venetian Gothic architecture, climb to the summit for a gorgeous church, medieval walls and incredible views, or just chill in the elegant main square, Tartinijev trg.

Stroll the centre of a lovely port

Most explorations of Piran begin in the graceful, oval-shaped, pastel-hued **Tartinijev trg**. The 'square' is named after Giuseppe Tartini (1692–1770), an 18th-century composer, violinist and Piran's favourite native son. A **statue** honours the great man in the centre of the square; his birthplace, **Tartini House** *(facebook.com/casatartini; entry free)*, hosts cultural events and exhibitions. Next door is the cute 1818 **Church of St Peter** with its twin Doric columns. Other highlights to enjoy from the outside include the grand **Court House** and the porticoed 19th-century **Municipal Hall**, home to the helpful **tourist information centre** at the western end of the square.

BEST SUNSET SPOTS IN PIRAN

Piran Town Walls: Soak in the amazing views from the preserved medieval walls high up above town.

Boat Harbour: Pick any vantage point along the coastal boardwalk, but this one is glorious in the late afternoon.

Hotel Piran Rooftop: The rooftop bar of Piran's iconic hotel is the classiest place in town for a sundowner.

Bell Tower: It may close just before sunset, but there are great views here; watch the spectacle over town from just outside the door.

Strunjan Landscape Park: About an hour's walk along the coast from Piran, this trail takes you up on 80m-high cliffs with amazing views.

 BEST FOR EATING IN PIRAN: OUR PICKS

Fritolin Pri Cantini: First choice of the places on Trg 1 Maja and a classic Old Town experience: order calamari under a cosy grape-wine canopy. *11am-9pm* €

Sarajevo 84: Order a plate of beans and some *čevapčiči* (spicy meatballs of beef or pork) with Bosnian bread and you'll be set for the day. *10am-10pm* €

Restaurant Neptune: Try delicious dondoli clams (sea truffles) and other top-notch seafood and pasta at this old-school joint. *noon-3pm & 6-10pm Wed-Mon* €€

Stara Gostilna: The home kitchen of young Michelin-starred chef Kristian Zule features lobster ravioli, perfect seafood and a huge wine list. *6am-midnight Mon-Sat* €€€

Places We Love to Stay

€ Budget €€ Midrange €€€ Top End

Ljubljana
MAP p263

Prešernov Trg

City Hotel Ljubljana €€ Good-value, central high-rise with clean rooms. It's a short walk from the train and bus stations and has an excellent breakfast buffet and a welcoming reception. Book ahead as it's popular in season.

AS Boutique Hotel €€€ Step inside a hidden courtyard just steps from Prešernov trg to find this upscale boutique, tastefully decorated with stunning contemporary art and a fashionable mid-century feel. Some rooms offer castle views.

Old Town

AdHoc Hostel € Well-situated, efficiently run hostel right on the Ljubljanica River has brightly painted, airy dorms and several private doubles. Good choice for hitting the coffee bars and restaurants along the riverbank.

Hotel Bloom €€ Lovely boutique below Gornji trg features eye-catching art deco styling and 10 newly refurbished rooms, with lovely hardwood floors and tasteful furnishings. Enjoy your breakfast or an evening drink in the hidden back garden.

Center

Urban Boutique Hotel €€ Great-value, upscale three-star with quiet, high-standard rooms

and an excellent breakfast that features lots of locally sourced items and made-to-order eggs. The Center location is close to the sights, yet removed from the noise of busy Slovenska cesta.

Hotel Mrak €€ Cosy, family-run hotel with 35 refurbished rooms set in an older building. Almost opposite the Križanke on Trg Francoske Revolucije, it's ideally located for culture vultures. The back courtyard is lovely for breakfast in nice weather.

Bled

Old Parish House €€ The former property of the Parish Church of St Martin has been transformed into a welcoming guesthouse with timber beams, hardwood floors and chic finishes.

Hotel Triglav Bled €€€ An historic facade hides modern touches and lakeside views, plus a fine restaurant that makes coming home after a day on the water a true pleasure.

Lake Bohinj

Boutique Hotel Majer'ca €€ Scandi cool rooms in Stara Fuzina with views of the mountains and private saunas for the lucky few who snag the suites.

Hotel Bohinj €€ Equal parts sumptuous and wacky, this restored lodge spares no

expense spoiling its guests while maintaining a true soul. Ask about the nightclub.

Postojna

Lipizzaner Lodge €€ Pleasant rural guesthouse run by a Welsh-Finnish couple with brilliant local expertise. You'll feel enveloped in the local countryside, but still close to everything.

Hotel Jama €€€ Literally atop Postojna Cave, this huge socialist-era hotel was renovated and turned into luxury lodging with great views; pay extra for a front-facing room.

Piran

Hostel Adriatic Piran € Offering dorms and rooms of varying sizes, this is one of the only budget options in Piran. Rooms are plain but nicely looked after. Shared bathrooms.

Guesthouse Rosemary €€ Tucked away in the back streets but within walking distance of everything, Rosemary has polished wooden floorboards, wrought-iron furnishings and great reviews from travellers.

PachaMama €€€ Built by travellers for travellers, this excellent guesthouse sits just off Tartinijev trg and has 12 fresh rooms, decorated with timber and lots of travel photography.

Practicalities

LGBTIQ+ Travellers

Slovenia is a largely tolerant destination and members of the LGBTIQ+ community are unlikely to face any overt forms of discrimination. Ljubljana is especially welcoming and same-sex couples holding hands on the street, for example, are unlikely to attract even a passing glance.

Health

Slovenia is a safe country, and travellers needn't worry about taking any special precautions. Tap water is safe to drink and of very good quality. Like much of Central Europe, Slovenia's forests and grasslands are filled with ticks. On hikes or treks, use repellent and cover up exposed skin.

Toilets

Public toilets, especially in Ljubljana, are plentiful and relatively easy to find. Unlike in many European countries, toilets are often free of charge. Authorities are working to make toilets accessible for travellers with disabilities.

Insurance

Consider a policy that covers flight cancellations and medical care. Alternatively, or additionally, EU travellers can apply for the European Health Insurance Card (EHIC) that covers emergency medical treatment outside their home country free of charge.

ALESSANDRO ZAPPALORTO/SHUTTERSTOCK

Tartinijev trg (p271), Piran

Opening Hours

Banks 8.30am–12.30pm & 2pm–5pm Monday to Friday
Pubs 11am–midnight Sunday to Thursday, to 2am Friday & Saturday
Restaurants 11am–10pm
Shops 8am–7pm Monday to Friday, to 1pm Saturday

Accessible Travel

Slovenia is reasonably accessible for travellers with disabilities. Facilities include public telephones with amplifiers, pedestrian crossings with beepers, Braille on maps at bus stops, sloped pavements, ramps in government buildings and reserved parking spaces.

Ljubljana is largely wheelchair-accessible. The centre is mostly flat; pavements have kerb cuts. Most buses are equipped with lifts. Old Town's cobblestone streets are a challenge.

Public Holidays

New Year's 1 and 2 January
Prešeren Day (Culture Day) 8 February
Easter & Easter Monday March/April
Insurrection Day 27 April
Labour Day 1 and 2 May
National Day 25 June
Assumption Day 15 August
Reformation Day 31 October
All Saints' Day 1 November
Christmas Day 25 December
Independence Day 26 December

Language

Slovene belongs to the South Slavic language family, along with Croatian and Serbian (although it is much closer to Croatia's northwestern and coastal dialects). It also shares some features with the more distant West Slavic languages through contact with a dialect of Slovak. Although most Slovene adults speak at least one foreign language, often English, German or Italian, any effort on your part to speak the local tongue will be rewarded.

Basics

Hello. Zdravo. *zdra·vo*
Goodbye. Na svidenje. *na svee·den·ye*
Excuse me. Dovolite. *do·vo·lee·te*
Sorry. Oprostite. *op·ros·tee·te*
Please. Prosim. *pro·seem*
Thank you. Hvala. *hva·la*
You're welcome. Ni za kaj. *nee za kai*
Yes. Da. *da*
No. Ne. *ne*
What's your name? Kako vam/ti je ime? (pol/inf) *ka·ko vam/tee ye ee·me*
My name is ... Ime mi je ... *ee·me mee ye ...*
Do you speak English? Ali govorite angleško? *a·lee go·vo·ree·te ang·lesh·ko*
I don't understand. Ne razumem. *ne ra·zoo·mem*

Directions

Where's the ...? Kje je ...? *kye ye ...*
What's the address? Na katerem naslovu je? *na ka·te·rem nas·lo·voo ye*
Can you show me (on the map)? Mi lahko pokažete (na zemljevidu)? *mee lah·ko po·ka·zhe·te (na zem·lye·vee·doo)*
How do I get to ...? Kako pridem do ...? *ka·ko pree·dem do ...*
Is it near/far? Ali je blizu/daleč? *a·lee ye blee·zoo/da·lech*
(Go) Straight ahead. (Pojdite) Naravnost naprej. *(poy·dee·te) na·rav·nost na·prey*

Time

What time is it? Koliko je ura? *ko·lee·ko ye oo·ra*
It's (one) o'clock. Ura je (ena). *oo·ra ye (e·na)*
half past seven pol osem *pol o·sem* (literally 'half eight')
in the morning zjutraj *zyoot·rai*
in the evening zvečer *zve·cher*
yesterday včeraj *vche·rai*
today danes *da·nes*
tomorrow jutri *yoo·tree*

Emergencies

Help! Na pomoč! *na po·moch*
Go away! Pojdite stran! *poy·dee·te stran*
I'm lost. Izgubil/Izgubila sem se. (m/f) *eez·goo·beew/ eez·goo·bee·la sem se*
Where are the toilets? Kje je stranišče? *kye ye stra·neesh·che*
I'm ill. Bolan/Bolna sem. *(m/f) bo·lan/boh·na sem*
Call ... Pokličite ...! *pok·lee·chee·te*
 a doctor zdravnika *zdrav·nee·ka*
 the police policijo *po·lee·tsee·yo*

Eating & Drinking

What would you recommend? Kaj priporočate? *kai pree·po·ro·cha·te*
Cheers! Na zdravje! *na zdrav·ye*
I'd like the ..., Želim ..., *zhe·leem ...*
please. prosim. *pro·seem*
 bill račun *ra·choon*
 menu jedilni list *ye·deel·nee leest*

NUMBERS

1
en *en*

2
dva *dva*

3
trije *tree·ye*

4
štirje *shtee·rye*

5
pet *pet*

6
šest *shest*

7
sedem *se·dem*

8
osem *o·sem*

9
devet *de·vet*

10
deset *de·set*

Ljubljana Airport

Arriving & Getting Around

Ljubljana Airport is the country's only international airport. The airport is 27km north of the city and well connected by taxi or shuttle bus. Slovenia is thoroughly integrated into European rail and bus networks.

Public Transport in Ljubljana
Central Ljubljana is walkable but use buses to reach outlying neighbourhoods. Buses operate from 5am to 10.30pm (fare €1.30). Pay fares with a contactless debit card or purchase a magnetic 'Urbana' card.

Driving
Before driving in Slovenia, purchase an **e-vignette** online (*evinjeta.dars.si*), required to drive on major highways. Vignettes can also be purchased at petrol stations near the border. The price is €16/32 per week/month.

Driving Essentials
Drive on the right.
The speed limit is 50km/h in urban areas, 90km/h on secondary roads and 130km/h on motorways.
Blood-alcohol limit is 0.05%.

Long-Haul Train & Bus Travel
Train and bus routes cover the entire country. Trains are generally more useful for covering longer distances, such as from Ljubljana to Maribor. Buses are more useful for shorter distances and on select routes, such as from Ljubljana to Lake Bled or to Piran. Trains and buses depart from the **Ljubljana Train Station**.

MONEY
Currency: Euro (€)

CHANGING MONEY
ATMs are ubiquitous and offer better rates for changing money than private exchange booths. That said, many banks, post offices, tourist offices and exchange bureaus do change money. Banks usually charge a commission of 1%. Other agencies charge 3%.

CARD & DIGITAL PAYMENTS
Paying with credit or debit cards is common around the country and often preferable to cash. The only exceptions might be smaller shops in outlying areas. Ticket machines in Ljubljana's buses now also accept card payments.

TIPPING
Hotels Gratuity for cleaning at your discretion.**Pubs** Not expected unless table service provided. **Restaurants** 10% for decent service.**Taxis** Round up fare to nearest euro.

Curated by
Nicola Williams

Switzerland

ALPINE TRADITION, OUTDOOR ACTION AND URBAN FUN

The Swiss don't do half measures: chocolate-box villages of film-set ilk, once-in-a-lifetime rail journeys, untamed nature off the charts...

No other place inspires exploration quite like Switzerland, a small country in western Europe that gave the world melt-in-the-mouth chocolate, cyberspace and an overdose of godlike landscapes. Where else can you follow flower trails around glittering lakes, cross glacial ice roped to a guide and corkscrew up vertiginous alpine passes like James Bond – all in one weekend?

How incredible and intoxicating it all is. But this is Sonderfall Schweiz ('special-case Switzerland'), a privileged neutral country, proudly idiosyncratic, insular and unique. Its four official languages alone speak volumes. French is spoken in Suisse Romande in the west, in Geneva and all around its lake, and in most of the split-personality canton of Valais. Moving east, Germanic Switzerland baffles with Swiss-German in avant-garde Swiss capital Bern; in the flush of art-rich cities north; and across the Swiss Alps, from extreme-sports hub Interlaken in the Bernese Oberland to the glitterati-infused ski slopes of ritzy St Moritz in Graubünden. It is here, shouldering up to Austria and Italy in the country's southeast, that you might get to hear Romansh – Switzerland's fourth national language few have ever heard of (or heard). This is where the mountains get really wild – if you want to tiptoe off-grid, the protected Swiss National Park is the sweet spot.

Then there is Ticino, a charismatic pocket of Italian-speaking exuberance and dolce vita in the hot south.

Sheer variety alone has you spellbound in Switzerland.

AARONCHENPS2/SHUTTERSTOCK

THE MAIN AREAS

GENEVA
Lakeside living and belle époque romance. **p280**

NORTHERN SWITZERLAND
World-class art in culture-rich cities. **p285**

THE SWISS ALPS
Bucket-list vistas and outdoor adventure. **p289**

TICINO
The country's 'dolce' Italianate soul. **p294**

For places to stay in Switzerland, see p297

SAIKO3P/SHUTTERSTOCK

Above: Matterhorn (p291) and Zermatt (p290); Right: Eiger Express (p292), Wetterhorn and Grindelwald

Find Your Way

Switzerland's ravishing landscapes inspire immediate action – grab boots, leap on board, toot bike bell and let spirits rip. However you choose to get around, the going is typically smooth and the scenery is XXL magnificent.

TRAIN, BUS, BOAT & CABLE CAR

Swiss trains, buses and paddle steamers on lakes all run like clockwork and connect seamlessly with mountain railways and cable cars. Transport is pricey – consider carefully the numerous discount-giving travel cards and tickets that are available.

CAR & MOTORCYCLE

A car is not essential, but can be useful for unearthing the country's nooks, crannies and most rural folds. Navigating steep relentless switchbacks is part of the joy of a summer road trip across high mountain passes in the Alps; check if open on *alpen-paesse.ch*.

Northern Switzerland, p285

Feel the edgy urban pulse of the country's Germanic roots in a flush of northern cities, from one of Europe's least-known capitals to wealthy, hard-working and increasingly hip Zürich.

Ticino, p294

Switzerland meets Italy: feast on pizza, gelato and a rich dose of dolce vita (the 'sweet life') in this Italian-speaking Swiss land of lakes, palm trees and more hours of sunshine than anywhere else in the country.

The Swiss Alps, p289

Soul-soaring mountain peaks, glacier, lakes and gorges stitch together this extraordinary swathe of the country, where the bulk of the action kicks off outside. Summer- or winter- sports fiends, this is your 'hood.

Geneva, p280

Meet French-speaking Switzerland. 'Big bang' secrets, beachside DJs and chocolate-box old towns: Lake Geneva's eponymous town and its belle époque shores delight and surprise.

Jet d'Eau (p280) and Lake Geneva, Geneva

Plan Your Time

Despite the gravity-defying geographical terrain at times, Switzerland distances are manageable, variety is within easy reach and pretty much everything runs with clockwork precision and efficiency.

A Quick Taster

● Spend a day in Francophone **Geneva** (p280), enjoying old-town flanerie and a lake swim. Venture east along Lake Geneva by rail or paddle steamer, stopping in art-rich **Lausanne** (p283) or music-mad **Montreux** (p283). Cross the famous *Röstigraben* (Switzerland's linguistic, cultural divide) to capital city **Bern** (p285). End on the Swiss-Italian Riviera (p296).

A Week in the Mountains

● Use metropolis **Zürich** (p287) as a stepping stone to **Grindelwald** (p292) for alpine scenery on skis or afoot, and take a ride of a lifetime up **Jungfraujoch** (p292). Consider a pit stop in **Lucerne** (p292), epitome of graceful lake living. Zip to **St Moritz** (p293) for more alpine action, then loop east into Italian Switzerland in medieval **Bellinzona** (p294).

SEASONAL HIGHLIGHTS

SPRING

Warm days: cafe terraces unfurl, flowers bloom along lake promenades, lake cruises spring into action.

SUMMER

Ski lifts open for hikers and mountain bikers, and high mountain passes are snow-free. Time to swim in lakes.

AUTUMN

Toast September's grape harvest at wine festivals. Ticino goes chestnut crazy. Mountain resorts hibernate in October.

WINTER

Carve through powder and scoff cheese fondue in an alpine resort. Ski season is mid-December to early April.

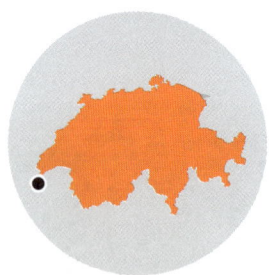

Geneva

CULTURE AND CHOCOLATE | OLD-TOWN FLANERIE | URBAN BEACHES

GETTING AROUND

Geneva is walkable, but **TPG** *(tpg.ch)* buses, trams and shuttle boats save tired legs; buy tickets *(three-stop single/hr/day Chf2/3/10)* at stops or on the TPG+ app.

Hotel guests receive a free **Geneva Transport Card**, covering unlimited public transport – also included in the **Geneva City Pass** *(geneve. com; Chf30/40/50 for 24/48/72hr).* Rent a bike via the **Donkey Republic** *(donkey. bike)* app.

☑ TOP TIP

To meet *chocolatiers* and taste their creations, buy a **Choco Pass** *(adult/ child Chf30/6)* at Geneva **tourist office** *(geneva.ch)* inside the train station or online; Chf1 goes towards Switzerland's climate protection/sustainable tourism. The 24-hour pass covers nine chocolate shops, Monday to Saturday.

French-speaking Geneva (Genève) is a rare breed. Glinting in the sun with the wealth of luxury jewellers, chocolate shops and investment banks, its flawless, glossy veneer can feel impenetrable. But meander away from the manicured lakeshore – into less touristy neighbourhoods like grungier Pâquis, village-like Carouge or along the postindustrial Rhône – and a rougher-cut diamond emerges, quietly humming with attitude.

A place of international diplomacy ever since persecuted Protestants from France sought refuge here during the Reformation in the 16th century, Geneva is home to 200-odd international and nongovernmental organisations, including the UN, World Health Organization and International Committee of the Red Cross. Getting a soaking on the pier beneath its emblematic Jet d'Eau pencil fountain, a 1951 rendition of the plume of water that shot into the sky for 15 minutes each Sunday to release pressure at the city's water station, is a rite of passage.

Feel Geneva's Antique Heartbeat

Explore the old town

Head to Gothic **Cathédrale St-Pierre** *(concerts-cathedrale. ch; towers adult/child Chf10/5)* and spiral up its towers to enjoy lake and old-town views. Next door at the **Musée International de la Réforme** *(musee-reforme.ch; adult/child Chf13/6),* closed Monday, learn how Geneva became a safe haven for Protestant refugees persecuted for their faith during the 16th-century Reformation. Uphill on **Grand-Rue**, philosopher Jean-Jacques Rousseau (1712–78) was born at the **Maison de Rousseau et de la Literature** *(m-r-l.ch/; adult/child Chf7/5).* End on **Place du Bourg-de-Four**, Roman forum, medieval-fair host and modern-day cafe-terrace hub.

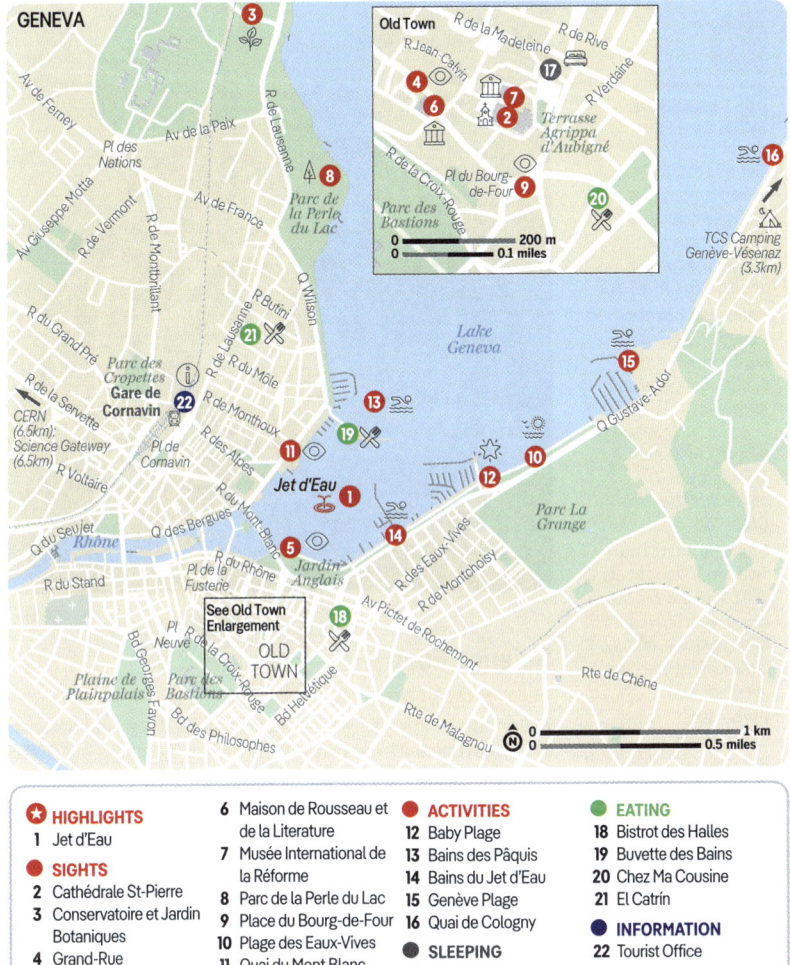

★ HIGHLIGHTS
1 Jet d'Eau

● SIGHTS
2 Cathédrale St-Pierre
3 Conservatoire et Jardin Botaniques
4 Grand-Rue
5 Horloge Fleurie
6 Maison de Rousseau et de la Literature
7 Musée International de la Réforme
8 Parc de la Perle du Lac
9 Place du Bourg-de-Four
10 Plage des Eaux-Vives
11 Quai du Mont Blanc

● ACTIVITIES
12 Baby Plage
13 Bains des Pâquis
14 Bains du Jet d'Eau
15 Genève Plage
16 Quai de Cologny

● SLEEPING
17 Hôtel Bel'Esperance

● EATING
18 Bistrot des Halles
19 Buvette des Bains
20 Chez Ma Cousine
21 El Catrín

● INFORMATION
22 Tourist Office

Venerate Mont Blanc

A waterfront walk along Quai du Mont Blanc

Satellites ensure Geneva's **Horloge Fleurie** (Flower Clock) next to **Pont du Mont Blanc** keeps perfect time, with the world's longest second hand (2.5m) and 6500 flowers. Across the bridge, views of Mont Blanc (4805m) encrust **Quai du Mont Blanc**. Promenade along the lakeshore to **Parc de la Perle du Lac**, where outdoor films are screened in summer *(cinetransat.ch; free)*. North again, the **Conservatoire et Jardin Botaniques** *(cjbg.ch; free)* showcases 11,000 species from around the world.

BEST LAKESIDE SWIM SPOTS

Genève Plage: May to September, this 1930s swimming-pool complex buzzes. *(geneve-plage.ch; adult/child Chf7/3.50)*

Bains des Pâquis: Vintage lake-water pool with retro vibe; sunrise concerts and full-moon swims in summer, saunas and lake dips in winter. *(aubp.ch; adult/child Chf2/1; extras Chf15–22)*

Bains du Jet d'Eau: Two small sleek pools in front of the Jet d'Eau, with lifeguards and snack bar. *(adult/child Chf2/1; Tue-Sun Jul–mid-Sep)*

Plage des Eaux-Vives: Human-made shingle beach with coffee trucks, showers, accessible ramps and family-friendly **Baby Plage** *(plagepublique deseauxvives.ge.ch; free).*

Quai de Cologny: Lounge on a ring-shaped wooden platform, suspended above the water.

DEYAN BARIC/ALAMY

CERN

Science Fest

Unravel the universe at CERN

Fathoming out particles that make up matter is what physicists at the European Organization for Nuclear Research or **CERN** do. This is where British scientist Tim Berners Lee invented the World Wide Web in 1989. **Science Gateway** *(visit.cern; free with online advance reservation)* shines light on CERN's incredulous work with science shows, films and exhibitions. Take tram 18 from Gare de Cornavin.

EATING IN GENEVA: GOOD-VALUE DINING

Buvette des Bains: Grab breakfast, salads, oysters and a superlative cheese fondue at Bains des Pâquis' trendy, no-frills buvette (snack bar). *7am-10.30pm €*

Chez Ma Cousine: Generous portions of chicken, potatoes and salad at the old town's much-loved rotisserie. *11am-11.30pm Mon-Sat, to 10.30pm Sun €*

Bistrot des Halles: Join locals at the zinc bar for *côte de boeuf* (steak), calf kidneys and other bistro classics in the covered market. *7.30-7pm Mon-Fri, 6am-4pm Sat €€*

El Catrín: Authentic tacos and party vibe at this fun-loving Mexican hangout near the station. *6-11.30pm Wed, noon-2pm & 6-11.30pm Thu-Sun €€*

Beyond Geneva

Gem villages, vineyards and castles bead the mythical northern shore of Europe's largest alpine lake.

Heading out of urban Geneva, join dots along the lakeshore between medieval villages, bijou pleasure ports and grassy 'beaches' cradling pebbly shores and summer bars. Rivalling Geneva in the dining and nightlife stakes is Lausanne (Switzerland's fourth-largest city), with an Olympian pedigree and vistas that pack a punch. A city of steps, its *escaliers* (staircases) link the hilltop old town and EPFL campus (Europe's version of Boston's MIT, where bold young scientists are engineering future brilliance) with belle époque beauty by the water. Continuing east, Lavaux vineyards so steep they are UNESCO-listed waltz along the shore to jazzy Montreux and the lake's emblematic château. Bicycle, e-bike or train, sailboat, vintage steamer or stand-up paddle: pick your means and level up with the local outdoor-action set.

Places

Lausanne
TIME FROM GENEVA: **45MIN**

Meet the watch at the cathedral

Atop Lausanne's steeply pitched, medieval Old Town, **Cathédrale de Notre Dame** *(cathedrale-lausanne.ch; belfry adult/child €5/2)* might lack the lightness of French Gothic buildings, but its 'backstage' encounters thrill. Visit after dark when you can accompany the *guet* (nightwatch) – floppy black hat, candlelit lantern – on his nightly climb up 153 steps to his lookout and spartan bunk room atop the 79m-tall **Tour du Beffroi** (Belfry Tower). In keeping with a medieval tradition dating to 1405, the nightwatchman (or, since 2021, a female *guette*) calls out the hours into the night from 10pm to 2am.

Aim for a full moon or a night around midsummer when starlit views of the city laid out at your feet glow gold. To join *le guet/guette* at 10pm, you must call their 'office' (+41 21 312 74 91) to reserve for the following day.

Montreux
TIME FROM GENEVA: **65MIN**

Follow a trail of flowers to Château de Chillon

Art, music and natural beauty collide in Montreux, 30km southeast of Lausanne. The elegant lakeside town has been a magnet for artists and celebrities since the 19th century. Pink Floyd, David Bowie, Elton John and Ella Fitzgerald have all played at

---

GETTING AROUND

Regular SBB trains trundle along the lake from Geneva and Lausanne to Montreux and beyond. CGN steamers from Lausanne (1¾ hours) and Montreux (15 minutes) dock right in front of Château de Chillon.

Use Lausanne's metro, buses and trolleybuses to tackle city hills. Hotel guests get a free **Lausanne Transport Card** covering transport; otherwise buy tickets on the TL app *(t-l.ch)*. Cut sightseeing costs with a **Lausanne City Pass** *(1/2/3 days Chf30/40/50)*, also covering transport.

Château de Gruyères, Gruyères

BEST LAUSANNE MUSEUMS

Olympic Museum: Sprint against Usain Bolt at this museum. Stacks of interactive exhibits for all ages.

Plateforme 10: Modern art in a trio of museums in an architecturally striking complex by Lausanne train station.

Collection de l'Art Brut: The world's original collection of Art Brut – subversive, 'raw art' by artists with no formal training – inside an 18th-century château.

Fondation de l'Hermitage: A 19th-century mansion with art exhibitions, gardens and a family-friendly cafe-bistro.

Palais de Rumine: Archaeology, geology and money museums inside the palace (1891–1906) where the treaty finalising the break-up of the Ottoman Empire after WWI was signed.

Montreux's world-famous music festival, an annual fixture since 1967. Poking around the recording studio where rock band Queen recorded several albums at **Queen: The Studio Experience** *(mercuryphoenixtrust.org/studioexperience; free)* is a tearjerker.

Soak up summer splendour along the **Chemin Fleuri**. The Flower Path unfurls along the waterfront for 2.5km to Switzerland's best-preserved medieval fortress **Château de Chillon** *(chillon.ch; adult/child Chf15/7)*. Spellbinding floral displays are positively tropical, and views of alpine mountain peaks across the water in France are Disney movie stuff. In odd years during summer's **Biennale Montreux** *(biennale.ch; Aug–Nov)*, sculptures by Swiss sculptors dot the lake path.

Gruyères

TIME FROM GENEVA: **90MIN**

On the trail of cheesemakers

A classic day trip for Genevans, this tiny chocolate-box village seduces with cobbled streets, flower-strewn wooden houses and 13th-century **Château de Gruyères** *(chateau-gruyeres.ch; adult/child Chf13/5)*. Come summer weekends, you might catch alpenhorn players in the streets. But cheese is the cherry on the cake – AOP Gruyère, to be precise. Get up close to the production process at two very different dairies: industrial **La Maison du Gruyère** *(lamaisondugruyere.ch, adult/family Chf8/12)* next to Gruyères train station, and 17th-century rustic wooden chalet **Fromagerie d'Alpage de Moléson** *(moleson.ch; adult/child Chf5/3)*, 5km south, where cheesemaker François still heats the milk each morning in a cauldron over a wood fire and presses curds by hand into the moulds. Book at both to bag a spot.

EATING & DRINKING IN LAUSANNE: OUR PICKS

Jetée de la Compagnie: Yoga, DJ sets, sunrise concerts at a 'beach' bar in an industrial container with tables by the water. *10am-midnight, from 9am Sun*

Great Escape: Grungy club-like interior and tree-shaded terrace above Place de Riponne. *10am-1am Mon-Thu, to 2am Fri, 11am-2am Sat, noon-1am Sun*

Le Barbare: Lausanne's best hot chocolate, plus superlative coffee, lunch and brunch year-round. *9am-midnight Tue & Wed, to 1am Thu-Sat, 10am-6pm Sun* €€

Café de l'Evêché: Dip into a traditional cheese fondue, laced with beer, in this old-school cafe by the cathedral. *7am-midnight Mon-Fri, from 11.30am Sat & Sun* €€

Northern Switzerland

ART AND ARCHITECTURE | CITIES | URBAN SWIMMING

Cradled by different beauty from the archetypal soaring mountains and alpine valleys, the Swiss Plateau in the north is Swisser than Swiss. Glacial meltwaters from the Bernese Alps trickle into the Aare River, a perfect ribbon of turquoise that wraps itself around Bern, the laid-back city few realise is Switzerland's capital. The holey cheese that couldn't be more Swiss if it tried hails from the surrounding Emmental countryside, as beautiful as Bern's cobbled picture-book Altstadt is enchanting.

Further north, velvety fields and rolling hills frame urban Basel. Nowhere is Switzerland's Franco-Germanic roots quite so apparent as in this multicultural powerhouse of a city, where Switzerland meets France and Germany at the heart of the Rhine confluence.

The metropolis vibes max out in Zürich, the country's hardworking financial centre which, being Swiss, softens the urban blow with a dreamy lake location and oversized nature right on its doorstep: the Rheinfall waterfall, mirrorlike Lake Constance, those whopping Swiss Alps on the horizon...

Places

Bern p285
Basel p286
Zürich p287

☑ TOP TIP

August is the month for Zürich's **Street Parade** *(streetparade.com/en)*, a techno celebration that has firmly become one of Europe's largest and wildest street parties. Join 800,000 revellers dancing to live music and DJ sets at one of eight stages and 29 'love mobiles'.

Bern

Bern will sweep you off your feet with its riverside location, World Heritage–listed **Altstadt** (Old Town), phenomenal art and views of snow-frosted Alps on the horizon. Catch bears,

⊚ GETTING AROUND

Efficient SBB trains link all the main towns and cities; a car is only needed if you want to meander completely off the urban beaten track. Bern, Basel and Zürich are all a delight to explore on foot; buses, trams and local trains cover longer distances (download public-transport apps at *bernmobil.ch, bvb.ch* and *svv.ch* respectively). Free or inexpensive bicycle-rental schemes make cycling fun – all three cities are part of the **PubliBike** *(publibike.ch)* bike-sharing scheme.

HOW SWISS CHEESE GETS ITS HOLES

Named for its birthplace in the Emme River valley, 15 minutes by train from Bern, Switzerland's Emmentaler cheese has a proud history dating back to the Middle Ages. Copycat cheesemakers around the world have appropriated the Emmental name, but only authentic Emmentaler Switzerland AOC conforms to the original production technique, using raw milk from grass-fed cows, cellar-ripened in giant wheels for at least 120 days.

Emmentaler's famous holes, known as 'eyes', result from the release of carbon-dioxide bubbles by bacteria during the ageing process. The larger the holes, the longer the cheese has matured, and the more pronounced its flavour.

a golden cockerel, jester and god of time Chronos twirling four minutes before the hour on Bern's historical **Zytglogge** clock tower.

Soak up Swiss art in technicolour

Take in Switzerland's answer to the Guggenheim. Rising like three rippling waves above farmland just outside town, Renzo Piano's striking **Zentrum Paul Klee** *(zpk.org; adult/child Chf20/7)* is a tribute to the visionary Swiss-German artist, born near Bern in 1879. Rotating exhibitions draw on a 4000-strong collection of Klee's colour-charged, music-inspired works, showcasing his prodigious career, from expressionism to Cubism and surrealism. Bus 12 runs from Bahnhof to the museum.

Swim down the Aare

Drifting past the historic landmarks of the Altstadt or dipping with locals during their lunch break in the city's shockingly cold turquoise water is a rite of passage. Providing you're an experienced swimmer, try the classic route: hike 2km upstream from **Marzili Pools** to **Camping Eichholz**, then drift back with the current to Marzili's brilliant (and free) lido to swim laps, sunbathe, play volleyball or grab an ice cream. The views of the domed **Bundeshaus** and the **Münster**'s medieval spire are spot on.

Basel

Basel draws culture fiends from far and wide with its exciting art museums, nightlife and cute Altstadt (Old Town) anchored by its colourful **Rathaus** and 13th-century Münster. One-third of its urban population being non-Swiss today assures a continuing international flavour.

Meet art masters at Basel's 'big three'

Basel's cultural scene is its biggest drawcard, with the **Kunstmuseum Basel** *(kunstmuseumbasel.ch; adult/child Chf30/12)* showcasing a world-class collection spread across three buildings in the heart of the city. Switzerland's largest collection of public art spans masters from the 15th century to present day.

Attack contemporary art next at the wacky **Museum Jean Tinguely** *(tinguely.ch; adult/child Chf18/free),* designed by Ticino architect Mario Botta. Arrive by ferry from the **Münster** (cathedral) or cross Mittlere Brücke (Middle Bridge) and walk east. The museum is above a pebble beach, pleasant for swimming or floating downstream with a *Wickelfisch* (sold at the tourist office) back to Mittlere Brücke.

 EATING & DRINKING IN BERN: OUR PICKS

Altes Tramdepot: Cavernous tram hall pairing schnitzel and *Bauernrösti* (fried potatoes topped with an egg) with microbrews. *11am-12.30am* €€

Kornhauskeller: Dine beneath vaulted frescoed arches at this cellar restaurant championing Mediterranean cuisine. *11.30am-11.30pm Mon-Sat, to 10pm Sun* €€

On Tap: Atmospheric vaulted cellar with 12 craft beers on tap and more by the bottle. Pair with antipasti. *4-11.30pm Mon-Wed, to 12.30am Thu-Sat*

Abflugbar: Slick, stylish, speakeasy-style cellar bar with knockout cocktails. Try the basil smash. *7.30pm-12.30am Wed-Sun*

Rathaus, Basel

Final calling card is **Fondation Beyeler** *(fondationbeyel
er.ch; adult/under 25 Chf25/free)*, in a light-filled, open-plan
building by Italian architect Renzo Piano. Exhibitions rotate
19th- and 20th-century works and ethnographic art from Africa, Alaska and Oceania.

Zürich
MAP p288

With a gorgeous location at the meeting of the Limmat River
and Zürichsee, Zürich is hip and culturally ambitious, too.
Pair old-world lanes in the cathedral-pinned Old Town with
postindustrial edge in the artsy Züri-West 'hood. May to
mid-September, swim at a lake- or riverside *badi* (lido) and
enjoy a lake cruise.

Gen up on Swiss history

Celebrate national history and culture at the **Landesmuseum
Zürich** *(landesmuseum.ch; adult/child Chf10/free)*. Elaborately carved and painted sleds, traditional costumes, reconstructed historical rooms and more are beautifully presented at the
main branch of the Swiss National Museum. Find exhibits
on archaeology, and Zürich's history and national identity.
The gift shop has one of the city's best choice of souvenirs.

🍸 EATING & DRINKING IN ZÜRICH: OUR PICKS
MAP p288

Haus Hiltl: A buffet of meatless delights or dine formally upstairs at the world's oldest vegetarian restaurant (1898). *7am-10pm Mon-Fri, 8am-11pm Sat, 10am-10pm Sun* €

Old Inn: Homemade pastrami and other delicacies in antique-style gastropub in art nouveau building. *11.30am-2pm Mon-Fri, 6pm-midnight Tue-Sat* €€

Frau Gerolds Garten: A focal point of the city's alfresco summer drinking scene, in Züri-West. This is one of Europe's best grownup playgrounds. *hours vary*

Clouds: Survey the city from the heady heights of this sophisticated bar on the 35th floor of the Prime Tower. *5pm-midnight Wed & Thu, to 1am Fri & Sat, noon-8pm Sun*

BEST ZÜRICH CHOCOLATE SHOPPING

Lindt Home of Chocolate: Buy Lindt at factory prices at this educational experience with showpiece 9m chocolate fountain.

Café Sprüngli: Try pralines, Luxemburgerli macarons and Grand Cru Absolu, a chocolate made only with cocoa beans and cocoa pulp, at this historic cafe from 1836.

Max Chocolatier: Stylishly packaged bars, truffles and pralines, made with 100% natural ingredients.

Berg und Tal: Artisan grocery stocking several brands of locally produced bean-to-bar chocolate, including Taucherli and Garçoa.

La Flor: Specialising in single-origin bars made from sustainably grown cacao sourced directly from farmers.

🟠 **HIGHLIGHTS**
1 Kunsthaus - Moser Building

🔴 **SIGHTS**
2 Landesmuseum Zürich

🟢 **EATING**
3 Café Sprüngli
4 Haus Hiltl
5 Old Inn
6 Restaurant Markthalle

🟢 **DRINKING & NIGHTLIFE**
7 Clouds

8 Frau Gerolds Garten

🔴 **SHOPPING**
9 Berg & Tal
10 Freitag
11 Im Viadukt
12 La Flor
13 Max Chocolatier

Admire great art at the Kunsthaus

Explore Switzerland's largest art collection at the superlative **Kunsthaus** *(kunsthaus.ch; adult/child Chf24/free)* museum, where thought-provoking exhibits span two main buildings, linked by an underground tunnel with an Ólafur Elíasson sculptural artwork on its ceiling. Seek out its unparalleled collection of the works by titans of the Swiss art world, including Augusto and Alberto Giacometti and Ferdinand Hodler.

Feel the pulse of Züri-West

Züri-West's **Im Viadukt** *(im-viadukt.ch)* is a trendy shopping and dining complex beneath old stone railway bridges. Stroll the viaduct's three blocks between Limmatstrasse and Geroldstrasse to see what catches your eye. Grab breakfast or dinner at **Restaurant Markthalle** *(restaurant-markthalle. ch)*. Inside a stack of shipping containers, **Freitag** *(freitag.ch)* sells colourful wallets and bags of all shapes and sizes made from recycled truck tarps.

The Swiss Alps

OUTDOOR SPORTS | INCREDIBLE SCENERY | PRISTINE PEACE

You have every right to feel petite in the Swiss Alps. Stretching from the canton of Valais above the Rhône Valley in the west to Graubünden in the east, they cut, slice and dice more than half of Switzerland into an astonishing outdoor playground of cloud-shredding snowy peaks, thunderous gorges, ice-blue glaciers and lakes – all ripe for summer hiking and winter skiing.

Switzerland's invisible *Röstigraben* (linguistic and cultural border) kicks in just beyond the French-speaking town of Verbier, where starlets sip cocktails and farmers craft AOP Raclette cheese. Arriving in Zermatt, tongues wag in Swiss-German as everyone stares, transfixed, at the famous Matterhorn. Moving north, the Bernese Oberland – shaped by a godlike hand – is another diva forcing visitors to constantly peer up in wonder. Whether flirting with mountaineering on a *via ferrata*, scaling new heights atop Jungfraujoch or thrilling out on Interlaken whitewater, be prepared to experience nature in overdrive.

Verbier

Ritzy Verbier is the diamond of the Valaisian Alps: small and expensive, it draws accomplished winter skiers and summertime mountain bikers. This French-speaking 'place to be' is an easy train from Geneva and its international airport to Verbier's valley station **Le Châble**, from where cable cars glide to the top.

Fly high on a Mont Fort sunrise

Watching the sun rise over pink peaks at dawn from **Mont Fort** (3330m) is a goosebump moment. If a 4.25am cable-car departure and Chf89 price tag (covering breakfast and all-day cable-car travel) is too extreme, ride a later bubble up to **Les Ruinettes** (2191m) and beyond to Mont Fort *(Chf22 with a free summertime VIP Pass, incl in hotel accommodation Jun-Oct)* from the **Médran cable-car station** on Verbier's main street. Harness the daredevil in you for the descent:

Places

GETTING AROUND

There are excellent SBB train services from the rest of Switzerland to mountain resorts such as car-free Zermatt and Interlaken; funiculars often cover the final leg up to resorts. Cable cars typically close for servicing in late April and late October.

If you are driving in winter, carry snow chains or use winter tyres. In early and late summer, check if mountain passes are open (signs at the bottom of access roads usually say so).

☑ **TOP TIP**

Remember the *Glacier Express* and other panoramic lines are mountain trains: last-minute cancellations due to blocked lines by snow or rockfall happen (your reserved journey still takes place, but on regular lines).

at 100km/h on the 1.4km-long **Mont 4 Zipline** *(adult/child over 8 Chf45/20)*. The bird's-eye view over the Tortin Glacier is of once-in-a-lifetime experience.

Mountain-bike in an alpine playground

Ski-celeb Verbier morphs into bike central in summer. Whether you're tearing down the mountainside as a family on chunky *trottinettes* (hairnet and helmet included in fat-tyre scooter rental; from eight years) from the top of the Savoleyres or Les Ruinettes cable cars, or tackling technical jumps with expert mountain bikers in a dedicated bike park, there is something to suit most abilities. June to mid-October, mountain bikers can transport wheels on the Médran cable car and La Chaux Express chairlift from Les Ruinettes to access 19km of down-hill descents in **Verbier Bike Park** *(verbierbikepark.ch; day pass adult/child Chf55/28, with VIP Pass Chf28/14)*.

Zermatt

Nothing prepares you for that first intoxicating glimpse of car-free Zermatt's peak rising majestically above the town and ski slopes. Step off the train and a puff cloud invariably

 DRINKING IN VERBIER: BEST APRÈS-SKI

Ice Cube: Summer or winter, watch paragliders paint rainbows in the sky from this slope-side 'cube' at Les Ruinettes. *9am-4.15pm Jun-Sep & Dec-Apr*

Le Rouge: Swoosh off the blue Le Rouge piste and into The Red for drinks, 'funky fondue' soirées and resident DJs spinning dance tunes. *noon-midnight*

Pub Mont Fort: Downtown's après-ski heavyweight: live music, DJ sets, terrace and pub grub (apricot chicken wings, fries in melted cheese). *3pm-2am*

Farinet: Less intimidating than other bars, the downtown lounge bar with sun terrace hosts a happy hour and live bands nightly in season. *3pm-2am*

clings to the 4478m hooked summit, making the sudden pop-up brilliance of a cloudless Matterhorn all the more wondrous.

Summit 3883m and glide into Italy

Admire ice sculptures in a palace 15m deep in a glacier, whoosh down ice slides and snow-tube atop **Klein Matterhorn** (3883m), accessed from Zermatt town by three cable cars culminating with the **Matterhorn Glacier Paradise** *(matterhornparadise.ch; adult/child return Chf125/62.50)*, the world's highest-altitude 3S cable car. The view of 14 glaciers and 35 other peaks over 4000m at the top is beyond breathtaking.

Assuming it's a bluebird day, hop aboard the 1.6km-long **Matterhorn Alpine Crossing** *(matterhornalpinecrossing.com; adult single/return from Zermatt Chf156/240)* for a spellbinding cable-car journey over a spectacular glacial world of ice – and across the world's highest alpine border crossing – to Testa Grigia (3458m) in Cervinia, Italy.

Ride Europe's highest cogwheel railway

The **Matterhorn** dominates the scenic ride aboard the **Gornergratbahn** *(gornergrat.ch; adult/child return summer Chf132/66, winter Chf96/48)* – an 1898 vintage – from Zermatt to **Gornergrat** (3089m). Larch forests and the Vispa River melt into snowfields as the train staggers up gradients of up to 20% for 9.4km. Alight at the top to a hypnotic panorama of the Gornergrat glacier, Monte Rosa massif and Switzerland's highest peak, Dufourspitze (Dufour Peak; 4634m). Toast your good fortune on the sun-blazed terrace of **Kulmhotel Gornergrat** *(gornergrat-kulm.ch)*.

Interlaken

Victorian-era glamour meets big mountains in Interlaken, which thrills with just about every heart-pumping alpine sport. Squished between the glacier-fed lakes of Thun and Brienz, this is the springboard to the Alps' fabled **Jungfrau Region**.

Hook up with a guide

Capped by the pearly white peaks of Eiger, Mönch and Jungfrau, this petite alpine town is second only to Queenstown, New Zealand, when it comes to extreme sports. **Outdoor Interlaken** *(outdoor.ch)* is a one-stop adventure shop for pretty much every buzz-inducing activity imaginable: tandem paragliding or skydiving, bungee jumping from a mountain gondola above a dazzling alpine lake, whitewater rafting and canyon swinging between gorge walls at speeds of 120km/h.

THE GLACIER EXPRESS

Gorging on cinematic shots of peaks, lakes, racing whitewater and other natural landscapes is what a day aboard the bucket-list **Glacier Express** *(glacierexpress.ch; single 1st/2nd class Chf159/272, plus reservation fee Chf49)* is about. Pulled by steam engine when it first puffed out of Zermatt in 1930, the iconic red train traverses 91 tunnels and 291 bridges on its slow journey to St Moritz (p293). Creeping along at 10km/h at times, the average speed on its 290km-long journey is just 42km/h. On the final leg between Chur and St Moritz, the six-arch, 65m-high Landwasser Viaduct on the UNESCO World Heritage–listed Albula railway line razzle-dazzles.

 EATING IN ZERMATT: OUR PICKS

Stefanie's Crêperie: Perfect crepes with sweet or savoury (cheese fondue with cherry brandy!) toppings. *1-7pm Mon & Tue, 11.30am-9.30pm Wed-Sun* €

Blatten: Follow a knowing crowd to this small family-run chalet cafe and prized lunch address, in Zermatt's peaceful Blatten hamlet since 1850. *10am-6pm* €

Zum See: Tuck into a cracking rösti and other top-drawer grassroots dishes at this centuries-old chalet in the Zum See hamlet. *8.30am-5pm* €€

Potato: With produce sourced within 99km and ceiling lamps crafted from wooden veg crates, you don't get more local – or brilliantly creative. *6-11pm Mon-Sat* €€€

MORE MYTHICAL TRAIN RIDES

Bernina Express: Plunge through 55 tunnels and across 196 bridges on this 156km journey through the Engadine, from Chur to Tirano (four hours) aboard panoramic coaches *(tickets.rhb.ch).*

Golden Pass Express: Variable-gauge bogies mean the journey between Interlaken and Montreux on Lake Geneva can be done in a single 3½-hour trip *(gpx.swiss).*

Centovalli Railway: Narrow-gauge line linking Locarno with Domodossola (Italy) in 1¾ hours *(vigezzina centovalli.com).*

Gotthard Panorama Express: Five-hour journey mixes a cruise across Lake Lucerne with a train through ravines and past mighty St Gotthard mountain range to Bellinzona and Lugano *(gotthard-panorama-express.ch).*

Grindelwald

Skiers and hikers cottoned onto the charms of this mountain resort in the late 19th century. The geranium-studded chalets, verdant pastures and Oscar-worthy backdrop (the Eiger's north face, glinting tongues of Oberer, crown-like peak of Wetterhorn) are as tantalising as ever.

Eternal ice at Europe's highest train station

Brave the crowds on the once-in-a-lifetime trip to Jungfraujoch, Europe's highest train station, at 3454m. From Grindelwald, the **Eiger Express** *(jungfrau.ch; round trip adult/child Chf97.80/20)* wings you up to Eigergletscher station, where you switch to the Jungfrau Railway up to UNESCO World Heritage–listed **Jungfraujoch** *(jungfrau.ch; round trip from Grindelwald adult/child Chf201/20)*. The summit is always snow white. From the Sphinx observation deck, spot the **Aletsch Glacier**. Grindelwald's **Outdoor Mountaineering School** *(outdoor.ch; 2-day hike Chf395)* organises summer roped hikes on the 23km-long sea of ice with a guide.

Pick up speed at First

Rising above Grindelwald, the 2184m summit of First gets hearts thumping with up-close views of Eiger's ferocious north face and the 4078m fang of Schreckhorn from **First Cliff Walk by Tissot** *(jungfrau.ch; free)*, a gravity-defying lookout platform jutting 45m into the void.

Less than an hour's walk from the First cable-car top station unveils the the calm sapphire waters of **Bachalpsee**. In winter, there's great powder for snowboarding and free-skiing. From **Faulhorn** (2681m), sledge 15km down to Grindelwald on the world's longest sledge run.

Lucerne

Lounging lakeside on the Swiss Alps' northernmost fringe, Lucerne (Luzern in German) has been on the map since the 13th century when merchants crossing the **St Gotthard Pass** traded their wares here. Mountains of myth ring its cobalt lake; Goethe, Queen Victoria, Wagner and more all waxed lyrical about the medieval Old Town.

Devour frescoes, fountains and medieval towers

Using the 14th-century covered wooden footbridge **Kapellbrücke**, cross the Reuss River into Lucerne's perfectly preserved **Altstadt**. Minutes from the train station, this warren

EATING IN GRINDELWALD: OUR PICKS

Cafe 3692: Grindelwald ingredients in tasty specials at this quirky, woodsy hut. Or try alpine teas with pastries. *9am-11pm Fri & Sat, to 6pm Sun €*

Stallbeizli–Heuboden: Fondue heaven at this mountain hut in a converted barn with summer terrace. *noon-10pm Tue-Sat, to 8pm Sun €€*

Glacier Fine Dining: Feast on foraged flowers, herbs and berries. Or Graubünden salmon marinated in gin made from Eiger glacier water. *6-11pm Thu-Mon €€€*

Airtime: In nearby Lauterbrunnen, chill over breakfast, gourmet sandwiches, coffee with cake and Staubbach beer. *9am-5pm Fri-Mon €*

Reuss River and Kapellbrücke, Lucerne

BEST LUCERNE MUSEUMS

Verkehrshaus: Switzerland's most visited museum, the interactive Swiss Museum of Transport is a family-must. *(verkehrshaus.ch)*

Sammlung Rosengart: View works by Paul Klee, Monet, Cézanne, Matisse and more in this world-class modern-art collection. *(rosengart.ch)*

Kunstmuseum Luzern: A hot spot for Swiss and international art. *(kunstmuseum luzern.ch)*

Zivilschutzanlage Sonnenberg: Tour a 1976 underground bunker large enough to accommodate 2000 people during the Cold War. *(unterir disch-ueberleben.ch)*

Bourbaki Panorama: Admire a huge circular painting by 19th-century Swiss artist Edouard Castres. *(bourbaki panorama.ch)*

of cobbled streets hides ornate fountains and frescoes illustrating city history and culture. Fill your water bottle at the colourful **Fritschibrunnen** on Kapellplatz, admire painted facades on **Hirschenplatz**, and nod to the stone fountain on historic market square **Weinmarkt**. End by the river to confront roof panels depicting the Dance of Death on 15th-century covered timber bridge **Spreuerbrücke** (1408).

St Moritz

Switzerland's cradle of alpine tourism, St Moritz has been luring royals, celebrities and moneyed wannabes since 1864. With its aquamarine lake, emerald forests and aloof mountains, the town looks a million dollars. Beyond the glamour, vast swathes of the surrounding Graubünden region are remote and ripe for exploring.

Dare to try extreme bobsledding and tobogganing

For buzz, try careering headfirst down glass-smooth ice at 135km/h on St Moritz's **Olympic Bob Run** *(olympia-bobrun. ch; bobsleigh guest ride Chf269)*. Handcrafted from natural ice in Celerina near St Moritz, this 1722m-long ice channel is the world's oldest bobsleigh run, dating from 1904. Or torpedo headfirst down the **Cresta Run** *(cresta-run.com; 1st 5 rides Chf700)*, a tobogganing course created by British visitors in 1885. In a lying down position, you use a rake on special boots to brake and steer at speeds of up to 140km/h.

 DRINKING AROUND LAKE LUCERNE: IDYLLIC SPOTS

Rigi Kulm Hotel: Modern incarnation of Switzerland's oldest mountain hotel has superlative views from Rigi's peak. *9am-4.30pm Mon-Fri, 8.30am-5pm Sat & Sun*

Restaurant Seerose: The shady lakeside terrace makes this a tempting spot for a post-hike spritz or beer in Weggis. *noon-10pm*

Bürgenstock Resort: If you're feeling flush, take the boat and funicular up to this luxury resort for a cocktail in its Lakeview Bar. *10am-midnight Sun-Thu, to 1am Fri & Sat*

Seehotel Waldstätterhof: The lakeside terrace of this Brunnen hotel is ideal for an aperitif or dinner as the sun sets. *11.30am-2pm & 6.30-10pm*

Ticino

ITALIAN DOLCE VITA | LAKES | HISTORY

GETTING AROUND

Geography dictates how you can explore this southern tip of Switzerland. A car allows you to go deep into its least-ventured folds – the steep switchbacks won't be to the taste of uncertain drivers. SBB trains connect towns with the rest of Switzerland and nearby Milan in Italy. Boats join the dots year-round between towns and villages on Lago Maggiore *(navigazionelaghi.it)* and Lago di Lugano *(lagolugano.ch).*

☑ **TOP TIP**

Locarno is the eastern terminus of the historic **Centovalli Railway** *(vigezzinacentovalli.com),* which trundles in slow motion through burrows via 34 tunnels and across 83 bridges to Domodossola in Italy. Dramatic alpine vistas are nonstop and mesmerising.

The Swiss Alps make their final descent into Italy's sunny plains in Ticino, Switzerland's only entirely Italian-speaking canton where glaciers meet palm trees and Swiss efficiency fuses with Italian flair. Here, on the country's southern tip, olive trees and palms ring alpine lakes. Narrow, twisting valleys sport stone-built villages little changed in two centuries. Gone are the fondue and rösti – think pasta, risotto and polenta instead. Mediterranean winter means sunny days and snow-free lakeshores. In August's sizzling heat, dine in a grotto – a traditional rural dining venue, in a cool shady spot. Earthy autumn ushers in September's grape harvest and Castagnata in October when local chestnuts are picked and celebrated in every guise.

At the heart of the canton rises Bellinzona, Ticino's head-turning capital and a UNESCO World Heritage site, with its fortified ramparts and medieval magic. Venturing south, the tranquil lake waters of Lugano and Locarno on the shared-with-Italy shores of Lago Maggiore quietly seduce.

Ticino's Medieval Capital

Fortress-hop in Bellinzona

Begin at Bellinzona's mighty **Castelgrande** *(fortezzabellinzo na.ch; adult/concession Chf28/18)*, with towers and ramparts free to scramble round. The defensive walls that barrel out for 450m to the west afford top-drawer panoramas of the town and mountains beyond. Continue up the other side of the valley to **Castello di Montebello**, with drawbridges, towers and archaeological exhibits. End with the long climb up switchbacks to **Castello di Sasso Corbaro**, perched high on a wooded hillside and exuding an austere beauty.

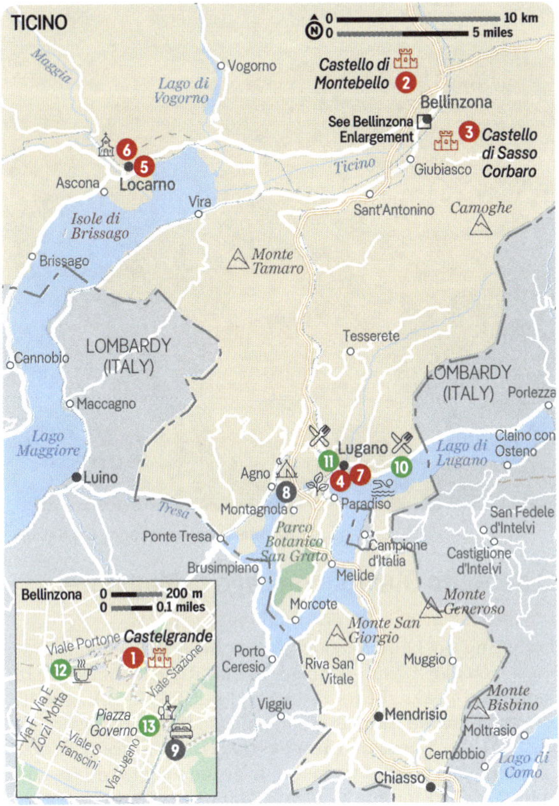

TICINO

Castello di Montebello 2

See Bellinzona Enlargement

3 Castello di Sasso Corbaro

Giubiasco *Corbaro*

Bellinzona

Vogorno

Lago di Vogorno

Locarno 6 5

Ascona

Vira

Isole di Brissago

Brissago

Ticino

Sant'Antonino

Camoghe

Monte Tamaro

Tesserete

Lago Maggiore

LOMBARDY (ITALY)

Cannobio

Maccagno

Luino

Tresa

Ponte Tresa

Montagnola

Agno 8

Paradiso 4 7

Lugano 11 10

Lago di Lugano

Claino con Osteno

San Fedele d'Intelvi

LOMBARDY (ITALY) Porlezza

Parco Botanico San Grato

Campione d'Italia

Castiglione d'Intelvi

Brusimpiano

Melide

Monte Generoso

Bellinzona 0 — 200 m / 0 — 0.1 miles

Viale Portone Castelgrande 1

Piazza Governo 13

12

9

Via F Via E Zorzi Motta

Viale S Franscini

Via Lugano

Morcote

Porto Ceresio

Riva San Vitale

Viggiù

Monte San Giorgio

Muggio

Monte Bisbino

Mendrisio

Moltrasio

Cernobbio

Lago di Como

Chiasso

10 km / 5 miles

HIGHLIGHTS
1 Castelgrande
2 Castello di Montebello
3 Castello di Sasso Corbaro

SIGHTS
4 Parco Ciani

5 Piazza Grande
6 Santuario della Madonna del Sasso

ACTIVITIES
7 Lido di Lugano

SLEEPING
8 Camping Lugano Lake

9 Ostello Montebello

EATING
10 Le Bucce di Gandria
11 Staglio

DRINKING & NIGHTLIFE
12 L'Arte del Caffè
13 Paprika Lounge Bar

PALMS, PARROTS & ICY PEAKS

Welcome to the 'Sunshine Capital of Switzerland'! With around 2300 hours of sunshine per year, Locarno is hands-down Switzerland's sunniest town. Thanks to its protected location on the northern rim of Lago Maggiore, ringed by mountains that block cold winds while retaining warmth, sunny days combine with a microclimate to create an almost Mediterranean environment. Palm trees, banana plants, olive trees and tropical flowers thrive in the mild climate here, as does the odd escaped pet parakeet that you occasionally see squawking in trees in city parks. Winter temperatures rarely drop below freezing here, in sharp contrast to Ticino's ice-bound valleys just a short drive away.

Savour the Difference on a Passeggiata

Chill out in Lugano

One of the joys of staying in Lugano is an evening stroll along the promenade, with palm trees and flowerbeds lacing the sparkling waters of Lago di Lugano. Inland, sculpture-dotted **Parco Ciani** is a gorgeous place for a gelato or picnic on a red bench. On hot days, swim in pools or from the sandy beach at **Lido di Lugano** (lugano.ch; adult/child Chf11/7). Meandering east, Piazza Manzoni anchors the old-world lanes and boutiques of the atmospheric **Old Town**.

TRABANTOS/SHUTTERSTOCK

Santuario della Madonna del Sasso

Cinematic Glamour on Lago di Maggiore

Dip into Locarno's historic cobblestone heart

Lounging on Lake Maggiore's northern tip, old spa town Locarno enjoys a sun-dappled 'Italian Riviera' vibe beneath mountain peaks. In its Città Vecchia (Old Town), arcaded **Piazza Grande** hosts film screenings after dark during August's 11-day **Locarno Film Festival** *(locarnofestival.ch)*.

Legend has it that Franciscan friar Bartolomeo d'Ivrea, inspired by a vision of the Virgin Mary in 1480, initiated the construction of **Santuario della Madonna del Sasso**, clinging to an outcrop in Locarno's Orselina suburb. To make the pilgrimage here, ride the Cardada **funicular** *(cardada.ch)* from just south of Locarno train station. Walk back down into town along the chapel-lined **Via Crucis** (Way of the Cross).

 EATING & DRINKING IN TICINO: OUR PICKS

Staglio: The best pizza slices in Lugano town that won't break the bank. Central location just back from the lakefront. *11am-9pm Mon-Thu, from noon Fri-Sun* €

Le Bucce di Gandria: In Gandria village above Lugano, feast on seasonal local flavours and sensational lake views. *7-10pm Thu-Sun, noon-2pm Sat & Sun* €€

Paprika Lounge Bar: Dive into inventive drinks and bites at this trendy spot in Bellinzona, perfect for a quick drink or lunch. *7am-10pm Mon-Fri, 8am-2pm Sat*

L'Arte del Caffè: This elegant cafe en route to Castelgrande is a great place for an Italian caffeine shot before the uphill castle hike. *8am-5.30pm Mon-Sat*

Places We Love to Stay

€ Budget €€ Midrange €€€ Top end

Geneva   MAP p281

TCS Camping Genève-Vésenaz € Campsite with cabins, tent pitches and van park overlooking a grassy beach on Pointe à la Bise, 7km north from downtown Geneva.

Hôtel Bel'Esperance €€ Single to family rooms sleeping four add extra appeal to this reliable midrange hotel. The icing on the cake: a rooftop terrace for lake-drooling.

Lausanne

Lausanne Jeunotel € Smart hostel a stone's throw from the lake, a Roman archaeological dig and the International Olympic Committee's shiny HQ. Dorms sleep two to six.

Mad House € The 'it' address in lively Flon (actually part of Accor's Ibis Styles brand), with rooftop bar, street-art deco and cool rooms from the team behind MAD club.

Montreux

Auberge de Jeunesse Montreux € Roll out of your bunk and into the lake at this modern hostel, midway between Montreux and Château de Chillon.

Hôtel La Rouvenaz €€ This boutique hotel–restaurant across from Montreux lakefront, with a down-to-earth contemporary ambience, is startling good value.

Gruyères

Fleur de Lys € Modern comfort with antique touches in a 17th-century building, plus a decent restaurant with a hidden terrace out the back.

Hotel de Gruyères €€ Cosy, traditional lodgings near the village entrance and car parks, with views of the surrounding mountains.

Bern

Am Pavillon € A pleasingly converted late-19th-century townhouse near the Hauptbahnhof, with bags of art-nouveau charm.

Hotel Marthahaus €€ In a leafy neighbourhood, this sweet and simple guesthouse is crisply designed, quiet and sprinkled with modern art.

Verbier

Map Hostel € Go vintage in the old vicarage, down the hill in Vieux Verbier. Bunk rooms sleep two to six.

Ride Inn €€ 'Chalet-style' B&B with shared bathrooms and summer garden. The bike-mad hosts are a mine of local information.

Zermatt

Jaëgerhof Hotel € Consistently reliable, this functional but attractive hotel sports three-star singles, doubles, twins and family rooms. Copious breakfast buffet.

Hotel Plateau Rose € Another brilliant deal, up a small hill by the Matterhorn Glacier Paradise cable car. Matterhorn views from its back garden are the finest in town.

Interlaken

Backpacker's Villa Sonnenhof € This slick, ecofriendly chalet and art-nouveau villa has immaculate dorms, a relaxed lounge and a well-equipped kitchen.

Salzano Hotel & Spa €€ This intimate chalet hotel on Interlaken's fringes has a quiet spa, big mountain views and outstanding Italian cooking.

Grindelwald

Gletschergarten €€ Brimming with pine, warmth and family heirlooms, this sweet family-run chalet has gorgeous mountain views.

Valley Hostel €€ A great activity base, this chilled hostel in Lauterbrunnen has pine-panelled dorms and a garden with compelling waterfall views.

Lucerne

Capsule Hotel € One-person enclosed sleeping booths, or 'capsules', in multi-capsule rooms, with shared bathrooms. Clean, comfortable alternative to dorm beds.

Hotel Continental Park €€ By pretty Vögeligärtli park in the new town, with stylish rooms and a Ticino-inspired restaurant. Bike hire available.

Mürren & Jungfrau

Mönchsjochhütte € Share the dinner table and dorm with rock climbers at Switzerland's highest serviced hut. Sensational sunrise.

Ticino   MAP p295

Ostello Montebello € Bellinzona's youth hostel occupies an enviable location between Castelgrande and Montebello. It has basic dorms and a large common room.

Camping Lugano Lake € One of four campsites clustered by Lake Lugano at the end of the runway of Lugano's small airport. High-standard facilities.

Practicalities

SAFE TRAVEL

Switzerland is very safe. Streets are well lit, and street crime and petty theft are uncommon. Check for ticks after a hike. As weather becomes increasingly fickle and extreme, a warming climate poses the greatest threat. Tap water is safe to drink; fill your bottle for free at fountains.

INSURANCE

If you're skiing, snowboarding or hiking, ensure your policy covers helicopter rescue and emergency repatriation.

Alternatively, summer or winter, when buying your lift pass online or in situ, most resorts offer optional insurance (usually Chf3 per day) covering emergency rescue off the mountain and medical care.

LGBTIQ+ TRAVELLERS

Switzerland is a tolerant country and reasonably progressive on LGBTIQ+ rights.

Zürich, Geneva, Lausanne, Bern and Lucerne have the liveliest LGBTIQ+ scenes. Pride kicks off on the snow in Verbier in April.

NATURAL DISASTERS

Download the Alert Swiss app or consult its website *(alert. swiss)* to receive national alerts, notifications, extreme weather warnings and information about a variety of hazards. The national service also issues relevant safety instructions.

LANGUAGES

German, French, Italian and Romansh are spoken in Switzerland.

AARONCHENPSZ/SHUTTERSTOCK

ALPINE HAZARDS

Mountain risks include snowstorms, avalanches, landslides, flooding and thunderstorms. Keep up-to-date with *natural-hazards.ch*.

Summer or winter, alpine weather is notoriously fickle. Even in August it can feel like four seasons in a day, with sun, fog, storms and snow. Before heading into the mountains, check weather forecasts on *meteoswiss.admin.ch*. Subscribe to alerts for your specific location.

OPENING HOURS

Museums 10am–6pm; many close Monday or Tuesday and some stay open late Thursday
Restaurants noon–2.30pm and 6pm–9.30pm (7.30pm–10.30pm in French-speaking Switzerland and Ticino); closed one or two days per week.
Shops 10am–6pm Monday to Friday, to 4pm Saturday (6pm or later in French-speaking Switzerland).

PUBLIC HOLIDAYS

Some cantons observe other holidays and religious days, eg 2 January, Labour Day (1 May), Assumption (15 August) and All Saints' Day (1 November).
New Year's Day 1 January
Good Friday March/April
Easter Sunday and Monday March/April
Ascension 40th day after Easter
Whit Sunday and Monday Seventh week after Easter
Swiss National Day 1 August
Christmas Day 25 December
Boxing Day 26 December

Swiss International Air Lines

Arriving & Getting Around

Zürich Airport, 9km north of the city centre, and Geneva Airport, 4km northwest of the town centre, both have a mainline train station, with speedy trains into town plus regular public transport.

Arriving by Road
Bordering France, Germany, Austria, Liechtenstein and Italy, Switzerland is easily accessible by road. High alpine passes are snow-blocked and closed in winter (October to May/June). Roads signs for motorways are green.

Driving Essentials
Drive on the right. Headlights must be turned on day and night. November to March, winter tyres are essential. Blood alcohol limit is 0.05%. To use motorways, pay an annual toll *(Chf40)* online at *vignette-schweiz.com*.

Cycling & E-Biking
Well-signposted, scenic cycling routes spaghetti across the country; find cycling and mountain-biking pages on *schweizmobil.ch*. With SBB Rent-a-Bike *(rentabike.ch),* collect at one train station and return to another.

Trains, Buses & Cable Cars
Interconnected trains, boats, yellow PostBuses and cable cars have most of the country within easy, car-free reach. Consult routes and buy tickets on *swissrailways.com* and *travelswitzerland.com*. Download the SBB app *(sbb.ch)* for train timetables and tickets.

MONEY

Currency: Swiss franc (CHF or Chf)

CONTACTLESS PAYMENT
Almost every hotel, shop, restaurant, cafe, bar and business supports contactless payments and Apple Pay – there is no minimum payment amount.

CARDS & ATMS
Credit cards are widely accepted; EuroCard/MasterCard and Visa are the most popular. ATMs are widespread and accessible 24 hours.

CASH
Swiss francs are divided into 100 centimes (*Rappen* in German-speaking Switzerland). Many shops and small businesses don't accept large-denomination notes – 100, 200 and 1000 franc notes. Businesses throughout Switzerland accept cash payments in euros. Change will be given in Swiss francs at the rate of exchange calculated on the day.

TOOLKIT

The chapters in this section cover the most important topics you'll need to know about in Central Europe. They're full of nuts-and-bolts information and valuable insights to help you understand and navigate Central Europe and get the most out of your trip.

Getting Around the Region
p302

Accommodation
p304

Family Travel
p306

Health & Safe Travel
p308

Food, Drink & Nightlife
p310

Responsible Travel
p312

LGBTIQ+ Travellers
p314

Accessible Travel
p315

Nuts & Bolts
p316

Todtnauer Wasserfall (p159), Germany
UNAI HUIZI PHOTOGRAPHY/SHUTTERSTOCK

Getting Around the Region

Travelling around Central Europe is surprisingly easy. Frequent train and bus connections link major and minor cities, and the highway network is comprehensive and well-maintained. Capitals and major cities are well linked by air.

TRAVEL COSTS

Train from Prague to Budapest
from €20

10-day Eurail/ Interrail pass
approx €400

Flight from London to Vienna
from €100

Petrol
€1.60 per litre

Air

Major Central European air hubs include Frankfurt, Munich, Zürich, Vienna, Prague, Budapest and Warsaw. Smaller cities like Kraków, Ljubljana, Bratislava and Graz are well connected to flights within Europe. Use planes to cover long distances; buses and trains are better and cheaper for covering shorter spans.

Train & Bus

Trains are generally the most atmospheric, comfortable and fun way to make tracks in Central Europe – that is, when they're running on time. All major cities are on the rail network, and many secondary cities are also served by rail. Overnight routes can save you a night's accommodation. Back on Track (back-on-track. eu) has a map of night trains.

Long-distance coach services, like Flixbus (flix.com), criss-cross the region. Buses are a cheap, handy way to move from place to place.

Car

Having your own wheels allows for greater flexibility. A car, however, can be a major inconvenience in crowded urban areas. In big cities, stow the car and rely on public transport. Work out parking details with your hotel in advance.

DRIVING ESSENTIALS

Drive on the right, overtake on the left.

Seatbelts are mandatory.

.05
Blood-alcohol (BAC) limit ranges from 0.0% to 0.05%.

Tip
Austria, Czechia, Hungary, Slovakia, Slovenia and Switzerland impose a road tax on all drivers and require pre-purchase of a 'vignette'. Fines for driving without a vignette can be steep.

RIVER CRUISES

Seasonal river cruises are a slow but easy way to visit Central Europe. You'll never have to worry about transport, accommodation or food. Several cruise lines operate multi-day trips along both the Danube and Rhine Rivers. Danube cruises generally start in Budapest and travel towards Vienna and on to Germany. Rhine cruises ply the river from Amsterdam to Basel.

EXPECT OCCASIONAL DELAYS

Travel within Central Europe is a breeze – except, of course, when it's not. Normally, the region's buses and trains hum with Teutonic efficiency, moving hundreds of thousands of people every day to their respective destinations. In recent years, however, the networks have been showing signs of strain. Delays and cancellations have become more common than they once were on systems like German Rail (Deutsche Bahn), the Austrian Federal Railways (ÖBB), and others. Don't get us wrong. These are still amazing systems, they're just not something you can set your watch to any more. On longer train or bus routes, leave extra time to make your connections. If things do go sideways, settle in and enjoy the ride.

Public Transport

Most Central European cities have excellent public-transport systems: usually a combination of metros (subways), trains, trams and buses. Indeed, cities like Vienna, Zürich, Prague, Munich and Warsaw regularly rank at the top of Europe's best transport infrastructure. Service is usually comprehensive and inexpensive. Buy day passes (instead of single tickets) to cut down on costs. Many systems now allow for contactless card payments. Major airports generally have express train, metro or bus links to the city centre.

BORDER CROSSINGS

All of the countries in this guide are part of the EU's common Schengen border and customs zone. That means travellers moving within the region are not subject to border passport or customs checks (though spot checks on some borders are still possible, so always carry your passport). Standard passport and customs checks still apply when entering the Schengen Zone from outside the EU. This includes at certain border road and rail crossings in Hungary (with Ukraine and Serbia), Poland (with Ukraine, Belarus and Russia), and Slovakia (with Ukraine). Lonely Planet is not recommending travel at this time to Belarus, Russia or Ukraine, and entering these countries often requires special visas and may entail significant waits at the border. Travellers flying into the Schengen Zone from outside the EU must show a valid passport and go through standard customs inspection. Travellers flying out of the Schengen Zone must produce a valid passport and boarding pass.

Beginning in late 2025, the EU began trialling a new Entry/Exit System (EES) for non-EU nationals travelling in and out of the Schengen Zone. Under the new system, border agents now collect enhanced biometric data (photos and fingerprints). The EES is ultimately intended to replace passport stamps, but travellers should expect significant delays at airports when entering or leaving the Schengen Zone until the kinks are worked out.

EURAIL/INTERRAIL PASSES

For some travellers, a rail pass might make sense. The two most popular passes include Interrail (interrail.eu) for European residents and Eurail (eurail.com) for non-European residents. Prices vary, so do the sums to see if you'll save money or not. Train travel here is still relatively inexpensive.

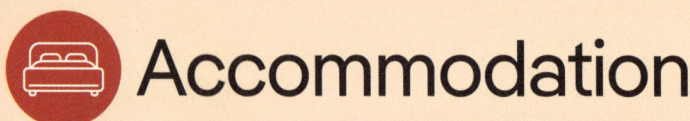

Accommodation

Hotels, hostels and apartment rentals are found all over Central Europe, but it's at privately owned pensions, guesthouses and farmhouses where you get a real feel for what life is like in this part of the world.

Camping

Camping provides the cheapest accommodation. In cities, most camping grounds will be some distance from the centre, and public transport may be limited. Expect a charge per tent or site, plus per person and per vehicle. In addition to tent sites, many camping grounds may offer bungalows, wooden cabins and caravan spaces. Note that wild camping is illegal across the region.

Glamping

Luxury tents, bungalows and futuristic pods featuring amenities like spas and gourmet dining are all part of the growing glamping phenomenon. Look for these in gorgeous spots in Austria, Switzerland and Slovenia. Check out tourist information portals or dedicated platforms like Glamping Hub *(glampinghub.com)*.

Mountain Huts

Mountain huts are a fixture in Austria, Switzerland, Slovenia, Slovakia and Poland. They're frequently run by local or national hiking clubs and conveniently placed along popular hiking trails. Standards are often basic – no more than a dorm bed and a hot meal. Book in advance when possible as they fill up quickly.

Hostels

Hostels offer a cheap roof over your head and you don't have to be young to take advantage of them. Accommodation is normally in multi-bunk dorm rooms (all-female dorms are often available), with a few higher-cost private singles or doubles. Amenities usually include a common room, kitchen, personal lockers and shared bathrooms. Big city hostels often cultivate their own vibe, with organised tours and themed party nights.

Seasons

High season is usually in July and August, with a winter peak season around Christmas. Hostels and cheap hotels fill up quickly, especially in popular backpacker or city-break destinations such as Kraków, Prague and Budapest.

Booking Sites

Many hotels list their properties on sites like Booking.com *(booking. com)* or Expedia *(expedia. com)*. These are handy for gauging prices and vacancy rates, though you might land a cheaper room by booking directly through the hotel.

Pensions & Guesthouses

Small pensions and guesthouses are common both in big cities and in smaller villages and rural areas across Central Europe. Priced lower than most hotels, they usually have loads more character. Most are small and family-owned with fewer than a dozen rooms, but some can be larger with saunas and other amenities. There may be a restaurant or bar attached. Breakfast is usually available and often factored into the room rate.

Hotels

Standards vary greatly from simple two-star places to luxury resorts. In general, the more facilities (restaurant, swimming pool etc), the higher the rate. Hotel parking may be tight or nonexistent in cities. Breakfast is often available and may be included in the rate (choose when booking). If travelling in mid-summer, check to see if air-conditioning is available. Not all hotels have it.

Flat Rentals & Airbnb

When travelling with family members or a group of friends, a short-term apartment rental may offer an affordable alternative to a hotel or guesthouse, and they frequently offer enticing extras like washing machines and kitchens. That said, quality can vary and the photos on a flat's website rarely match what the place actually looks like. Additionally, in cities like Vienna, Berlin, Prague and Ljubljana, short-term rental apartments have exerted an upward pressure on local renters, leading to calls for stricter regulation.

HOW MUCH FOR A NIGHT IN A...

Dorm bed in a hostel
€25–40

Pitch for two in a campground
€20–30

Double room in a decent hotel
€125–225

Resort splurge
€175–300

Van Life

The allure of van life – roaming at whim through beautiful surroundings in a camper van – has taken off in Central Europe in a big way. It's especially popular in Switzerland, given the sheer variety of gorgeous locations there. Get started by downloading the helpful 'park4night' app to see what's available.

Rural Homestays

Rural home- and farmstays offer a distinctly local experience, often in picturesque areas. Some work may or may not be expected; in return, you might get fresh milk straight from the cow. In Slovenia and Switzerland, you can also stay in a hay barn. Reaching these remote outposts almost always requires having your own transport. National tourism portals like My Switzerland (farm.myswitzerland.com) or I Feel Slovenia (slovenia.info) have good overviews.

SUSTAINABLE CHOICES

Sustainability has taken off in a big way in Central European hotels and guesthouses, and many places now tout their dedication to recycling solid waste, limiting water waste and restricting single-use plastics, among many other virtues. In Austria, look out for Bio- or Öko- ('eco') hotels (biohotels.info). Most of these are set in pretty countryside or mountains. In Slovenia, keep an eye out for hotels with the 'Slovenia Green' label, awarded to properties that pledge responsible resource usage and place an emphasis on serving seasonal and local food. Each country has its own national equivalent.

TOP: ROMIEG/SHUTTERSTOCK; LEFT: NOAH STRYCKER/SHUTTERSTOCK

Family Travel

Central European countries are family-orientated and travelling here with kids is generally hassle-free. Family discounts and reduced prices are common, and there are plenty of kid-friendly attractions.

Travelling with Children

The region is filled with attractions geared towards kids of all ages. Traditional sights like castles, fortresses, and museums have been refreshed and outfitted with attention-grabbing audio-visual effects and other electronic highlights to make them more appealing to younger minds. Add to that the many reliably family-friendly outings like zoos, parks and playgrounds, plus dazzling natural wonders like mountains, caves and canyons, and you'll never run short of things to do.

Dining Out

Outside of a few fancier options, restaurants around Central Europe generally open their arms to family diners. Many midrange restaurants have high chairs and can offer special children's menus (often a chicken schnitzel or hot dog). Some may even have a special children's play area to give parents a moment to eat in peace. Pizza and burger joints abound, as do places selling cakes and gelato.

Cribs & Cots

Cribs and cots are widely available in hotels and pensions, but make your requests known in advance.

BEST ATTRACTIONS FOR FAMILIES

Lake Balaton, Hungary
Central Europe's largest lake has slides and paddleboats. (p201)

Postojna Cave, Slovenia
Ride an underground mini train and spot stalagmites and stalactites. (p270)

Eisriesenwelt, Austria
A real-life Narnia at the world's largest accessible ice caves. (p67)

Science Gateway, Switzerland
Older kids will enjoy the films and exhibitions at the CERN research lab. (p282)

Techmania, Czechia
Interactive science museum. (p100)

FAMILY TRAVEL ON A BUDGET

Save money on transport, which is often free or heavily discounted for children. Prague's excellent system of trams and metros, for example, is free for kids under 6 years; fares are discounted to age 15. Similarly, on national railways, kids under six (or older) often travel free. Be sure to carry photo IDs as proof of age. Those same discounts often carry over to museums and other attractions. Additionally, many museums offer reduced-price family tickets (two adults, two children). Teens or older children may be able to show their student ID cards for other reductions.

TOP: APRILPHOTO/SHUTTERSTOCK; LEFT: PIXEL-SHOT/SHUTTERSTOCK

MAYBE NOT APPROPRIATE?

Central Europe has seen more than its share of tragedy over the years, and not every historical site will be appropriate for kids or younger teens. The **Auschwitz-Birkenau Memorial & Museum** (p223) in Poland, for example, where more than one million people were systematically murdered, sensibly recommends that visitors be at least 14 years of age to enter (though this is simply a suggestion, not a rule).

On Your Best Behaviour

Everyone appreciates the special challenges of parenting. That said, kids (and their parents) are still expected to adhere to certain standards of behaviour when in public. When at a fancy restaurant or more formal outing at a concert or theatre, for example, children running around or making lots of noise is certain to elicit the side-eye from nearly everyone around. On public transport, kids should be prepared to give their seats to the elderly or mobility-impaired riders. Expectations of proper behavior loosen up significantly when outdoors. Here, Central European parents are quite laissez-faire and kids are often free to be as loud and expressive as they want.

Tip

Most car-hire firms provide children's safety seats for a fee, but make sure to book these ahead.

Just Ask

Don't be afraid to ask staff for a high-chair or a passerby to help carry a stroller up a flight of stairs in the metro station. You may be surprised at how accommodating strangers can be in this part of the world.

Public Breastfeeding

Public breastfeeding is legal across the region, though attitudes vary. It's widely accepted in Germany and many larger cities, but less so in the eastern countries or in rural areas. In Poland, for example, a 2020 study found almost half of Polish women would not feel comfortable breastfeeding in public.

NECESSITIES

Find infant formula, baby food, milk (soy and cow), nappies and other essentials at pharmacies, drugstores and supermarkets.

SANTA CLAUS IS COMING TO…

In many parts of Central Europe, Santa Claus (Svatý Mikuláš in Czech, Mikulás in Hungarian, Święty Mikołaj in Polish) traditionally comes to town a little earlier than you might think – on the evening of 5 December, ahead of the feast day of St Nicholas – and brings gifts to well-behaved children. St Nicholas is often accompanied by two helpers: an angel and the mean, hairy and horned creature Krampus, who disciplines the naughty ones. That night, children typically leave their clean, shiny boots on the windowsill or by the doorstep, which are magically filled with goodies by the next morning. On Christmas Eve, it's often Baby Jesus who decorates the tree and leaves gifts for children. This means that various kid-friendly events start taking place in early December.

Health & Safe Travel

While Central Europe is generally safe for travellers, it's important to take certain precautions and consider health and safety factors to ensure your trip goes smoothly.

TRAVEL INSURANCE

For peace of mind, a travel-insurance policy to cover theft, loss and medical problems is always a good idea. Some insurance policies will specifically exclude 'dangerous activities', such as scuba diving, motorcycling and even hiking, while winter sports and car-rental coverage is sometimes limited. Always check the fine print, and see if your policy covers ambulances and an emergency flight home as well.

Quality of Healthcare

Healthcare standards are high across the countries of Central Europe. All of the capitals and large cities covered here will have major hospitals, often with English-speaking staff. Hospitals in smaller cities and rural areas will likely have fewer facilities, but are staffed by well-trained doctors and medical personnel. When visiting a hospital, be sure to bring your passport and a credit or debit card for any costs that may not be covered by your insurance. Healthcare costs can vary greatly by country, but are generally lower, for example, than in North America. Pharmacists are well trained and can give valuable advice and sell over-the-counter medication for minor illnesses. If more specialised help is needed, they'll be able to point you in the right direction.

European Health Insurance

Residents of all EU countries, as well as Switzerland, Iceland, Norway and Liechtenstein, holding a European Health Insurance Card (EHIC) are entitled to free or reduced-cost emergency healthcare throughout Central Europe under the same conditions as afforded to local residents. The same benefit applies to UK holders of the GHIC (Global Health Insurance Card). Note that the coverage is limited to urgent, temporary care, such as emergency treatment for acute conditions, but does not cover planned medical treatment or private care. For that you'll need private health or travel insurance.

Vaccinations

There are no mandatory vaccinations for entering Central Europe, but some are recommended. Routine vaccinations to consider are MMR (measles, mumps and rubella), DTP (diphtheria, tetanus, pertussis), Hepatitis A and B, and TBE for tick-borne encephalitis. While rabies is rare, always go to a hospital immediately if there is a chance that you have been exposed. Most vaccines don't produce immunity until two weeks after they are administered, so visit your doctor in advance to ensure you are up to date.

TAP WATER

Tap water is generally safe to drink. If you're unsure, especially in rural areas, check with locals.

Petty Crime & Scams

Central Europe is generally safe, but petty crime and tourist scams can happen anywhere, so it's best to be vigilant. Be mindful of your belongings in crowded areas, especially on public transport, and avoid people aggressively selling stuff on the street. Don't leave anything of value, including luggage, on car seats. In big cities like Prague, Budapest or Warsaw, taxi drivers may occasionally try to overcharge riders, so always use a reputable taxi company or book through rideshare apps like Uber or Bolt. Be wary of anyone approaching you with an offer to 'change money' – particularly in countries like Poland, Czechia and Hungary, which do not use the euro. This is always a scam.

High-Altitude Hiking

Central Europe abounds with beautiful mountains, but high-altitude trekking comes with its own dangers: avalanches, extreme weather and, of course, tumbles over sheer rock faces. Always seek local advice before attempting an unfamiliar hike, check the weather forecast, pack accordingly and let other people know where you're going.

Ticks

Ticks are an ever-present danger in fields and woodlands, particularly in outlying parts of Austria, Czechia, Poland and Slovenia. Ticks are normally active from April to October. They can carry two serious diseases: tick-borne encephalitis and Lyme disease. Use repellents, cover exposed legs and periodically check your skin for bites.

PHARMACIES VERSUS DRUGSTORES

Confusingly, Central Europe is home to both pharmacies, identified by a green cross out front, and drugstores *(drogerien)*, bearing ubiquitous retail names like DM or Rossmann. Bear in mind that pharmacies are usually the only outlets that can dispense medications. These include both prescription *and* over-the-counter meds, like aspirin or cough syrup. Drugstores are for picking up cosmetics, personal-care items like toothpaste and health foods. It's best to bring whatever medications you'll need from home.

CANNABIS & HARD DRUGS

The use and sale of hard drugs is illegal in every country in Central Europe. The region generally takes a zero-tolerance policy toward substances like cocaine, heroin, ecstasy/MDMA and other street drugs.

Cannabis occupies a grey zone. As of 2026, Germany and Czechia had taken steps to legalise cannabis, though only for personal use and in relatively small quantities. Even here, buying and selling cannabis remains illegal. That goes as well for the many cannabis and weed shops you see in Prague and other places. These shops sell products with a diluted amount of THC permitted by law. Everywhere else, cannabis remains either strictly illegal or partly decriminalised. Possession might merit a prison sentence in harder-line countries like Slovakia and Hungary, while eliciting a misdemeanour charge or fine in other countries.

Never buy drugs on the street. You're breaking the law.

Food, Drink & Nightlife

When to Eat

Breakfast (7am–10am) Can be light or substantial, mixing bread, cold cuts, eggs, cheese, yoghurt and coffee or tea.

Lunch (noon–2pm) Often the biggest meal of the day, consisting of soup, meat, potatoes and dessert.

Coffee & Cake (3pm–4pm) Light afternoon snack in Austria.

Dinner (6pm–9pm) Home dinners tend to be a lighter meal than lunch, often made up of leftovers.

Where to Eat

Restaurants From pizzerias to Michelin-starred finery.

Coffeehouses Fancy in Vienna, Budapest and Bratislava. Great for coffee and cake or a more filling meal.

Street kiosks Snacks or takeaway, the most famous being the *Würstelstand* (sausage stand).

Canteens Self-service, with simple inexpensive dishes. Polish 'milk bars' are a local staple.

Bakeries From breads and pastries to fresh-made sandwiches.

Pubs or Inns Popular everywhere in Central Europe, with an emphasis on home cooking.

Sweet shops Traditional spot to order cake and coffee.

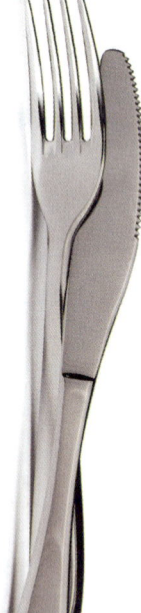

MENU DECODER

Goulash Hearty beef- or pork-based soup, popular in Hungary, Czechia, Slovakia and Austria.

Pork Knee (Pork Knuckle) Broiled or grilled pork hock (*koleno* in Czech, *Schweinshaxe* in German), served with bread and mustard or with potatoes and sauerkraut.

Dumplings Can be a bread-based side, as in Czechia, Austria or Slovakia, or stuffed dough pockets (pierogi) in Poland.

Sausage A staple in Germany (*Würst*), Austria and Poland (*kiełbasa*), with too many varieties to count.

Schnitzel Pork, veal or chicken that's been breaded and fried.

Chimney cakes Cylindrical dough, baked and rolled in sugar and cinnamon. Ubiquitous in Hungary (*kürtőskalács*) and Prague (*trdelník*).

Pancakes Thin and crepe-like, normally served as a dessert. Look for *palačinky* (Czech) or *Palatschinken* (Austria).

HOW TO... Dine Like a Local

Reservations At trendy restaurants, especially at weekends, book at least a few days in advance. More informal inns, pubs or beer halls are less strict and can usually squeeze you in at a moment's notice.

Settling up Request the bill directly from the server, who will bring it to the table.

Cash or card? Your server will ask whether you want to pay by cash or card. In most places you'll pay the waiter directly.

Splitting the tab Sometimes the person who invites will pay, but generally bills are split. Most restaurants can handle separate payments.

Tipping Gratuity is usually not included on bills and reflects customer satisfaction. In restaurants, 10% is standard; in cafes and bars, round to the nearest euro or two. Don't name the tip amount, instead specify the total amount you wish to pay (tip included) or the total change you want back.

HOW MUCH FOR A...

Pint of beer
€1.50–4

Glass of wine
€2–8

Sausage (street food)
€3–5

Espresso
€2–4

Midrange meal
€10–25

Michelin-starred meal
€100–250

Ice cream (one scoop)
€2–4

Public-transport ticket
€1.50–3

HOW TO... ### Order Coffee in a Grand Coffee House

Swing open the heavy wooden door of one of Central Europe's grand coffee houses, especially in Vienna, but also in Budapest, Bratislava and Prague, and it's as though the clocks stopped in 1910. The waiters are just as aloof, the menu still baffles and newspapers outnumber smartphones. Outside life rushes ahead, but the coffee house is a world unto itself, immune to time and trends. Try the following:

Brauner Black, served with a splash of milk; comes in *gross* (large) or *klein* (small)
Einspänner With whipped cream, served in a glass
Kapuziner With a splash of milk and perhaps a sprinkling of grated chocolate
Maria Theresia (pictured) With orange liqueur and whipped cream
Masagran Cold coffee with ice and Maraschino liqueur
Mocca, Mokka, Schwarzer Black coffee
Türkische (Turkish) In a copper pot with coffee grounds and sugar
Verlängerter Brauner Weakened with hot water
Wiener Eiskaffee Cold coffee with vanilla ice cream and whipped cream

Coffee House Style

Wait to be seated in formal places, or take your pick of the tables in casual coffee houses. You're welcome to linger over a cup if you wish.

EXCELLENT BEER & WINE

Whether you call it *bier* or *pivo*, *wein* or *vino*, Central Europe's beer and wine are worth talking about. Germany and Czechia, especially, are known worldwide for their hoppy brews and beer halls, and the wine cellars of Austria and Hungary provide an excellent alternative for imbibing. In towns and cities across Czechia, beer gardens and halls are the establishments of choice for enjoying a good Czech brew. And you can always go straight to the factory – for 'Pilsner Urquell' in Plzeň and 'Budvar' in České Budějovice. Germany has more types and styles of beer than you can count. Munich, the home of Oktoberfest, is well-known, but look out too for regional beers, like Rauchbier (smoked beer) in Bamberg or Cologne's signature Kölsch, a pale, clear fermented brew that has its own beer-ordering etiquette.

For wine, Hungary's Tokaj dessert wines have been famous for centuries; sample them from a 600-year-old cellar. Even more fun are the outdoor tasting tables in Eger's wine valley, which produces a full-bodied red called Bikavér (Bull's Blood). Austrian wine is enjoying its own moment, with wine bars popping up all over the country and quality continuing to rise. Austrian wine hails from 17 wine-growing areas, mostly situated in Lower Austria and Burgenland (known as the Weinland Österreich region), Styria and the vine-strewn fringes of Vienna. Well-known varieties to look for include crisp Grüner Veltliner and Weissburgunder (pinot blanc) whites, fruity Blauburgunder (pinot noir) and full-bodied Zweigelt reds, and sweet Eiswein, made from grapes that have frozen on the vines.

Responsible Travel

Climate Change & Travel

It's impossible to ignore the impact we have when travelling; Lonely Planet urges all travellers to engage with their travel carbon footprint, which will mainly come from air travel. While there often isn't an alternative, travellers can look to minimise the number of flights they take, opt for newer aircrafts and use cleaner ground transport, such as trains. One proposed solution – purchasing carbon offsets – unfortunately does not cancel out the impact of individual flights. While most destinations will depend on air travel for the foreseeable future, for now, pursuing ground-based travel where possible is the best course of action.

The **UN Carbon Offset Calculator** shows how flying impacts a household's emissions

The **ICAO's carbon emissions calculator** allows visitors to analyse the CO2 generated by point-to-point journeys

Eco-friendly walks and cycling tours are available across Central Europe. In the mountains, seek out tours that prioritise responsible tourism.

Instead of frequenting touristy shops that sell the same souvenirs in every city, look for genuinely local artisans and support the community.

Sleep Sustainably

Central Europe is filled with privately owned pensions and guesthouses, so stay with locally run accommodation over big-name hotels. Many countries award sustainability certificates to lodgings that pledge to reduce single-use plastic and water waste.

Use Public Transport

In most countries, especially in major capitals, the public transport system is well developed and affordable. Where possible, opt for buses, trams or metros over taxis or private cars.

HIKING ETIQUETTE

Keep Central Europe's hiking trails pristine by taking home everything from an outdoor adventure. If you see plastic bottles or anything else that doesn't belong, take those out with you and bin/recycle them in the next village.

USE LONG-HAUL BUSES & TRAINS

Central Europe is well connected by international bus and train lines. These often offer cheaper and quicker connections than short-hop flights and are much easier on the environment.

Stick to Marked Trails

Central Europe abounds with beautiful landscapes and colourful flora and fauna. When hiking in or visiting natural parks or reserves, always stay on marked trails.

Travel Off-Peak

Bucket-list destinations like Vienna, Salzburg, Budapest and Prague get crowded in mid-summer, so plan your trip for the spring or autumn if possible to avoid contributing to (and dealing with) overtourism.

Eat Local

Restaurants that claim 'locally sourced' or 'farm fresh' can make it sound like a tired cliché. That said, there's much to be said for eateries and markets that legitimately prioritise organic ingredients and support small-scale farmers.

Respect Recycling Rules

Across Central Europe, cities and towns have leaned into stringent recycling requirements and targets. Look for special, colour-marked bins where you can separate waste into glass, plastics and paper.

Ukrainian Refugees

Countries like Poland, Czechia and Slovakia have done more than most to help their war-torn neighbour. Any initiatives you notice helping Ukrainian refugees in these countries are likely to be worth supporting.

Bike-share schemes are common in big cities and are easy on the environment.

Many cities and towns have drinking fountains where you can refill your water bottle.

Green Capital

Heilbronn (Germany), north of Stuttgart, was crowned European Green Capital for 2027, recognising the city's commitment to sustainability, climate action and smart urban development.

RESOURCES

Seat 61
Useful ideas on navigating Europe's rail system.

Worldpackers
Volunteer work in eco-villages around Europe.

Green Traveller
Helpful ideas for lowering your carbon footprint.

LGBTIQ+ Travellers

Local attitudes towards public displays of same-sex affection vary widely, both by country and between cities and rural areas. Berlin, Munich and Vienna have vibrant and active gay scenes. It's a different story in the eastern countries: most capital cities there have small LGBTIQ+ scenes centred on a few bars or clubs. LGBTIQ+ venues are almost nonexistent outside urban centres.

At a Crossroads

The LGBTIQ+ community finds itself at a crossroads and nowhere more so than in Central Europe. A few years ago, progress towards achieving greater public acceptance of same-sex relationships and enacting supportive legal-rights frameworks appeared to be a given. With the rise of populist governments in countries like Hungary, Poland and Slovakia, but also to some extent in Czechia and Austria, this progress has slowed. The result is a patchwork of tolerant major cities surrounded by less-accepting pockets of smaller towns and rural areas.

PRIDE

Pride parades are held in cities throughout Central Europe. Indeed, these events have taken on renewed significance in view of the ever-changing political landscape. The best-attended Pride events take place in Prague (August), Budapest (March), Warsaw (June), Berlin (July), Vienna (June) and Ljubljana (June). In German cities, look for 'Christopher Street Day' events from June to August.

From Conservative Hungary...

While Budapest has a solid gay scene and LGBTIQ+ visitors generally have a good time in Hungary, the Hungarian government's stance on LGBTIQ+ issues continues to be at odds with other parts of Europe. While travellers aren't generally affected, be aware that PDAs may attract unwanted attention.

...TO PROGRESSIVE SWITZERLAND

Switzerland has long been progressive on LGBTIQ+ rights. Homosexuality was decriminalised nationally in 1942, and in some cantons it has been legal since the late 18th century. In 2021 laws were passed allowing same-sex marriage, same-sex adoption and IVF access for queer couples.

RESOURCES

Gay CH *(gay.ch)* Swiss listings and features in German for Zürich and surrounds.
Queer DE *(queer.de)* One of Germany's most-popular LGBTIQ+ websites.
Prague Saints *(praguesaints.cz)* Popular Prague site with lots of local tips.
Visit Ljubljana *(visitljubljana.com)* Official tourist portal for Ljubljana; loads of helpful info.
Patroc *(patroc.com)* Europe-wide gay travel guide.

Same-Sex Partnerships

Austria, Germany, Slovenia and Switzerland allow same-sex partners to marry. Czechia and Hungary recognise same-sex partnerships that fall short of full marriage, while Poland and Slovakia do not recognise same-sex partnerships.

Accessible Travel

Central Europe can be challenging for travellers with disabilities, though it depends greatly on the destination. Countries like Switzerland, Austria and Germany are ahead of the curve, while the east is still catching up.

Cobblestones

Cobblestones and uneven pavements make Central European old towns challenging for the mobility-impaired. Tourist information offices can help plan mobility-friendly routes or offer special resources.

Airport

Nearly all major airports across Central Europe are accessible and offer assistance in terminals, the use of wheelchairs and aid with boarding. Airlines must usually be notified at least 48 hours in advance.

Accommodation

Accessible accommodation is widely available in major cities, especially at hotel chains. Regional examples also exist, but specific research is necessary. **Euan's Guide** *(euansguide. com)*, a disabled access review, can be handy.

RESOURCES

Accessable *(disabledaccessible travel.com)* Wide range of bespoke services for travellers in need of adapted solutions.

Wheelchair Traveling *(wheelchairtravel. org)* Personal website of accessible-travel advocate John Morris, with tips on wheelchair travel.

Accessible Prague *(accessibleprague. com)* A Prague-based travel agency for people living with disabilities, with info on accommodation and tours.

Visit Ljubljana *(visitljubljana.com)* Tourist information portal has a special section devoted to visitors with mobility issues.

LJUBLJANA CASTLE

Ljubljana Castle (p262) is a top sight that's nearly fully accessible. Holders of the EU Disability Card are eligible for free entry (together with one accompanying person).

'BE MY EYES'

The 'Be My Eyes' app *(bemyeyes.com)* connects people who are blind or have impaired vision with volunteers and companies worldwide through live video chat. You can connect to a volunteer anytime for help.

Accessible Cities

The best cities in Central Europe in terms of awareness of accessibility issues include Ljubljana (Slovenia), Bratislava (Slovenia), Vienna (Austria), Geneva (Switzerland), Munich (Germany) and Warsaw (Poland).

Friendly Festival

Budapest's **Sziget Festival** *(szigetfestival. com)* is largely accessible and home to XS Land, an interactive experience park with a focus on disabilities.

Metro, tram and bus systems in major cities across Central Europe have made major strides in improving accessibility, but gaps remain. Don't expect every metro station to have a lift or every bus to have roll-in access.

Nuts & Bolts

TIME ZONES

GMT/UTC +1

COUNTRY CODES

Austria
+43
Czechia
+420
Germany
+49
Hungary
+36
Poland
+48
Slovakia
+421
Slovenia
+386
Switzerland
+41

EMERGENCY NUMBER

112

POPULATION

169.1 million

Public Toilets

Public toilets are normally available in heavily touristed areas, though cleanliness standards vary. You'll also find public toilets in trains and bus stations, metro stations, petrol stations, restaurants, fast-food chains, museums and malls. Expect to pay a small fee (€0.50–€1), so have small coins ready.

Smoking

Smoking is generally banned across Central Europe in all enclosed public spaces, including hotels, restaurants, bars, workplaces, hospitals, public-transport terminals and educational institutions. Smoking is generally permitted on outdoor terraces at cafes, bars and restaurants, though restrictions vary by country and region. The situation is different in Germany, where smoking is legislated by each individual state. In Bavaria, for example, smoking is banned practically everywhere; while in Berlin and Hamburg, smoker-friendly bars abound. Look for a sign out front reading *Raucherkneipe* (smoking bar).

OPENING HOURS

Banks & Post Offices 9am–4pm Monday to Friday; may also open Saturday mornings

Museums & Castles 9am–6pm Tuesday to Sunday; may be closed additional days or completely from October to April

Offices 9am–6pm Monday to Friday

Pubs & Bars 6pm–midnight

Restaurants 11am–11pm

Shops 9am–7pm, reduced hours on Saturday and/or closed entirely on Sunday, depending on the country

Electricity

220/240V

Type C

Type E

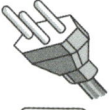

Type F

Type J

Most of Europe uses a variation of the 'europlug' with two round pins. Switzerland uses a third round pin in a way that the two-pin plug usually – but not always – fits. Buy an adapter before leaving home or at the airport.

Internet Access

Wi-fi is commonly available in cafes, hotels, restaurants, malls, hostels, libraries and other public spaces. In rural areas, especially mountainous ones, connections may be slow or even drop. Major telecoms operators like T-Mobile, Vodafone or local carriers will have coverage throughout cities and large towns. SIM cards are often inexpensive and can be bought at the airport or online, and should include prepaid data.

Embassies & Consulates

If you happen to run into serious trouble during your visit, your home-country embassy or consulate has resources to help. It's important, though, to know what embassies can and cannot do for you while abroad. Generally speaking, they won't be much help if you're in trouble for something that is your own fault, in which case you are bound by the laws of the country you are visiting. Nations such as Australia, Canada, New Zealand, the UK and the US have embassies and consulates across Central Europe in capitals and major cities.

ETIQUETTE

Greetings A firm but friendly handshake is a common greeting, especially when meeting somebody for the first time. Women generally give each other air kisses, but it depends on familiarity and personal preference.

Gifts If you're invited to a local household, it's polite to bring something small and thoughtful as a gift. For men, it's generally a bottle of alcohol. For women, a bouquet of flowers will do – make sure you give an odd number of flowers, as even numbers are generally reserved for funerals.

Shoes In many countries in Central Europe – particularly Czechia, Slovakia, Poland and Slovenia – it's customary to remove your shoes on entering someone's house. To be on the safe side, always ask your host for guidance. Prepare ahead of time and choose your socks accordingly; you may be spending the evening standing around in them.

PUBLIC HOLIDAYS

The following common holidays are celebrated in all of the countries covered in this guide, but this list is by no means exhaustive. Each country will have at least one national or founder's holiday, as well as other religious holidays or saints' days. Many countries also celebrate Boxing Day (St Stephen's Day, 26 December) and Easter Monday, when all government offices and many shops will be closed.

New Year's Day 1 January

Easter Late March or April, depending on the year

Labour Day 1 May

Christmas Day 25 December

Time

The time zone is GMT+1 hour. Central European countries employ daylight saving. Clocks usually go forward one hour on the last Sunday in March and go back one hour on the last Sunday in October. The 24-hour time system is common.

Emergency Numbers

The EU emergency number (112) is used widely in Central Europe. It works for all urgent services, including the police, fire and medical emergencies.

STORYBOOK

Our writers delve deep into different aspects of Central European life

A History of Central Europe in 15 Places

Central Europe is a fascinating overlay of castles and cityscapes alongside the battle scars of monumental struggles

Mark Baker

p320

The Hills Are Alive: Overtourism in the Alps

Communities are facing challenges in the form of overtourism and global warming

Vesna Maric

p324

Party Time of the Season

At avant-garde festivals across Central Europe, creativity is sky-high, but these events are grounded in regional traditions

Barbara Woolsey

p328

A HISTORY OF CENTRAL EUROPE IN
15 PLACES

Central Europe is the historical home of some of the world's most prosperous empires, as well as its most destructive political and ideological cataclysms. For modern visitors, the region presents a fascinating overlay of wonderfully preserved castles, cathedrals and cityscapes perched alongside the surviving battle scars of monumental struggles. By Mark Baker

THE COUNTRIES IN this guide stand at the heart of Europe and define the cleavage in our collective consciousness between east and west. In Roman times, the Germans and other peoples to the east were the 'barbarians'. Starting with Emperor Charlemagne in 800 CE, those barbarians had the last laugh, though, with the gradual formation of the prosperous Holy Roman Empire, which would grow to encompass modern-day Germany, Austria and Czechia. The Vienna-based Habsburg monarchy, in the late Middle Ages, took this sprawling empire further and created a vast entity that would include much of continental Europe and parts of the New World. To the east, the Polish and Hungarian kingdoms – one originally centred in Kraków and the other in Pest (Budapest) – were building giant fiefdoms of their own. The destructive world wars of the 20th century ripped apart these old empires and tragically pitted many of the countries covered here against one another. From the end of WWII to 1989, the Iron Curtain ran straight down the middle, separating communist-era Czechoslovakia (Czechia and Slovakia), East Germany, Poland, Hungary and Yugoslavia (Slovenia) from their brethren to the west.

1. Hallstatt, Austria
BACK TO THE BRONZE AGE

With its glass-blue lake and lofty mountains lifting your gaze to postcard heaven, Hallstatt is prime fodder for Instagrammers. But its history runs deep, for it was here that a proto-Celtic civilisation – the Hallstatt culture – took root in the late Bronze Age around 800 BCE, centring on burial sites in the high alpine valley above town. These proto-Celts mined salt and traded with the Mediterranean. A spin through the cavernous Salzwelten salt mines, which are the world's oldest, and a visit to the Weltkulturerbe Museum wing you through Hallstatt's long and fascinating history.

For more on Hallstatt, see p68.

2. Budapest, Hungary
THE MAGYAR CONQUEST

The Grand Prince of the Hungarians, Árpád, led the Magyars into Central Europe in in 895 CE, crushing the First Bulgarian Tsardom and settling in the Great Hungarian Plain. They soon secured the territory and in 1000 established the Kingdom of Hungary, which would become a significant Christian power in Central Europe for centuries. From the crowning of Saint Stephen, the first king of Hungary, the Árpád Dynasty ruled for 300 years. Today's Millennium Monument in Budapest's Heroes' Square is a key sight related to the Hungarian conquest.

For more on Heroes' Square, see p197

3. Wawel Royal Castle, Poland
KRAKÓW'S ROYAL RESIDENCE

For centuries, Warsaw was little more than a fortified farmstead while Kraków served as the ostentatious capital of a confident European power. The seat of that power was Wawel Royal Castle, the residence of a long list of Polish kings going back as far as the 10th century. During WWII, the Nazi governor-general Hans Frank lived in the castle. In 1978 it was declared a World Cultural Heritage site, one of the first behind the Iron Curtain. The complex is a textbook of European architectural styles, while the art collections are second to none in Poland.

For more on Kraków's Wawel Royal Castle, see p221.

4. Dürnstein, Austria
A FAIRYTALE FORT

Medieval castles guard many a hilltop in Austria, but few have such a gripping past as Kuenringerburg, whose romantic, rocky ruins cling to a steeply forested crag in the Wachau. Richard the Lionheart was incarcerated here in 1192 and 1193. His crime was insulting Leopold V; his misfortune was to be recognised when journeying through Austria on his way home from the Holy Lands. His liberty was granted only upon payment of an enormous ransom of 35,000kg of silver. This sum partly funded the building of Wiener Neustadt.

For more on Kuenringerburg, see p62.

5. Cologne, Germany
MAGNIFICENT GOTHIC ARCHITECTURE

Germany's most visited landmark, Cologne Cathedral (Kölner Dom), is a masterpiece of high-medieval Gothic church architecture. Construction commenced in 1248 CE, but the cathedral was only completed to its full, original plan in 1880. To this day, it remains the world's tallest twin-spired cathedral, reaching 157m into the sky above the city. This site on the Rhine has been significant throughout the entire course of German Christian history, and was occupied in the 4th century by the 'first cathedral', commissioned by the first bishop of Cologne. Today, it remains an icon of German spiritual architecture.

For more on Cologne Cathedral, see p131.

6. Piran, Slovenia
INSPIRED BY VENICE

Beginning in the 13th century, the Venetian Republic established dominion over the coast of Istria, founding a pseudo empire along the eastern Adriatic in modern-day Slovenia, Croatia and Albania. They shaped the region's architecture, culture and maritime trade: in Piran, for example, flourishing salt commerce fostered an economic, architectural and spiritual boom. At one point before the Venetian Republic collapsed in 1797, little Piran had over 23 churches, plus a monastery. To this day, the town remains a repository of Venetian Gothic architecture, and it's hard to imagine a more romantic spot anywhere.

For more on Piran, see p271.

7. Lübeck, Germany
MEDIEVAL ECONOMIC POWERHOUSE

The northern city of Lübeck was once known as Queen of the Hanseatic League – the powerful, predominantly German

Dürnstein (p62)

PAUL KUBALEK/GETTY IMAGES

confederation of cities that dominated Baltic and North Sea trade between the 13th and 15th centuries. Founded in 1143 CE by Adolf II, the Count of Schauenburg and Holstein, Lübeck grew rapidly in wealth and magnificence and was, in 1375, declared one of the five 'Glories of the Empire' by Emperor Charles IV. Its wonderfully preserved medieval heart retains a taste of this early prosperity.

For more on Lübeck, see page 144.

8. Hofburg, Austria
RULER OF THE REALM

Imagine what you could do with unlimited riches and Austria's top architects at hand for 640 years: this is the Vienna of the Habsburgs. The crown jewel is the Hofburg, HQ of the Habsburgs from 1273 to 1918, with a flabbergasting stash of cultural and art treasures. The oldest section is the 13th-century Schweizerhof (Swiss Courtyard), named after the Swiss guards who protected its precincts. Marvel at the treasury's imperial crowns and religious relics, the equine ballet of snow-white Lipizzaner stallions and the chandelier-lit apartments fit for a rather fussy Empress Elisabeth.

For more on Vienna's Hofburg, see p58.

9. Olomouc, Czechia
FRANZ JOSEPH ASSUMES THE THRONE

Unlike much of the rest of Bohemia and Moravia, the stately college town of Olomouc served as a bastion of support for Austria's ruling Habsburg family for centuries. During the revolution of 1848, when the emerging middle classes across the empire revolted against their rulers, the Habsburgs fled here for their personal safety. Austrian Emperor Franz Joseph I was even crowned emperor at Olomouc's Archbishop's Palace later that year at the tender age of 18.

For more on Olomouc, see p106.

10. Soča Valley, Slovenia
HORRORS OF WWI

WWI began on 28 July 1914, when the Austro-Hungarian monarchy declared war on Serbia. Though the assassination of Archduke Franz Ferdinand in Sarajevo a month earlier was the catalyst, a complex system of alliances quickly drew other European nations into the conflict,

turning it into a global war. The Isonzo Front in the Soča Valley saw some of the war's bloodiest battles. Today, a long-distance hiking trail from the Julian Alps to Trieste on the Adriatic connects Slovenia and Italy's WWI heritage sites. Museums, cemeteries, memorials and chapels pay homage to the lives lost.

For more on the Soča Valley, see p269.

11. Auschwitz-Birkenau Memorial & Museum, Poland
THE HOLOCAUST

There's hardly a better example of the horrors of WWII than Auschwitz-Birkenau. German occupiers established the extermination camp in prewar Polish army barracks on the outskirts of Oświęcim in April 1940. The much larger camp at Birkenau (Brzezinka) was built 2km west of the original site in 1941 and 1942, followed by another one in Monowitz (Monowice), several kilometres to the west. More than a million Jews, and many Poles and Roma, were murdered here by German Nazis during WWII. It's essential to visit both to appreciate the extent and horror of the place.

For more on Auschwitz-Birkenau, see p223.

Monument to the Fallen Shipyard Workers (p232), Gdańsk

FROM LEFT: DANUTA HYNIEWSKA/SHUTTERSTOCK, JAMES O'NEIL/GETTY IMAGES

Aletsch Glacier (p292)

12. Plzeň, Czechia
LIBERATED BY THE US ARMY

At the start of WWII, Nazi Germany occupied Bohemia and Moravia, while Slovakia became an independent Nazi puppet; they all remained under German domination until the final days of the war, in May 1945. Much of Czechoslovakia was liberated by the Soviet Red Army. The exception was the extreme western part of the country, around Plzeň, which was freed by the US Army, led by General George S Patton. The people of Plzeň have never forgotten and celebrate the liberation with an annual festival in early May.

For more on Plzeň, see p98.

13. Gdańsk, Poland
WHERE COMMUNISM HIT THE BUFFERS

Travellers interested in the history of 20th-century Europe should make a pilgrimage to the Gdańsk shipyard area, a place that played a major role in the fall of communism across Eastern Europe. Though protests against the communist regime took place throughout Poland at various times from the mid-1950s onwards, it was the birth of the Solidarity Movement at the Lenin Shipyard in 1980 that gave the region's opposition to Kremlin rule a name, a face and even a logo. The face was that of Lech Wałęsa, a shipyard electrician who went on to serve as Poland's first post-communist president.

For more on the Gdańsk, see p229.

14. Geneva, Switzerland
DIGITAL REVOLUTION

In 1989, Tim Berners Lee, a British scientist working at Geneva's European Organization for Nuclear Research (CERN), developed a computer language to automate sharing information between fellow scientists and academics around the world. At the time, he did not realise the impact his language (HTML) would go on to have. HTML could link text to graphics and create pages for the World Wide Web – all with the intention of creating a shared information system for CERN's 17,000-odd scientists in 100 different countries. By 1990, the world's first web server and browser was functioning in Geneva.

For more on Geneva's CERN, see p282.

15. Aletsch Glacier, Switzerland
WARMING CLIMES

There's no more visible sign of global warming than a melting glacier – and approximately half of Europe's glaciers are in Switzerland. Swiss glaciers lost half their volume between 1931 and 2016, another 10% in 2022 and 2023, and are feared to disappear completely by 2100. This includes the country's iconic giant, the Aletsch Glacier in Valais, which has lured the curious onto its magnificent ice-sculpted tongue since the 19th century. Nearby, on 28 May 2025, the mountain village of Blatten was obliterated after a nearby glacier collapsed, burying the 600-year-old community in falling rubble and rocks in a matter of seconds.

For more on the Aletsch Glacier, see p292.

THE HILLS ARE ALIVE: OVERTOURISM IN THE ALPS

Alpine communities are facing increasing challenges in the form of overtourism and global warming. What can we do to help?
By Vesna Maric

EACH YEAR, ROUGHLY 120 million people visit the Alps. They come to hike, ski and cycle in the shadows of these majestic peaks and to witness the inimitable natural beauty. But climate change has had a significant impact on the Alpine environment, leading many to wonder what the future has in store.

A Vital Environment

Many of the Alps' highest peaks are found in Switzerland and Austria, and these are the only two countries that are considered to be fully Alpine – meaning that the mountain range is the most important natural feature inside their borders. The highest peak in the Alps, and Western Europe, is Mont Blanc (4809m), which straddles Italy and France. But it is Switzerland where the range is at its most emblematic, with iconic peaks like the Matterhorn (4478m), with its distinctive pyramid-like shape, and the Eiger (3967m), whose north face is con-

sidered to be one of the most challenging technical climbs in Europe.

The Alps are more than just an extended series of stunning landscapes, however. They are one of Europe's most significant natural environments and many of Earth's ecosystems can be found somewhere in these mountains. The Alps are also the source of many major European rivers, such as the Rhône, Rhine, Po and many tributaries of the Danube, and the range's snowmelt waters flow into the North, Mediterranean, Adriatic and Black Seas.

In short, the Alps are one of Europe's most important environmental features, but they are also heavily developed and thus face a growing number of challenges.

Increasing Numbers

Tourism in the Alps started in the 19th century, but it wasn't until after the 1950s that activities like skiing became affordable enough to become a mainstream

phenomenon. Today, there are around 600 Alpine ski resorts, with more than 270 in Austria alone. And while mass tourism has brought significant economic benefits to local communities, it has also ratcheted up the pressure on local resources, through increased transport (the largest single source of greenhouse gas emissions in Europe), waste management challenges and environmental degradation. In addition, popular adventure sports such as mountain biking, canyoning, and paragliding are bringing increasing numbers of people into previously isolated natural areas, causing disturbances to the wildlife and posing threats to biodiversity.

In many valleys, visitors outnumber locals during the peak months. For instance, the Sustainable Tourism Observatory, a monitoring body set up in conjunction with the UN, produces an annual report that investigates tourism's impact on the South Tyrol region of Italy, a well-known ski destination. While South Tyrol's permanent population is just 530,000, it recorded a new all-time high of 37.1 million overnight stays in 2024, an increase of 2.6% from the previous year.

And it's not only skiing that draws people to the Alps – as summer temperatures get hotter, growing numbers of people fleeing the heat head to the mountains. For example, in August 2024, more than six million tourists visited South Tyrol. Popular ski regions have adapted to this increasing demand by offering more and more summer activities, like downhill mountain-bike parks.

And, of course, it's impossible to talk about overtourism without mentioning social media, which is a key driver in funnelling huge numbers of people into one very specific location.

In 2022, for example, the Swiss lakeside village of Iseltwald was swamped by an unexpected influx of fans of the Netflix series *Crash Landing on You*. Thousands of tourists turned up daily to take a selfie on a wooden pier on Lake Brienz, which happened to be the location of a particularly romantic scene in the series. Every day 12 packed coaches would arrive in this small village – which has a permanent population of just 400 – leading residents to introduce a new reservation system that limited visitors to 2000 per day, in addition to imposing a CHF5 selfie fee.

Warmer Temperatures & Decreasing Snowfall

As global temperatures continue to rise, reliable snowfall in the Alps has continued to decrease. It is estimated that many ski areas below 1500m in elevation will have little to no snowfall in the coming years. Smaller ski resorts at lower elevations will likely become unsustainable, which will lead to increasing demand at the larger resorts at higher elevations. The larger areas are now faced with a tricky balancing act: they want to continue to attract skiers while also preserving the environment that draws people to the resorts to begin with. Ski lifts are now being built at higher elevations in the hopes of guaranteeing reliable snow coverage, but this development is not without cost. There has been a significant impact on local ecosystems, through soil erosion, deforestation and the fragmentation of wildlife habitats.

And yet, efforts at sustainable development are under way. Some of Austria's top resorts – Ski Arlberg and Lech Zürs – are transitioning to renewable energy, using their own independent hydroelectric plants to power cable cars, lifts and restaurants. And some snow groomers are now powered by a renewable fossil-free diesel substitute, made from natural waste products such as used cooking oil. Another notable improvement is the addition of free shuttles (many electric) that connect the valley stations.

Nevertheless, melting glaciers continue to pose a threat, and as permafrost soil begins to thaw more rapidly, it brings with it a greater risk of landslides, rockfall and avalanches in both winter and summer. June 2023 saw the collapse of part of the summit of Fluchthorn Mountain in the Austrian state of Tyrol: more than a million cubic meters of rock came crashing into the valley below, followed by mudslides.

A Strained Infrastructure

Overtourism also affects housing and infrastructure. The rising demand for short-term holiday rentals is driving up prices, making it increasingly difficult for locals to afford housing. In Chamonix, the situation has become so acute that the local government voted to change the law in May 2025, with new regulations restricting the number of short-term lets.

Waste management and public transport networks are also struggling to keep up with seasonal numbers, and there are fears that some mountain towns are now at a tipping point. In 2025, poignant graffiti left near the main cable car at the Italian ski resort of Alpe di Siusi read, 'Too Much. Too Much. Too Much. Too Much'. The message is clear: there are too many tourists.

The picture in the Alps is part of a bigger trend across Europe, where protests are now widespread in those places that bear the brunt of overtourism. And while the climate crisis is a global problem, its effects are felt most acutely by those who live in these overtouristed areas. But the economic double bind is real. When tourism is a community's main economic driver, how do you reduce visitor numbers without creating a negative impact on local livelihoods?

SOME OF AUSTRIA'S TOP RESORTS – SKI ARLBERG, ST ANTON AND LECH ZÜRS – ARE TRANSITIONING TO RENEWABLE ENERGY, USING THEIR OWN INDEPENDENT HYDROELECTRIC PLANTS TO POWER CABLE CARS, LIFTS AND RESTAURANTS

St Anton am Arlberg
PANDORA PICTURES/SHUTTERSTOCK

tribution to overtourism, and our aim is to inform our readers of issues facing individual destinations and to suggest travel alternatives that might help mitigate these issues, along with those related to climate change.

Travellers to the Alps can take action by rethinking plans to go downhill skiing and snowboarding, and instead try out cross-country skiing, ski touring, snowshoeing and winter walking, since these activities have a lighter environmental impact. Another helpful strategy is to avoid the glitzy big resorts and stay in smaller communities. And consider hiring local guides, as they are likely to be more aware of environmental issues and can ensure that you don't accidentally stray into sensitive habitat or dangerous terrain. Informed local guides can also point out to visitors where and how the warming climate is reshaping the landscape, at the same time providing a glimpse of places in the Alps that downhill skiers will never see.

Ultimately, the tourist industry and the governments of Alpine countries need to ensure appropriate legislation is passed to protect this fragile and precious environment. Meanwhile, it remains to be seen how the ski industry adapts to the growing challenges of overtourism and climate change.

Sustainable Tourism

Sustainable tourism and an increased awareness on the part of visitors can help protect the natural areas in the Alps. At Lonely Planet, we are aware of our con-

PARTY TIME
OF THE SEASON

At avant-garde arts and music festivals across Central Europe, creativity is sky-high. Yet these events remain grounded in regional values and traditions. By Barbara Woolsey

GERMANY'S BUCHT DER Träumer (Dreamer's Bay) exemplifies all the summer magic of Central Europe's festival circuit. Near Frankfurt an der Oder, by the Polish border, around 20,000 glitter- and sequin-covered festival-goers revel in five days of avant-garde, countercultural art.

Berlin-based artists and music collectives transform the former open-pit coal mine into a surrealistic funfair of tiki DJ stages and interactive art. Imagination is everywhere, from an open-air roller disco to tea parties, and a 'human car wash' where dust-covered partygoers get (optionally) naked and are non-sexually suds-upped and hosed down by volunteers dressed as giant sponges. Bucht represents a certain kind of grassroots festival that's unique to Central Europe, and particularly regions such as Poland, Czechia and eastern Germany. And yet, these festivals hark back to older regional traditions and centuries-spanning beliefs that highlight the best of the human experience.

Overcoming the Cold War Divide

The era spent behind the Iron Curtain frames today's festival circuit with a deep-rooted historical and cultural context. Decades of Cold War oppression – of individuality, creativity and open knowledge – has been subverted through these indie social gatherings, which are intent on pushing boundaries.

Berlin's post-Wall counterculture, consisting of warehouse techno raves, artist squats, and graffiti, was the catalyst for today's regional festivals. The movement turned the city into the nightlife powerhouse it is today: the world capital of electronic beats and club culture. Seeking freedom from urban constraints, festivals began popping up outside of Berlin and throughout the east. Vacated Soviet land and crumbling buildings became the perfect DIY incubators for open-air dance floors and multi-day escapes that extended beyond one-off club nights.

Germany's largest gathering is the Fusion Festival. Over five days in July, some 70,000 Fusion-goers descend upon a disused Soviet airbase in Lärz (160km northeast of Berlin) to celebrate alternative, anti-establishment art. Across 500 acres (about 10 times the size of Coachella), lumber stages and chill spaces, adorned in handcrafted deco, offer a variety of experiences – breathwork, gardening, circus training, you name it.

The former Eastern Bloc is fertile soil for festivals – a different 'temporary city' goes up every weekend in June, July and August. Attendance ranges from small Familienfest ('family festivals', which attract hundreds of people) to ragers that draw tens of thousands. Standouts include the aforementioned Bucht and Zurück zu den Wurzeln (Back to the Roots) in Brandenburg. Diverse, open-air electronic-music floors include a mirror-balled Studio 54 disco space and a decommissioned train carriage where you can bounce to beats on passenger seats. Experiential art, big and small, is everywhere, from wooden postboxes where you can leave notes for other festival-goers to magnifying telescopes and ball pits. Notably, Wurzeln's 'secret forest' paths and dance areas

are wheelchair-friendly. It's one of the most accessible festivals in Europe.

In the last decade or so, festivals across the border in Poland have proliferated. They're cheaper to organise and have fewer bureaucratic regulations than in Germany. The most famous is Garbicz, a spiritual sibling to Fusion with a more psychedelic hippie vibe and a cosier 7000-person attendance.

The centrepiece of most of these festivals is usually electronic music, but not always. At Wave-Gotik-Treffen (Leipzig), the world's largest goth festival, 20,000 black-clad, head-banging enthusiasts indulge in a subcultural spectacle spanning industrial metal concerts and an extraordinary Victorian Picnic (a steampunk tea-sipping fashion show). Meanwhile, an example of the tiniest of niche festivals is the atMOERSphere in Moers, where 200 people enter the mosh pits for psychedelic doom and desert rock.

Nestled in Nature

Mystical festivals are grounded in the idea of nature as magic. These experiences are as much about gathering together as they are about solo reflection in the great outdoors. Fusion's doorstep, Müritz National Park, abounds with lush flora and fauna-filled forests, lakes, meadows and wetlands. Bicycles are a festival lover's best friend for indulging in the contrast of energetic, neon-popping nightlife with daytime *Waldeinsamkeit* (the age-old German principle of 'forest solitude', which is good for the soul).

Open-air spaces provide unforgettable moments, from dancing shoeless at sunrise to discovering fields where makeshift rotundas and cabins form indelible hideaways. And there's always at least one lake as a fixture, no matter the festival. Skinny-dipping (especially after sweaty grooving) is preferred to queuing at cubicle showers. In Brandenburg forests the sandy soils become squishy dance floors by night and prime leisure spots by day.

Campsites can be party bases too, with revellers bringing their own makeshift wagons and generator-powered DJ equipment. Small Bluetooth speakers also incite impromptu dance floors amid the retro VW and Soviet camper vans poking up among the tents.

Sustainability is a uniting ethos, emphasising cultural respect for co-existing with nature. Biodegradable and recycled materials abound, and compost toilets include innovations like female-catering 'pussoirs'. Some festivals, including Brandenburg's Wurzeln and Wilde Möhre, only have plant-based food trucks (think *pommes* and lots of lentil curry).

Connecting with nature is a key aspect of the modern festival experience, though cultural roots go back generations. The concept harks back to long-established regional beliefs of nature as leading to soul and self. This is a concept well explored through the philosophy, poetry and art that has defined German, Polish and Czech intellectual history.

In former Soviet regions, outdoors exploration is also connected to indulging in once repressed freedoms. During socialism, hiking, mountaineering and rural retreats offered a sense of autonomy, whether through gardening and foraging for one's own ingredients or holding dissident meetings beyond observant eyes.

Reclaiming History

Dynamic art and music infuses new life into once decrepit buildings that have fallen out of use. Festivals held in industrial warehouses and aristocratic residences represent an important form of sustainable development – especially in disenfranchised rural areas that have been left behind by modern urbanisation.

In Poland, medieval and baroque fortresses such as the Bolków Castle, near the German and Czech borders, or Las Balance, a century-old manor turned socialist farming headquarters that's a four-hour train ride from Berlin, vibrate with subwoofers and shuffling guests. Chandeliered dining halls and former throne rooms sparkle with neon lights, flashy decorations and, of course, guests decked out in lamé and feathers. In a tiny Saxon-Anhalt village in Germany, the Giebichenstein Castle, once a residence of the Holy Roman Emperor, hosts year-round festivals staged by artist collectives. Around 300 guests bunk in castle rooms and meet up with the castle's owner on the dance floor.

Meanwhile, Czechia's Dolní oblast Vítkovice and Germany's Hive Festival are electronic music weekends held at former mining and steelwork sites. The latter is held at Ferropolis, a converted 'City of Iron' where leftover machinery and towering girders imbue a fittingly dystopian Mad Max atmosphere, with fast-pumping techno and psytrance.

While rural eastern areas remain strongholds of conservative ideals, these countercultural festivals are mostly welcomed by locals. Like a travelling carnival, party-goers bring excitement in their wake – not to mention tourism. Villagers and visitors coexisting harmoniously during festival days is a microcosm of the tolerance and open-mindedness that uphold European unity.

Community Spirit

Perhaps most impressive of all is that most of the aforementioned festivals are volunteer- and community-driven. Some are run by for-profit entities, but cooperation with collectives is key so that performing artists are paid. Most festivals sell tickets on a sliding scale, with more affordable day passes and reduced prices for marginalised groups. Volunteering is one of the best experiences such festivals have to offer, and often it gets you in for free. Spend a few hours washing dishes and handing out wristbands before dancing the night away. Being part of an awareness team (vested individuals strolling around to help those who are unsafe or unwell) or hammering and decorating structures in the days before the main event is always enriching – after all, you're making an important contribution.

Fusion and Garbicz stages are designed and built by artists' collectives. Despite the overwhelming size of Fusion, the festival has never advertised or accepted any corporate sponsors. It also stays true to a fair, anticapitalist ethos through its ticketing process – a randomised raffle known as a tombola.

The tombola, and other rules such as a one-ticket-per-person limit, are distinguishing features that have set Fusion apart from other festivals. The possibility of getting a golden ticket is an equalising process that is not predicated on your internet speed during a ticket drop. However, this means that the possibility that all of your friends will be among the lucky few is slim. But this is, perhaps, the thing that makes Fusion so wonderful – many festival-goers arrive alone, which fosters much mixing and mingling outside of pre-formed social bubbles. One of the finest parts of any festival, Fusion included, is getting lost on the grounds with barely-there wi-fi. That's how fast, and often lifelong, friends are made. Such togetherness, when framed against the historical separation of the Iron Curtain and its toppling by collective resistance, is a thing of great power.

Heartland Traditions

Contemporary bohemian impulses and sensualism aside, Central Europe's arts and music festivals maintain the ritualistic nature of the summer solstice festivals that came before. Communities gathered after the planting season to give thanks for agricultural bounties. They feasted, drank and danced, and ultimately, this hasn't changed.

Even the eclecticism of today's festival rituals holds an echo of how harvest and midsummer rural celebrations blended pre-Christian rites with regional folk customs. Colourful pageantry and chaotic fanfare, once represented by symbolic traditions such as maypoles and huge bonfires, held the same function of bringing people together. Casting out evil spirits and winter chills were different ambitions, but wishing for the growth and prosperity of entire communities has stayed the same.

Music, dance and artisanship have taken new forms in modern times. There are now ambient, euphoria-inducing beats, yoga sessions and wooden jungle gyms for the frolicking child within us all. The adornments might be avant-garde, but they carry through regional values which proclaim that the best parts of being human are often what's most simple and liberating.

Sculpture, Wilde Möhre
WILDE MÖHRE

331

INDEX

Map Pages **000**

Mapping data sources:
© Lonely Planet
© OpenStreetMap http://openstreetmap.org/copyright

THIS BOOK

The 11th edition of Lonely Planet's Central Europe guidebook was written and researched by Mark Baker, Marc Di Duca, Kata Fári, Kerry Walker, Luke Waterson, Nicola Williams and Barbara Woolsey. The previous edition was written and researched by Ryan Ver Berkmoes, Mark Baker, Kerry Christiani, Steve Fallon, Tim Richards, Andrea Schulte-Peevers and Luke Waterson. This guidebook was produced by the following:

Destination Editor
Shauna Daly

Production Editors
Sofie Andersen, Kat Rowan, Jeremy Toynbee

Image Researchers
Dominic Allen, Dermot Hegarty

Cartographers
Dorothy Davidson, Julie Dodkins, Mark Griffiths, Jennifer Johnston, Valentina Kremenchutskaya, Chris Lee-Ack, Daniela Machová, Anthony Phelan

Coordinating Editors
Christopher Pitts, Brana Vladisavljevic

Assisting Editors
Imogen Bannister, Natalie Butler, Liana Cafolla, Nigel Chin, Melanie Dankel, Helen Koehne, Anne Mulvaney, Karyn Noble, Holly Proctor, Fionnuala Twomey

Contributing Writers
Rudolf Abraham, Isabel Albiston, Alexis Averbuck, Kat Barber, Oliver Berry, Joe Bindloss, Caroline Bishop, Abigail Blasi, Federica Bocco, Shaun Busuttil, Jean-Bernard Carillet, Daniel James Clarke, Fionn Davenport, Natalia Diaz, Virginia DiGaetano, Jamie Ditaranto, Kathy Donaghy, Peter Dragicevich, Keith Drew, Mark Elliott, Becki Enright, Mark Eveleigh, Daniel Fahey, Fabienne Fong Yan, Esme Fox, Michael Frankel, Duncan Garwood, Benedetta Geddo, Kay Gillespie, Laurie Goodlad, Anthony Haywood, Sandra Henriques, Rooksana Hossenally, Felicity Hughes, Sarah Irving, Anna Kaminski, Lauren Keith, Cyrena Lee, Daphné Leprince-Ringuet, Lucy Lovell, Emily Luxton, Mike MacEacheran, Vesna Maric, Marlene Marques, Chrissie McClatchie, Hugh McNaughtan, Mélissa Monaco, Mary Winston Nicklin, John Noble, Nanjala Nyabola, Stephanie Ong, Lorna Parkes, Ashley Parsons, Marisa Megan Paska, Samantha Priestley, Isabel Putinja, Leonid Ragozin, Kevin Raub, Joseph Reaney, Simon Richmond, Daniel Robinson, Madeleine Rothery, Eva Sandoval, Andrea Schulte-Peevers, Sarah Souli, Regis St Louis, Paul Stafford, Nicola Leigh Stewart, Monica Suma, Rowan Twine, Sara van Geloven, Ryan Ver Berkmoes, Tasmin Waby, Neil Wilson, Peter Yeung, Angelo Zinna

Cover Researcher
Katelyn Perry

Thanks Kate Chapman, Kate James, Kellie Langdon, Darren O'Connell, Saralinda Turner

MIX
Paper | Supporting responsible forestry
FSC
www.fsc.org   FSC™ C021741

Paper in this book is certified against the Forest Stewardship Council™ standards. FSC™ promotes environmentally responsible, socially beneficial and economically viable management of the world's forests.

Published by Lonely Planet Global Limited
CRN 554153
11th edition – June 2026
ISBN 978 1 74321 396 4
© Lonely Planet 2026 Photographs © as indicated 2026
10 9 8 7 6 5 4 3 2 1
Printed in Malaysia